RED THORN

MAD GODS AND SCOTSMEN

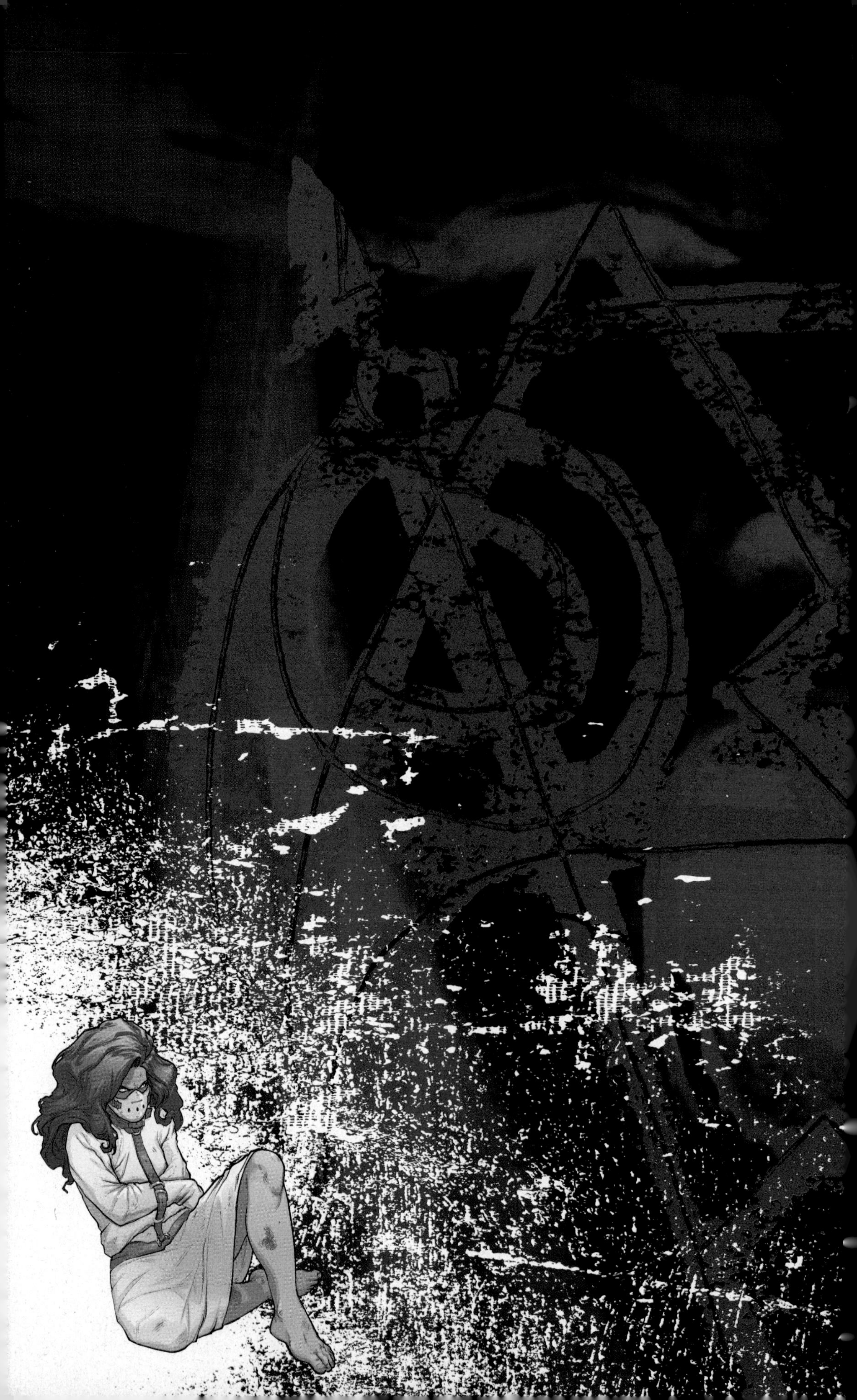

RED THORN
MAD GODS AND SCOTSMEN

DAVID BAILLIE WRITER
MEGHAN HETRICK ARTIST

RYAN KELLY GUEST ARTIST (ISSUE #12)

NICK FILARDI COLORIST

TODD KLEIN LETTERER

CHOONG YOON COVER ART
AND ORIGINAL SERIES COVERS

SPECIAL THANKS TO
PETER GROSS AND MIKE CAREY

RED THORN CREATED BY
DAVID BAILLIE AND MEGHAN HETRICK

Logo design by Nancy Ogami

For Isla
—David Baillie

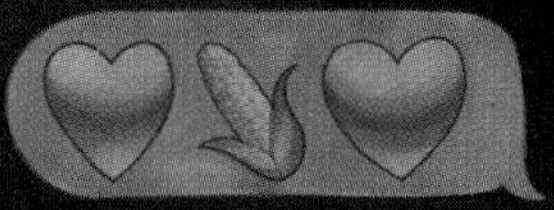

—Meghan

RED THORN VOL. 2: MAD GODS AND SCOTSMEN

DC Comics
2900 West Alameda Avenue
Burbank, CA 91505
Printed in the USA. First Printing.
ISBN: 978-1-4012-6725-4

Library of Congress Cataloging-in-Publication Data is available.

FSC
www.fsc.org
MIX
Paper from responsible sources
FSC® C016956

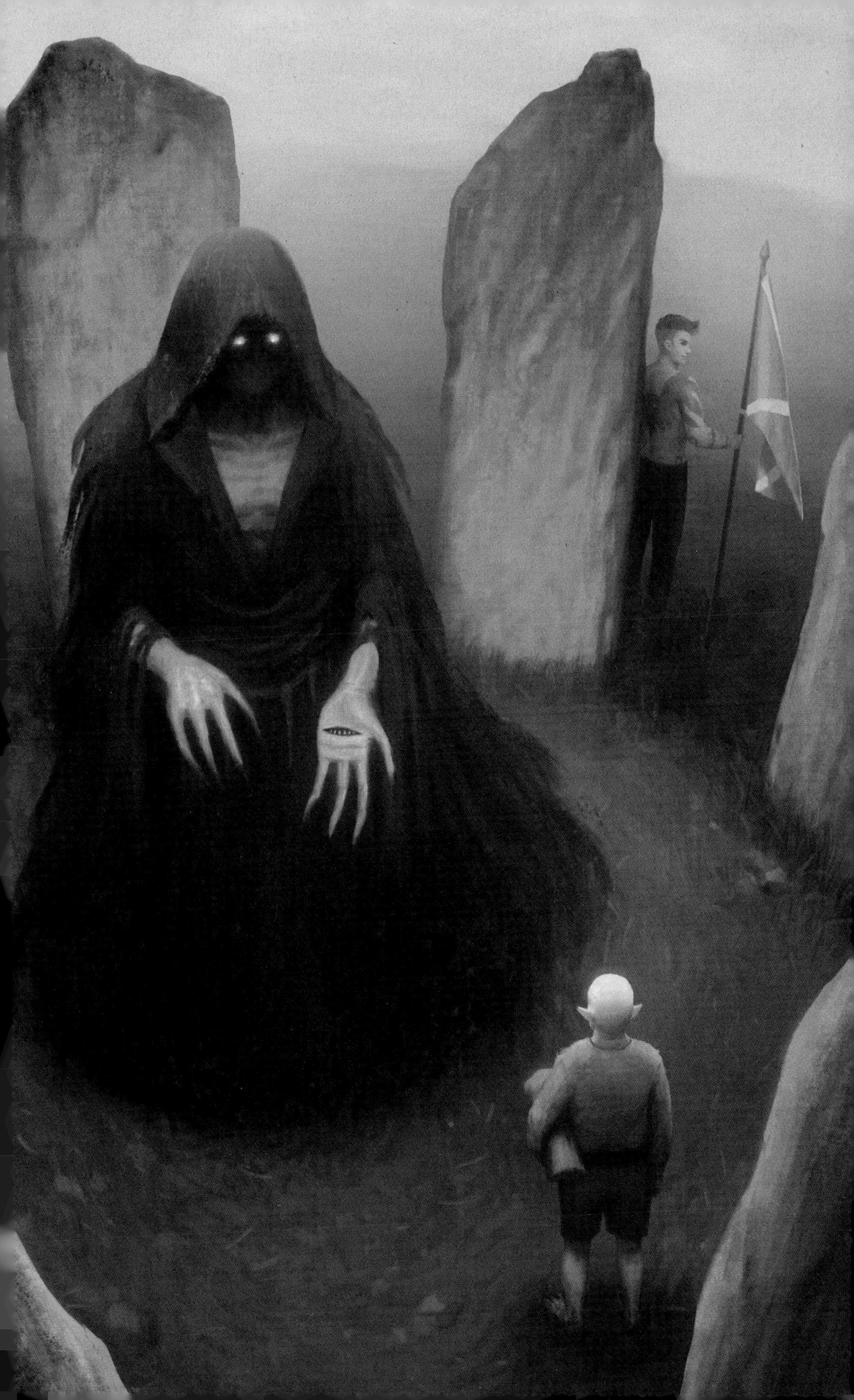

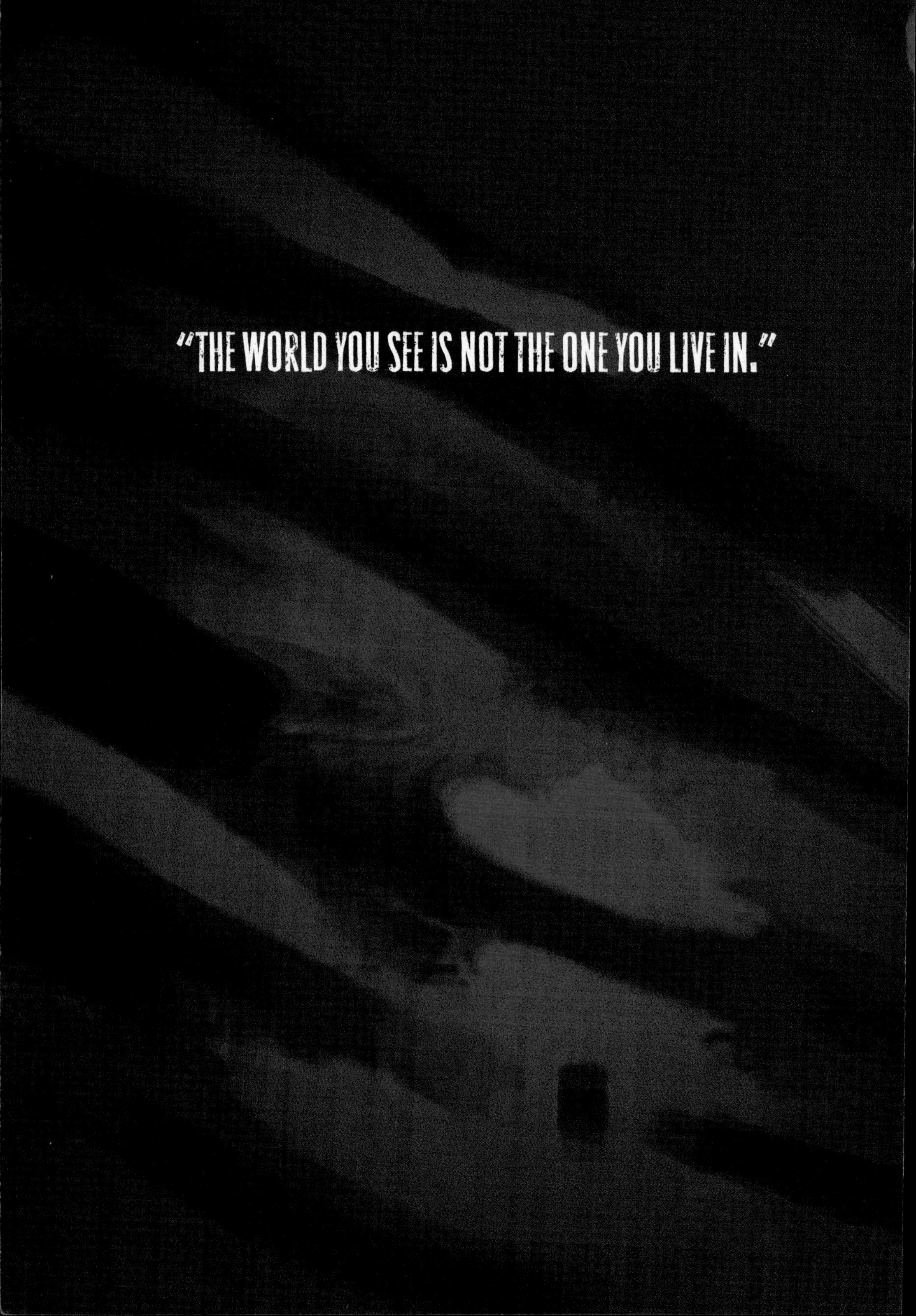
"THE WORLD YOU SEE IS NOT THE ONE YOU LIVE IN."

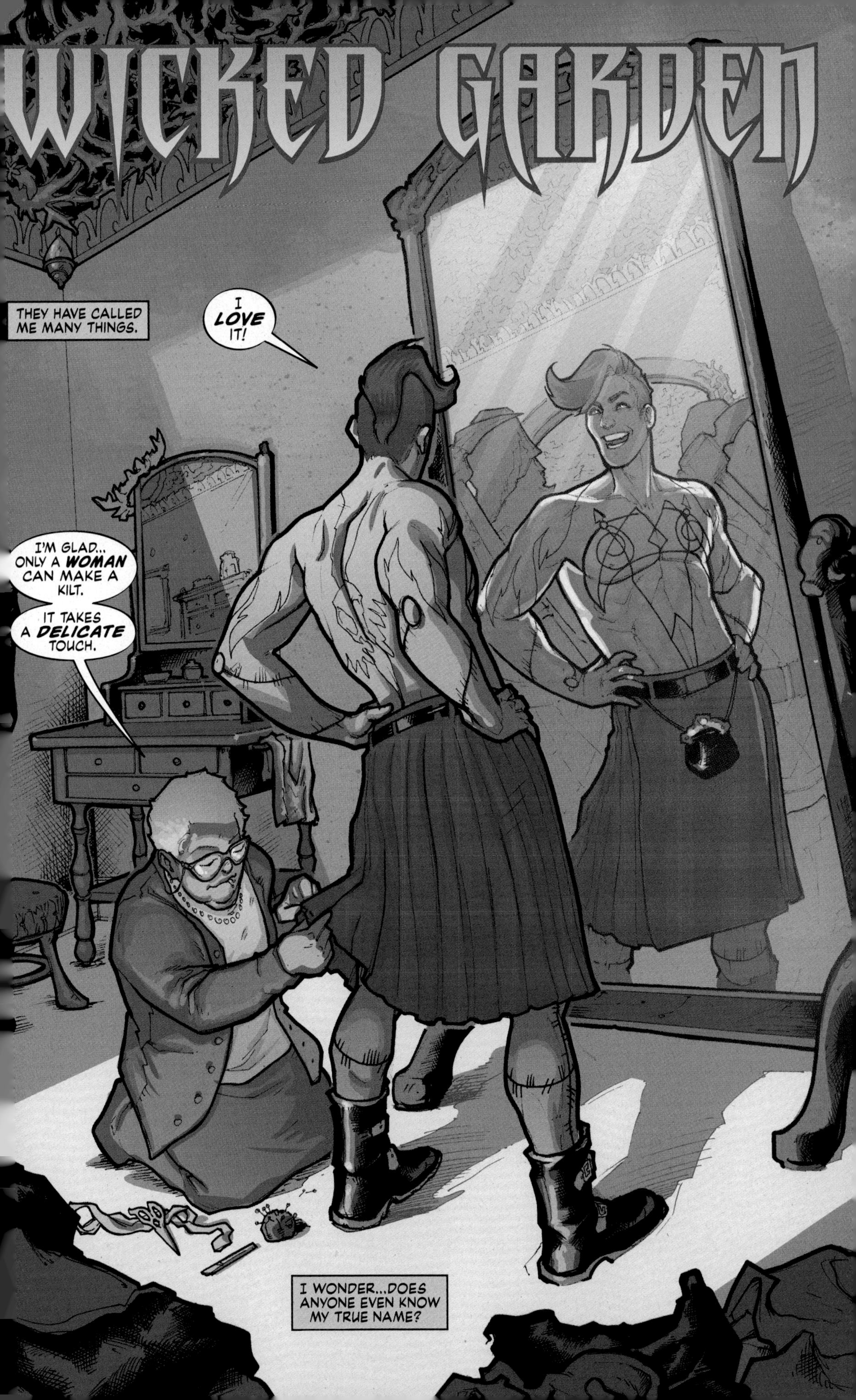

WICKED GARDEN
THEY HAVE CALLED ME MANY THINGS.
I *LOVE* IT!
I'M GLAD... ONLY A *WOMAN* CAN MAKE A KILT.
IT TAKES A *DELICATE* TOUCH.
I WONDER...DOES ANYONE EVEN KNOW MY TRUE NAME?

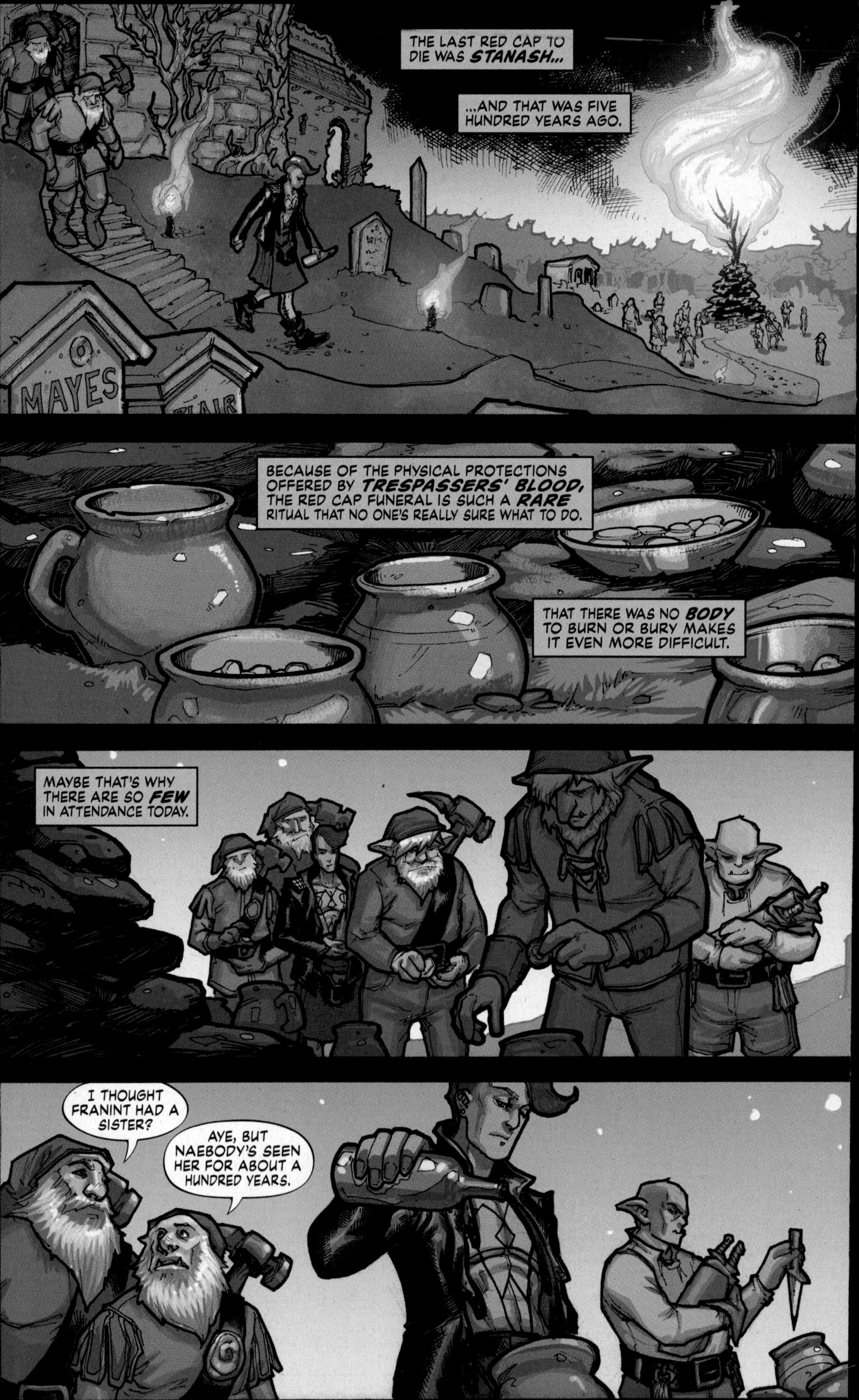
THE LAST RED CAP TO DIE WAS STANASH...
...AND THAT WAS FIVE HUNDRED YEARS AGO.
MAYES
BECAUSE OF THE PHYSICAL PROTECTIONS OFFERED BY TRESPASSERS' BLOOD, THE RED CAP FUNERAL IS SUCH A RARE RITUAL THAT NO ONE'S REALLY SURE WHAT TO DO.
THAT THERE WAS NO BODY TO BURN OR BURY MAKES IT EVEN MORE DIFFICULT.
MAYBE THAT'S WHY THERE ARE SO FEW IN ATTENDANCE TODAY.
I THOUGHT FRANINT HAD A SISTER?
AYE, BUT NAEBODY'S SEEN HER FOR ABOUT A HUNDRED YEARS.

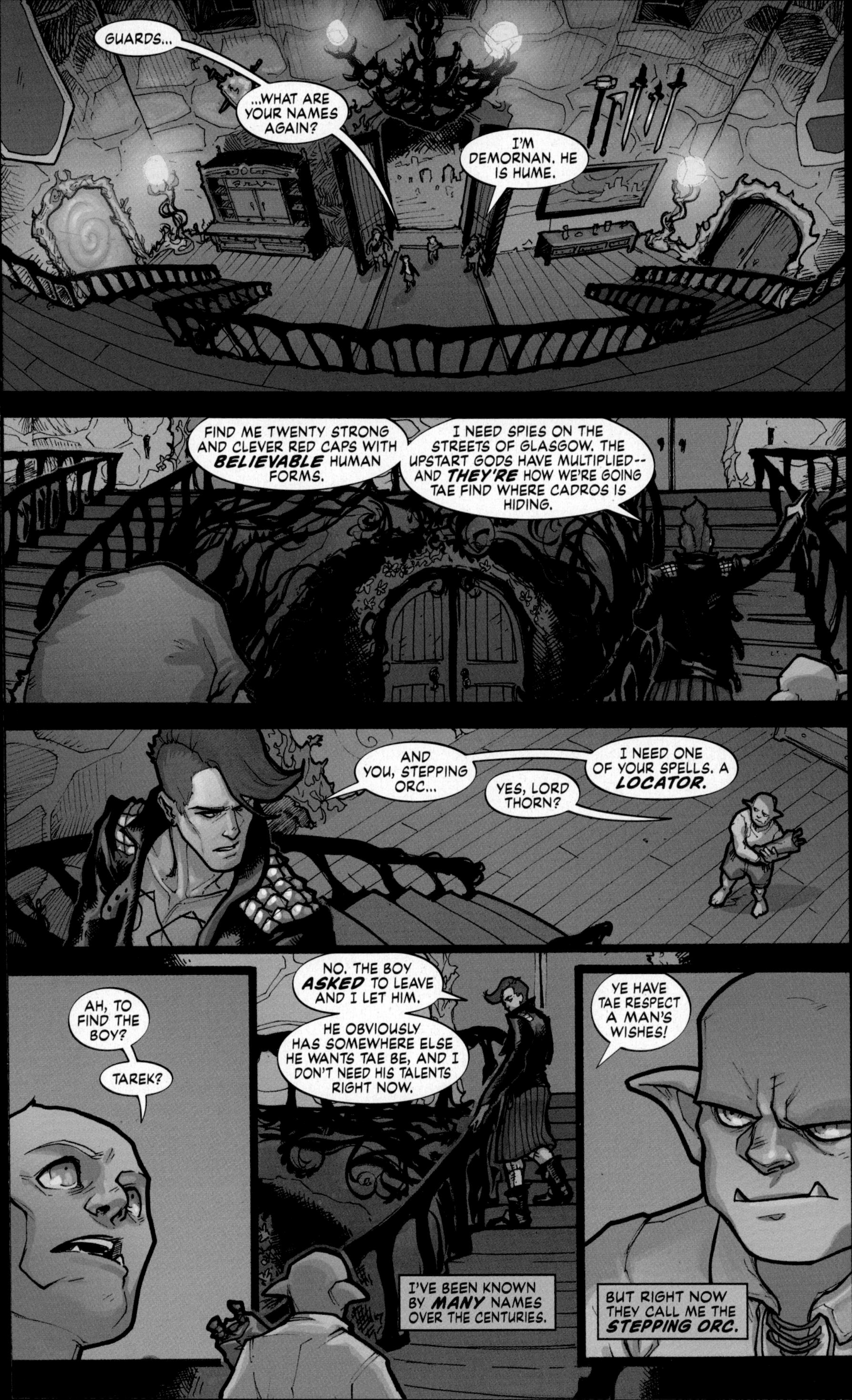
GUARDS...
...WHAT ARE YOUR NAMES AGAIN?
I'M DEMORNAN. HE IS HUME.
FIND ME TWENTY STRONG AND CLEVER RED CAPS WITH **BELIEVABLE** HUMAN FORMS.
I NEED SPIES ON THE STREETS OF GLASGOW. THE UPSTART GODS HAVE MULTIPLIED-- AND **THEY'RE** HOW WE'RE GOING TAE FIND WHERE CADROS IS HIDING.
AND YOU, STEPPING ORC...
YES, LORD THORN?
I NEED ONE OF YOUR SPELLS. A **LOCATOR.**
AH, TO FIND THE BOY?
TAREK?
NO. THE BOY **ASKED** TO LEAVE AND I LET HIM.
HE OBVIOUSLY HAS SOMEWHERE ELSE HE WANTS TAE BE, AND I DON'T NEED HIS TALENTS RIGHT NOW.
I'VE BEEN KNOWN BY **MANY** NAMES OVER THE CENTURIES.
YE HAVE TAE RESPECT A MAN'S WISHES!
BUT RIGHT NOW THEY CALL ME THE **STEPPING ORC.**

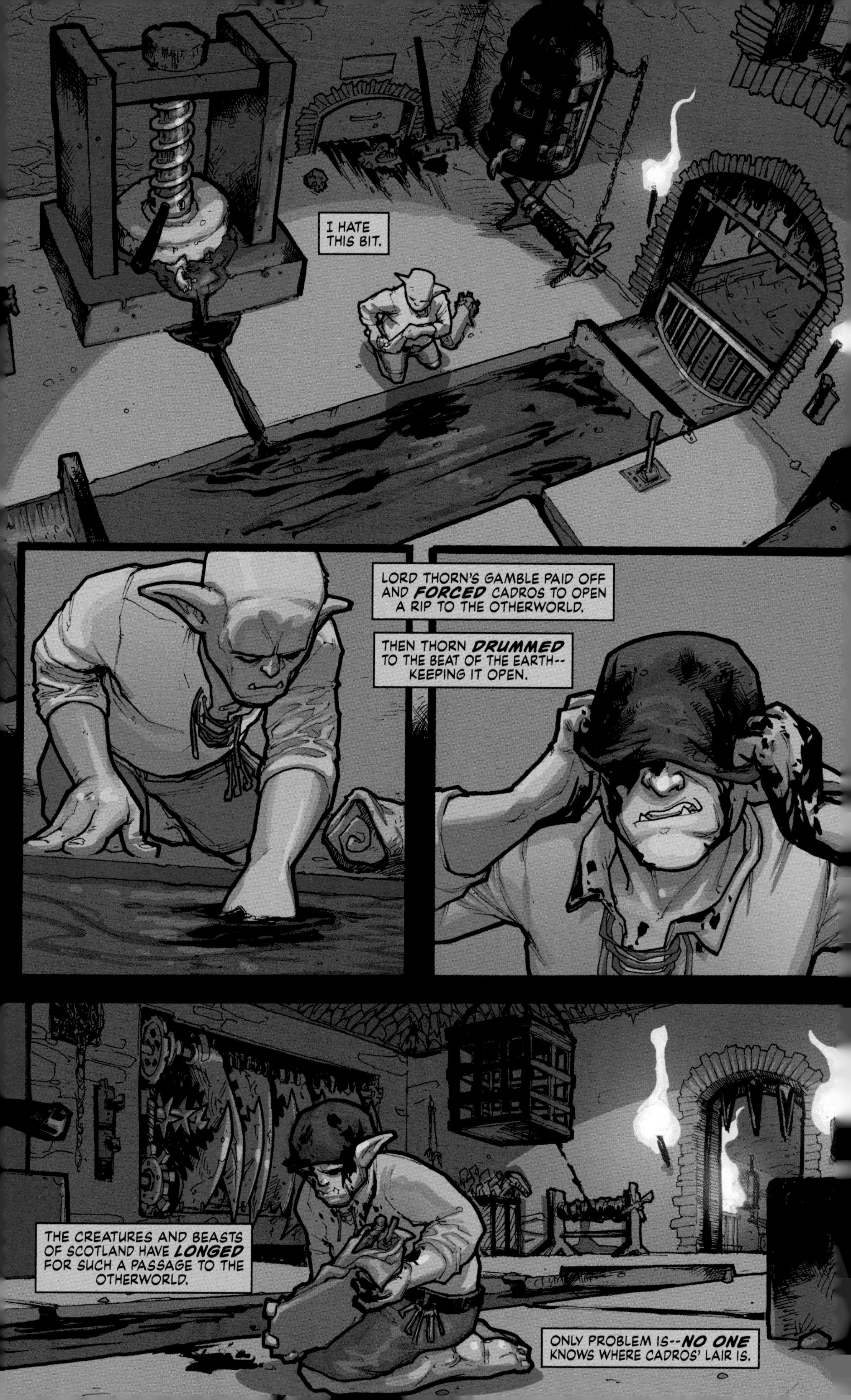
I HATE THIS BIT.
LORD THORN'S GAMBLE PAID OFF AND FORCED CADROS TO OPEN A RIP TO THE OTHERWORLD.
THEN THORN DRUMMED TO THE BEAT OF THE EARTH-- KEEPING IT OPEN.
THE CREATURES AND BEASTS OF SCOTLAND HAVE LONGED FOR SUCH A PASSAGE TO THE OTHERWORLD.
ONLY PROBLEM IS--NO ONE KNOWS WHERE CADROS' LAIR IS.

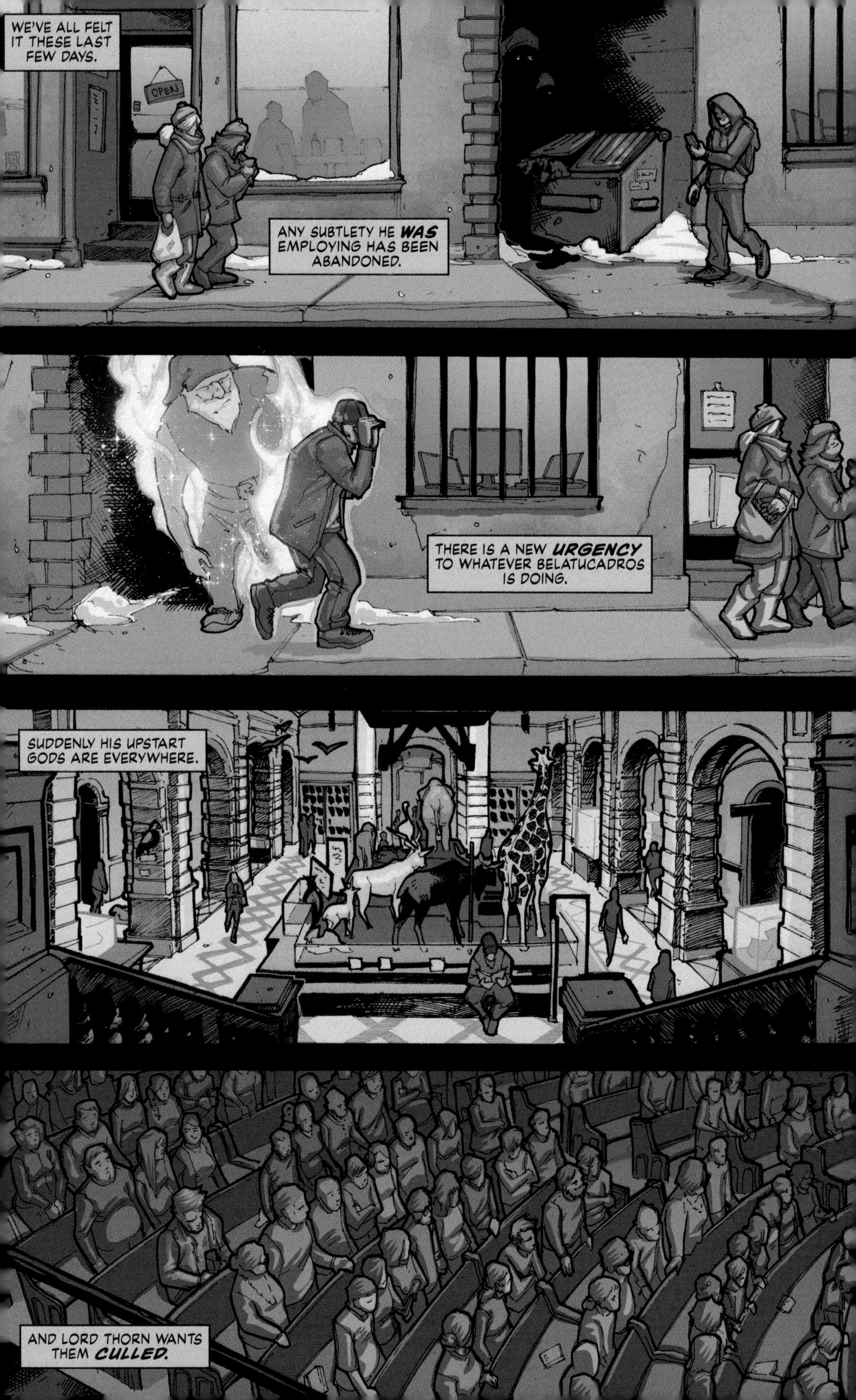
WE'VE ALL FELT IT THESE LAST FEW DAYS.
OPEN
ANY SUBTLETY HE WAS EMPLOYING HAS BEEN ABANDONED.
THERE IS A NEW URGENCY TO WHATEVER BELATUCADROS IS DOING.
SUDDENLY HIS UPSTART GODS ARE EVERYWHERE.
AND LORD THORN WANTS THEM CULLED.

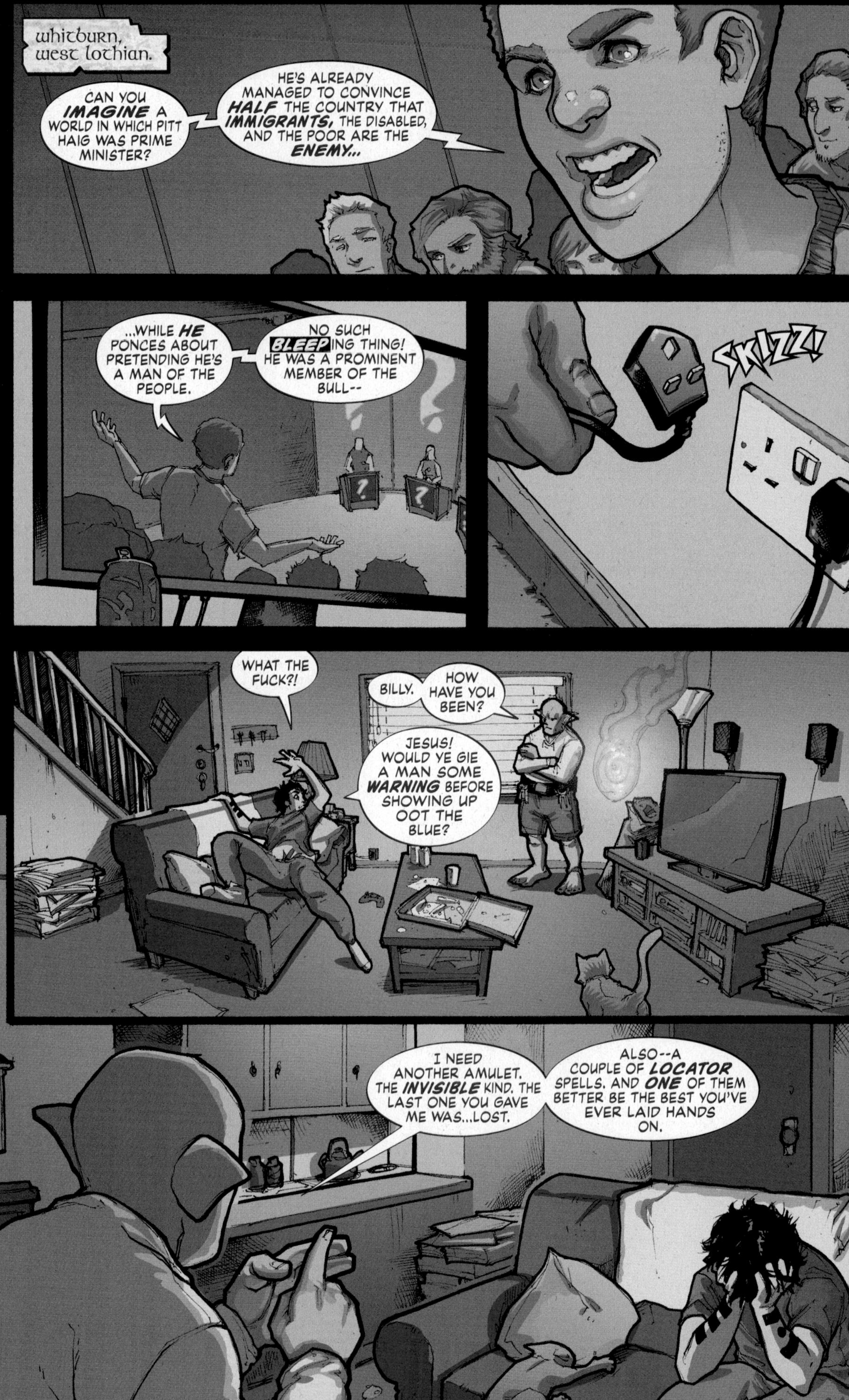
whitburn, west lothian.
CAN YOU IMAGINE A WORLD IN WHICH PITT HAIG WAS PRIME MINISTER?
HE'S ALREADY MANAGED TO CONVINCE HALF THE COUNTRY THAT IMMIGRANTS, THE DISABLED, AND THE POOR ARE THE ENEMY...
...WHILE HE PONCES ABOUT PRETENDING HE'S A MAN OF THE PEOPLE.
NO SUCH BLEEPING THING! HE WAS A PROMINENT MEMBER OF THE BULL--
SKIZZZ!
WHAT THE FUCK?!
BILLY.
HOW HAVE YOU BEEN?
JESUS! WOULD YE GIE A MAN SOME WARNING BEFORE SHOWING UP OOT THE BLUE?
I NEED ANOTHER AMULET. THE INVISIBLE KIND. THE LAST ONE YOU GAVE ME WAS...LOST.
ALSO--A COUPLE OF LOCATOR SPELLS, AND ONE OF THEM BETTER BE THE BEST YOU'VE EVER LAID HANDS ON.

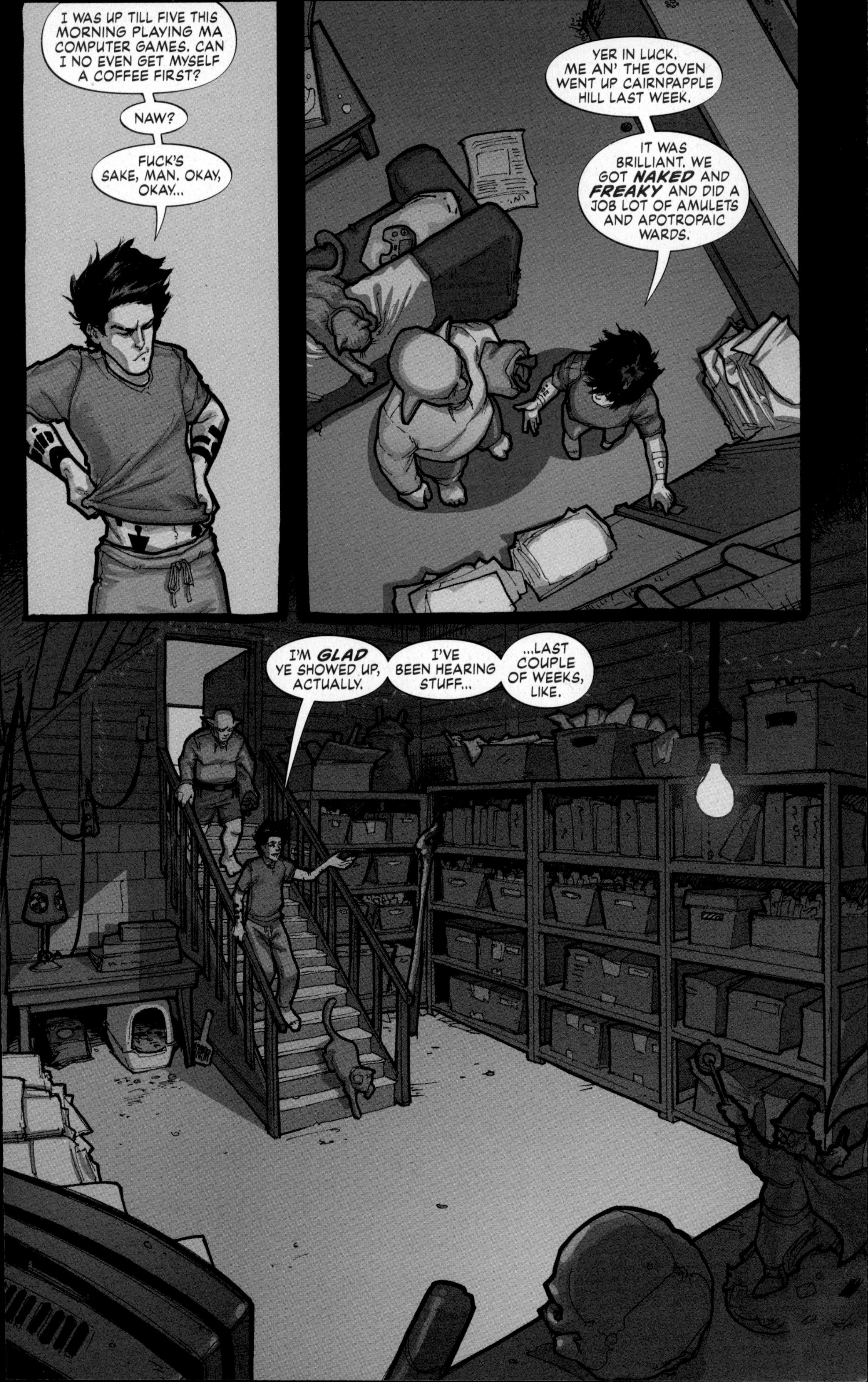

I WAS UP TILL FIVE THIS MORNING PLAYING MA COMPUTER GAMES. CAN I NO EVEN GET MYSELF A COFFEE FIRST?
NAW?
FUCK'S SAKE, MAN. OKAY, OKAY...
YER IN LUCK. ME AN' THE COVEN WENT UP CAIRNPAPPLE HILL LAST WEEK.
IT WAS BRILLIANT. WE GOT NAKED AND FREAKY AND DID A JOB LOT OF AMULETS AND APOTROPAIC WARDS.
I'M GLAD YE SHOWED UP, ACTUALLY.
I'VE BEEN HEARING STUFF...
...LAST COUPLE OF WEEKS, LIKE.

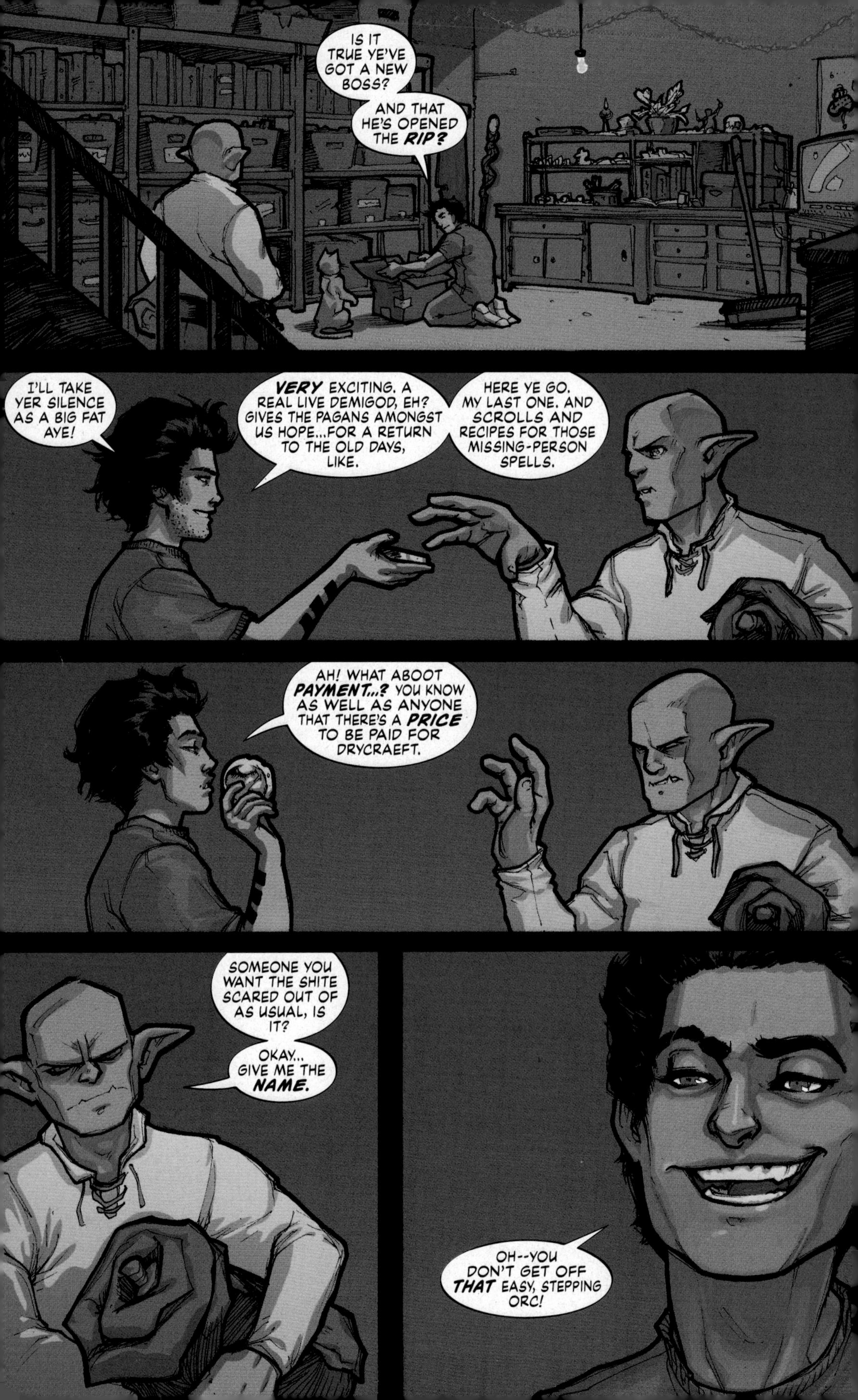
IS IT TRUE YE'VE GOT A NEW BOSS?
AND THAT HE'S OPENED THE RIP?
I'LL TAKE YER SILENCE AS A BIG FAT AYE!
VERY EXCITING. A REAL LIVE DEMIGOD, EH? GIVES THE PAGANS AMONGST US HOPE...FOR A RETURN TO THE OLD DAYS, LIKE.
HERE YE GO. MY LAST ONE. AND SCROLLS AND RECIPES FOR THOSE MISSING-PERSON SPELLS.
AH! WHAT ABOOT PAYMENT...? YOU KNOW AS WELL AS ANYONE THAT THERE'S A PRICE TO BE PAID FOR DRYCRAEFT.
SOMEONE YOU WANT THE SHITE SCARED OUT OF AS USUAL, IS IT?
OKAY... GIVE ME THE NAME.
OH--YOU DON'T GET OFF THAT EASY, STEPPING ORC!

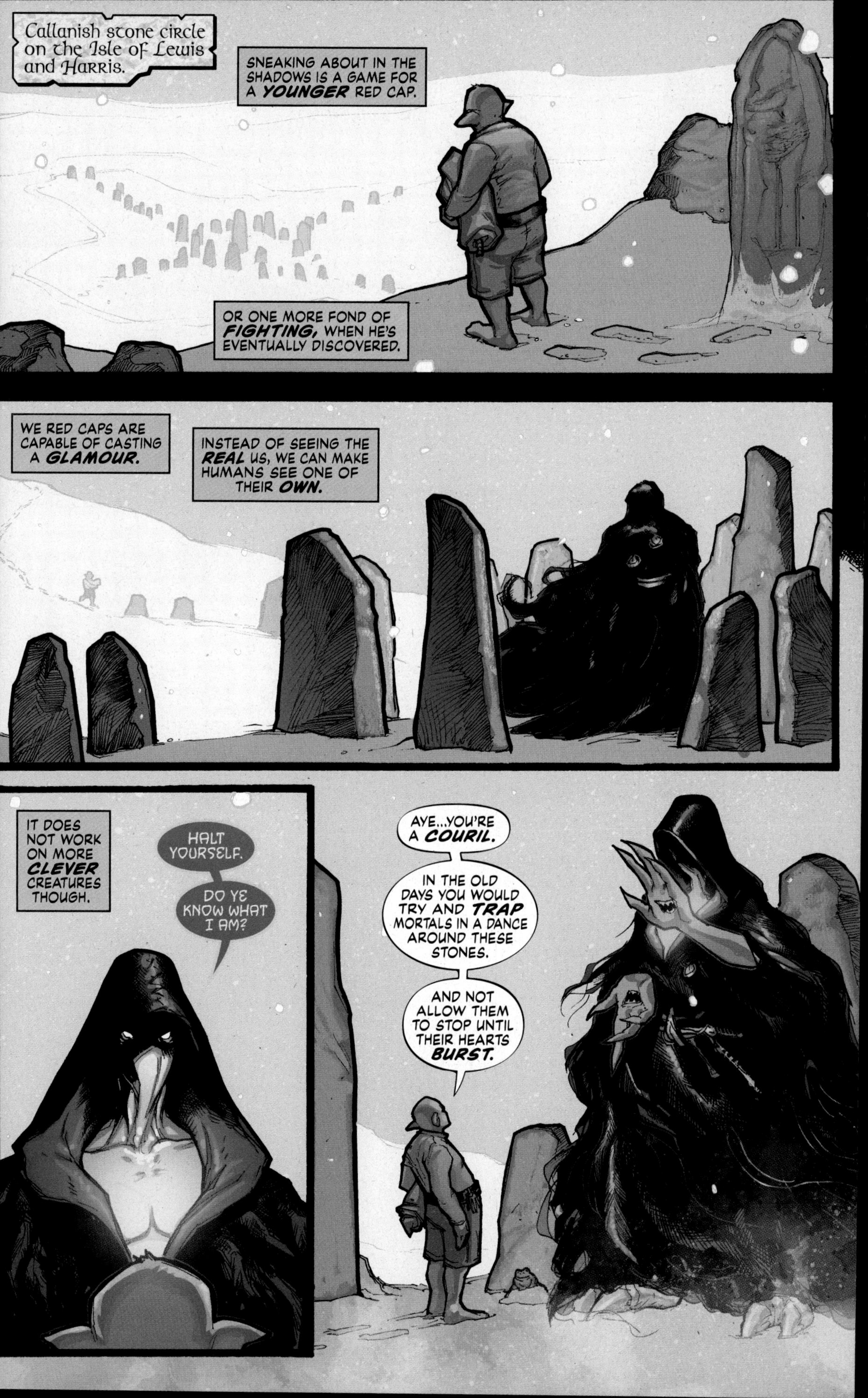
Callanish stone circle on the Isle of Lewis and Harris.
SNEAKING ABOUT IN THE SHADOWS IS A GAME FOR A YOUNGER RED CAP.
OR ONE MORE FOND OF FIGHTING, WHEN HE'S EVENTUALLY DISCOVERED.
WE RED CAPS ARE CAPABLE OF CASTING A GLAMOUR.
INSTEAD OF SEEING THE REAL US, WE CAN MAKE HUMANS SEE ONE OF THEIR OWN.
IT DOES NOT WORK ON MORE CLEVER CREATURES THOUGH.
HALT YOURSELF.
DO YE KNOW WHAT I AM?
AYE...YOU'RE A COURIL.
IN THE OLD DAYS YOU WOULD TRY AND TRAP MORTALS IN A DANCE AROUND THESE STONES.
AND NOT ALLOW THEM TO STOP UNTIL THEIR HEARTS BURST.

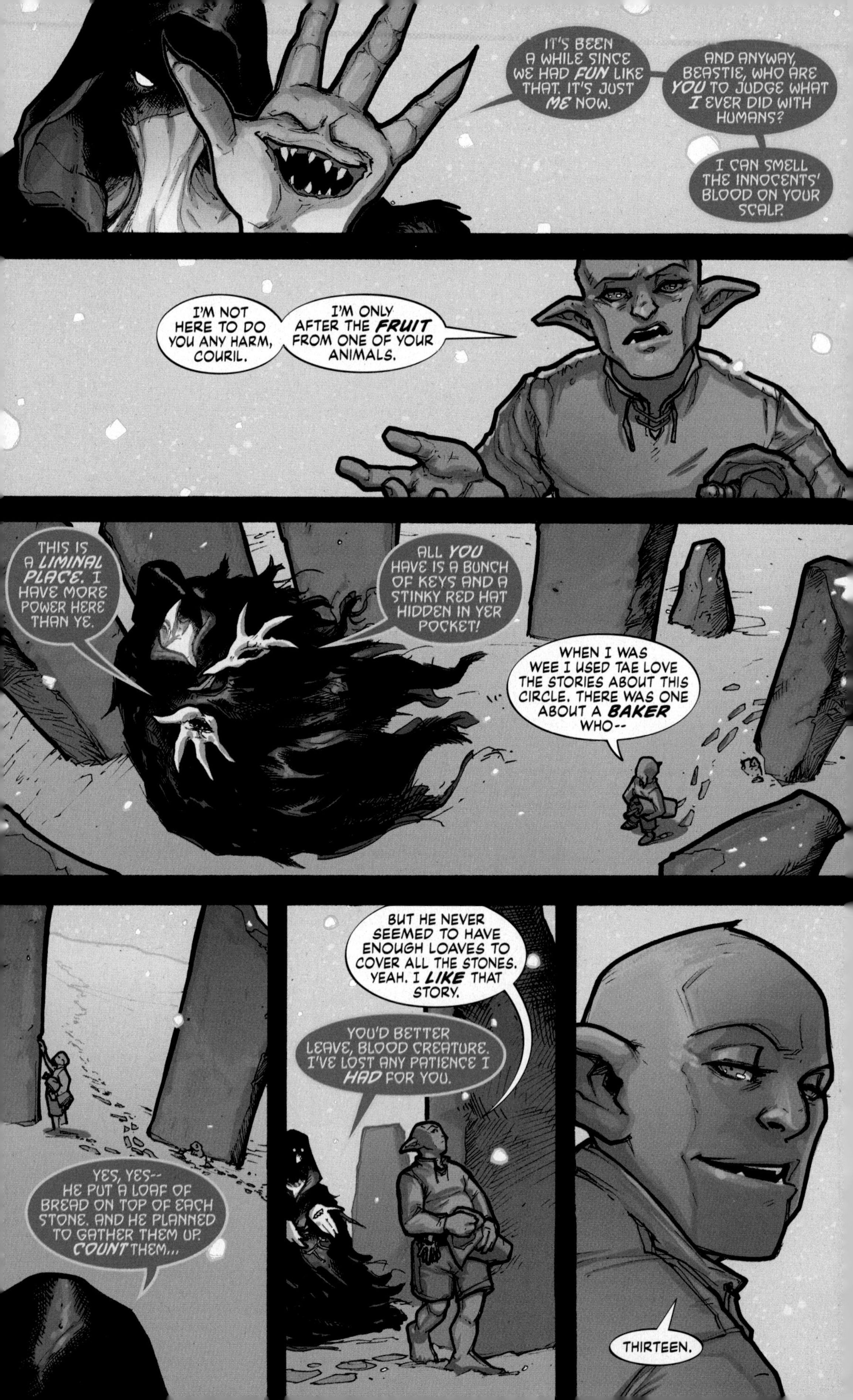
IT'S BEEN A WHILE SINCE WE HAD FUN LIKE THAT. IT'S JUST ME NOW.
AND ANYWAY, BEASTIE, WHO ARE YOU TO JUDGE WHAT I EVER DID WITH HUMANS?
I CAN SMELL THE INNOCENTS' BLOOD ON YOUR SCALP.
I'M NOT HERE TO DO YOU ANY HARM, COURIL.
I'M ONLY AFTER THE FRUIT FROM ONE OF YOUR ANIMALS.
THIS IS A LIMINAL PLACE. I HAVE MORE POWER HERE THAN YE.
ALL YOU HAVE IS A BUNCH OF KEYS AND A STINKY RED HAT HIDDEN IN YER POCKET!
WHEN I WAS WEE I USED TAE LOVE THE STORIES ABOUT THIS CIRCLE. THERE WAS ONE ABOUT A BAKER WHO--
YES, YES-- HE PUT A LOAF OF BREAD ON TOP OF EACH STONE. AND HE PLANNED TO GATHER THEM UP. COUNT THEM...
BUT HE NEVER SEEMED TO HAVE ENOUGH LOAVES TO COVER ALL THE STONES. YEAH. I LIKE THAT STORY.
YOU'D BETTER LEAVE, BLOOD CREATURE. I'VE LOST ANY PATIENCE I HAD FOR YOU.
THIRTEEN.

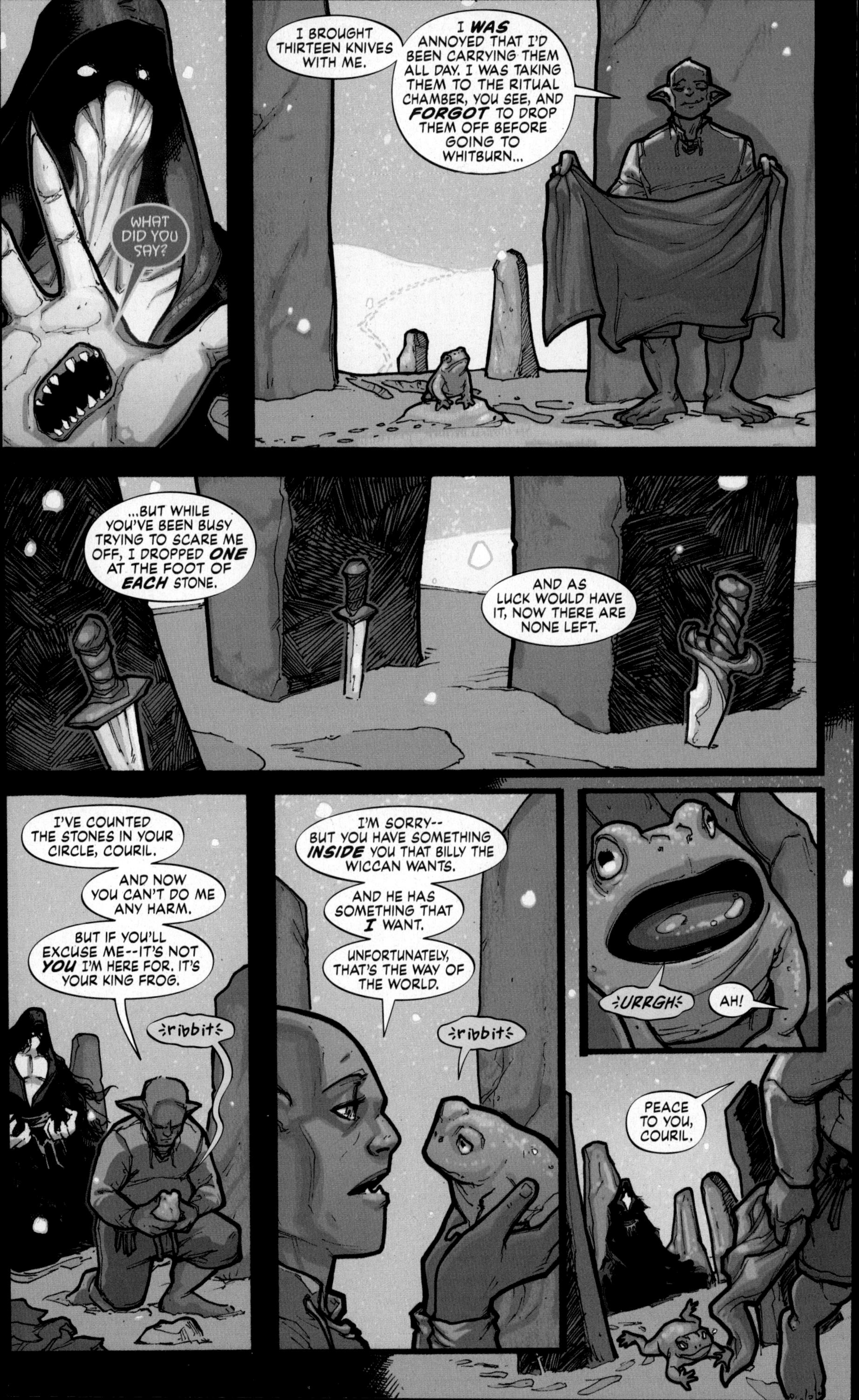
WHAT DID YOU SAY?
I BROUGHT THIRTEEN KNIVES WITH ME.
I WAS ANNOYED THAT I'D BEEN CARRYING THEM ALL DAY. I WAS TAKING THEM TO THE RITUAL CHAMBER, YOU SEE, AND FORGOT TO DROP THEM OFF BEFORE GOING TO WHITBURN...
...BUT WHILE YOU'VE BEEN BUSY TRYING TO SCARE ME OFF, I DROPPED ONE AT THE FOOT OF EACH STONE.
AND AS LUCK WOULD HAVE IT, NOW THERE ARE NONE LEFT.
I'VE COUNTED THE STONES IN YOUR CIRCLE, COURIL.
AND NOW YOU CAN'T DO ME ANY HARM.
BUT IF YOU'LL EXCUSE ME--IT'S NOT YOU I'M HERE FOR. IT'S YOUR KING FROG.
ribbit
I'M SORRY-- BUT YOU HAVE SOMETHING INSIDE YOU THAT BILLY THE WICCAN WANTS.
AND HE HAS SOMETHING THAT I WANT.
UNFORTUNATELY, THAT'S THE WAY OF THE WORLD.
ribbit
URRGH
AH!
PEACE TO YOU, COURIL.

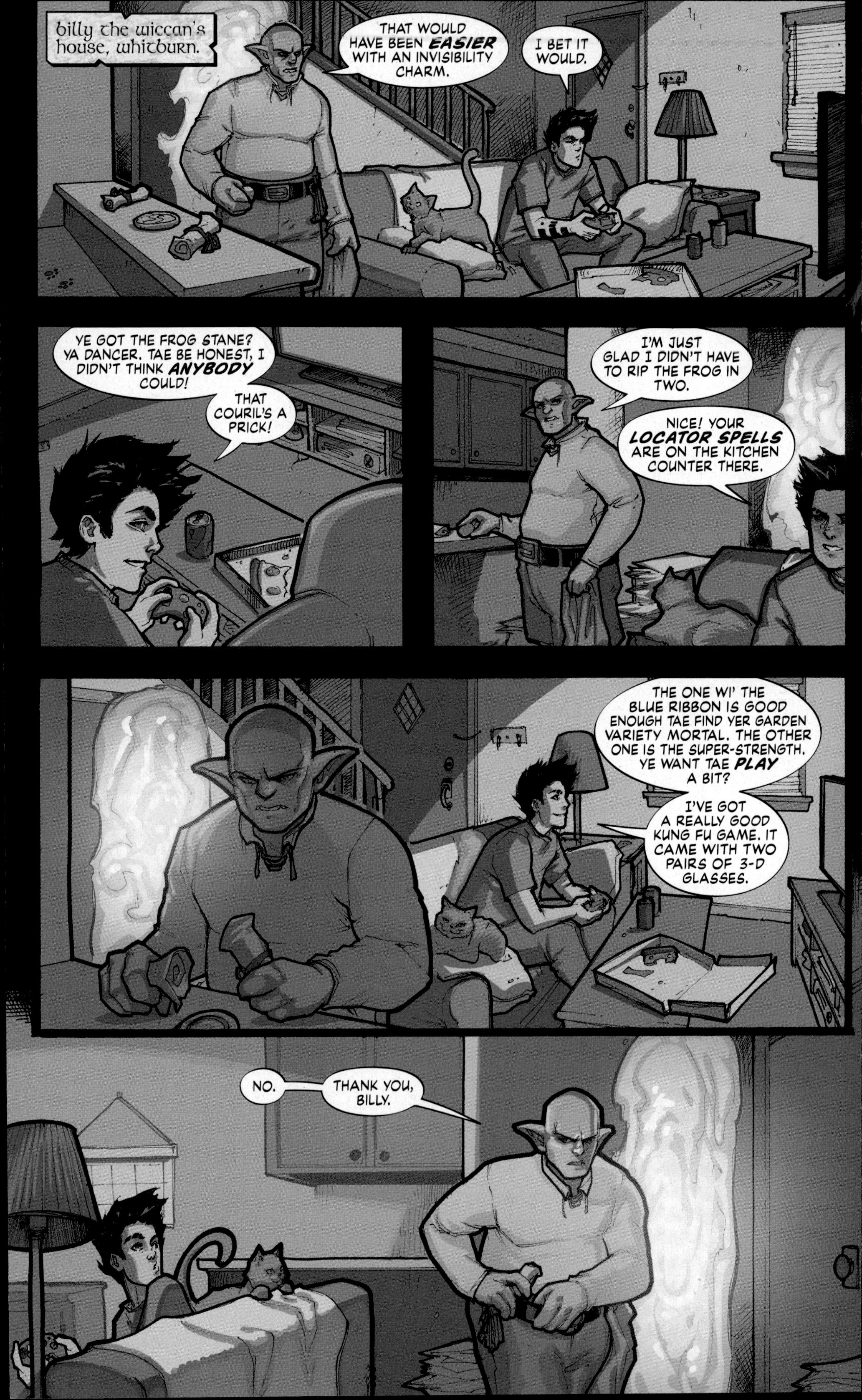
billy the wiccan's house, whitburn.
THAT WOULD HAVE BEEN EASIER WITH AN INVISIBILITY CHARM.
I BET IT WOULD.
YE GOT THE FROG STANE? YA DANCER. TAE BE HONEST, I DIDN'T THINK ANYBODY COULD!
THAT COURIL'S A PRICK!
I'M JUST GLAD I DIDN'T HAVE TO RIP THE FROG IN TWO.
NICE! YOUR LOCATOR SPELLS ARE ON THE KITCHEN COUNTER THERE.
THE ONE WI' THE BLUE RIBBON IS GOOD ENOUGH TAE FIND YER GARDEN VARIETY MORTAL. THE OTHER ONE IS THE SUPER-STRENGTH. YE WANT TAE PLAY A BIT?
I'VE GOT A REALLY GOOD KUNG FU GAME. IT CAME WITH TWO PAIRS OF 3-D GLASSES.
NO.
THANK YOU, BILLY.

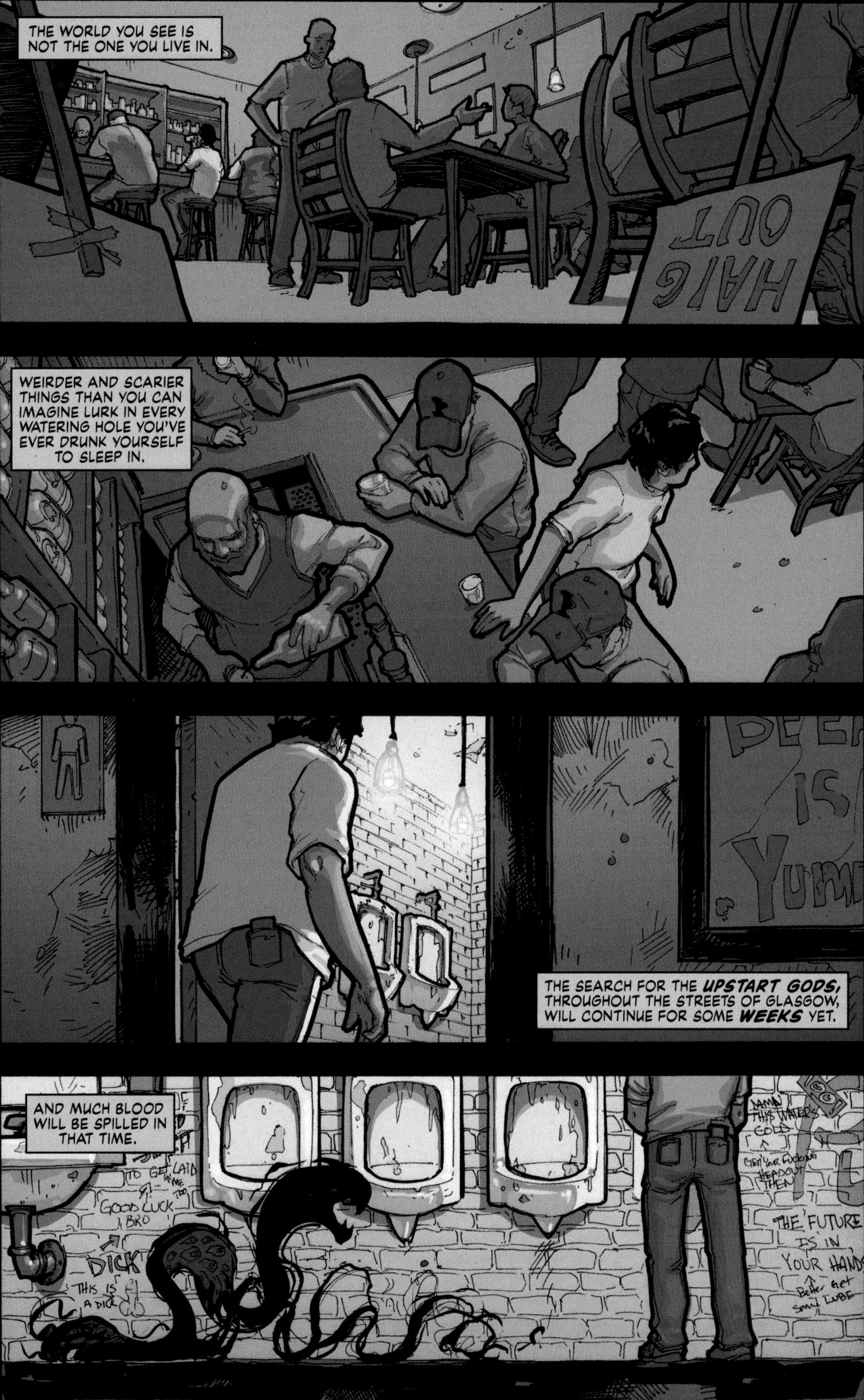
THE WORLD YOU SEE IS NOT THE ONE YOU LIVE IN.
WEIRDER AND SCARIER THINGS THAN YOU CAN IMAGINE LURK IN EVERY WATERING HOLE YOU'VE EVER DRUNK YOURSELF TO SLEEP IN.
THE SEARCH FOR THE UPSTART GODS, THROUGHOUT THE STREETS OF GLASGOW, WILL CONTINUE FOR SOME WEEKS YET.
AND MUCH BLOOD WILL BE SPILLED IN THAT TIME.
TO GET LAID
ME TOO
GOOD LUCK BRO
DICK
THIS IS A DICK
DAMN THIS WATER'S COLD
GET YOUR FUCKING HEAD OUT THEN
THE FUTURE IS IN YOUR HANDS
Better get some LUBE

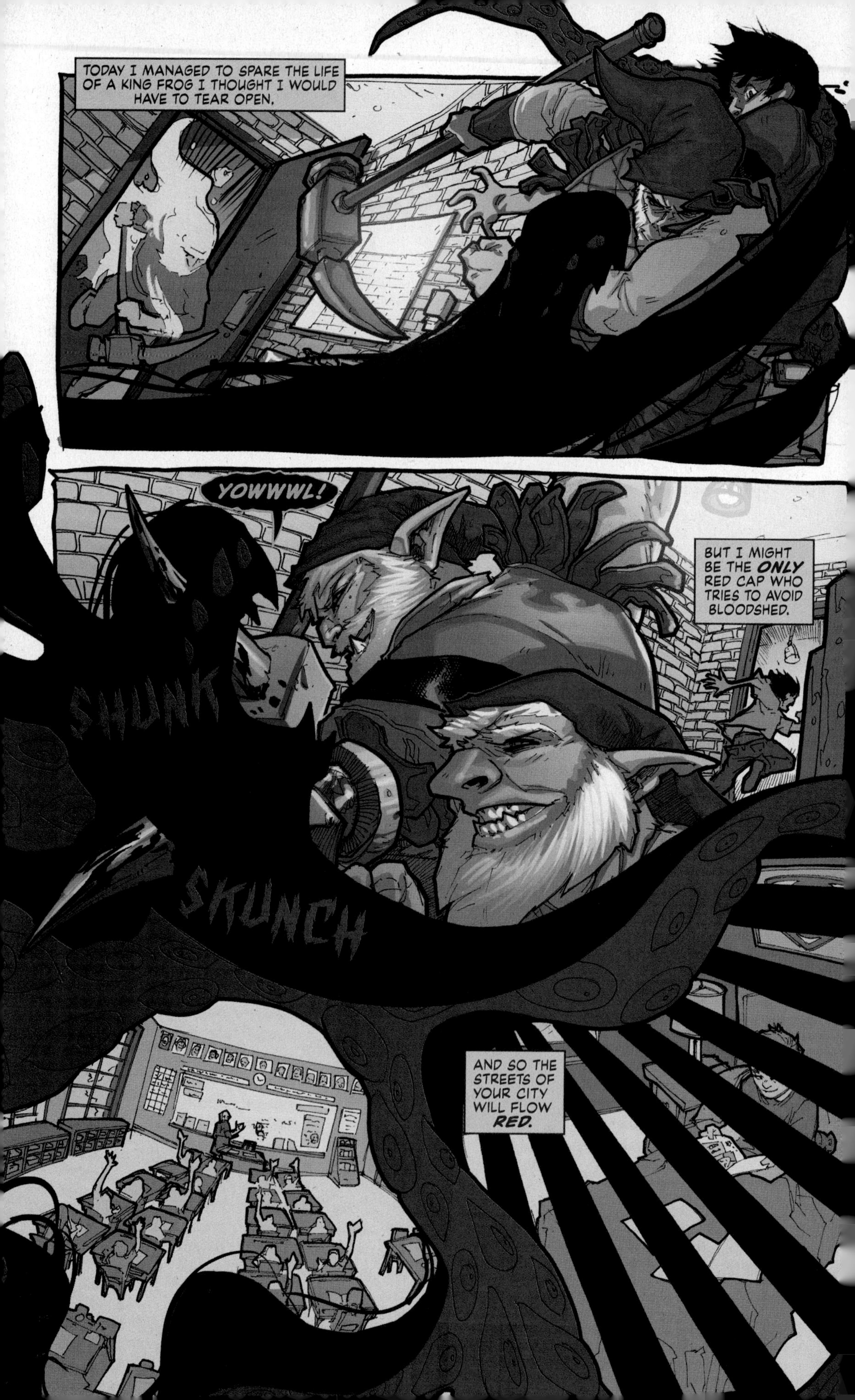
TODAY I MANAGED TO SPARE THE LIFE OF A KING FROG I THOUGHT I WOULD HAVE TO TEAR OPEN.
YOWWWL!
BUT I MIGHT BE THE ONLY RED CAP WHO TRIES TO AVOID BLOODSHED.
SHUNK
SKUNCH
AND SO THE STREETS OF YOUR CITY WILL FLOW RED.

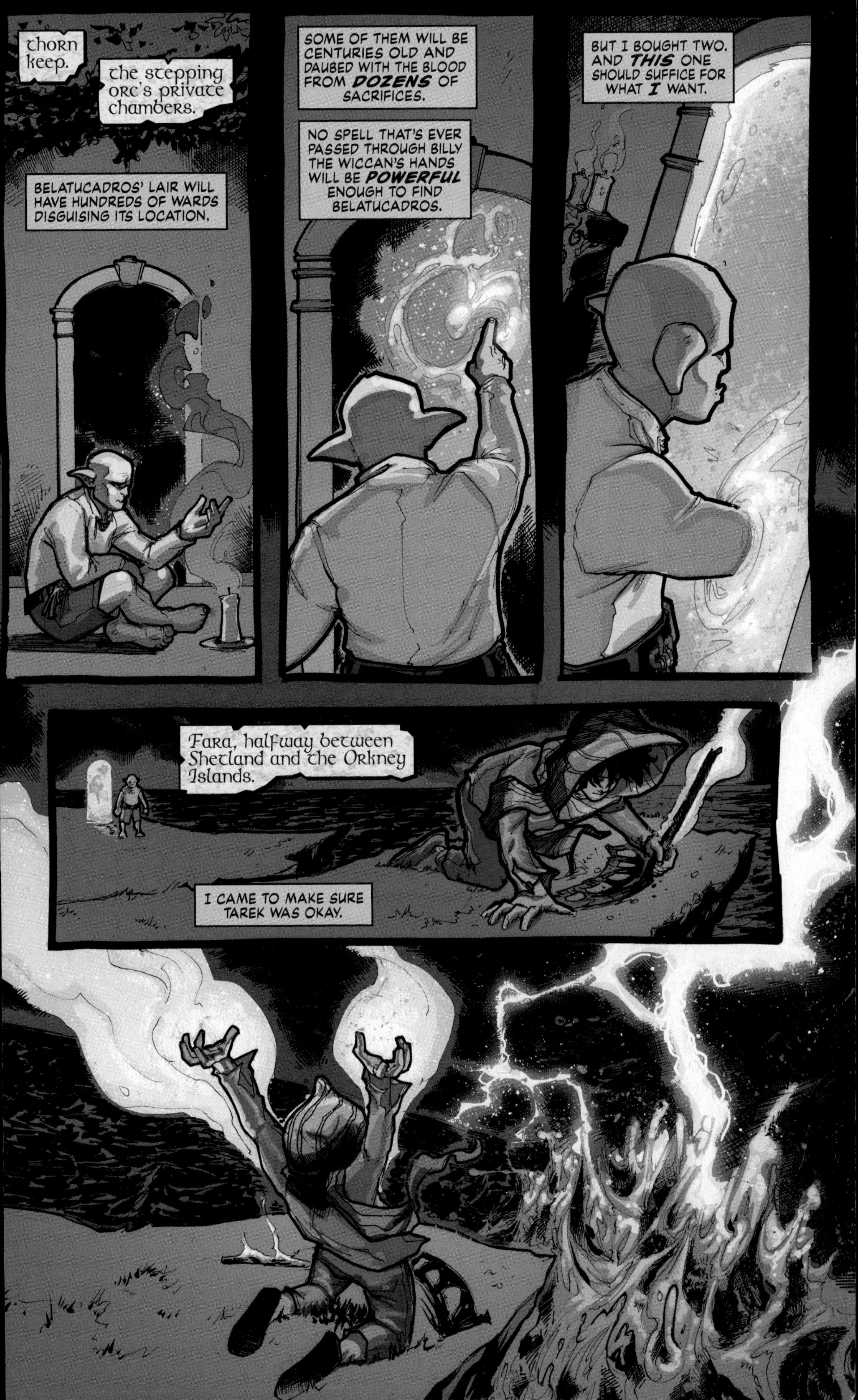
Thorn keep.
the stepping orc's private chambers.
BELATUCADROS' LAIR WILL HAVE HUNDREDS OF WARDS DISGUISING ITS LOCATION.
SOME OF THEM WILL BE CENTURIES OLD AND DAUBED WITH THE BLOOD FROM DOZENS OF SACRIFICES.
NO SPELL THAT'S EVER PASSED THROUGH BILLY THE WICCAN'S HANDS WILL BE POWERFUL ENOUGH TO FIND BELATUCADROS.
BUT I BOUGHT TWO. AND THIS ONE SHOULD SUFFICE FOR WHAT I WANT.
Fara, halfway between Shetland and the Orkney Islands.
I CAME TO MAKE SURE TAREK WAS OKAY.

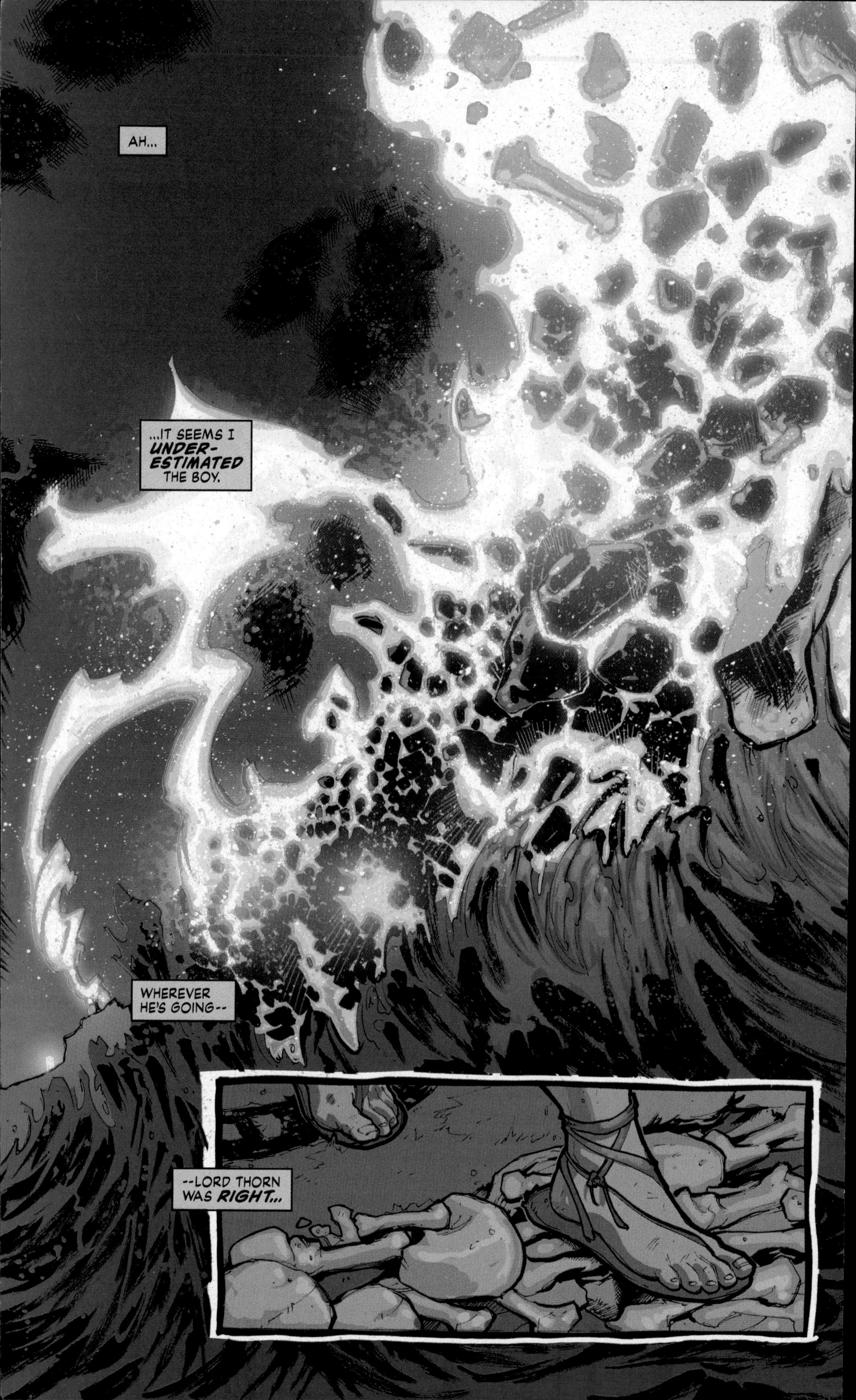
AH...
...IT SEEMS I UNDER-ESTIMATED THE BOY.
WHEREVER HE'S GOING--
--LORD THORN WAS RIGHT...

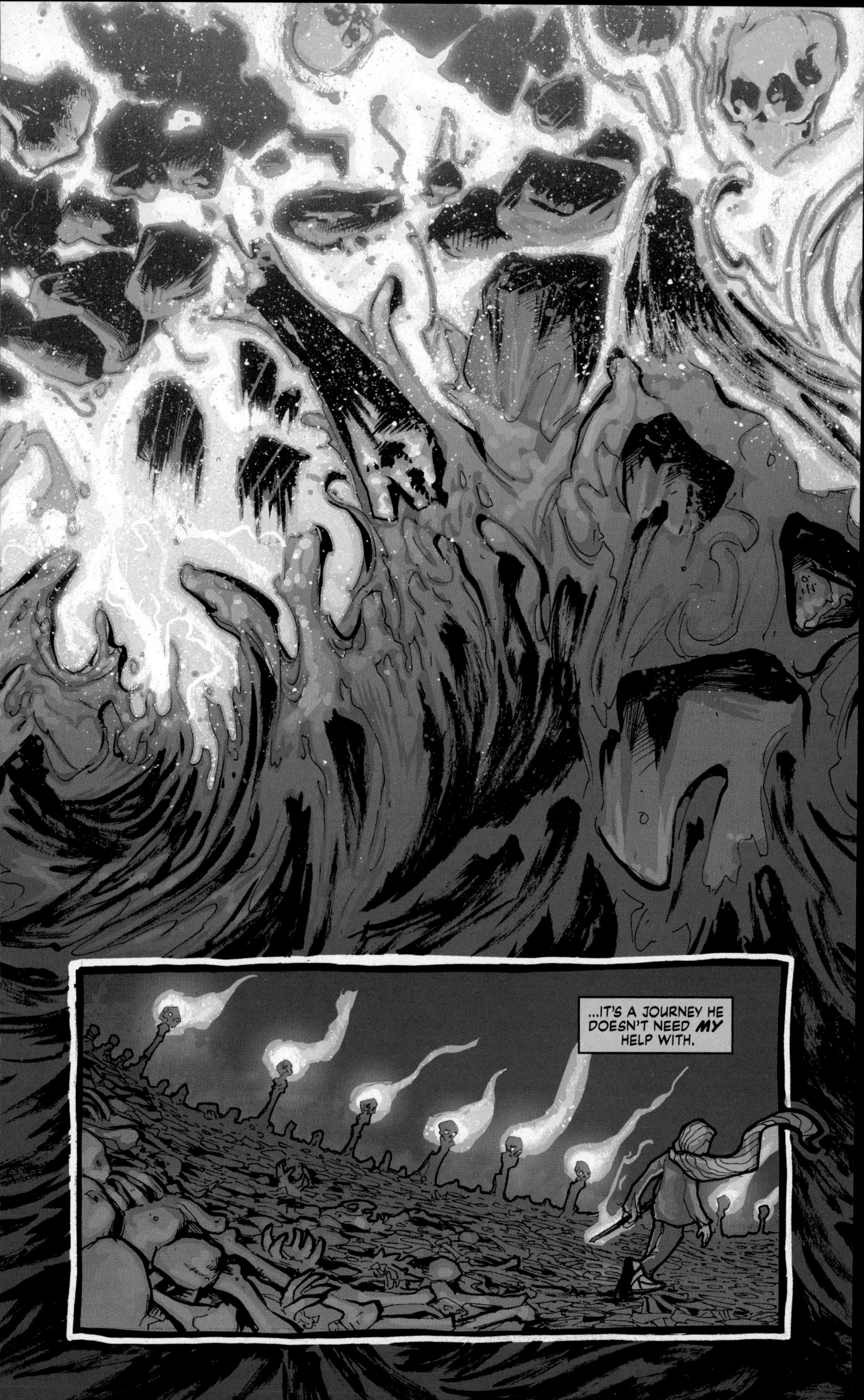
...IT'S A JOURNEY HE DOESN'T NEED MY HELP WITH.

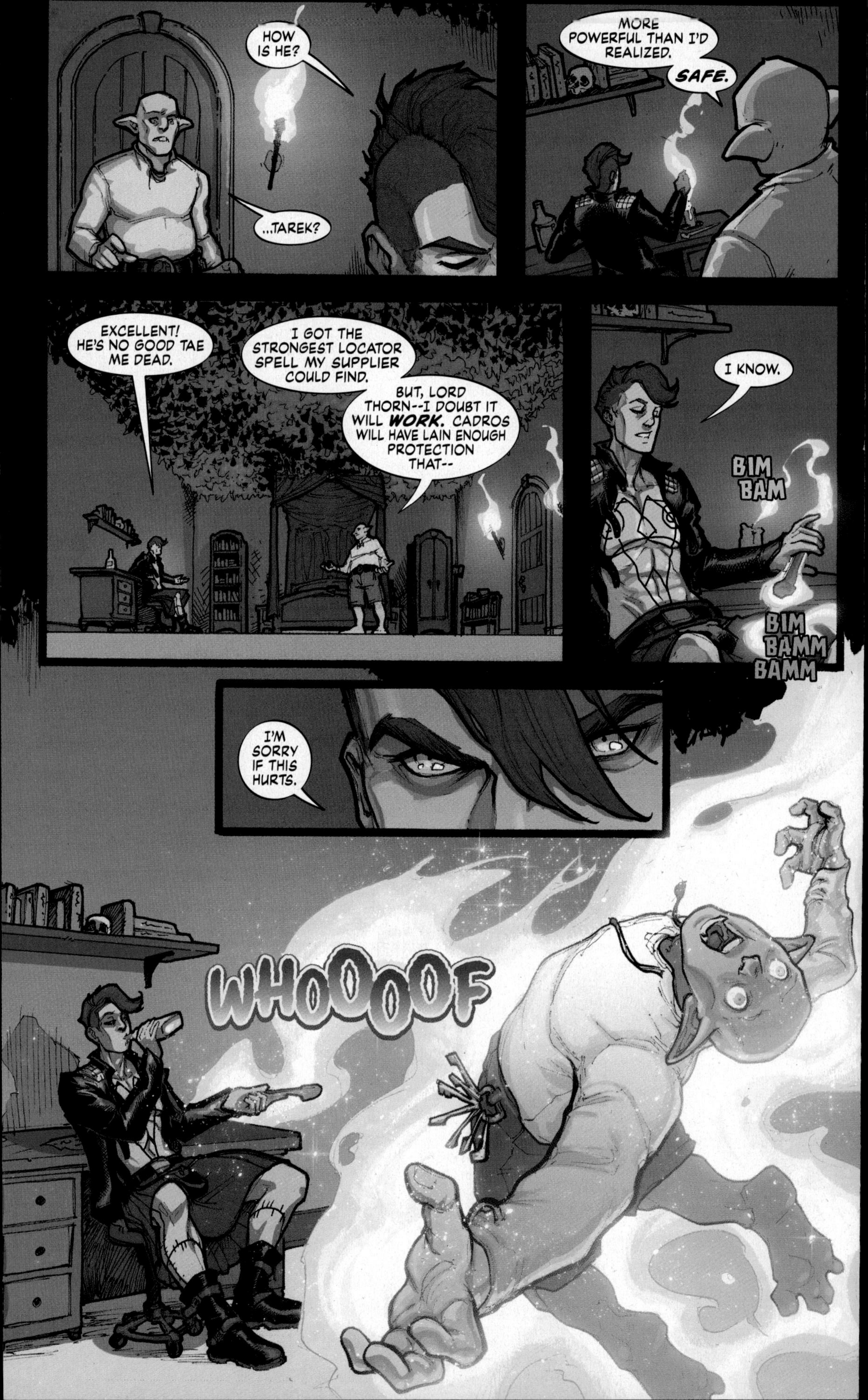
HOW IS HE?
...TAREK?
MORE POWERFUL THAN I'D REALIZED.
SAFE.
EXCELLENT! HE'S NO GOOD TAE ME DEAD.
I GOT THE STRONGEST LOCATOR SPELL MY SUPPLIER COULD FIND.
BUT, LORD THORN--I DOUBT IT WILL WORK. CADROS WILL HAVE LAIN ENOUGH PROTECTION THAT--
I KNOW.
BIM BAM
BIM BAMM BAMM
I'M SORRY IF THIS HURTS.
WHOOOOF

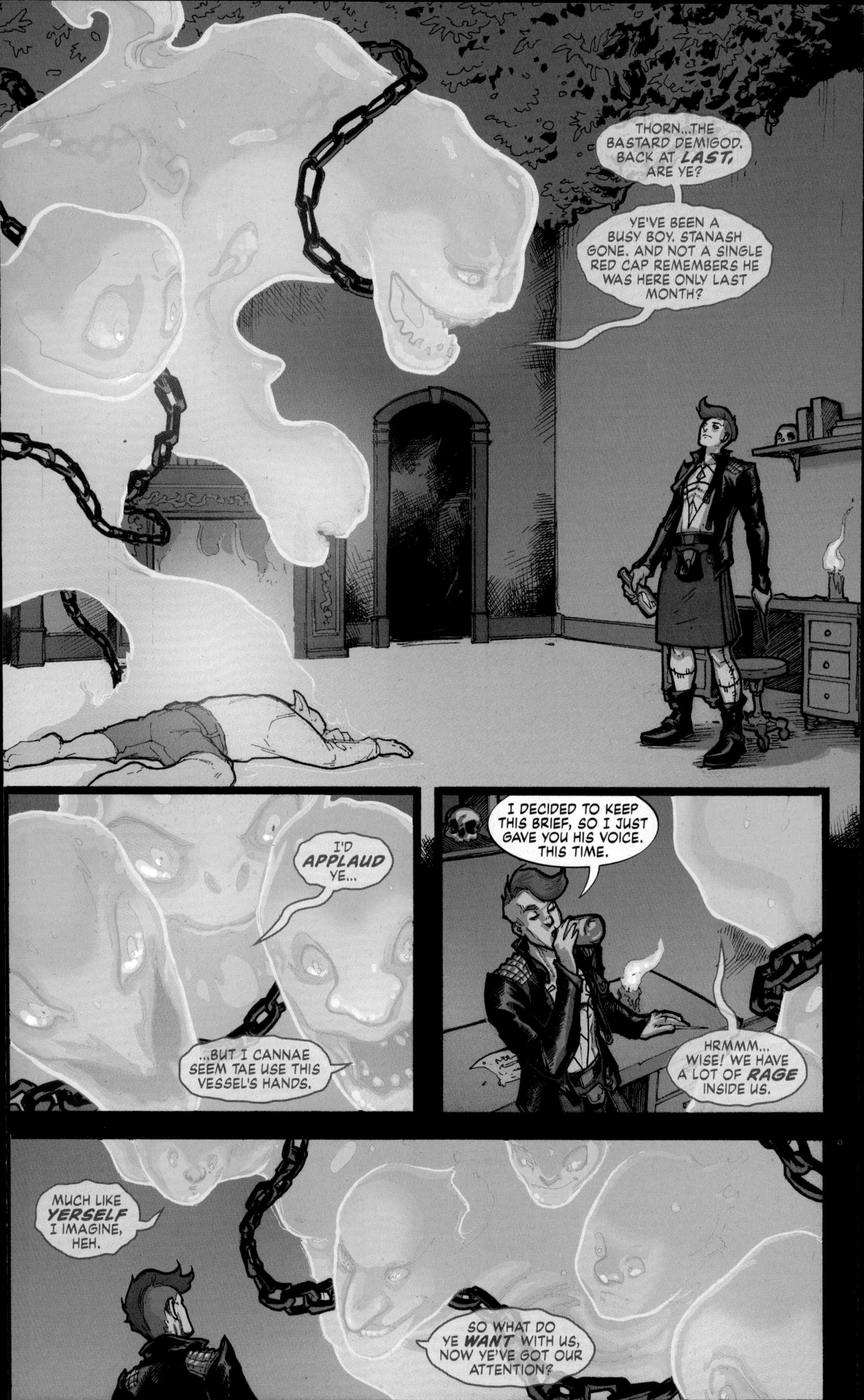
THORN...THE BASTARD DEMIGOD. BACK AT LAST, ARE YE?
YE'VE BEEN A BUSY BOY. STANASH GONE. AND NOT A SINGLE RED CAP REMEMBERS HE WAS HERE ONLY LAST MONTH?
I'D APPLAUD YE...
...BUT I CANNAE SEEM TAE USE THIS VESSEL'S HANDS.
I DECIDED TO KEEP THIS BRIEF, SO I JUST GAVE YOU HIS VOICE. THIS TIME.
HRMMM... WISE! WE HAVE A LOT OF RAGE INSIDE US.
MUCH LIKE YERSELF I IMAGINE, HEH.
SO WHAT DO YE WANT WITH US, NOW YE'VE GOT OUR ATTENTION?

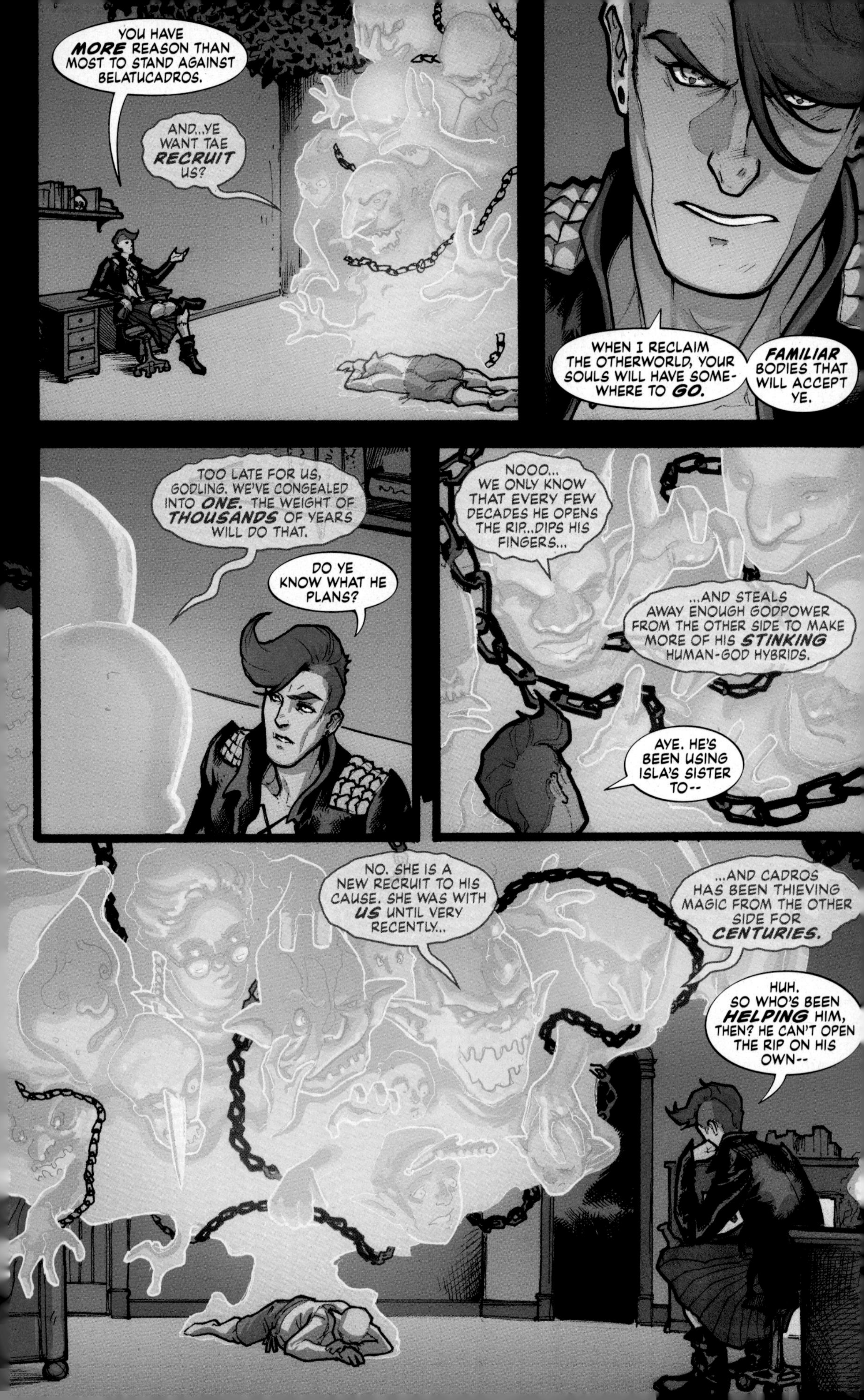

YOU HAVE MORE REASON THAN MOST TO STAND AGAINST BELATUCADROS.
AND...YE WANT TAE RECRUIT US?
WHEN I RECLAIM THE OTHERWORLD, YOUR SOULS WILL HAVE SOME-WHERE TO GO.
FAMILIAR BODIES THAT WILL ACCEPT YE.
TOO LATE FOR US, GODLING. WE'VE CONGEALED INTO ONE. THE WEIGHT OF THOUSANDS OF YEARS WILL DO THAT.
DO YE KNOW WHAT HE PLANS?
NOOO... WE ONLY KNOW THAT EVERY FEW DECADES HE OPENS THE RIP...DIPS HIS FINGERS...
...AND STEALS AWAY ENOUGH GODPOWER FROM THE OTHER SIDE TO MAKE MORE OF HIS STINKING HUMAN-GOD HYBRIDS.
AYE. HE'S BEEN USING ISLA'S SISTER TO--
NO. SHE IS A NEW RECRUIT TO HIS CAUSE. SHE WAS WITH US UNTIL VERY RECENTLY...
...AND CADROS HAS BEEN THIEVING MAGIC FROM THE OTHER SIDE FOR CENTURIES.
HUH. SO WHO'S BEEN HELPING HIM, THEN? HE CAN'T OPEN THE RIP ON HIS OWN--

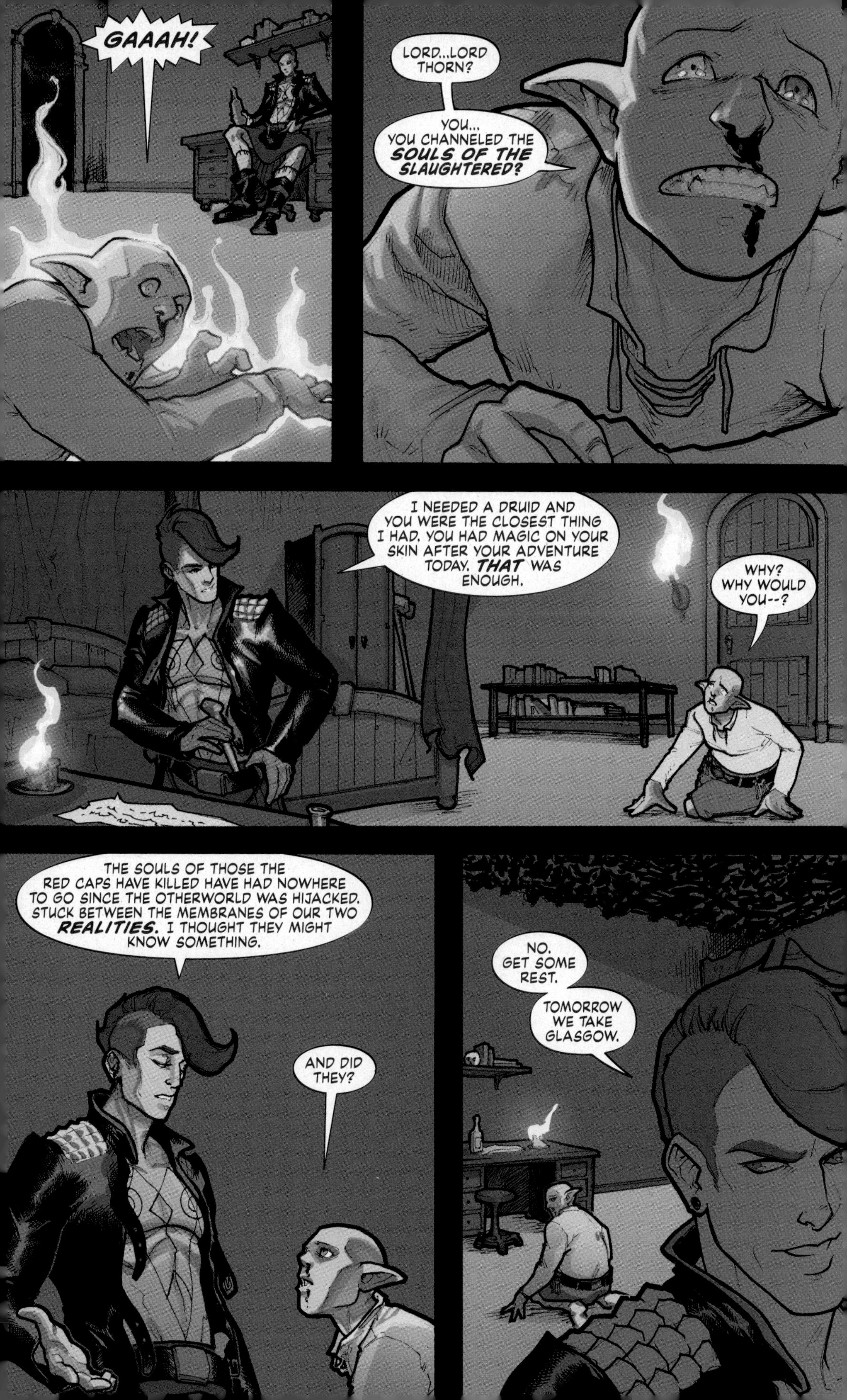
GAAAH!
LORD...LORD THORN?
YOU... YOU CHANNELED THE SOULS OF THE SLAUGHTERED?
I NEEDED A DRUID AND YOU WERE THE CLOSEST THING I HAD. YOU HAD MAGIC ON YOUR SKIN AFTER YOUR ADVENTURE TODAY. THAT WAS ENOUGH.
WHY? WHY WOULD YOU--?
THE SOULS OF THOSE THE RED CAPS HAVE KILLED HAVE HAD NOWHERE TO GO SINCE THE OTHERWORLD WAS HIJACKED. STUCK BETWEEN THE MEMBRANES OF OUR TWO REALITIES. I THOUGHT THEY MIGHT KNOW SOMETHING.
AND DID THEY?
NO. GET SOME REST.
TOMORROW WE TAKE GLASGOW.

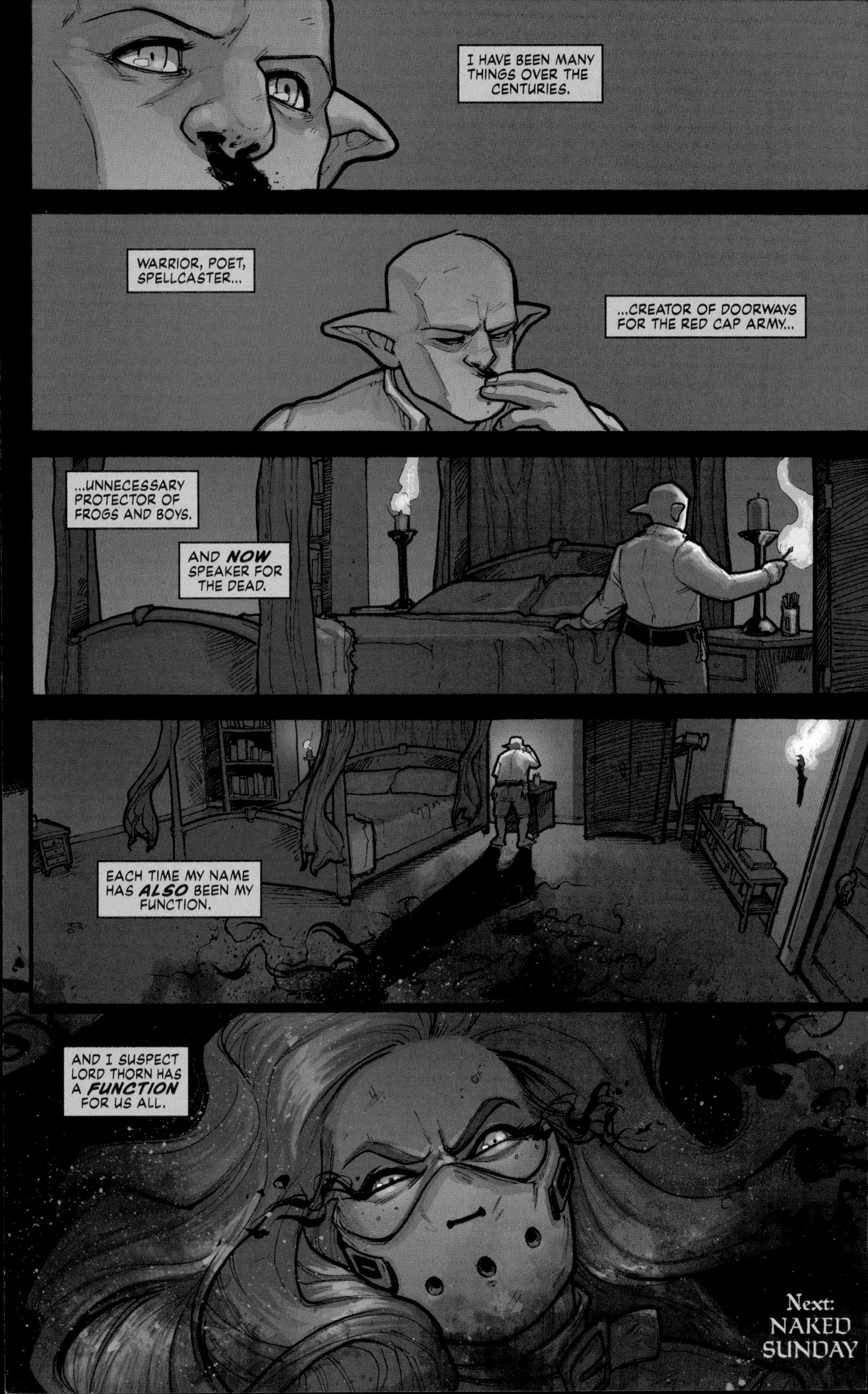
I HAVE BEEN MANY THINGS OVER THE CENTURIES.
WARRIOR, POET, SPELLCASTER...
...CREATOR OF DOORWAYS FOR THE RED CAP ARMY...
...UNNECESSARY PROTECTOR OF FROGS AND BOYS.
AND NOW SPEAKER FOR THE DEAD.
EACH TIME MY NAME HAS ALSO BEEN MY FUNCTION.
AND I SUSPECT LORD THORN HAS A FUNCTION FOR US ALL.
Next: NAKED SUNDAY

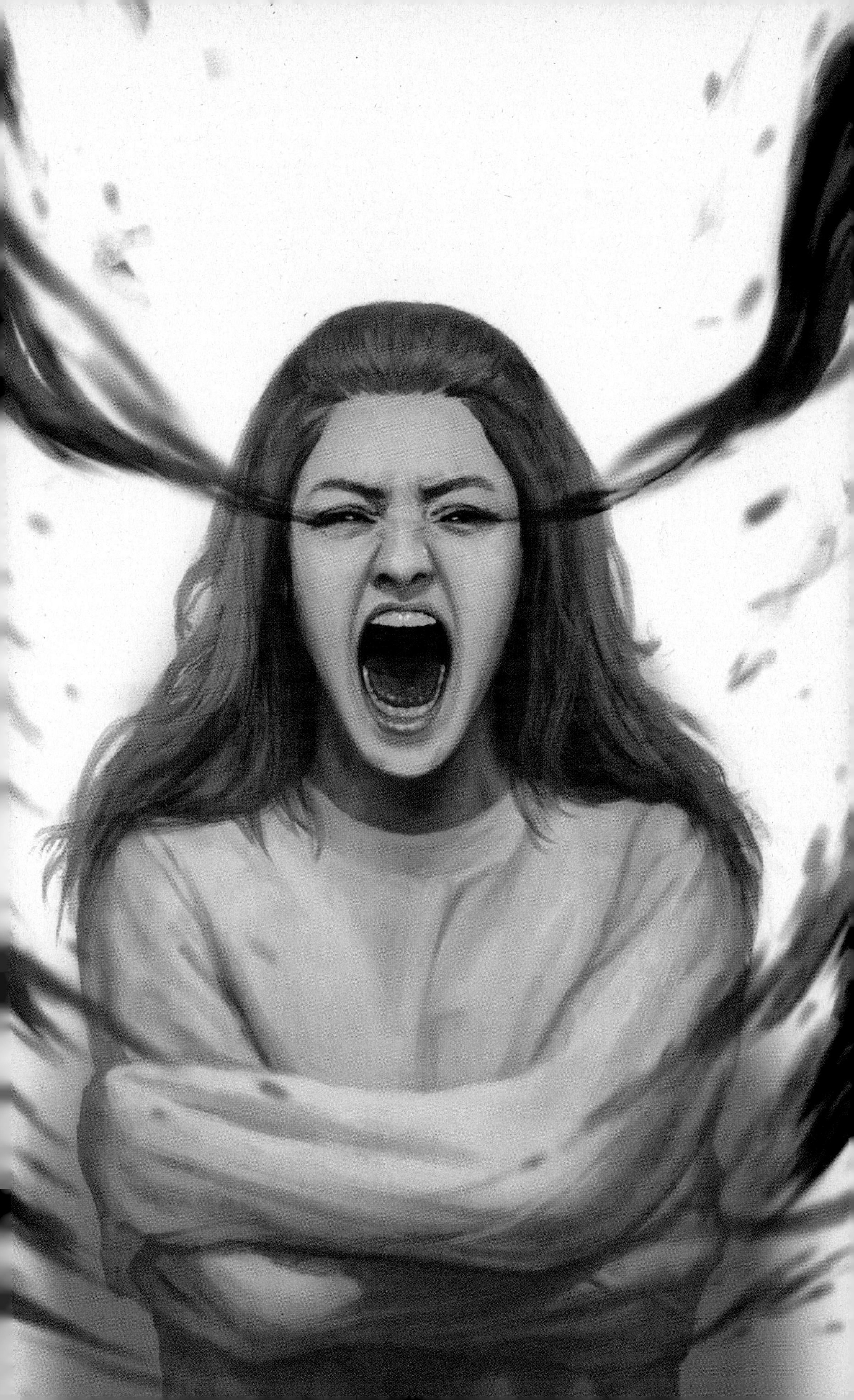

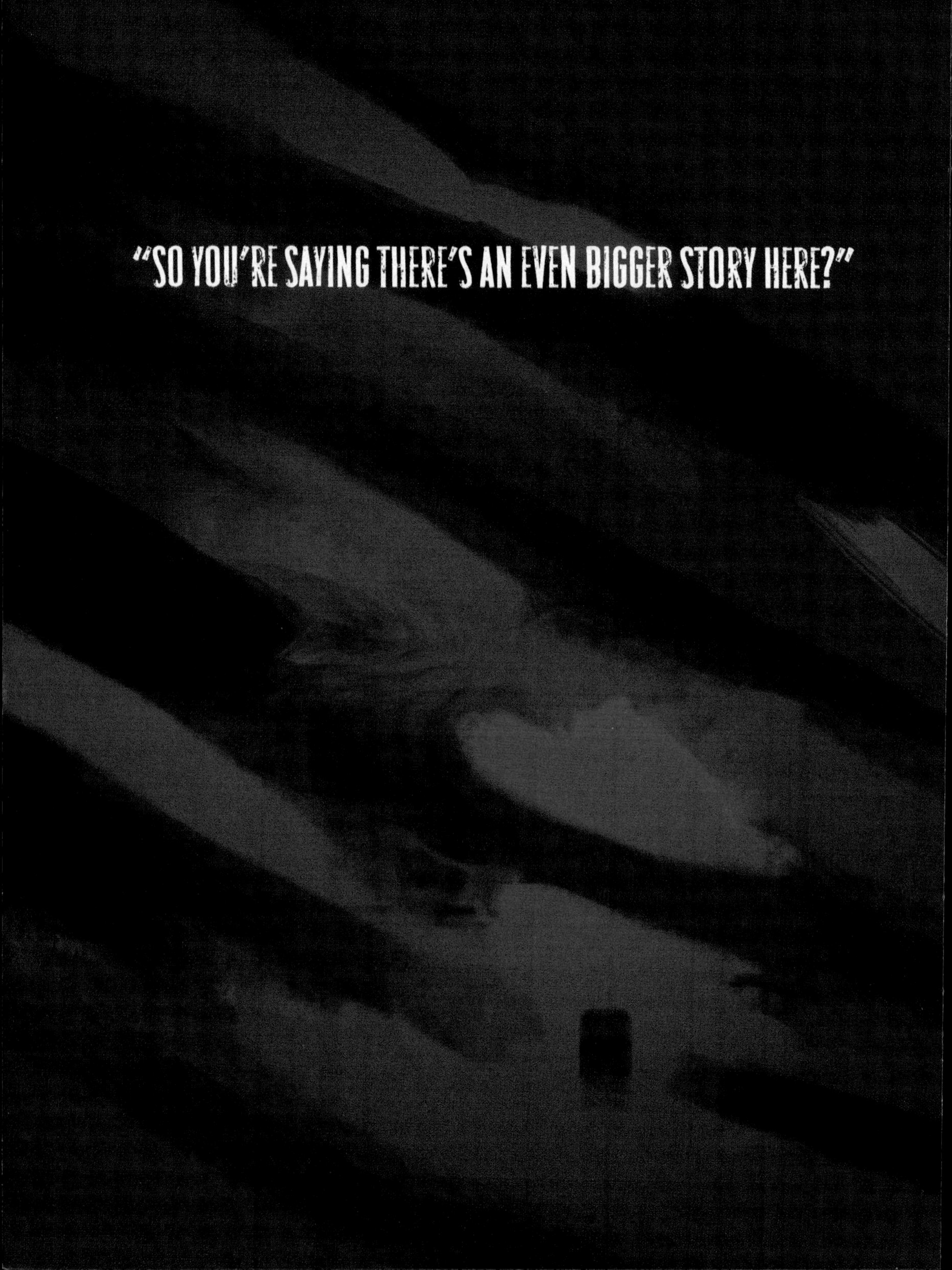
"SO YOU'RE SAYING THERE'S AN EVEN BIGGER STORY HERE?"

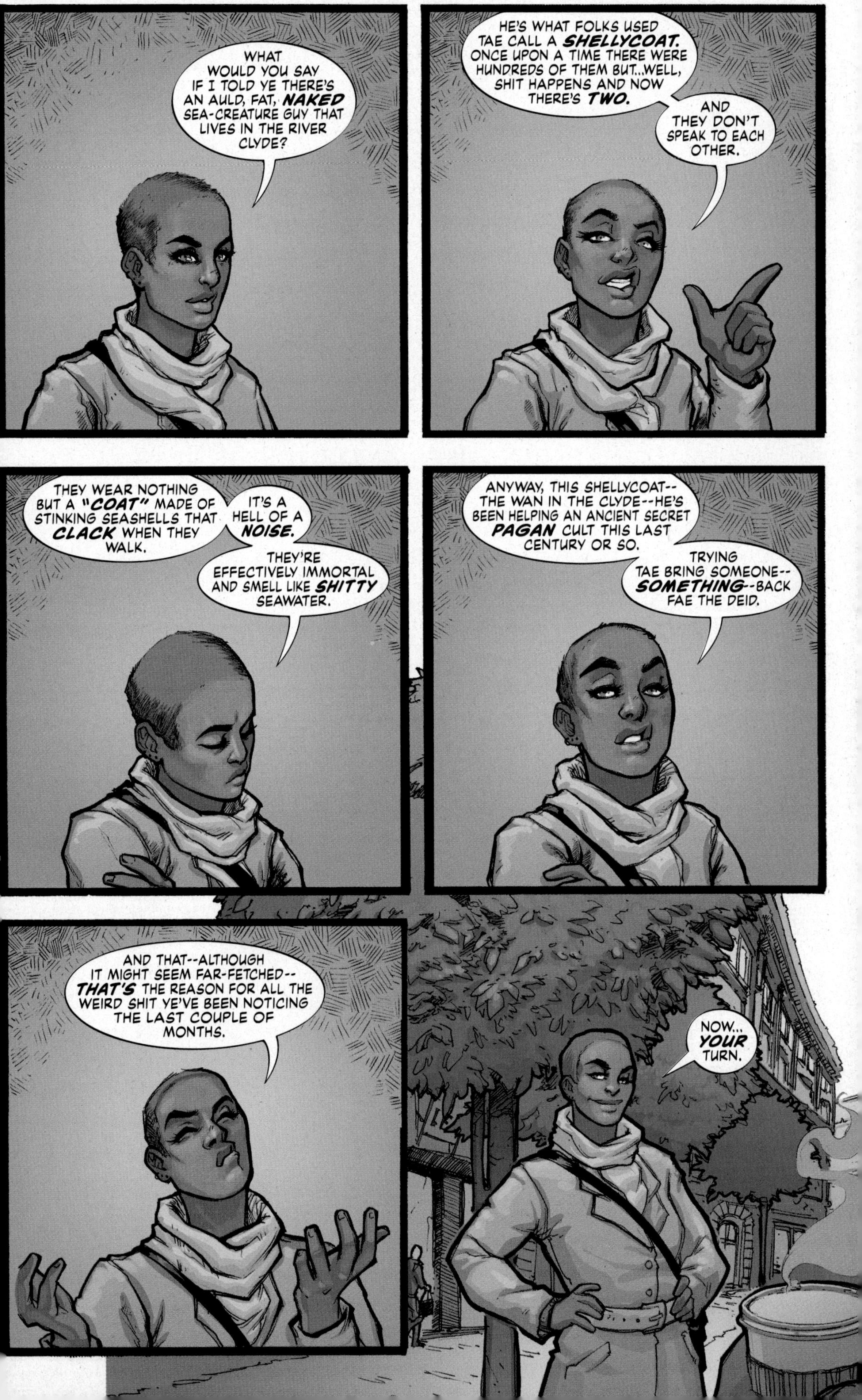
WHAT WOULD YOU SAY IF I TOLD YE THERE'S AN AULD, FAT, NAKED SEA-CREATURE GUY THAT LIVES IN THE RIVER CLYDE?
HE'S WHAT FOLKS USED TAE CALL A SHELLYCOAT. ONCE UPON A TIME THERE WERE HUNDREDS OF THEM BUT...WELL, SHIT HAPPENS AND NOW THERE'S TWO.
AND THEY DON'T SPEAK TO EACH OTHER.
THEY WEAR NOTHING BUT A "COAT" MADE OF STINKING SEASHELLS THAT CLACK WHEN THEY WALK.
IT'S A HELL OF A NOISE.
THEY'RE EFFECTIVELY IMMORTAL AND SMELL LIKE SHITTY SEAWATER.
ANYWAY, THIS SHELLYCOAT-- THE WAN IN THE CLYDE--HE'S BEEN HELPING AN ANCIENT SECRET PAGAN CULT THIS LAST CENTURY OR SO.
TRYING TAE BRING SOMEONE-- SOMETHING--BACK FAE THE DEID.
AND THAT--ALTHOUGH IT MIGHT SEEM FAR-FETCHED-- THAT'S THE REASON FOR ALL THE WEIRD SHIT YE'VE BEEN NOTICING THE LAST COUPLE OF MONTHS.
NOW... YOUR TURN.

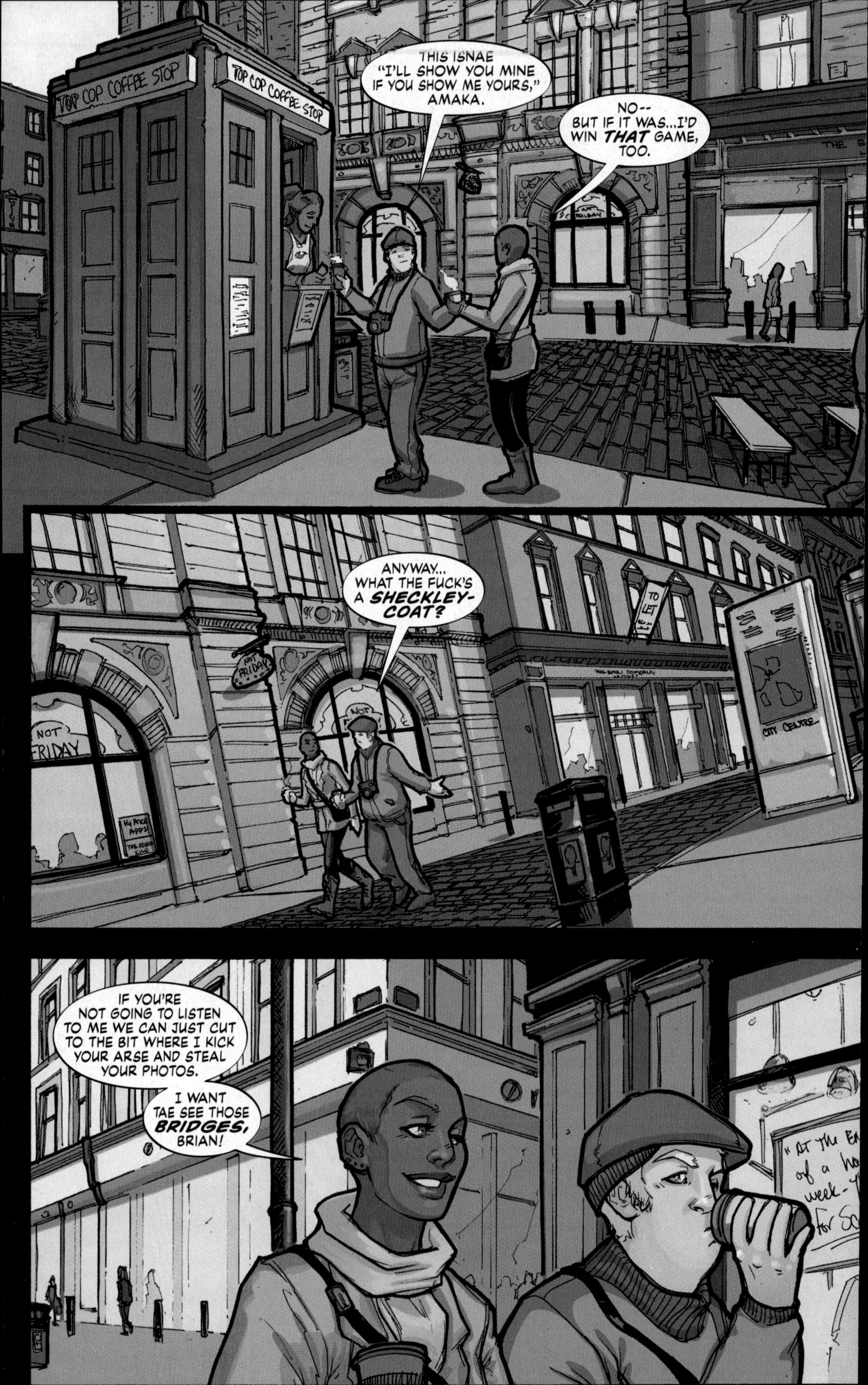
TOP COP COFFEE STOP
THIS ISNAE "I'LL SHOW YOU MINE IF YOU SHOW ME YOURS," AMAKA.
NO-- BUT IF IT WAS...I'D WIN *THAT* GAME, TOO.
ANYWAY... WHAT THE FUCK'S A *SHECKLEY-COAT?*
NOT FRIDAY
TO LET
CITY CENTRE
IF YOU'RE NOT GOING TO LISTEN TO ME WE CAN JUST CUT TO THE BIT WHERE I KICK YOUR ARSE AND STEAL YOUR PHOTOS.
I WANT TAE SEE THOSE *BRIDGES,* BRIAN!

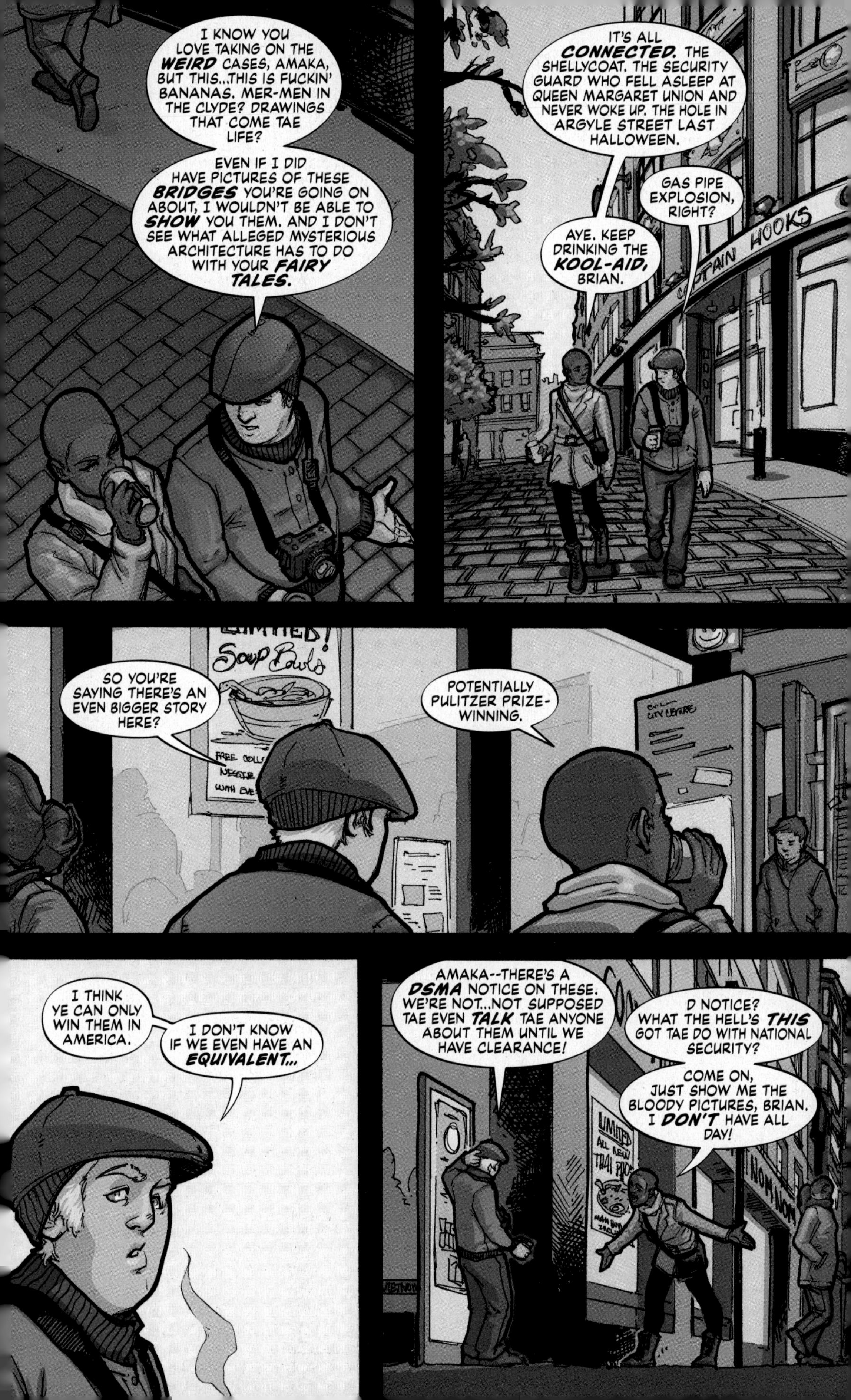
I KNOW YOU LOVE TAKING ON THE WEIRD CASES, AMAKA, BUT THIS...THIS IS FUCKIN' BANANAS. MER-MEN IN THE CLYDE? DRAWINGS THAT COME TAE LIFE?
EVEN IF I DID HAVE PICTURES OF THESE BRIDGES YOU'RE GOING ON ABOUT, I WOULDN'T BE ABLE TO SHOW YOU THEM. AND I DON'T SEE WHAT ALLEGED MYSTERIOUS ARCHITECTURE HAS TO DO WITH YOUR FAIRY TALES.
IT'S ALL CONNECTED. THE SHELLYCOAT. THE SECURITY GUARD WHO FELL ASLEEP AT QUEEN MARGARET UNION AND NEVER WOKE UP. THE HOLE IN ARGYLE STREET LAST HALLOWEEN.
GAS PIPE EXPLOSION, RIGHT?
AYE. KEEP DRINKING THE KOOL-AID, BRIAN.
CAPTAIN HOOKS
SO YOU'RE SAYING THERE'S AN EVEN BIGGER STORY HERE?
POTENTIALLY PULITZER PRIZE-WINNING.
I THINK YE CAN ONLY WIN THEM IN AMERICA.
I DON'T KNOW IF WE EVEN HAVE AN EQUIVALENT...
AMAKA--THERE'S A DSMA NOTICE ON THESE. WE'RE NOT...NOT SUPPOSED TAE EVEN TALK TAE ANYONE ABOUT THEM UNTIL WE HAVE CLEARANCE!
D NOTICE? WHAT THE HELL'S THIS GOT TAE DO WITH NATIONAL SECURITY?
COME ON, JUST SHOW ME THE BLOODY PICTURES, BRIAN. I DON'T HAVE ALL DAY!

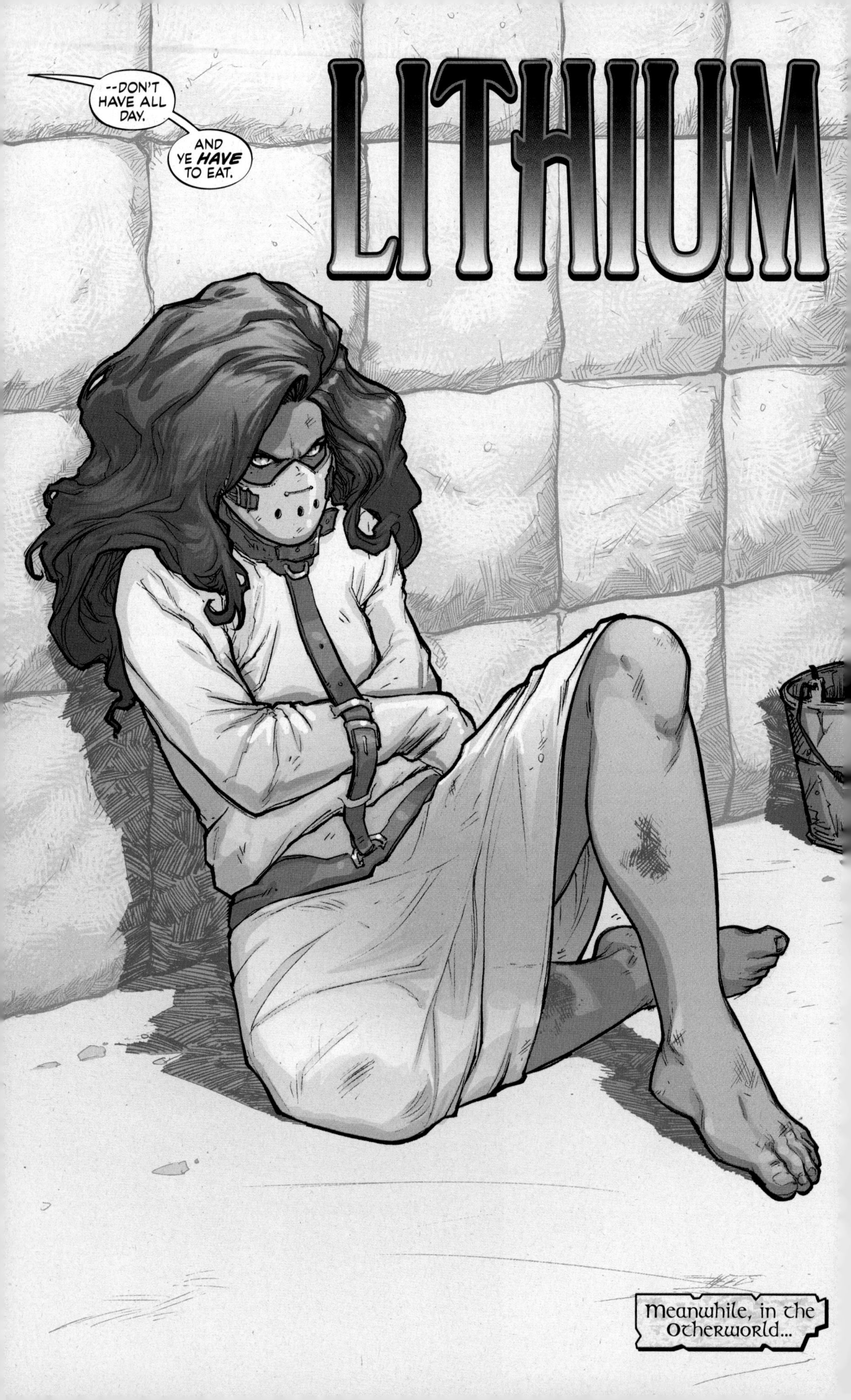
--DON'T HAVE ALL DAY.
AND YE HAVE TO EAT.
LITHIUM
Meanwhile, in the Otherworld...

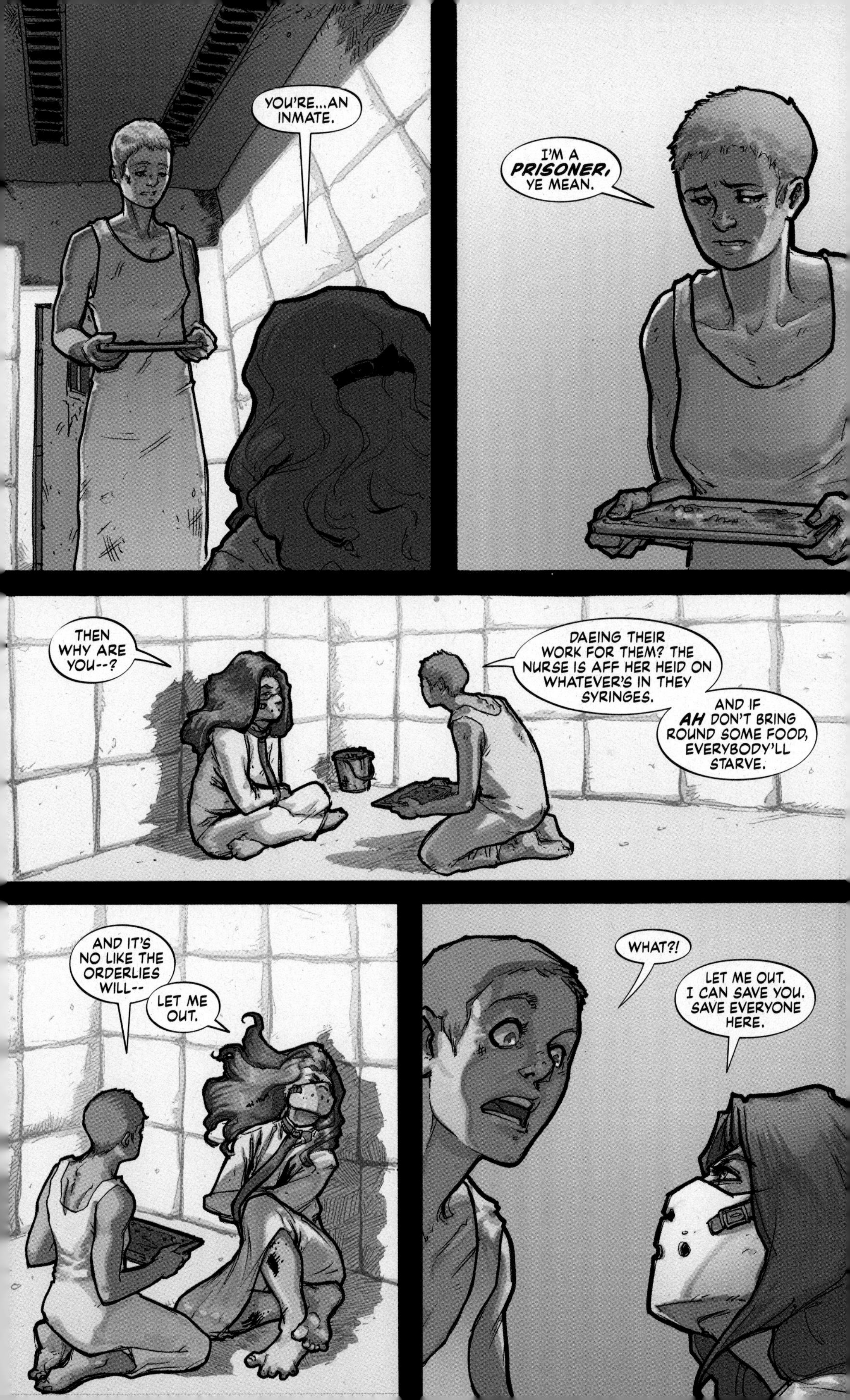
YOU'RE...AN INMATE.
I'M A PRISONER, YE MEAN.
THEN WHY ARE YOU--?
DAEING THEIR WORK FOR THEM? THE NURSE IS AFF HER HEID ON WHATEVER'S IN THEY SYRINGES.
AND IF AH DON'T BRING ROUND SOME FOOD, EVERYBODY'LL STARVE.
AND IT'S NO LIKE THE ORDERLIES WILL--
LET ME OUT.
WHAT?!
LET ME OUT. I CAN SAVE YOU. SAVE EVERYONE HERE.

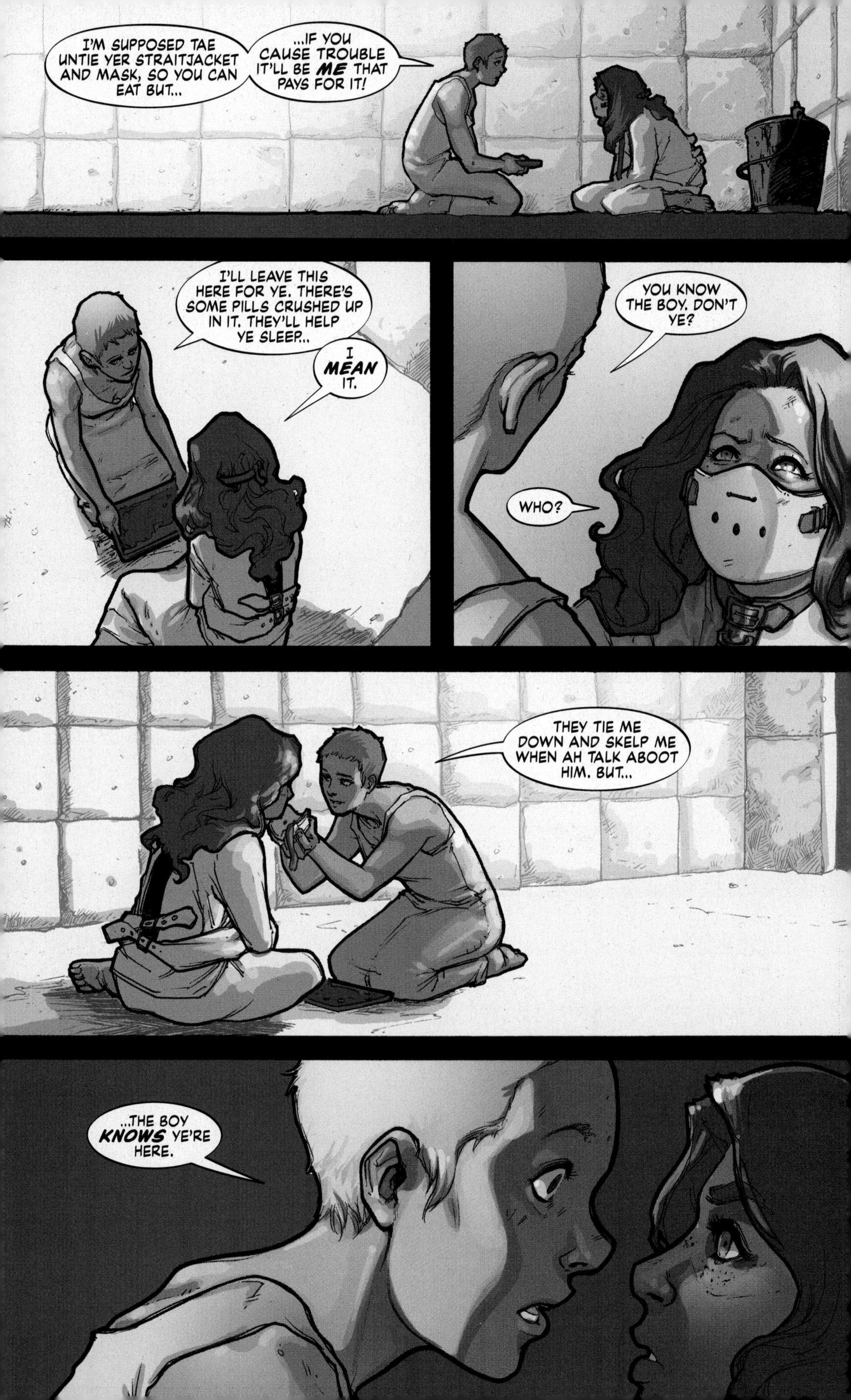
I'M SUPPOSED TAE UNTIE YER STRAITJACKET AND MASK, SO YOU CAN EAT BUT...
...IF YOU CAUSE TROUBLE IT'LL BE ME THAT PAYS FOR IT!
I'LL LEAVE THIS HERE FOR YE. THERE'S SOME PILLS CRUSHED UP IN IT. THEY'LL HELP YE SLEEP...
I MEAN IT.
YOU KNOW THE BOY, DON'T YE?
WHO?
THEY TIE ME DOWN AND SKELP ME WHEN AH TALK ABOOT HIM. BUT...
...THE BOY KNOWS YE'RE HERE.

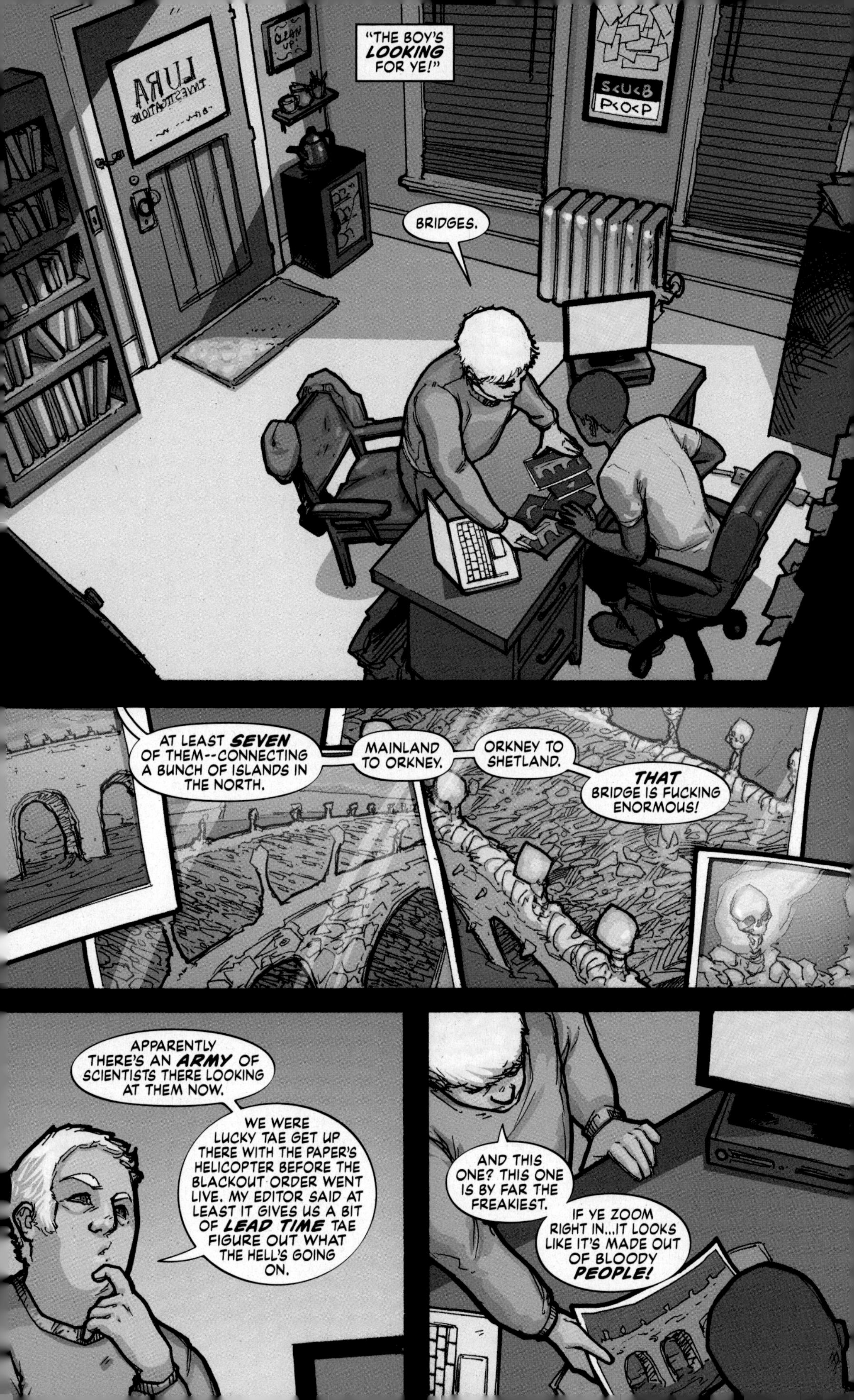

"THE BOY'S LOOKING FOR YE!"
LURA INVESTIGATIONS
CLEAN UP!
BRIDGES.
AT LEAST SEVEN OF THEM--CONNECTING A BUNCH OF ISLANDS IN THE NORTH.
MAINLAND TO ORKNEY.
ORKNEY TO SHETLAND.
THAT BRIDGE IS FUCKING ENORMOUS!
APPARENTLY THERE'S AN ARMY OF SCIENTISTS THERE LOOKING AT THEM NOW.
WE WERE LUCKY TAE GET UP THERE WITH THE PAPER'S HELICOPTER BEFORE THE BLACKOUT ORDER WENT LIVE. MY EDITOR SAID AT LEAST IT GIVES US A BIT OF LEAD TIME TAE FIGURE OUT WHAT THE HELL'S GOING ON.
AND THIS ONE? THIS ONE IS BY FAR THE FREAKIEST.
IF YE ZOOM RIGHT IN...IT LOOKS LIKE IT'S MADE OUT OF BLOODY PEOPLE!

MAKES NO SENSE... THEY'VE EVACUATED THE ISLANDS...AND *NONE* OF THIS HAS TURNED UP ON SOCIAL MEDIA--NOT EVEN ON SOME TEENAGER'S BLOG?

AYE. TOTAL SHUTDOWN.

NEVER SEEN ANYTHING LIKE IT.

SO GO ON-- HOW DOES THIS RELATE TO *YOUR* STORY? IT'S A CASE YOU'RE WORKING, IS IT?

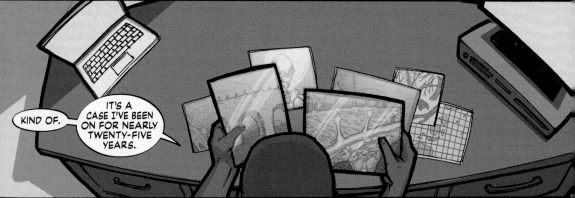

KIND OF.

IT'S A CASE I'VE BEEN ON FOR NEARLY TWENTY-FIVE YEARS.

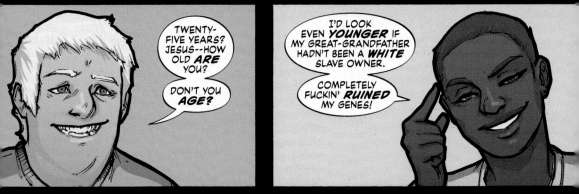

TWENTY-FIVE YEARS? JESUS--HOW OLD *ARE* YOU?

DON'T YOU *AGE*?

I'D LOOK EVEN *YOUNGER* IF MY GREAT-GRANDFATHER HADN'T BEEN A *WHITE* SLAVE OWNER.

COMPLETELY FUCKIN' *RUINED* MY GENES!

LET ME TELL YOU A STORY. IT WAS 1991...

...MY BEST FRIEND, LAUREN, WAS KILLED.

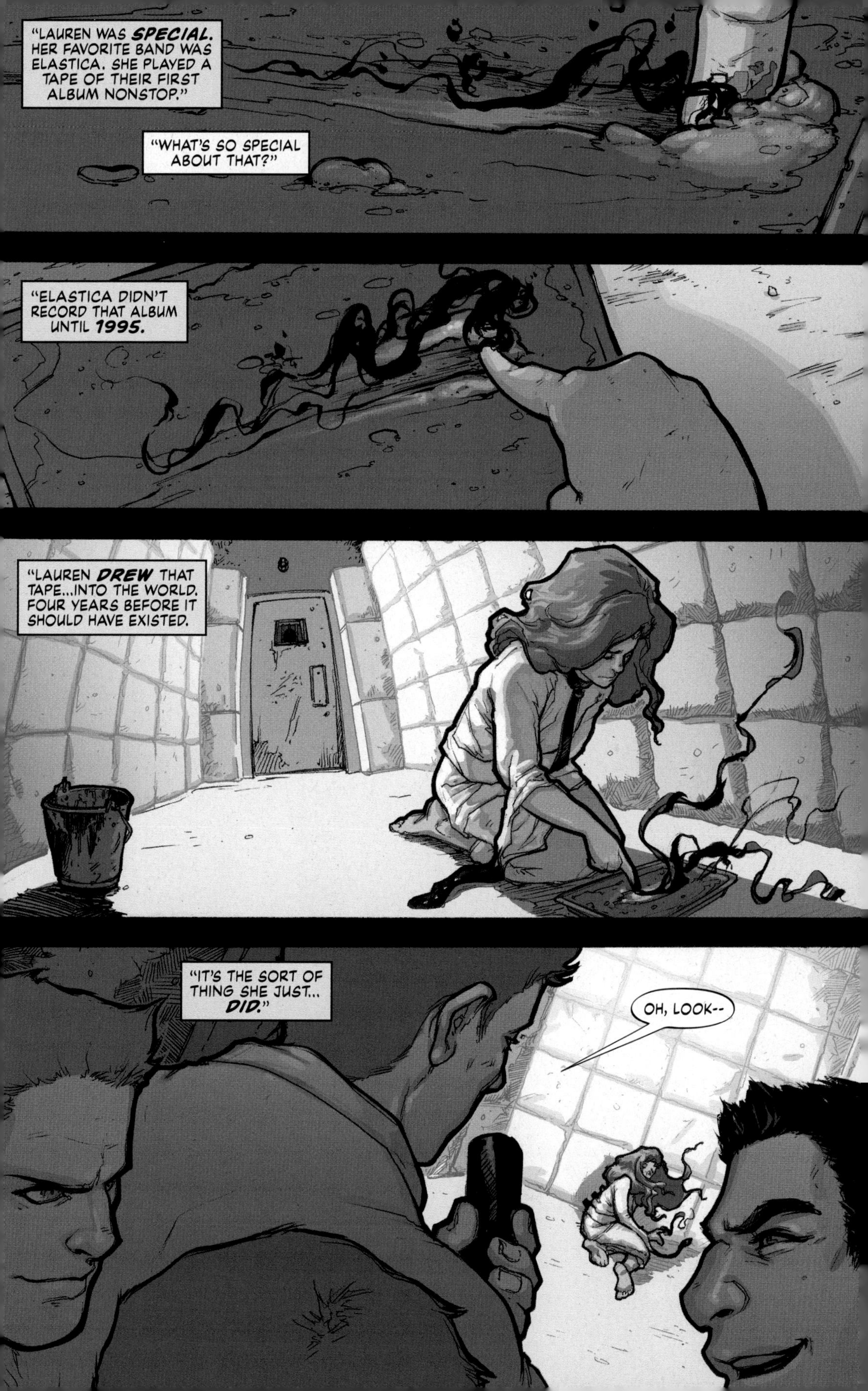
"LAUREN WAS SPECIAL. HER FAVORITE BAND WAS ELASTICA. SHE PLAYED A TAPE OF THEIR FIRST ALBUM NONSTOP."
"WHAT'S SO SPECIAL ABOUT THAT?"
"ELASTICA DIDN'T RECORD THAT ALBUM UNTIL 1995.
"LAUREN DREW THAT TAPE...INTO THE WORLD. FOUR YEARS BEFORE IT SHOULD HAVE EXISTED.
"IT'S THE SORT OF THING SHE JUST... DID."
OH, LOOK--

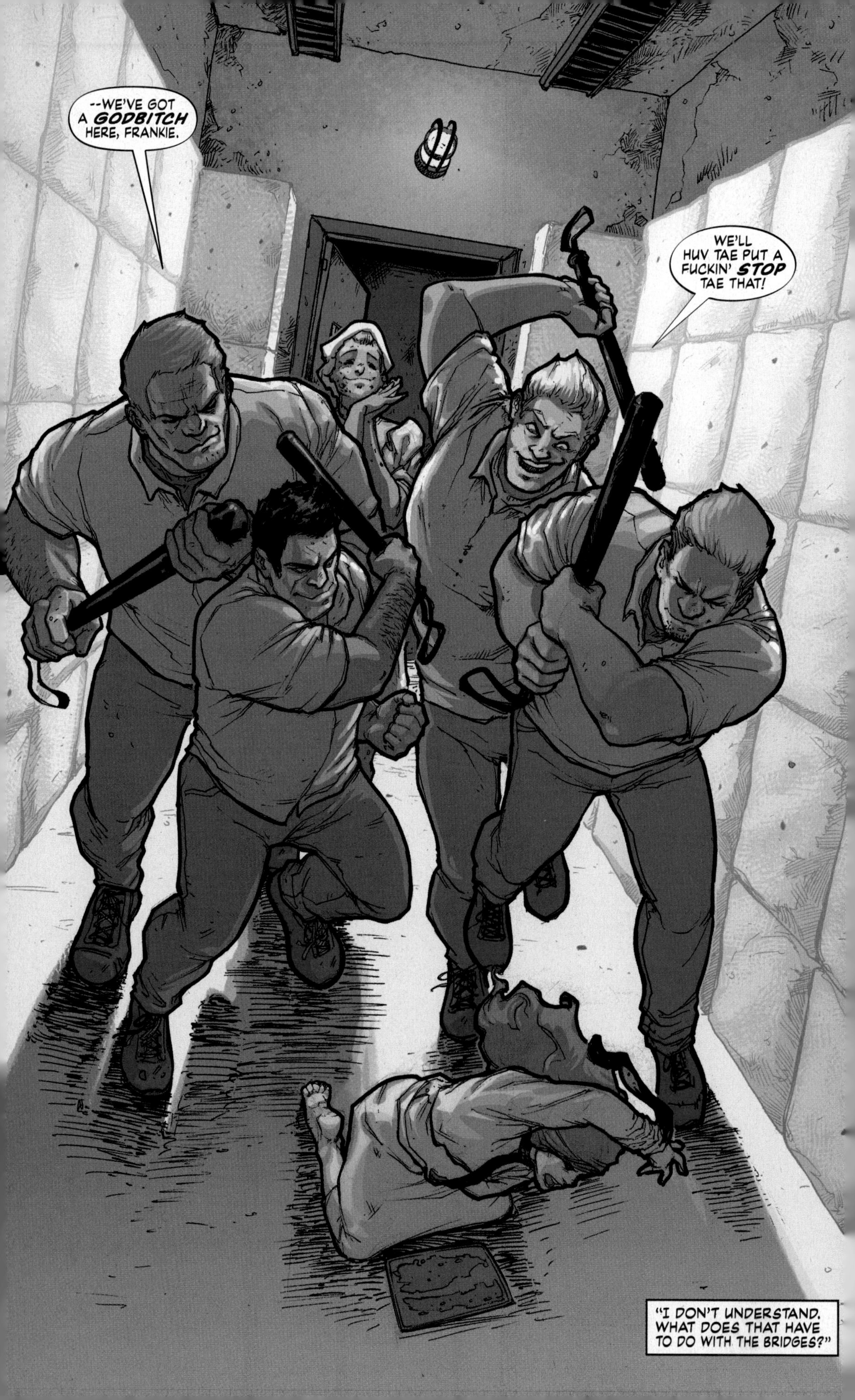
--WE'VE GOT A GODBITCH HERE, FRANKIE.
WE'LL HUV TAE PUT A FUCKIN' STOP TAE THAT!
"I DON'T UNDERSTAND. WHAT DOES THAT HAVE TO DO WITH THE BRIDGES?"

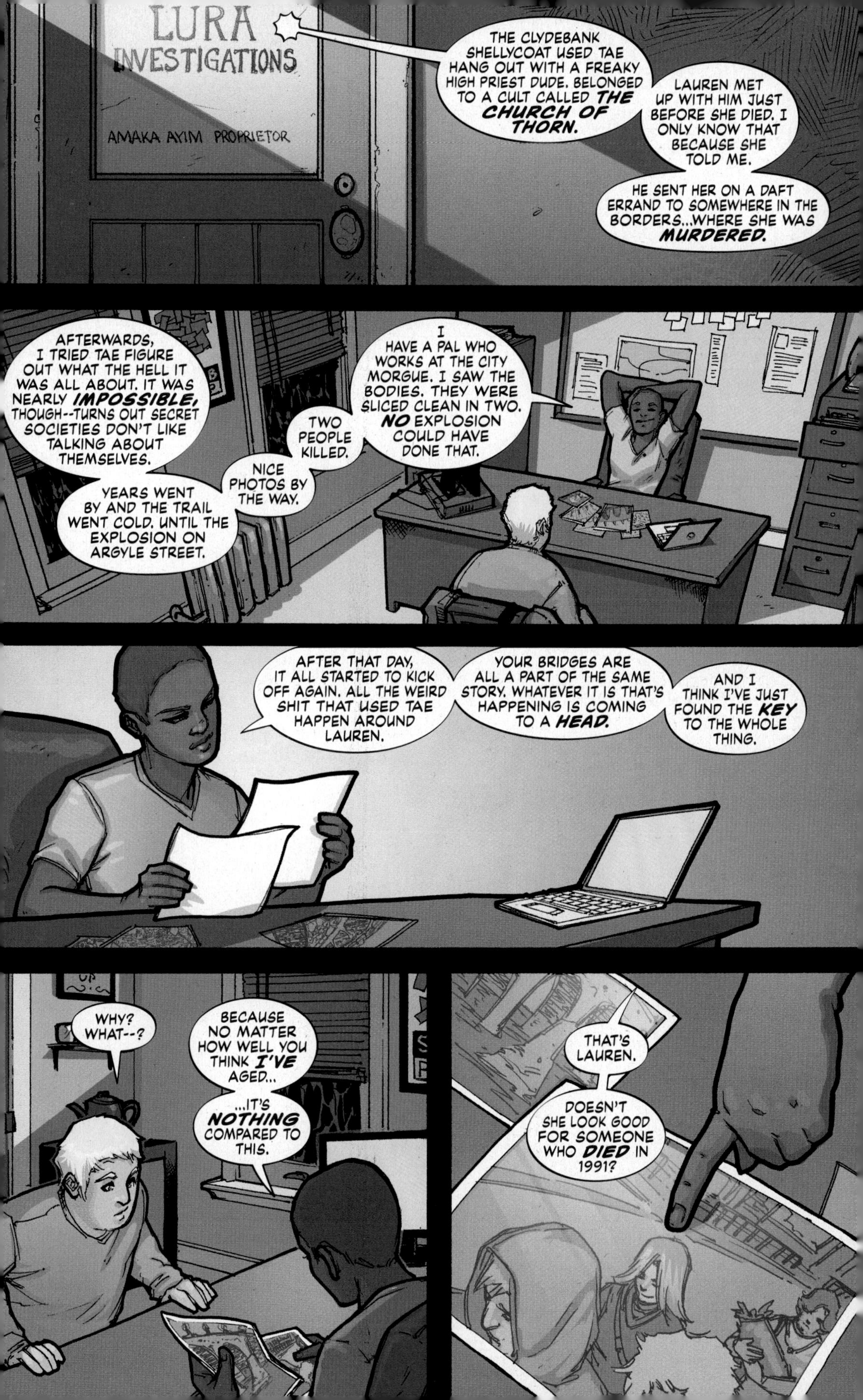
LURA INVESTIGATIONS
AMAKA AYIM PROPRIETOR
THE CLYDEBANK SHELLYCOAT USED TAE HANG OUT WITH A FREAKY HIGH PRIEST DUDE. BELONGED TO A CULT CALLED **THE CHURCH OF THORN.**
LAUREN MET UP WITH HIM JUST BEFORE SHE DIED. I ONLY KNOW THAT BECAUSE SHE TOLD ME.
HE SENT HER ON A DAFT ERRAND TO SOMEWHERE IN THE BORDERS...WHERE SHE WAS **MURDERED.**
AFTERWARDS, I TRIED TAE FIGURE OUT WHAT THE HELL IT WAS ALL ABOUT. IT WAS NEARLY ***IMPOSSIBLE,*** THOUGH--TURNS OUT SECRET SOCIETIES DON'T LIKE TALKING ABOUT THEMSELVES.
YEARS WENT BY AND THE TRAIL WENT COLD. UNTIL THE EXPLOSION ON ARGYLE STREET.
NICE PHOTOS BY THE WAY.
TWO PEOPLE KILLED.
I HAVE A PAL WHO WORKS AT THE CITY MORGUE. I SAW THE BODIES. THEY WERE SLICED CLEAN IN TWO. ***NO*** EXPLOSION COULD HAVE DONE THAT.
AFTER THAT DAY, IT ALL STARTED TO KICK OFF AGAIN. ALL THE WEIRD SHIT THAT USED TAE HAPPEN AROUND LAUREN.
YOUR BRIDGES ARE ALL A PART OF THE SAME STORY. WHATEVER IT IS THAT'S HAPPENING IS COMING TO A ***HEAD.***
AND I THINK I'VE JUST FOUND THE ***KEY*** TO THE WHOLE THING.
WHY? WHAT--?
BECAUSE NO MATTER HOW WELL YOU THINK ***I'VE*** AGED...
...IT'S ***NOTHING*** COMPARED TO THIS.
THAT'S LAUREN.
DOESN'T SHE LOOK GOOD FOR SOMEONE WHO ***DIED*** IN 1991?

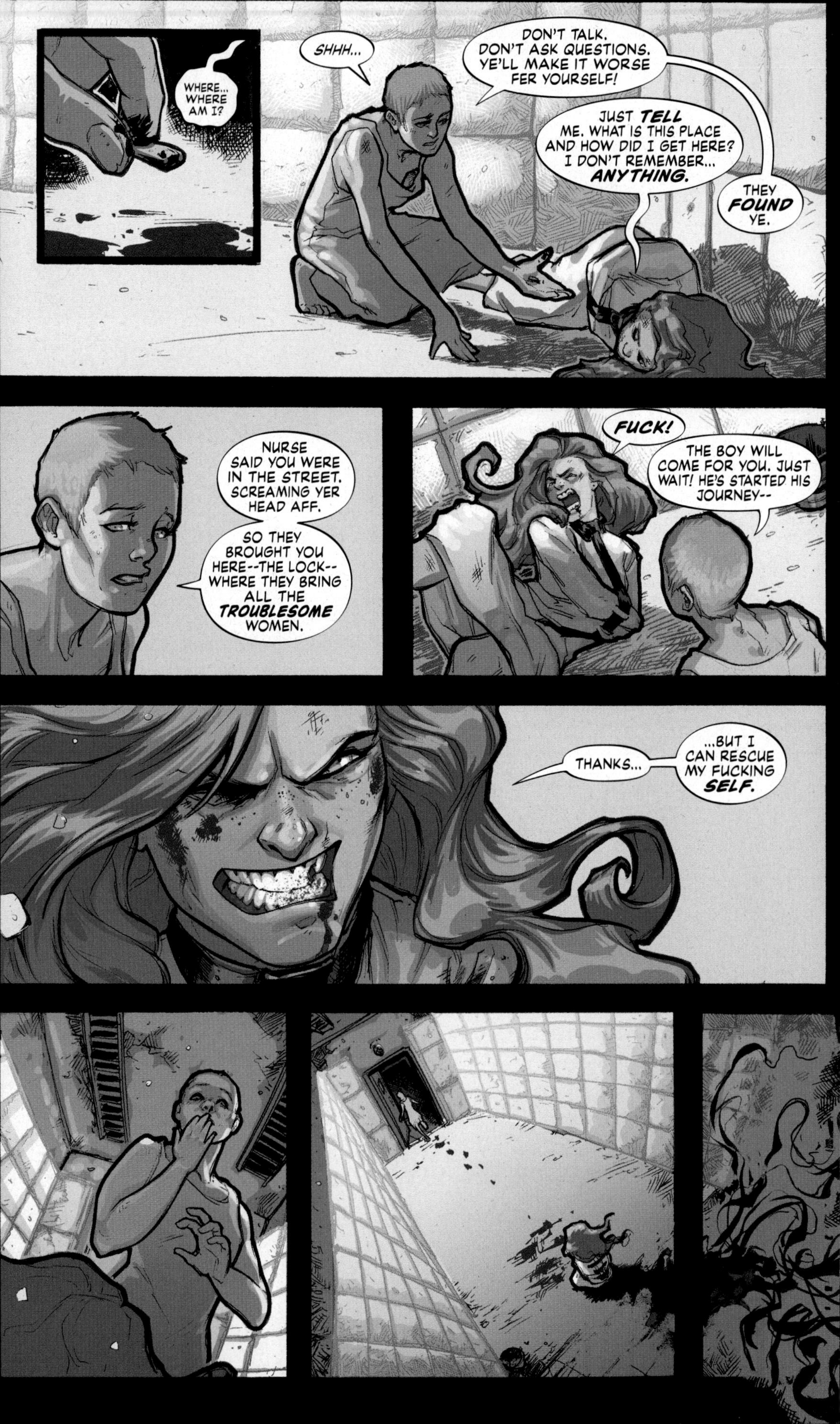
WHERE... WHERE AM I?
SHHH...
DON'T TALK. DON'T ASK QUESTIONS. YE'LL MAKE IT WORSE FER YOURSELF!
JUST TELL ME. WHAT IS THIS PLACE AND HOW DID I GET HERE? I DON'T REMEMBER... ANYTHING.
THEY FOUND YE.
NURSE SAID YOU WERE IN THE STREET. SCREAMING YER HEAD AFF.
SO THEY BROUGHT YOU HERE--THE LOCK--WHERE THEY BRING ALL THE TROUBLESOME WOMEN.
FUCK!
THE BOY WILL COME FOR YOU. JUST WAIT! HE'S STARTED HIS JOURNEY--
THANKS...
...BUT I CAN RESCUE MY FUCKING SELF.

CCTV

KEEP DOOR SHUT

KNOCK
KNOCK

HIYA!

AMAKA! LONG TIME NO SEE, HEN!

YOU TOO, BETH. YE'RE LOOKING GOOD!

HOW'S THAT NEW FACIAL RECOGNITION SOFTWARE WORKING FOR YOU GUYS?

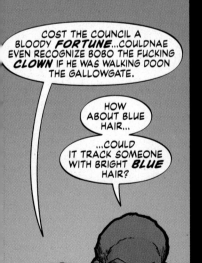

COST THE COUNCIL A BLOODY *FORTUNE*...COULDNAE EVEN RECOGNIZE BOBO THE FUCKING *CLOWN* IF HE WAS WALKING DOON THE GALLOWGATE.

HOW ABOUT BLUE HAIR...

...COULD IT TRACK SOMEONE WITH BRIGHT *BLUE* HAIR?

KEEP DOOR SHUT

I WAS ONLY JOKING ABOUT THE CLOWN BIT. BUT LET'S SEE... THERE'S PROBABLY PLENTY OF BLUE HAIR WALKING ABOOT THE CITY CENTER.

TIK TAK TAK TAK

ACTUALLY... NO...IT'S A BIT RARER THAN YE'D THINK.

THERE. THAT'S *HER!*

TAK TAK

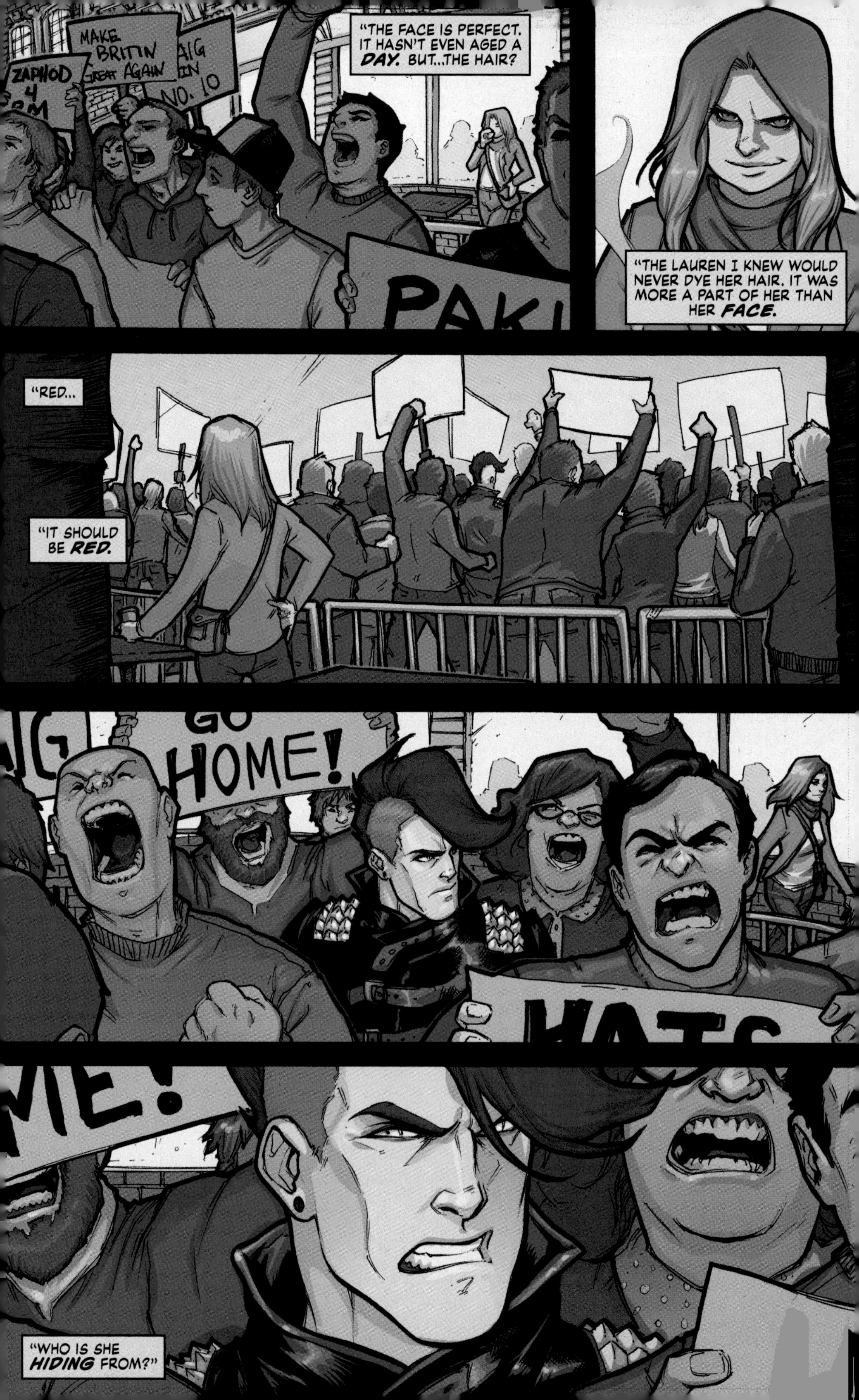

MAKE BRITIN GREAT AGAIN
ZAPHOD 4
NO. 10
"THE FACE IS PERFECT. IT HASN'T EVEN AGED A DAY. BUT...THE HAIR?
"THE LAUREN I KNEW WOULD NEVER DYE HER HAIR. IT WAS MORE A PART OF HER THAN HER FACE.
"RED...
"IT SHOULD BE RED.
GO HOME!
"WHO IS SHE HIDING FROM?"

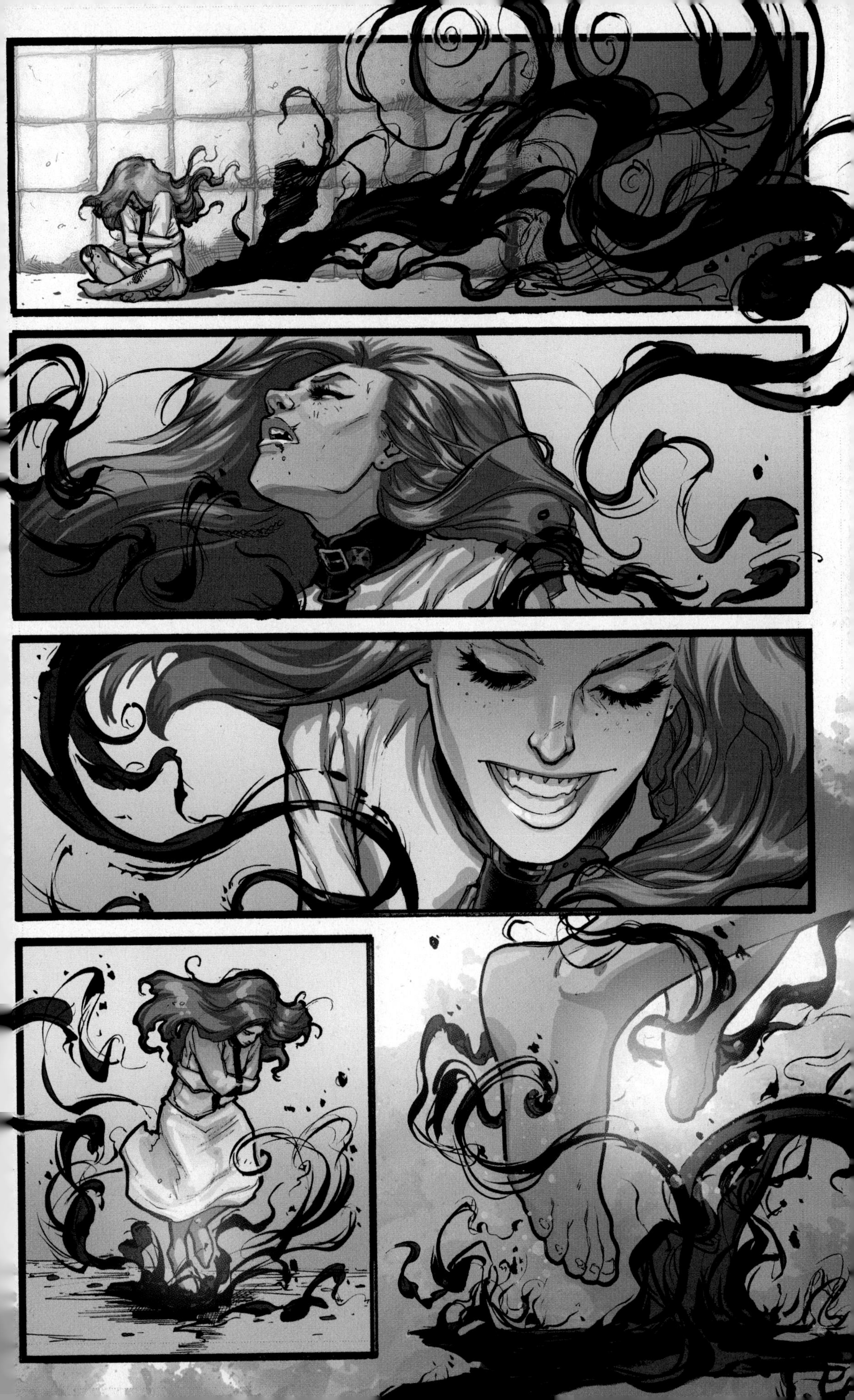

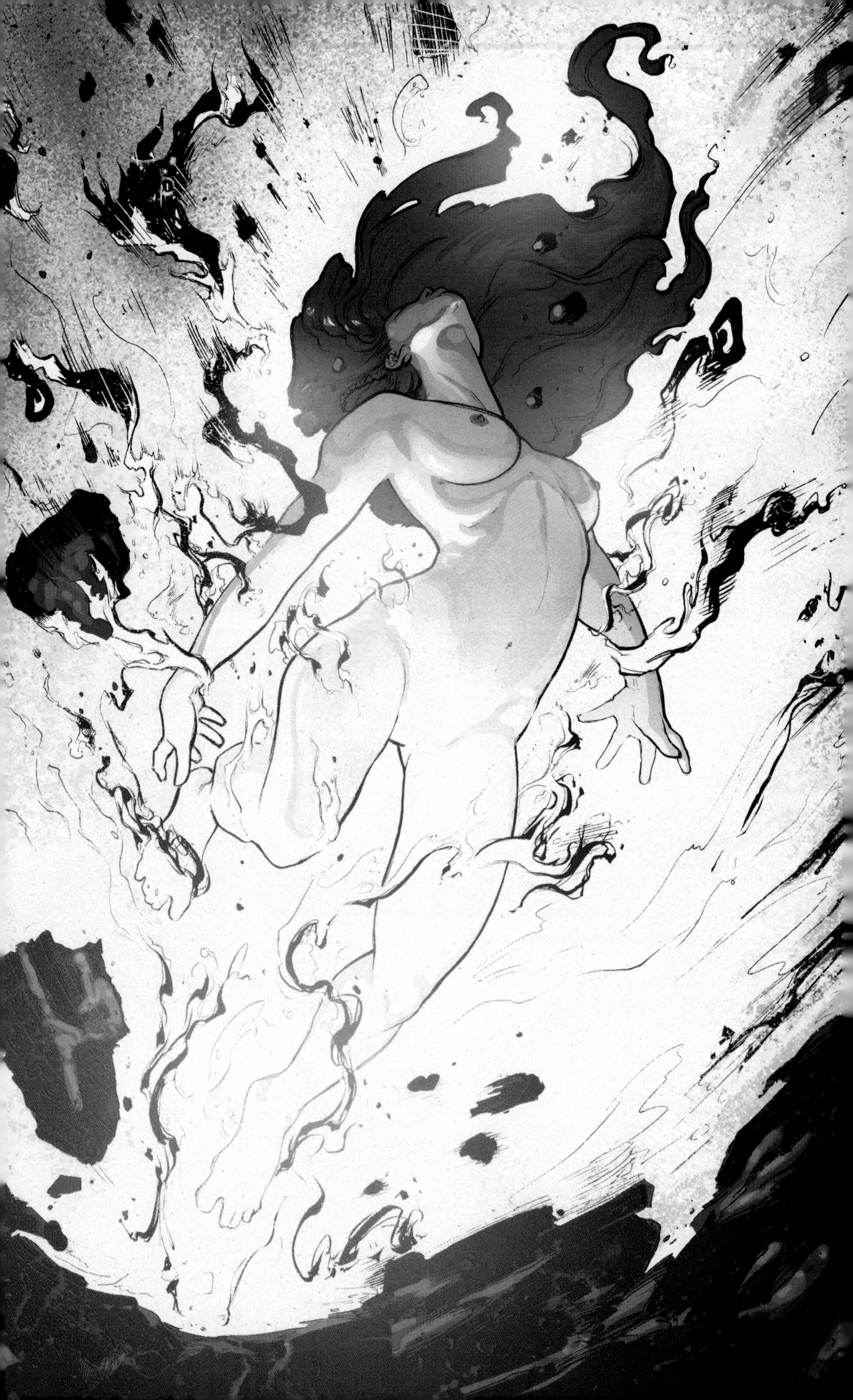

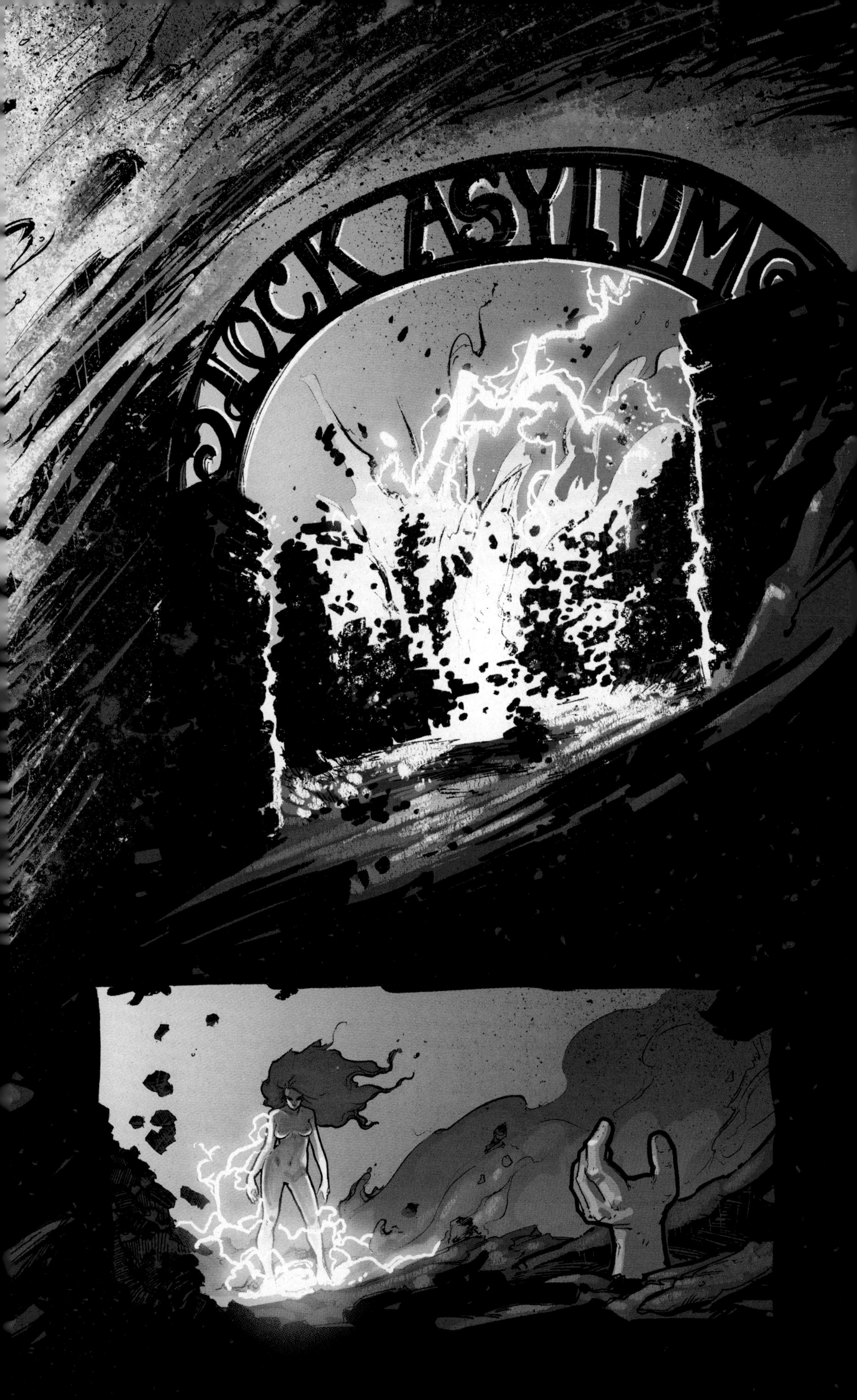
HOCK ASYLUM

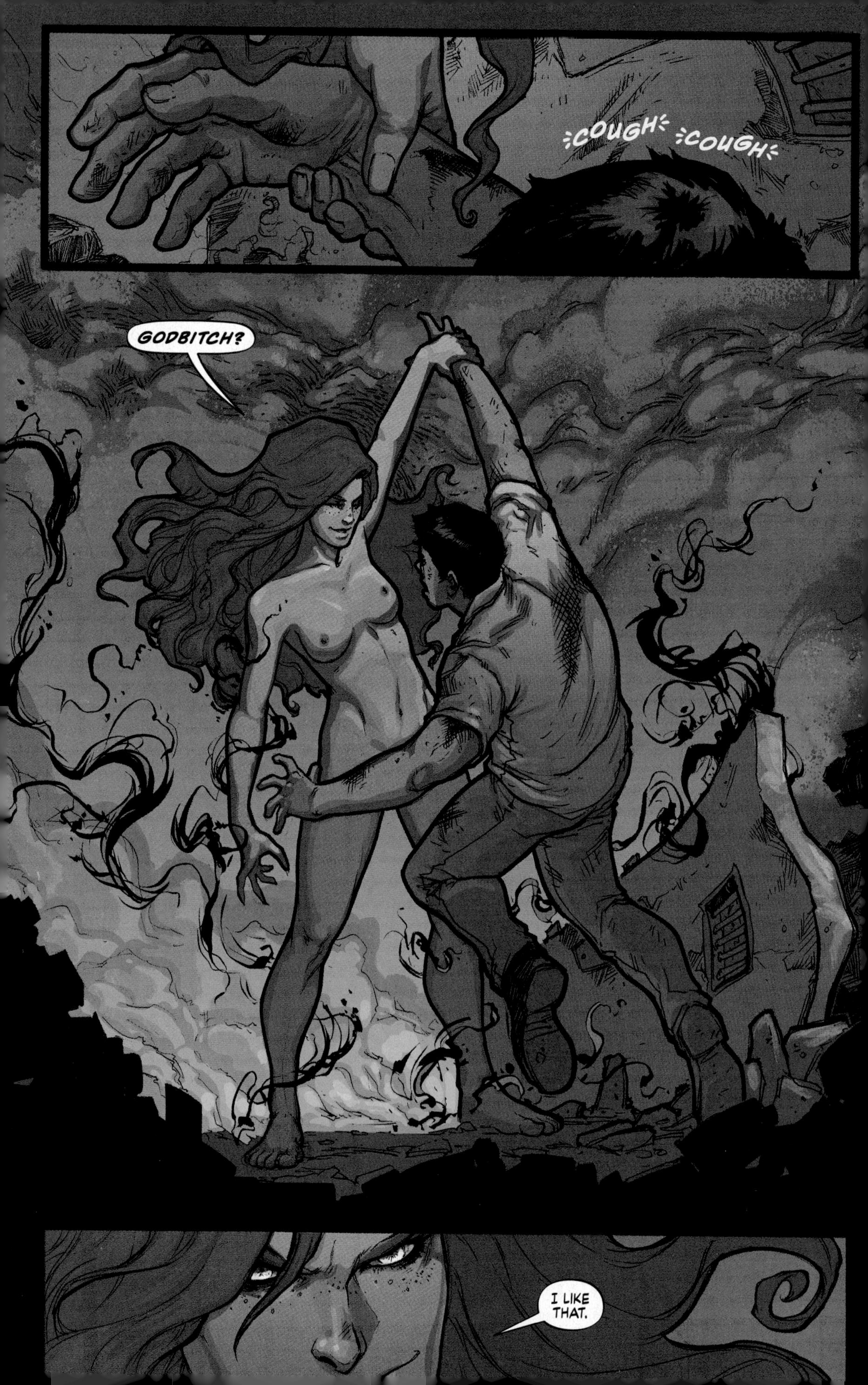
COUGH COUGH
GODBITCH?
I LIKE THAT.

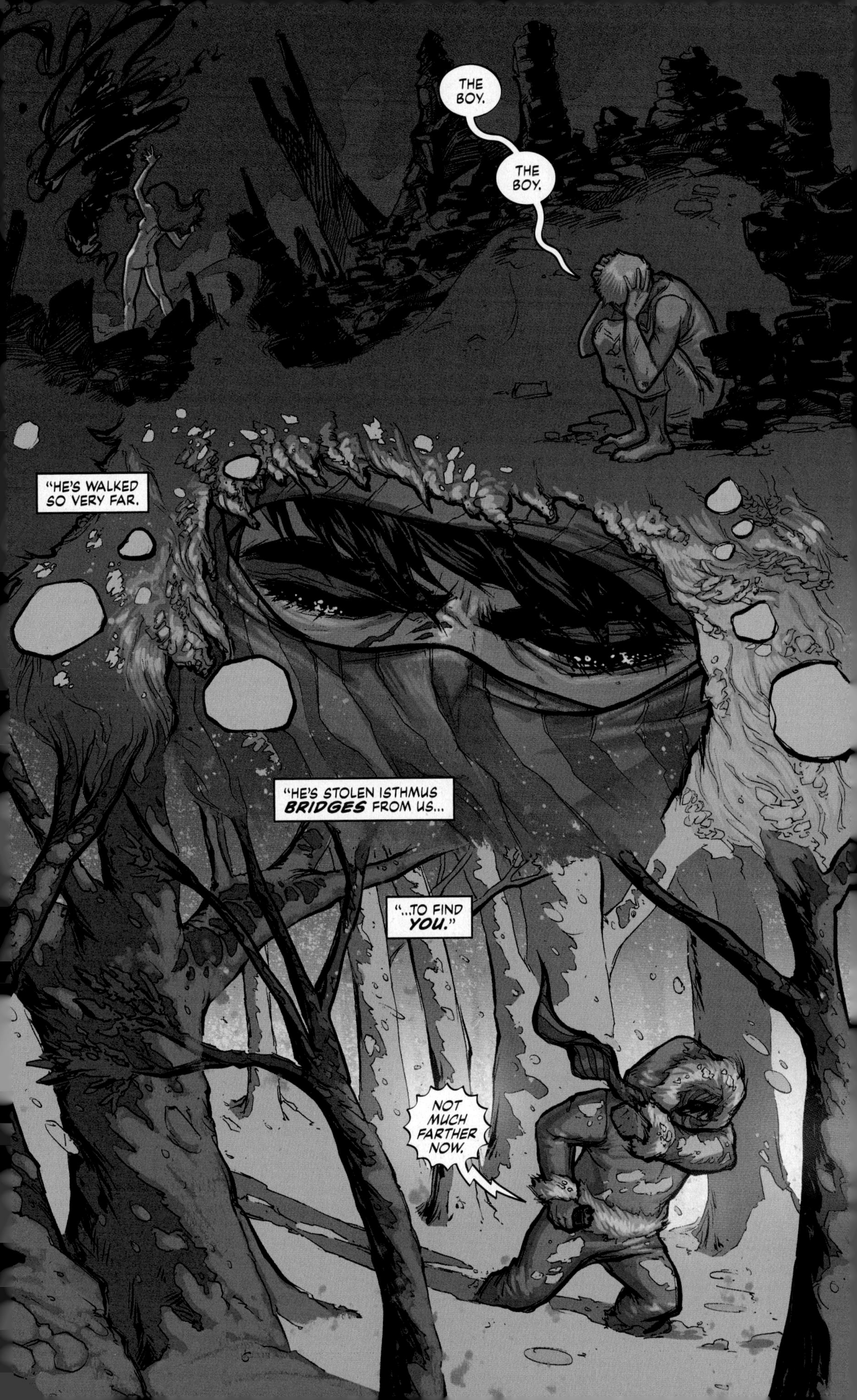
THE BOY.
THE BOY.
"HE'S WALKED SO VERY FAR.
"HE'S STOLEN ISTHMUS BRIDGES FROM US...
"...TO FIND YOU."
NOT MUCH FARTHER NOW.

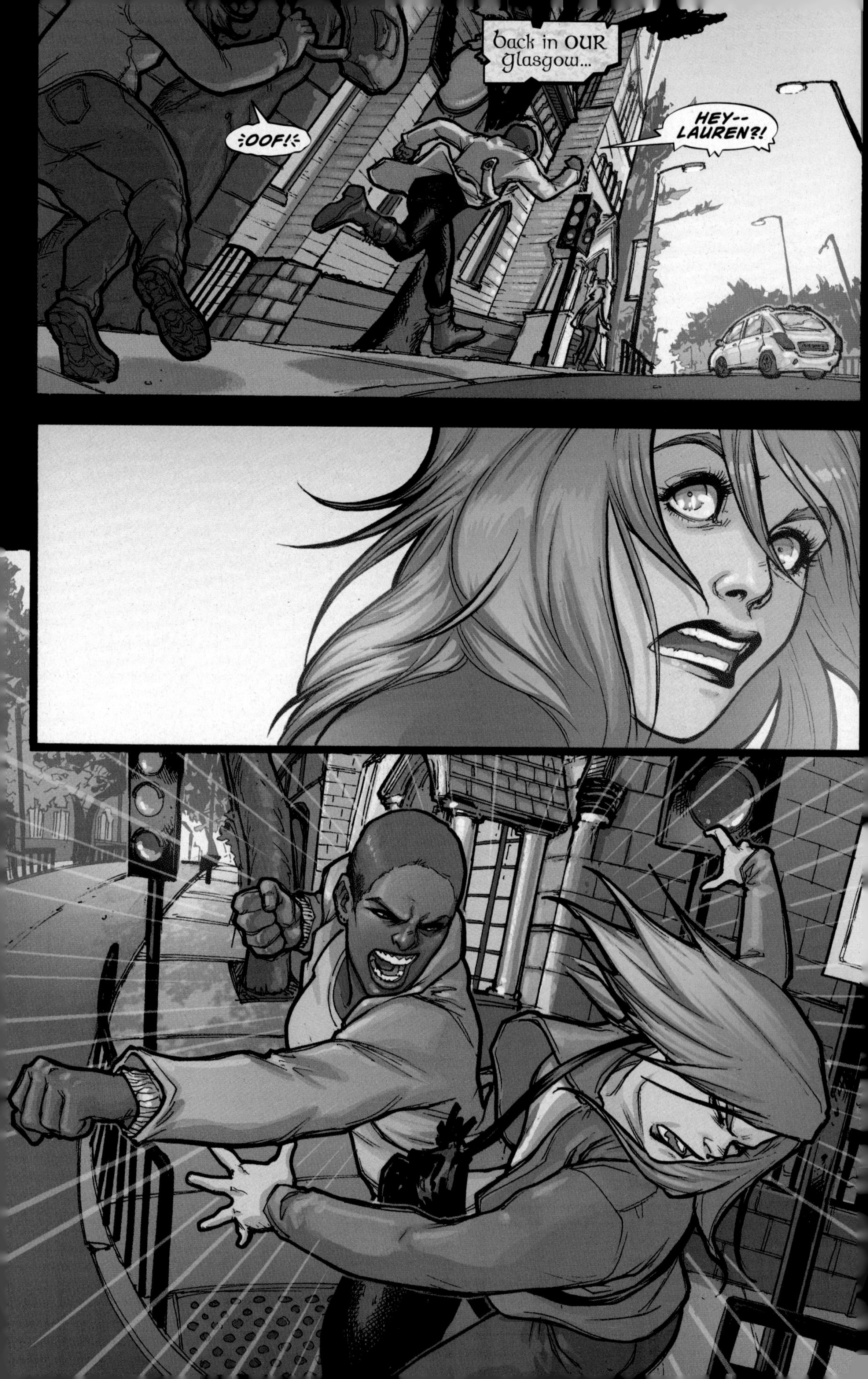
back in OUR Glasgow...
OOF!
HEY-- LAUREN?!

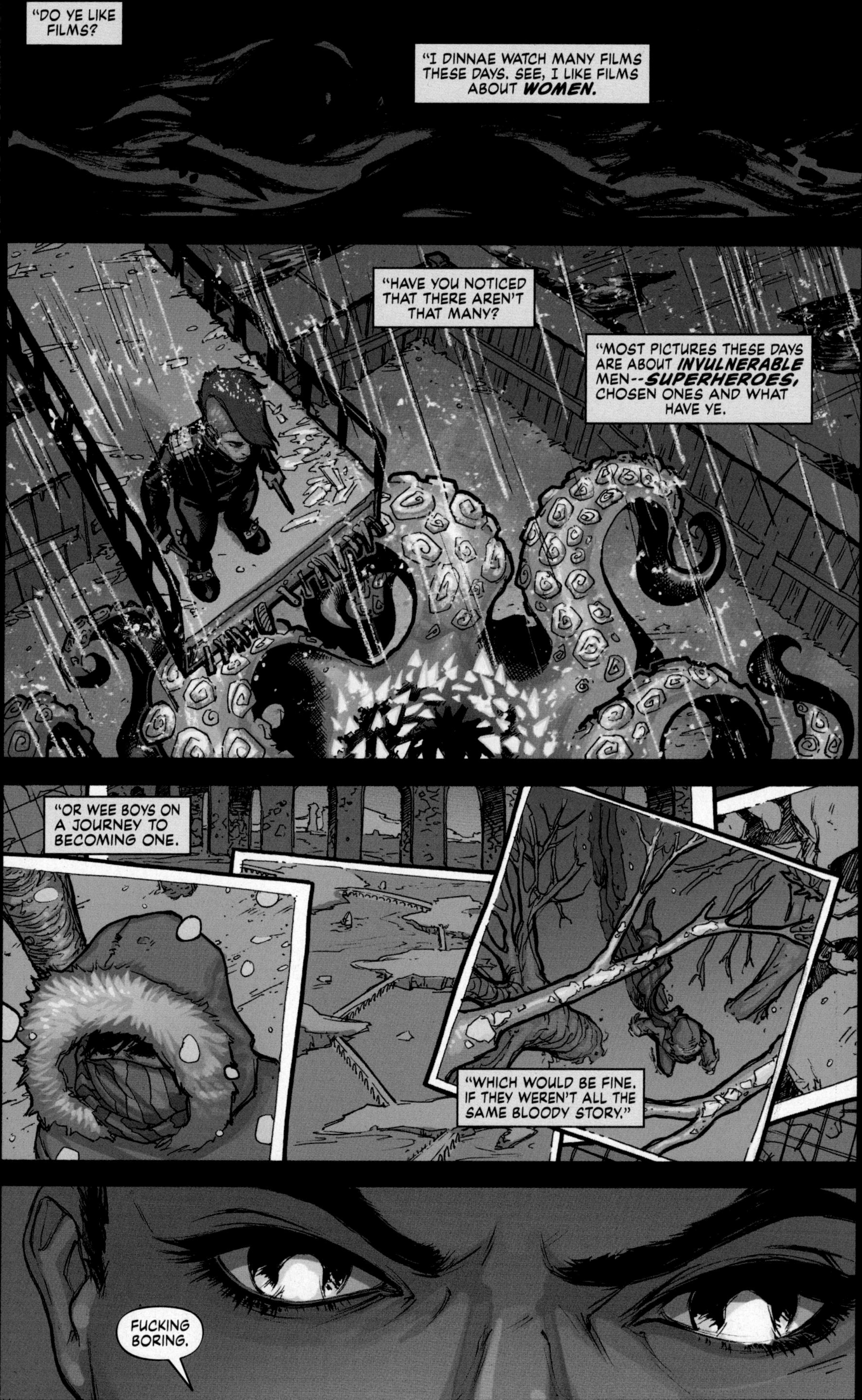
"DO YE LIKE FILMS?
"I DINNAE WATCH MANY FILMS THESE DAYS. SEE, I LIKE FILMS ABOUT WOMEN.
"HAVE YOU NOTICED THAT THERE AREN'T THAT MANY?
"MOST PICTURES THESE DAYS ARE ABOUT INVULNERABLE MEN--SUPERHEROES, CHOSEN ONES AND WHAT HAVE YE.
"OR WEE BOYS ON A JOURNEY TO BECOMING ONE.
"WHICH WOULD BE FINE. IF THEY WEREN'T ALL THE SAME BLOODY STORY."
FUCKING BORING.

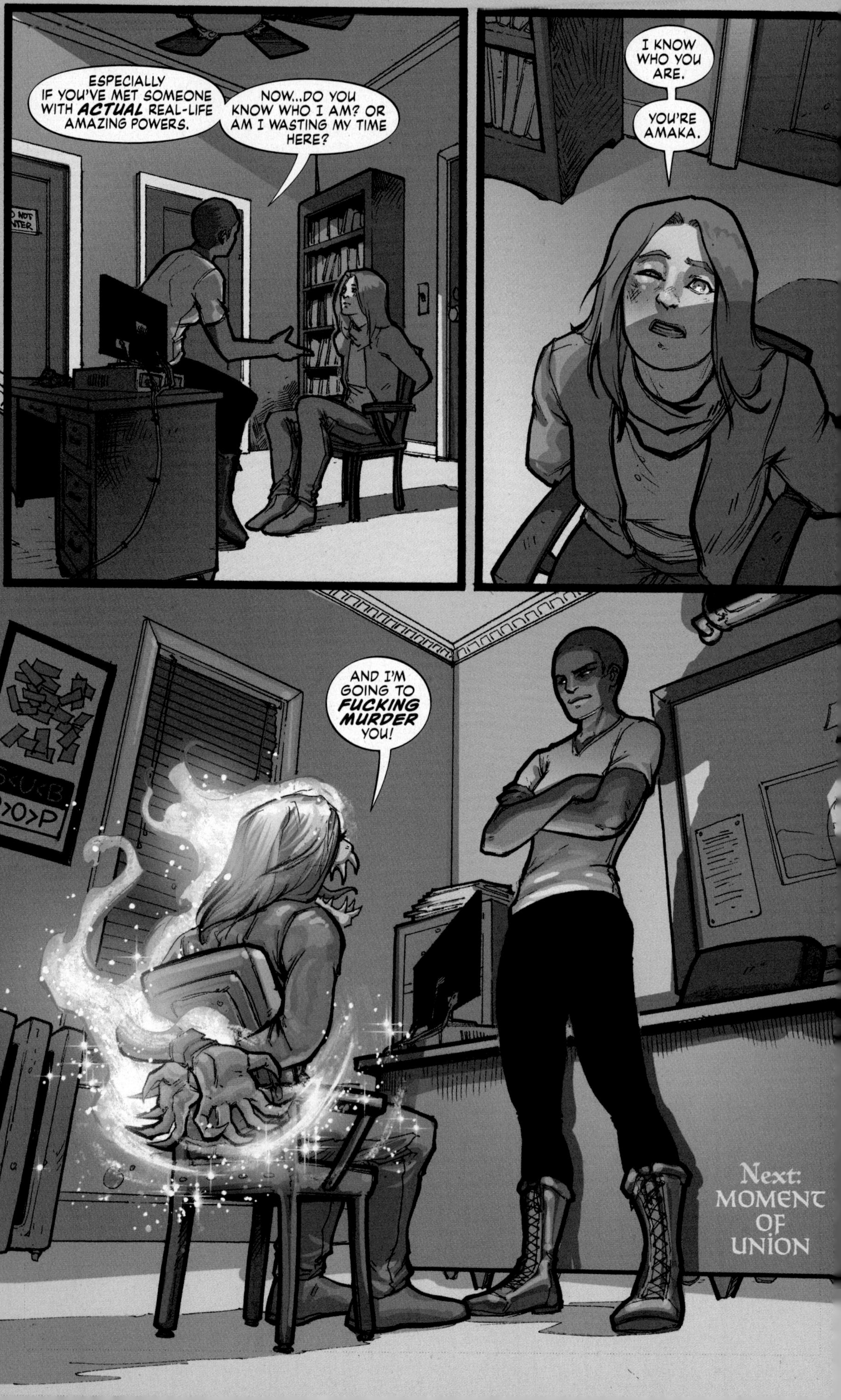
ESPECIALLY IF YOU'VE MET SOMEONE WITH **ACTUAL** REAL-LIFE AMAZING POWERS.
NOW...DO YOU KNOW WHO I AM? OR AM I WASTING MY TIME HERE?
I KNOW WHO YOU ARE.
YOU'RE AMAKA.
AND I'M GOING TO ***FUCKING MURDER*** YOU!
S<U<B
P>O>P
Next: MOMENT OF UNION

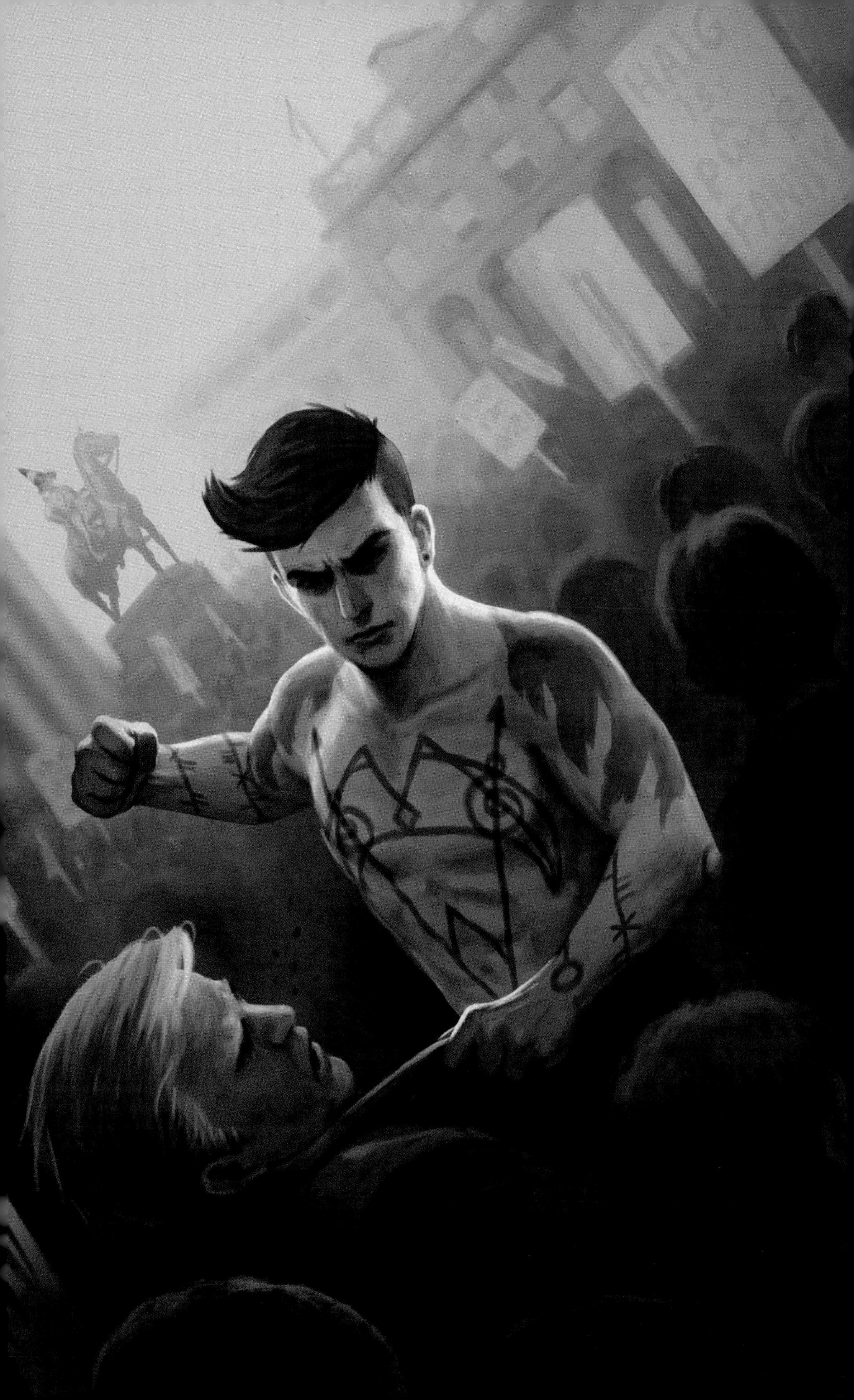

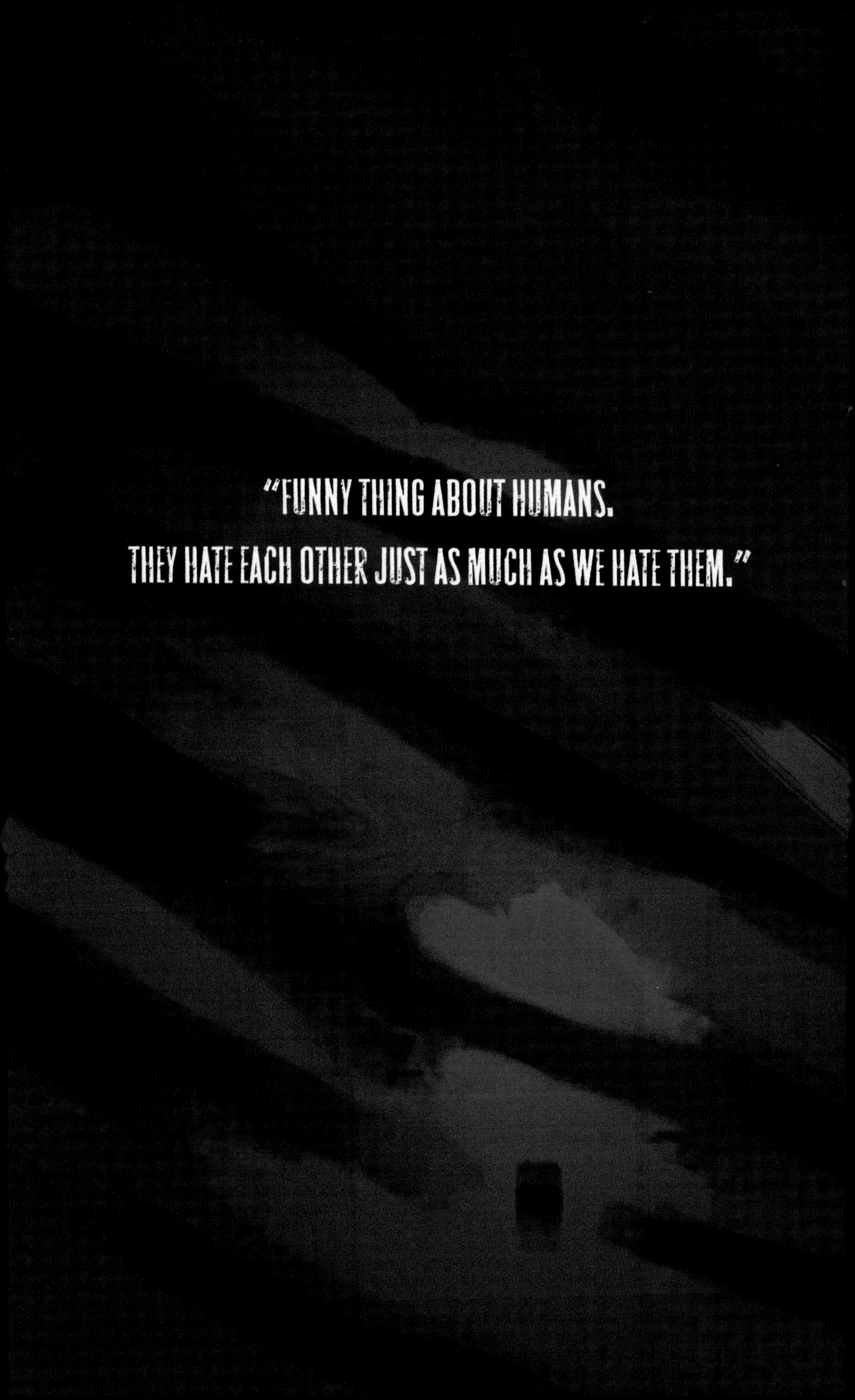
"FUNNY THING ABOUT HUMANS.
THEY HATE EACH OTHER JUST AS MUCH AS WE HATE THEM."

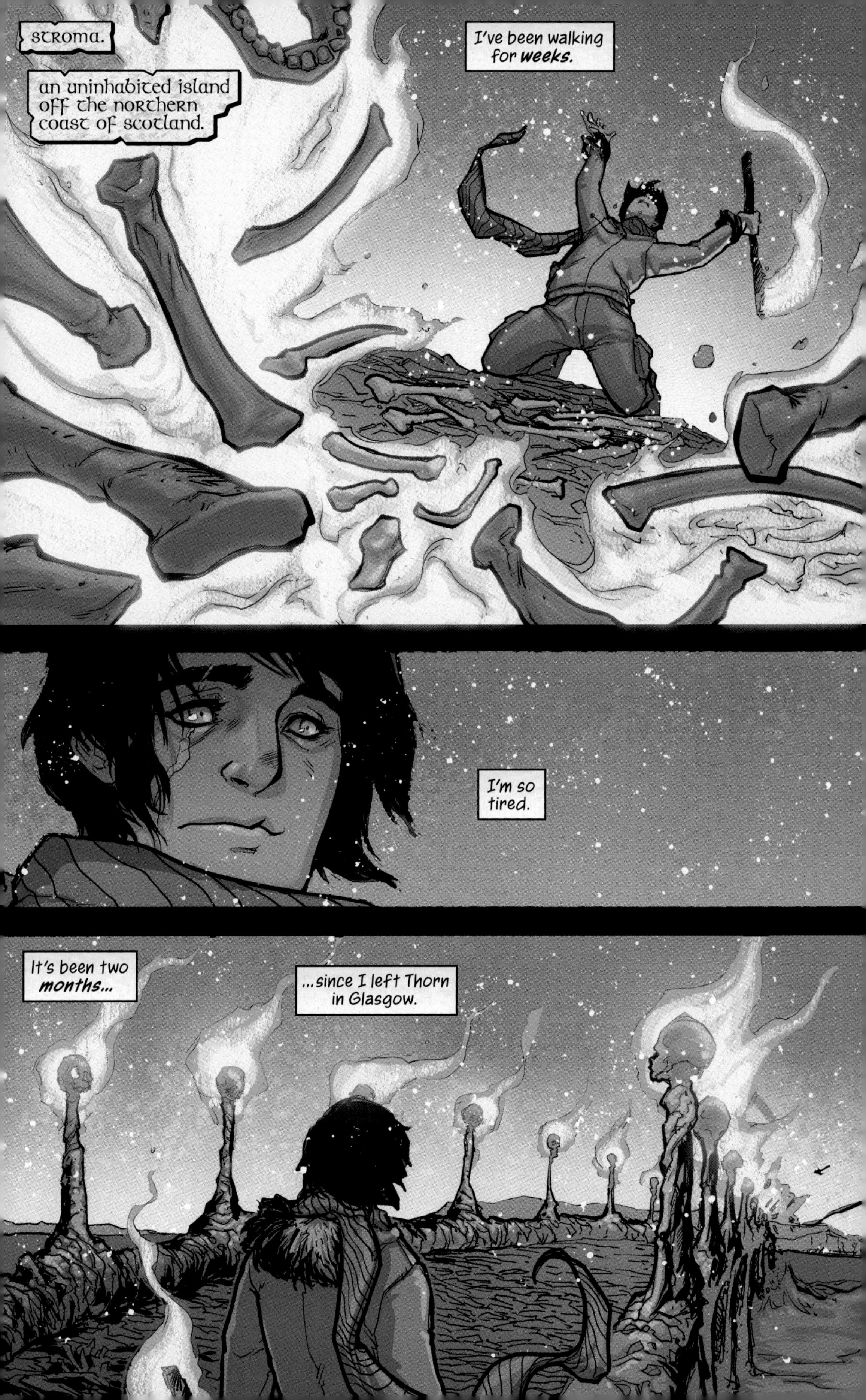
stroma.
an uninhabited island off the northern coast of scotland.
I've been walking for weeks.
I'm so tired.
It's been two months...
...since I left Thorn in Glasgow.

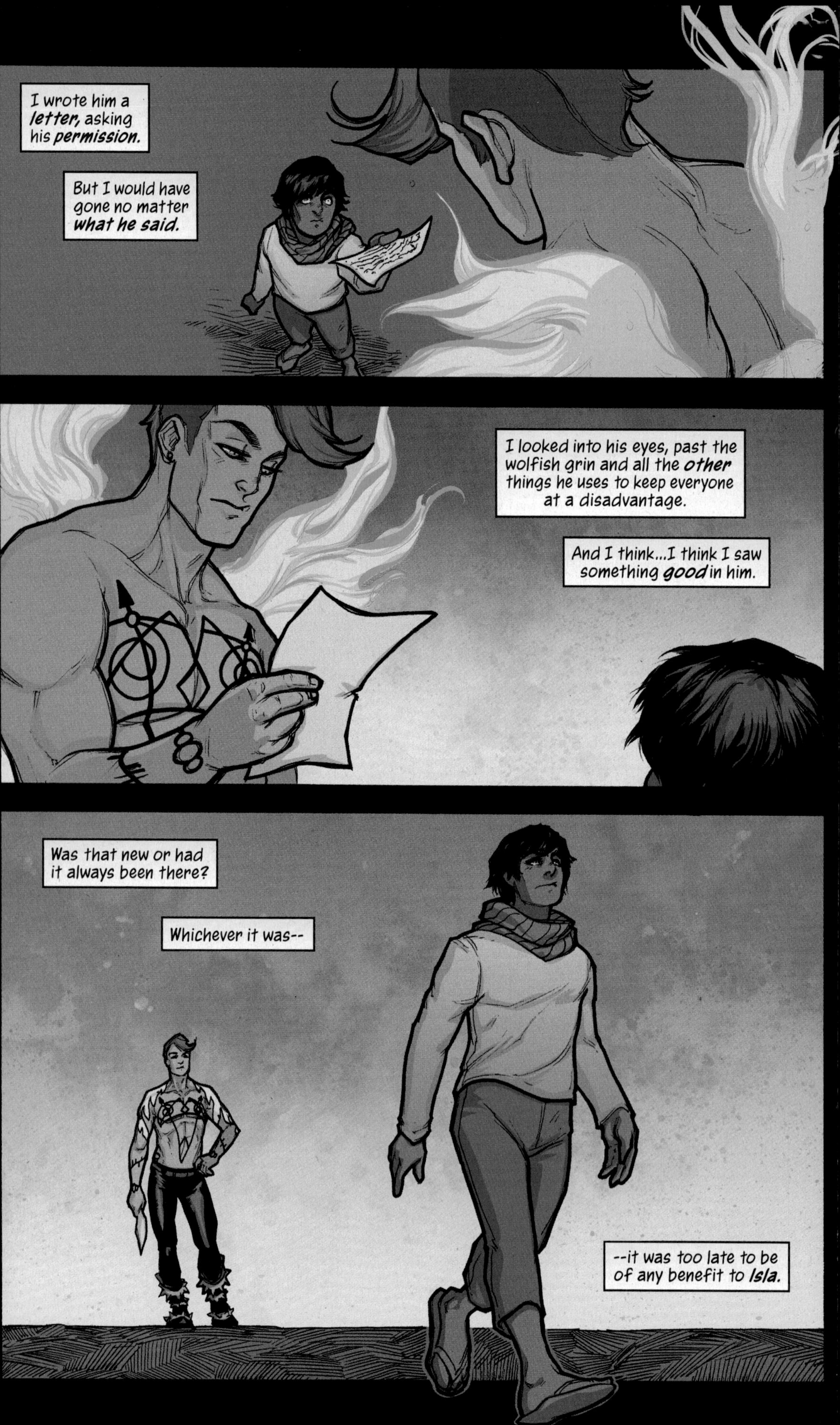
I wrote him a letter, asking his permission.
But I would have gone no matter what he said.
I looked into his eyes, past the wolfish grin and all the other things he uses to keep everyone at a disadvantage.
And I think...I think I saw something good in him.
Was that new or had it always been there?
Whichever it was--
--it was too late to be of any benefit to Isla.

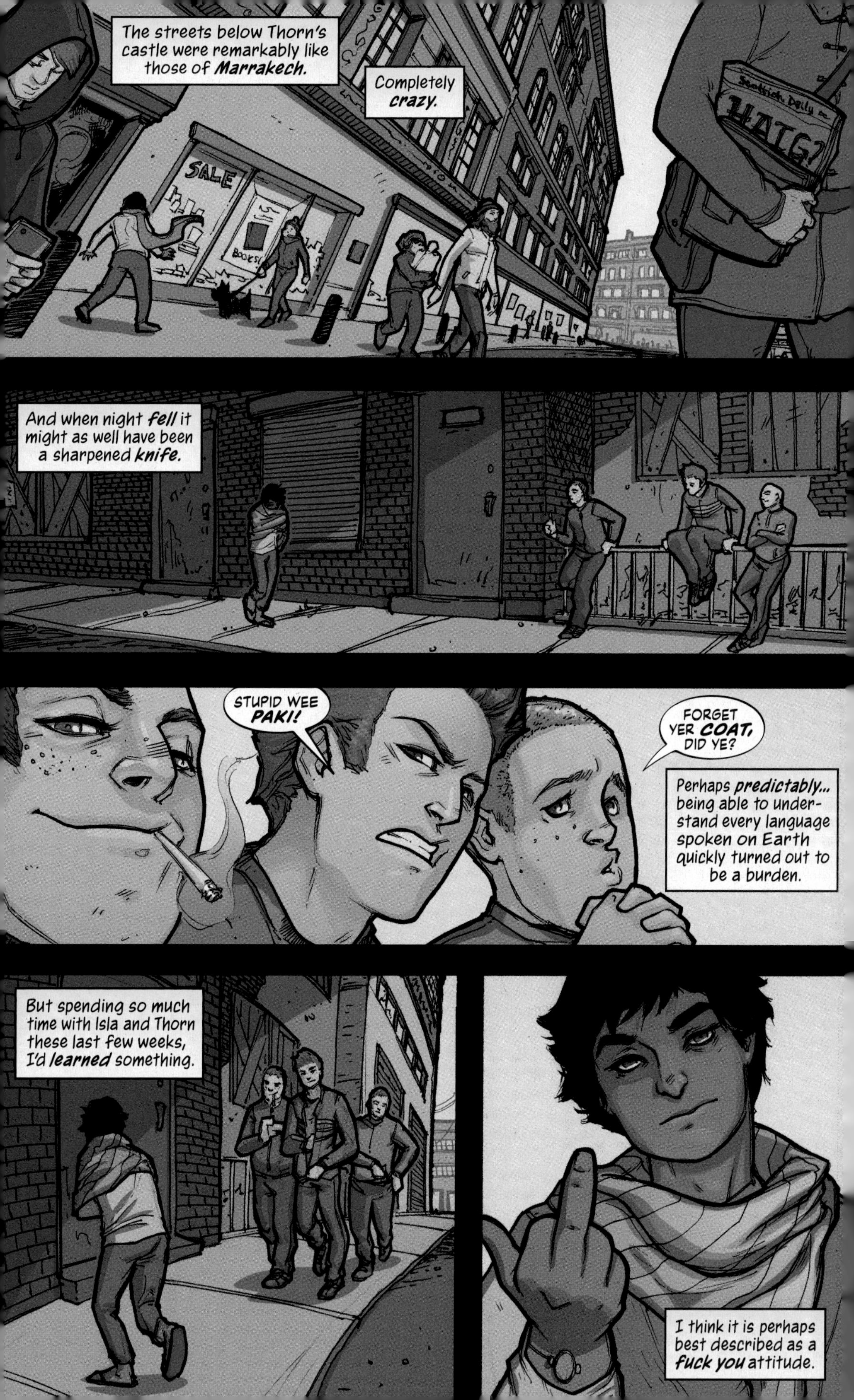

The streets below Thorn's castle were remarkably like those of *Marrakech.*
Completely *crazy.*
SALE
BOOKS!
Scottish Daily
HAIG?
And when night *fell* it might as well have been a sharpened *knife.*
STUPID WEE *PAKI!*
FORGET YER *COAT,* DID YE?
Perhaps *predictably...* being able to understand every language spoken on Earth quickly turned out to be a burden.
But spending so much time with Isla and Thorn these last few weeks, I'd *learned* something.
I think it is perhaps best described as a *fuck you* attitude.

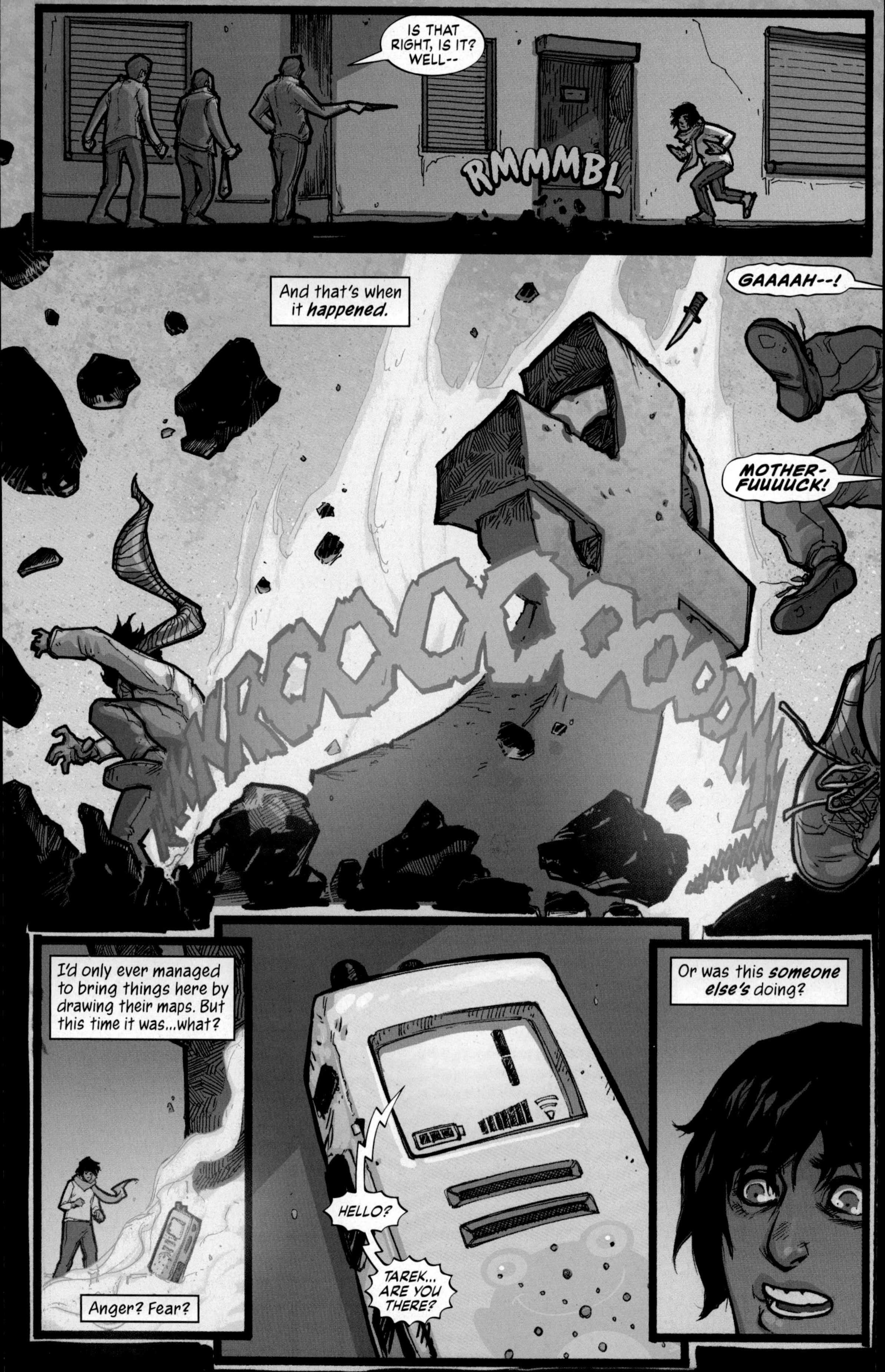
IS THAT RIGHT, IS IT? WELL--
RMMMBL
And that's when it *happened.*
GAAAAH--!
MOTHER-FUUUUCK!
I'd only ever managed to bring things here by drawing their maps. But this time it was...what?
Anger? Fear?
HELLO?
TAREK... ARE YOU THERE?
Or was this *someone else's* doing?

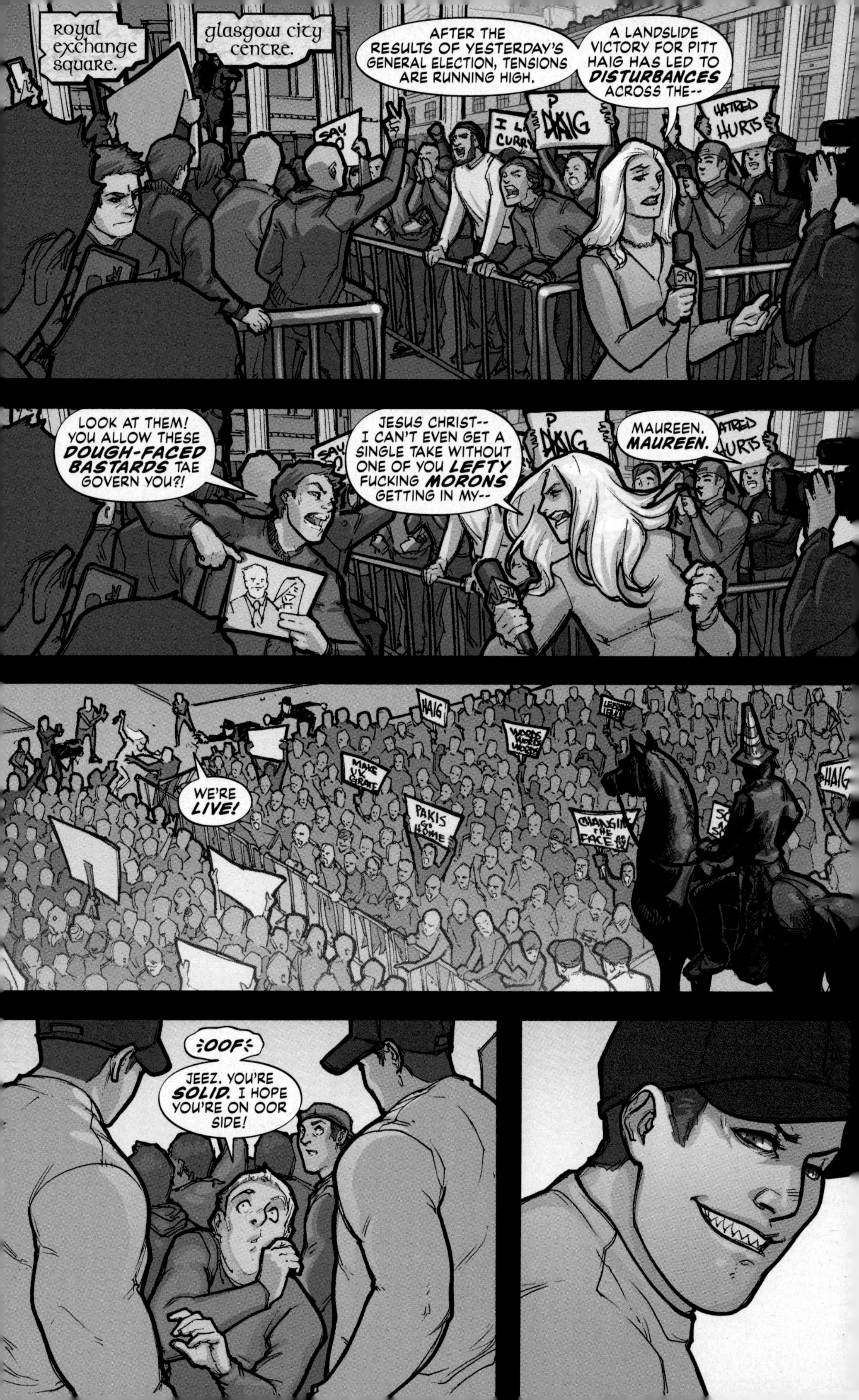
Royal exchange square.
glasgow city centre.
AFTER THE RESULTS OF YESTERDAY'S GENERAL ELECTION, TENSIONS ARE RUNNING HIGH.
A LANDSLIDE VICTORY FOR PITT HAIG HAS LED TO DISTURBANCES ACROSS THE--
HATRED HURTS
LOOK AT THEM! YOU ALLOW THESE DOUGH-FACED BASTARDS TAE GOVERN YOU?!
JESUS CHRIST-- I CAN'T EVEN GET A SINGLE TAKE WITHOUT ONE OF YOU LEFTY FUCKING MORONS GETTING IN MY--
MAUREEN. MAUREEN.
HAIG
PAKIS GO HOME
WE'RE LIVE!
OOF
JEEZ. YOU'RE SOLID. I HOPE YOU'RE ON OOR SIDE!

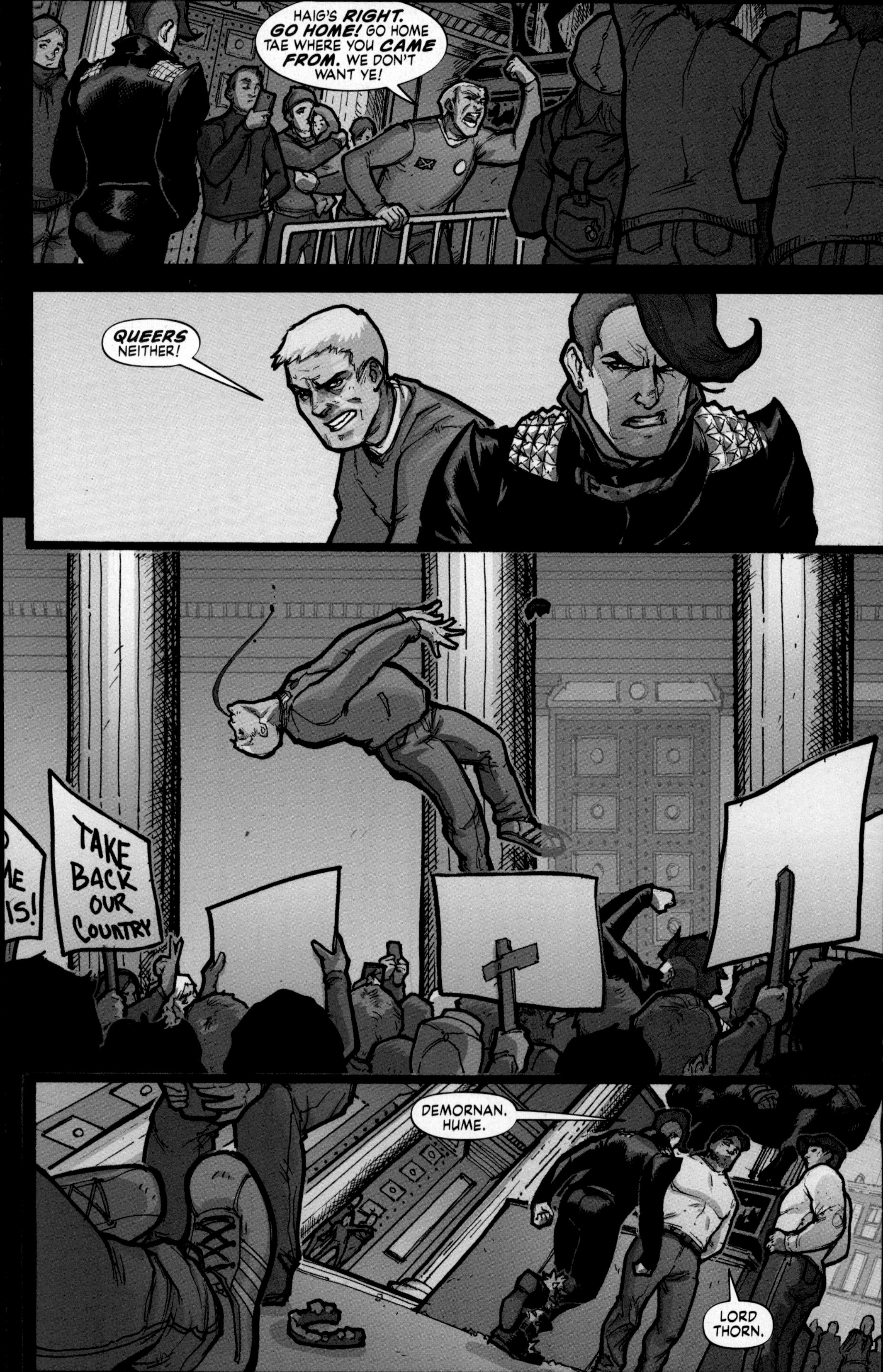
HAIG'S **RIGHT.** **GO HOME!** GO HOME TAE WHERE YOU **CAME FROM.** WE DON'T WANT YE!
QUEERS NEITHER!
TAKE BACK OUR COUNTRY
DEMORNAN. HUME.
LORD THORN.

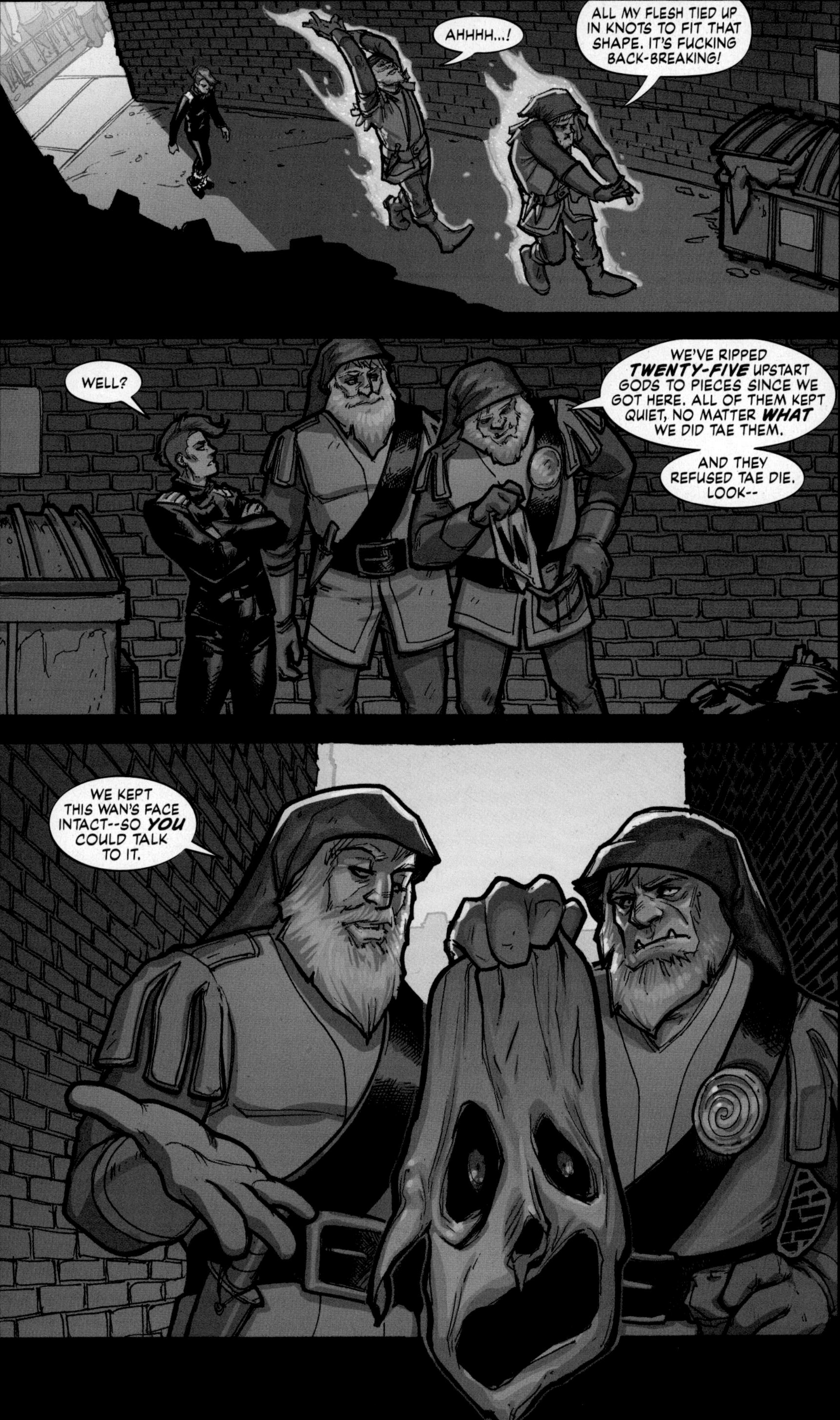
AHHHH...!
ALL MY FLESH TIED UP IN KNOTS TO FIT THAT SHAPE. IT'S FUCKING BACK-BREAKING!
WELL?
WE'VE RIPPED **TWENTY-FIVE** UPSTART GODS TO PIECES SINCE WE GOT HERE. ALL OF THEM KEPT QUIET, NO MATTER **WHAT** WE DID TAE THEM.
AND THEY REFUSED TAE DIE. LOOK--
WE KEPT THIS WAN'S FACE INTACT--SO **YOU** COULD TALK TO IT.

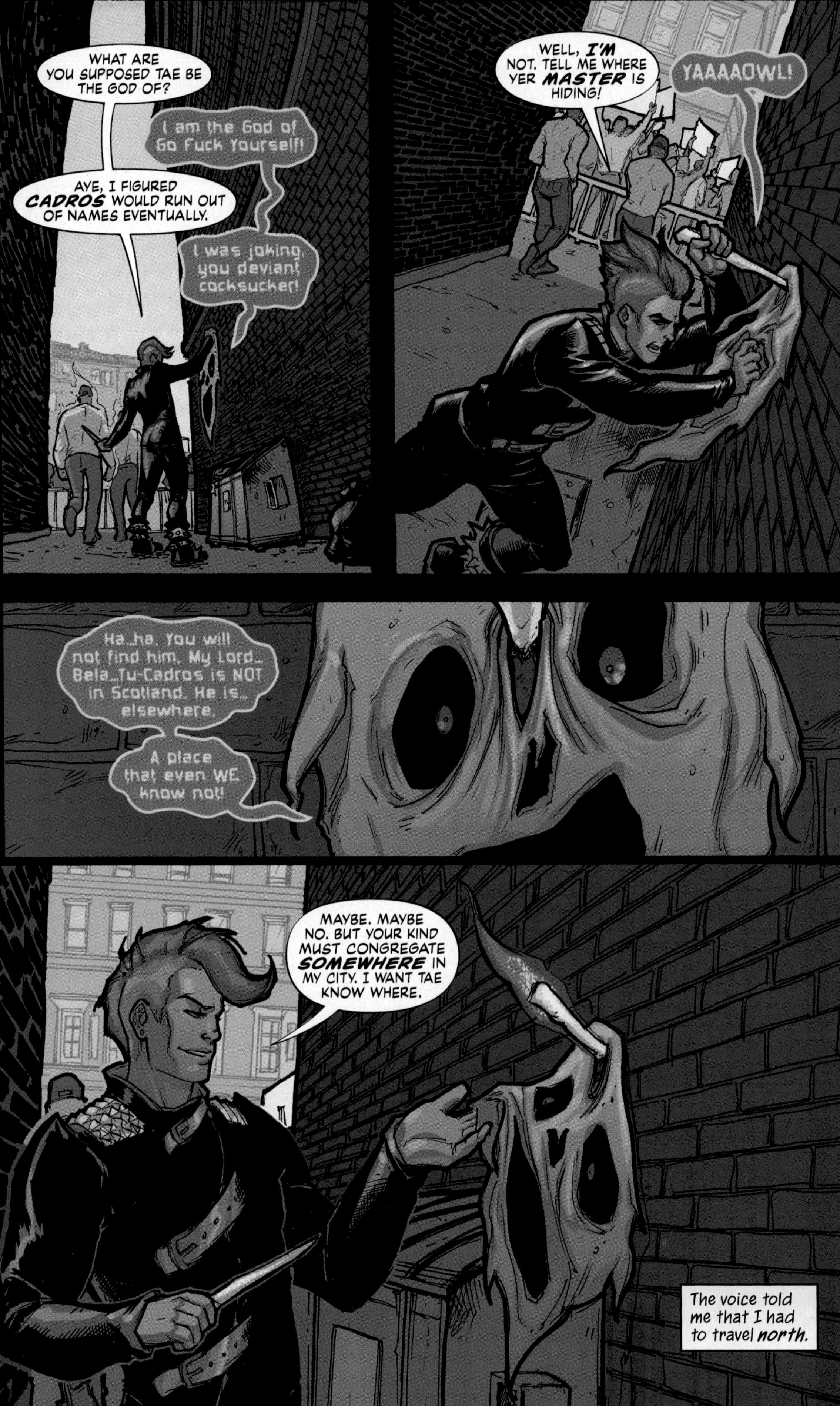
WHAT ARE YOU SUPPOSED TAE BE THE GOD OF?
I am the God of Go Fuck Yourself!
AYE, I FIGURED CADROS WOULD RUN OUT OF NAMES EVENTUALLY.
I was joking, you deviant cocksucker!
WELL, I'M NOT. TELL ME WHERE YER MASTER IS HIDING!
YAAAAOWL!
Ha...ha. You will not find him. My Lord... Bela...Tu-Cadros is NOT in Scotland. He is... elsewhere.
A place that even WE know not!
MAYBE. MAYBE NO. BUT YOUR KIND MUST CONGREGATE SOMEWHERE IN MY CITY. I WANT TAE KNOW WHERE.
The voice told me that I had to travel north.

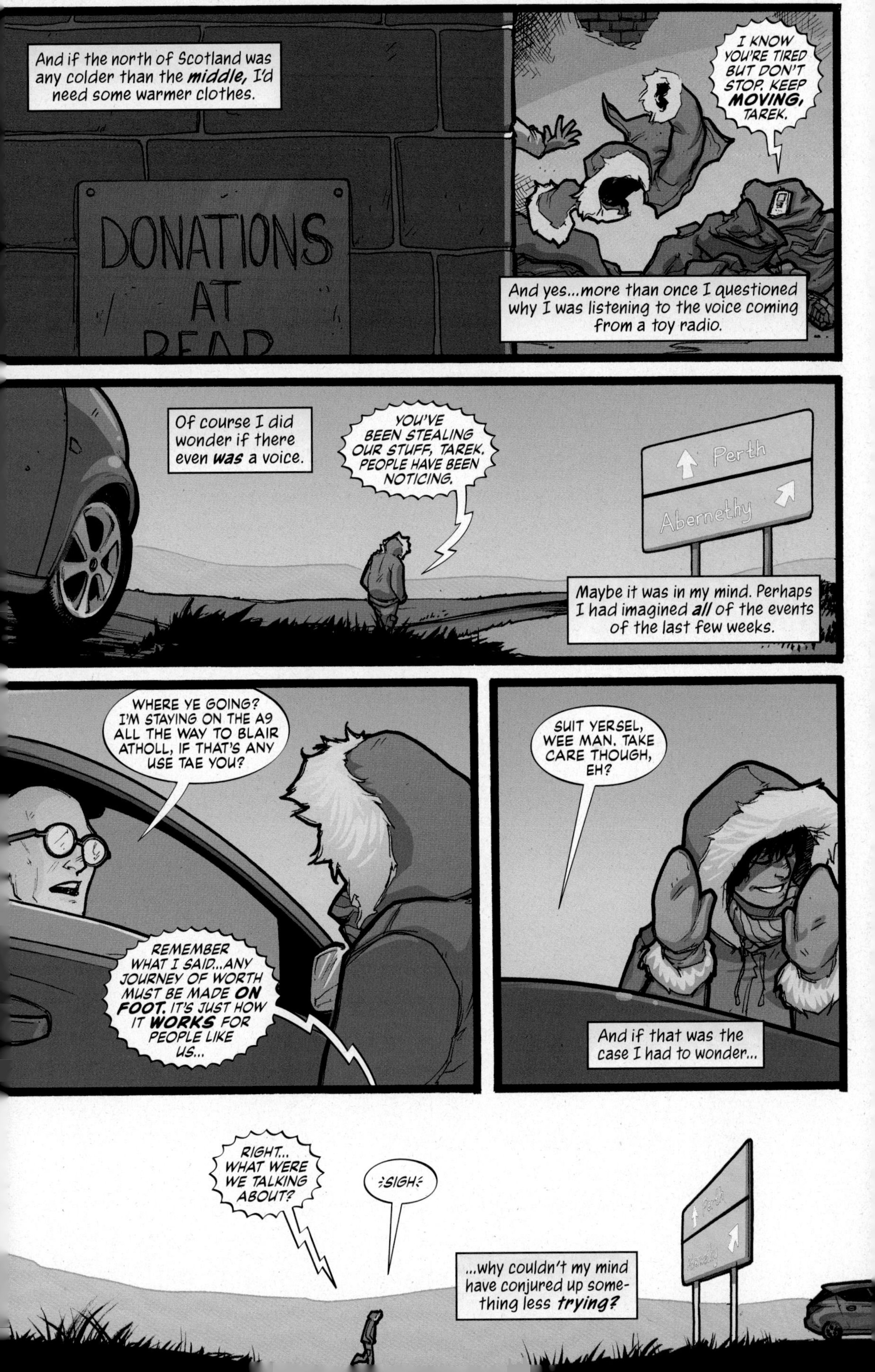

And if the north of Scotland was any colder than the *middle*, I'd need some warmer clothes.
DONATIONS AT REAR
I KNOW YOU'RE TIRED BUT DON'T STOP. KEEP **MOVING,** TAREK.
And yes...more than once I questioned why I was listening to the voice coming from a toy radio.
Of course I did wonder if there even *was* a voice.
YOU'VE BEEN STEALING OUR STUFF, TAREK. PEOPLE HAVE BEEN NOTICING.
Perth
Abernethy
Maybe it was in my mind. Perhaps I had imagined *all* of the events of the last few weeks.
WHERE YE GOING? I'M STAYING ON THE A9 ALL THE WAY TO BLAIR ATHOLL, IF THAT'S ANY USE TAE YOU?
REMEMBER WHAT I SAID...ANY JOURNEY OF WORTH MUST BE MADE **ON FOOT.** IT'S JUST HOW IT **WORKS** FOR PEOPLE LIKE US...
SUIT YERSEL, WEE MAN. TAKE CARE THOUGH, EH?
And if that was the case I had to wonder...
RIGHT... WHAT WERE WE TALKING ABOUT?
SIGH
...why couldn't my mind have conjured up something less *trying?*

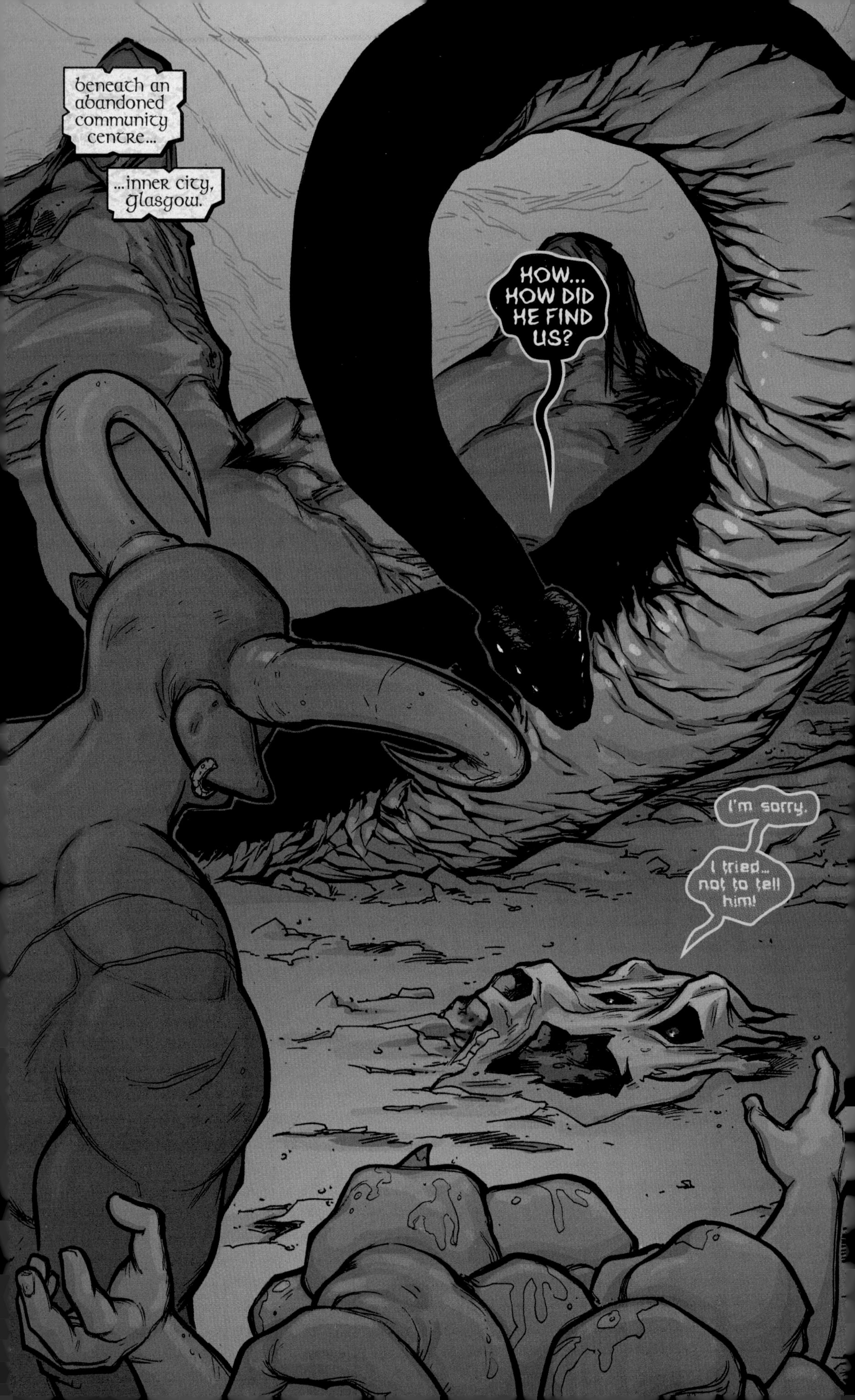
beneath an abandoned community centre...
...inner city, glasgow.
HOW... HOW DID HE FIND US?
I'm sorry.
I tried... not to tell him!

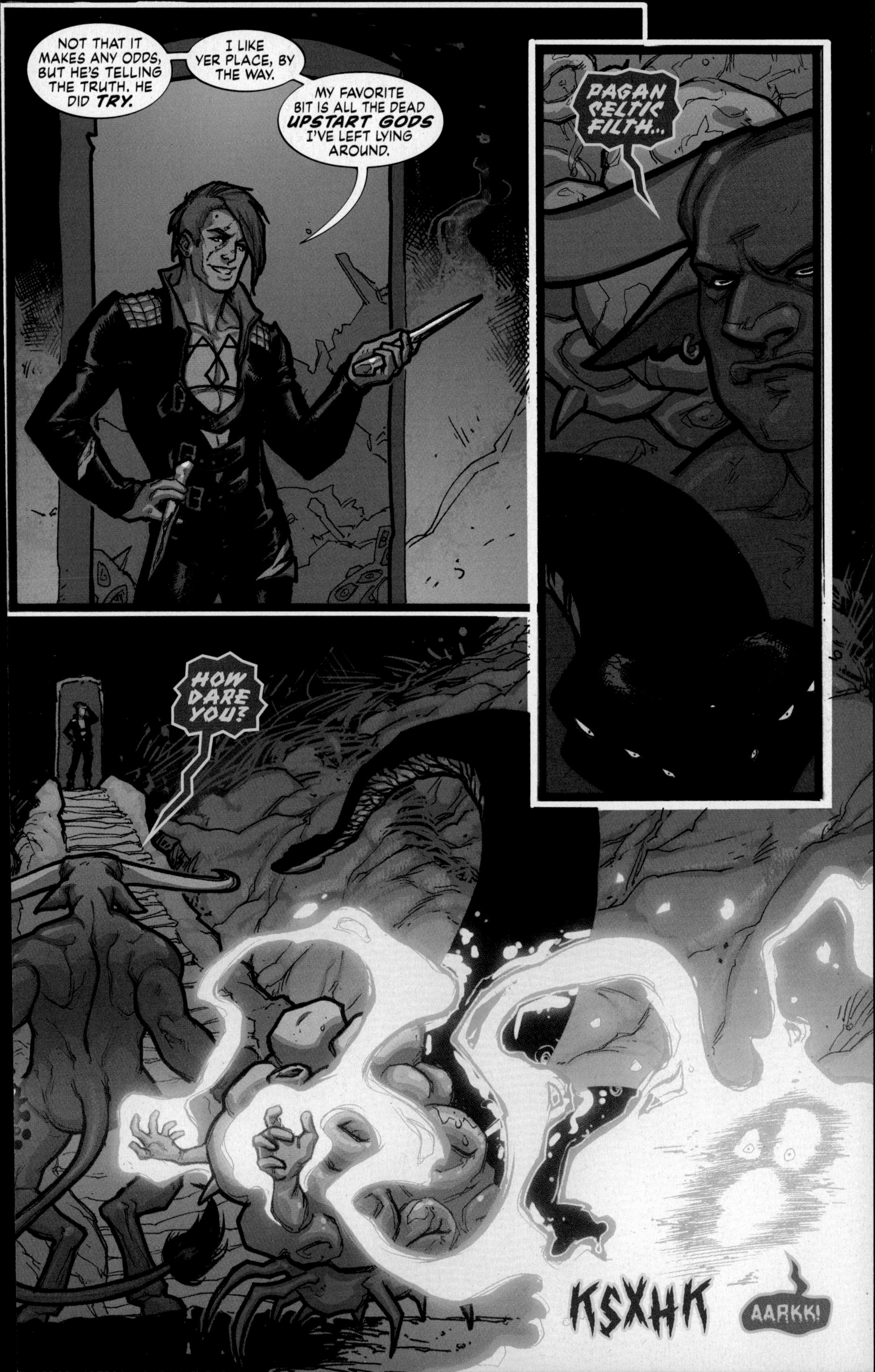
NOT THAT IT MAKES ANY ODDS, BUT HE'S TELLING THE TRUTH. HE DID TRY.
I LIKE YER PLACE, BY THE WAY.
MY FAVORITE BIT IS ALL THE DEAD UPSTART GODS I'VE LEFT LYING AROUND.
PAGAN CELTIC FILTH...
HOW DARE YOU?
KSXHK
AARKK!

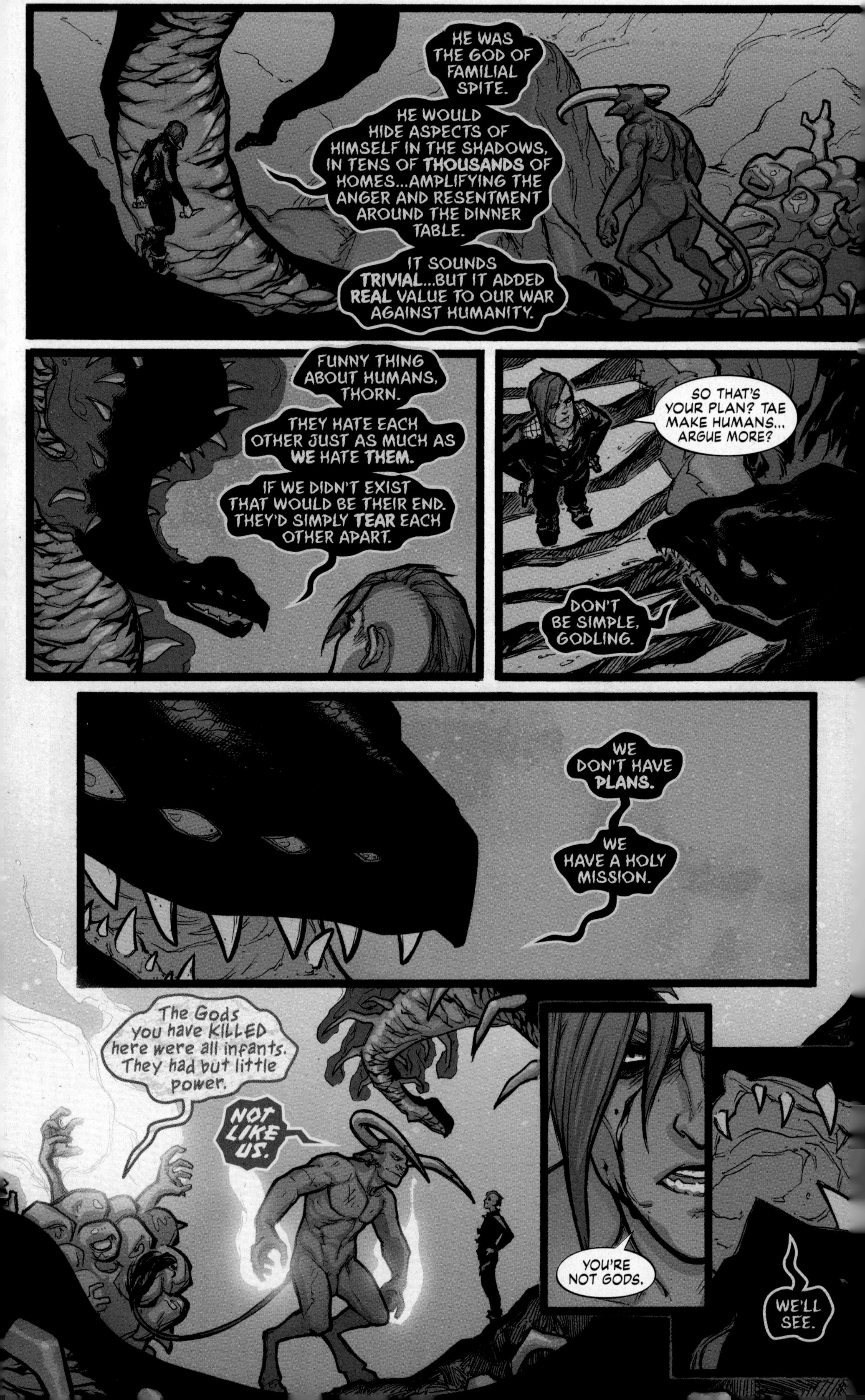
HE WAS THE GOD OF FAMILIAL SPITE.
HE WOULD HIDE ASPECTS OF HIMSELF IN THE SHADOWS, IN TENS OF THOUSANDS OF HOMES...AMPLIFYING THE ANGER AND RESENTMENT AROUND THE DINNER TABLE.
IT SOUNDS TRIVIAL...BUT IT ADDED REAL VALUE TO OUR WAR AGAINST HUMANITY.
FUNNY THING ABOUT HUMANS, THORN.
THEY HATE EACH OTHER JUST AS MUCH AS WE HATE THEM.
IF WE DIDN'T EXIST THAT WOULD BE THEIR END. THEY'D SIMPLY TEAR EACH OTHER APART.
SO THAT'S YOUR PLAN? TAE MAKE HUMANS... ARGUE MORE?
DON'T BE SIMPLE, GODLING.
WE DON'T HAVE PLANS.
WE HAVE A HOLY MISSION.
The Gods you have KILLED here were all infants. They had but little power.
NOT LIKE US.
YOU'RE NOT GODS.
WE'LL SEE.

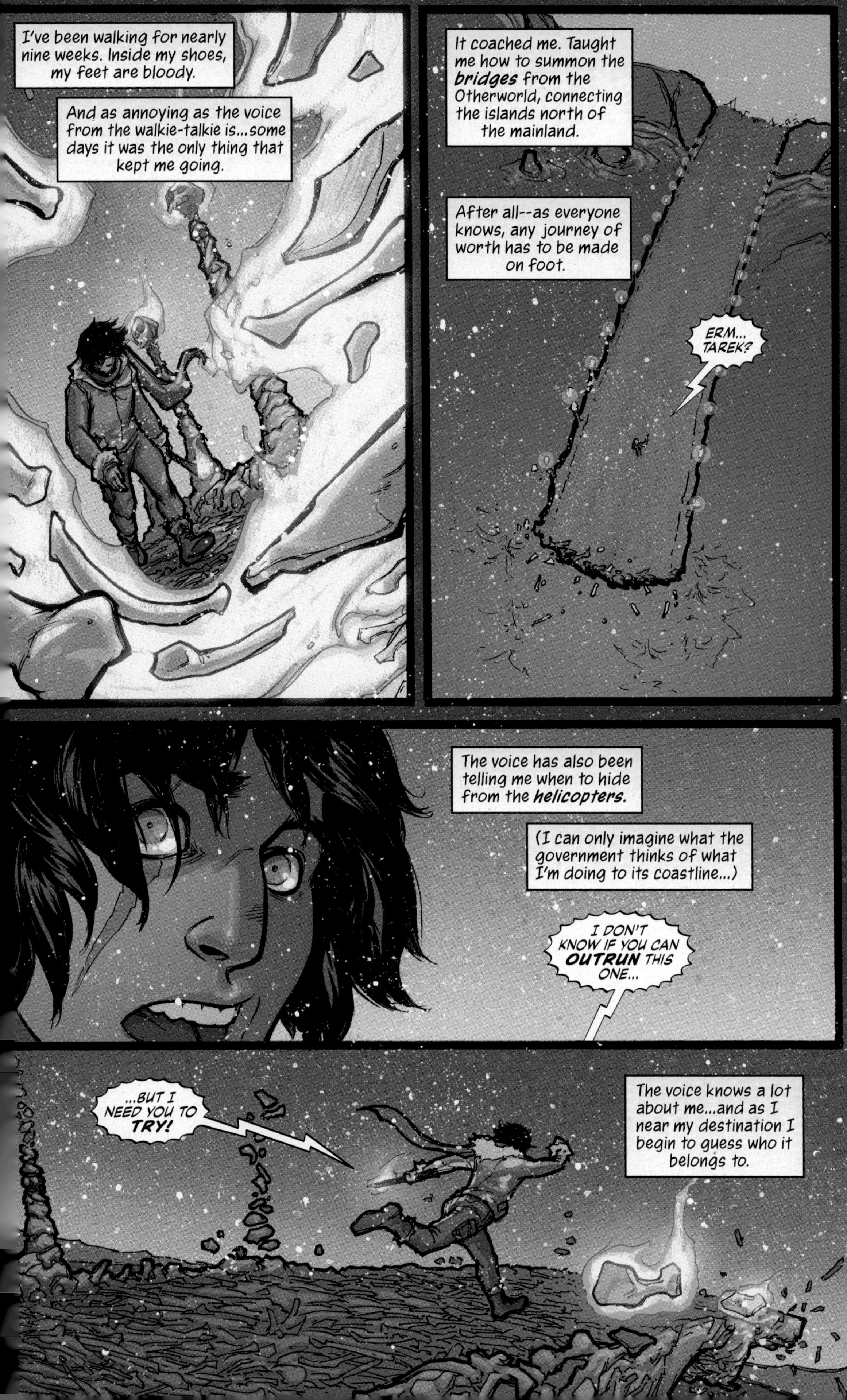

I've been walking for nearly nine weeks. Inside my shoes, my feet are bloody.
And as annoying as the voice from the walkie-talkie is...some days it was the only thing that kept me going.
It coached me. Taught me how to summon the ***bridges*** from the Otherworld, connecting the islands north of the mainland.
After all--as everyone knows, any journey of worth has to be made on foot.
ERM... TAREK?
The voice has also been telling me when to hide from the ***helicopters.***
(I can only imagine what the government thinks of what I'm doing to its coastline...)
I DON'T KNOW IF YOU CAN ***OUTRUN*** THIS ONE...
...BUT I NEED YOU TO ***TRY!***
The voice knows a lot about me...and as I near my destination I begin to guess who it belongs to.

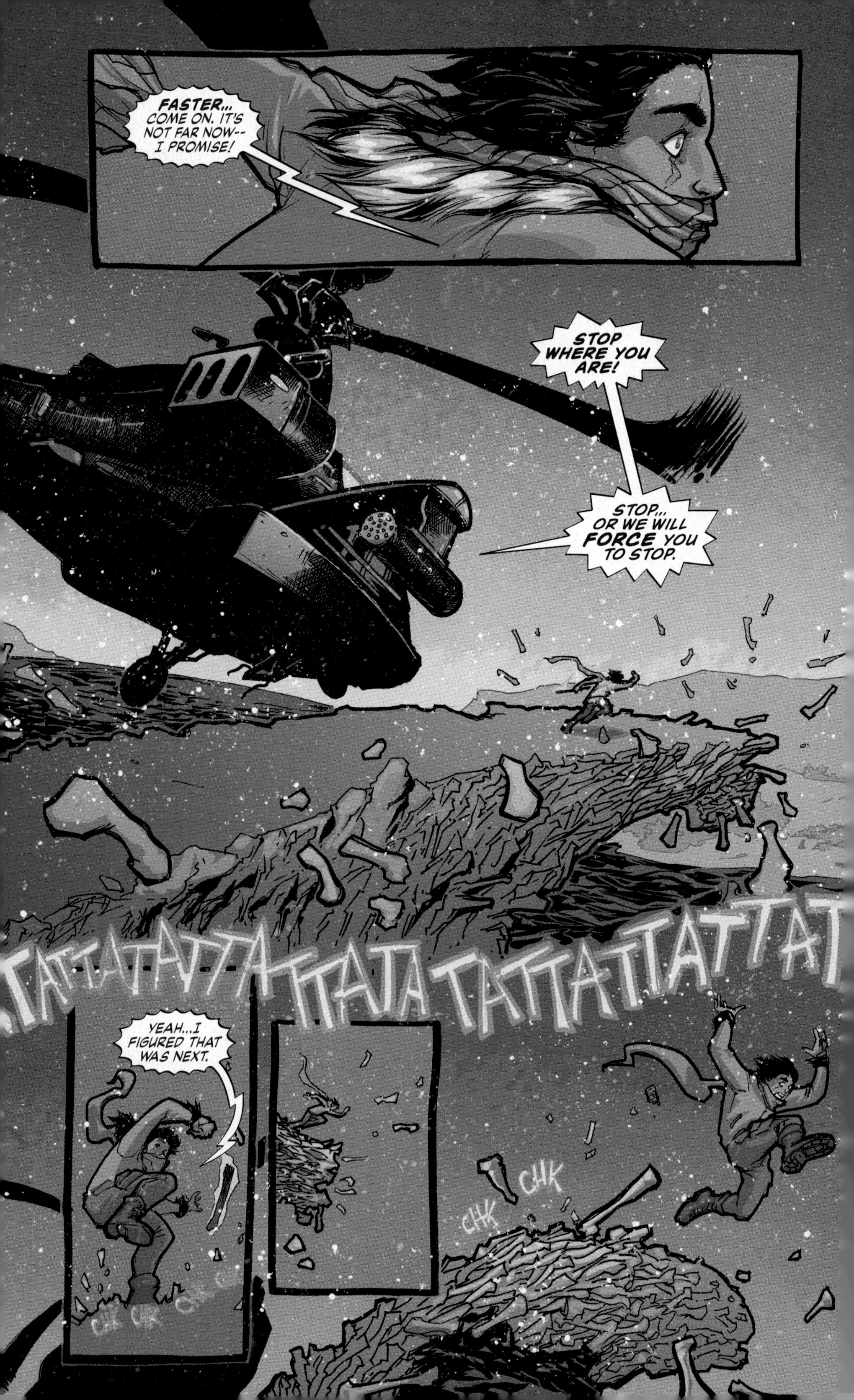
FASTER... COME ON. IT'S NOT FAR NOW-- I PROMISE!
STOP WHERE YOU ARE!
STOP... OR WE WILL FORCE YOU TO STOP.
TATTATATTATATTATATATTATTATTAT
YEAH...I FIGURED THAT WAS NEXT.
CHK CHK
CHK
CHK

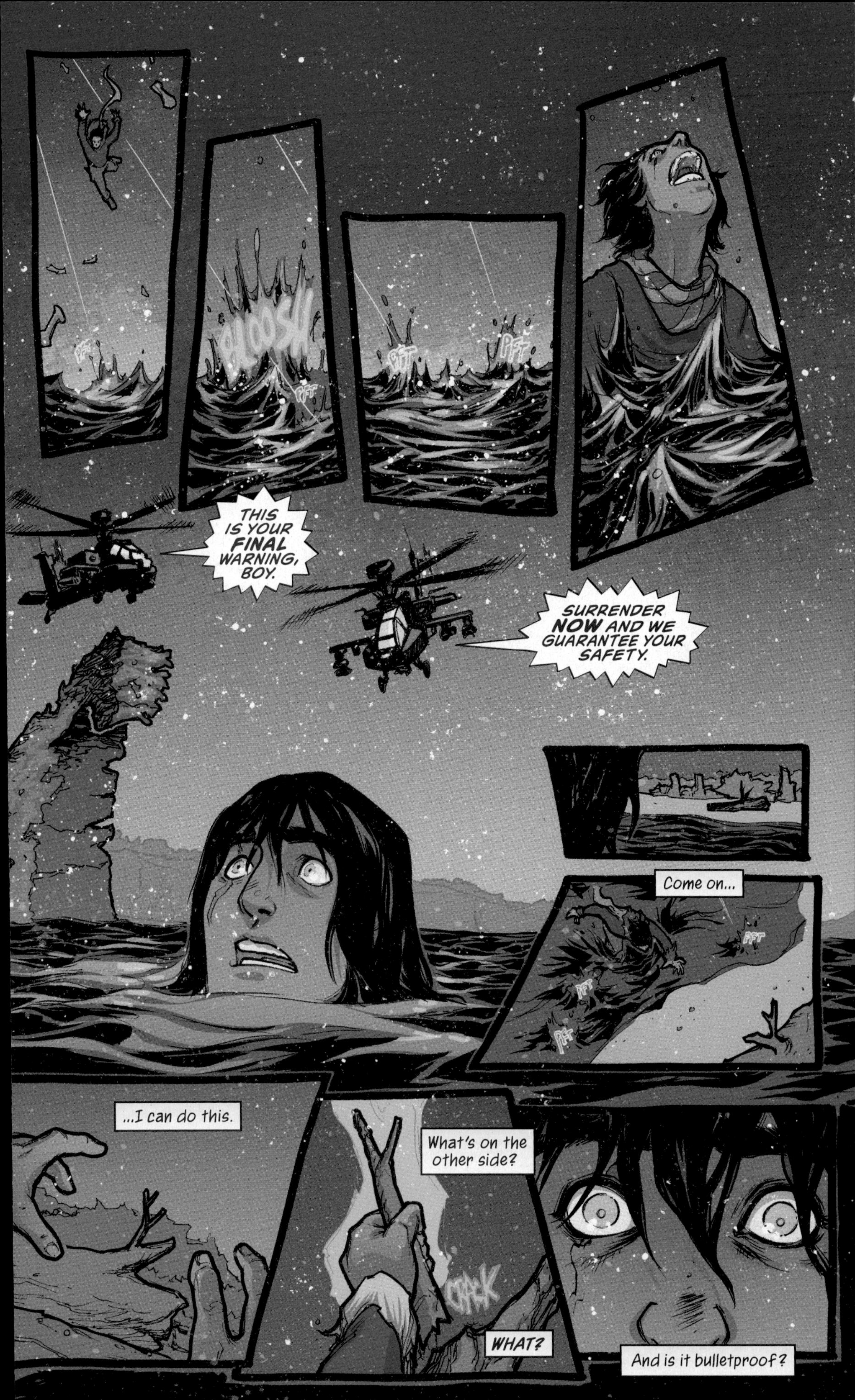

PFT
BLOOSH
PFT
PFT
PFT
THIS IS YOUR FINAL WARNING, BOY.
SURRENDER NOW AND WE GUARANTEE YOUR SAFETY.
Come on...
PFT
PFT
PFT
...I can do this.
What's on the other side?
CRACK
WHAT?
And is it bulletproof?

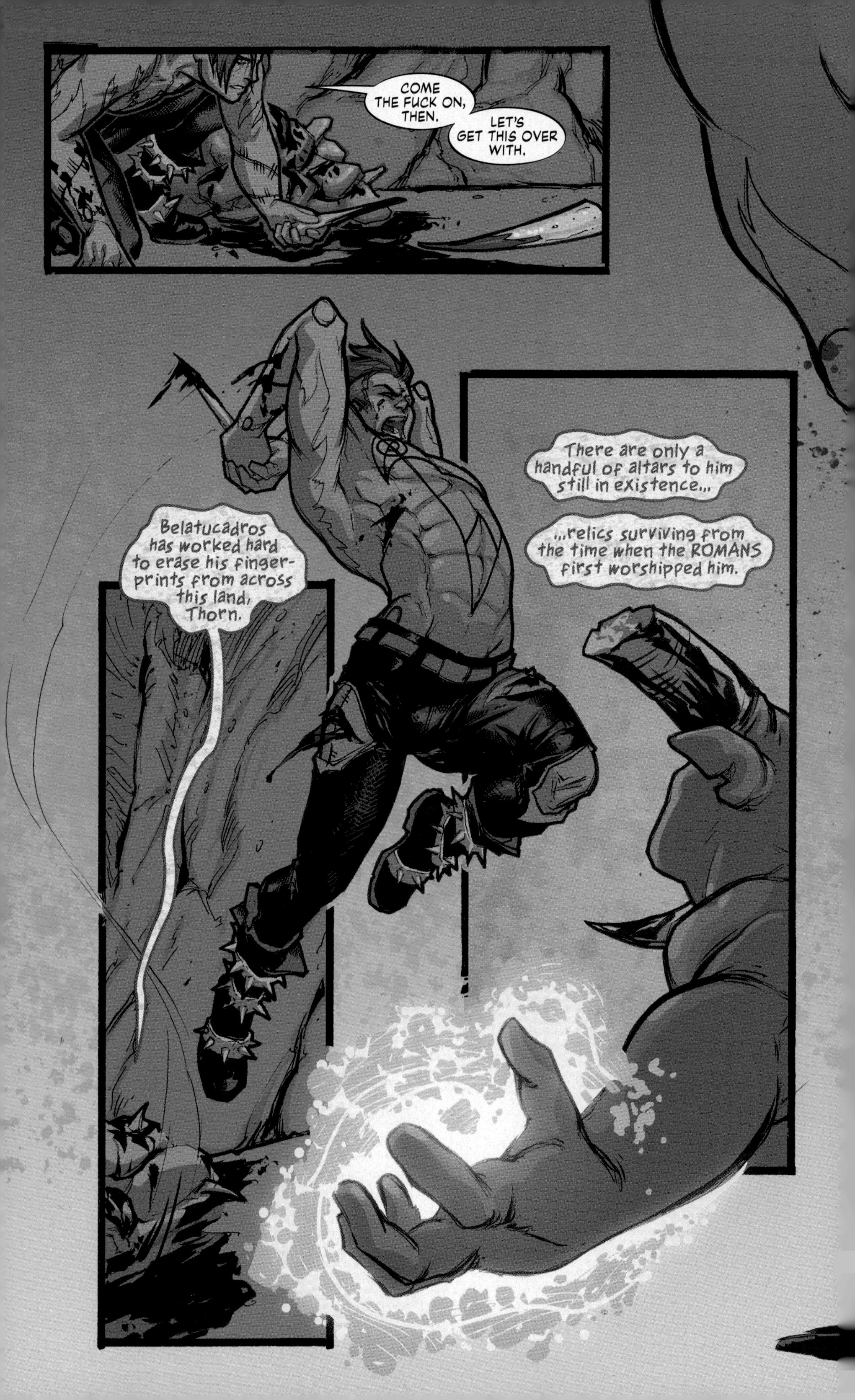

COME THE FUCK ON, THEN.
LET'S GET THIS OVER WITH.
Belatucadros has worked hard to erase his finger-prints from across this land, Thorn.
There are only a handful of altars to him still in existence...
...relics surviving from the time when the ROMANS first worshipped him.

As he stole more and more CONTROL for himself, he scorched away all other clues to his identity.

Since returning to this mortal Earth, did you ever think to wonder why that was so?

Human archaeologists believe Belatucadros to be a God of War. Of revolution.

A God of the Working Classes.

Of course none of that is true.

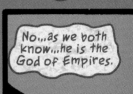

No...as we both know...he is the God of Empires.

NOOO--!

YAAAAAARGHH!

WRONG...

...HE IS THE GOD OF *PSYCHOPATHY.*

Yes. Yes, he is.

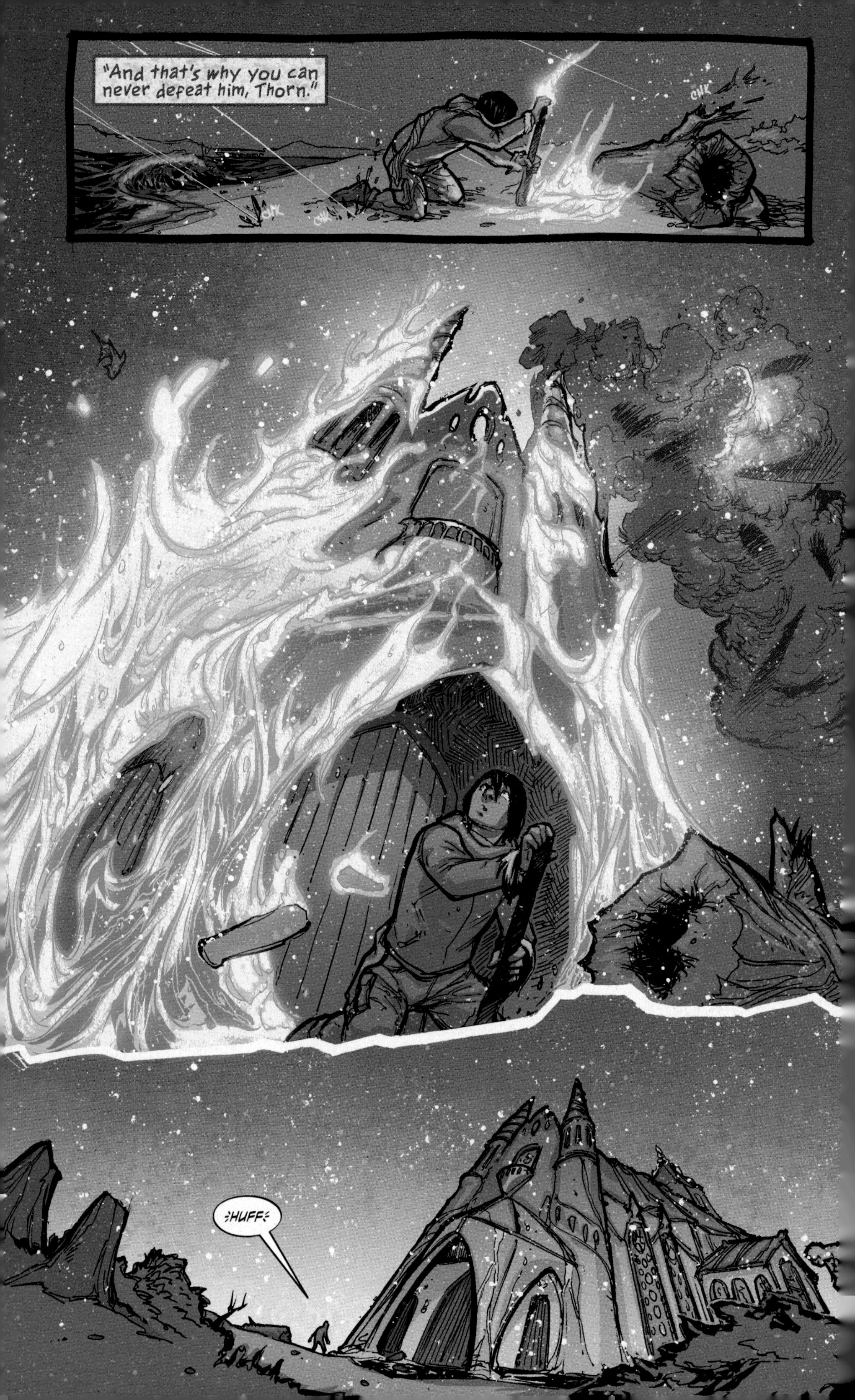
"And that's why you can never defeat him, Thorn."
CHK
CHK
CHK
HUFF

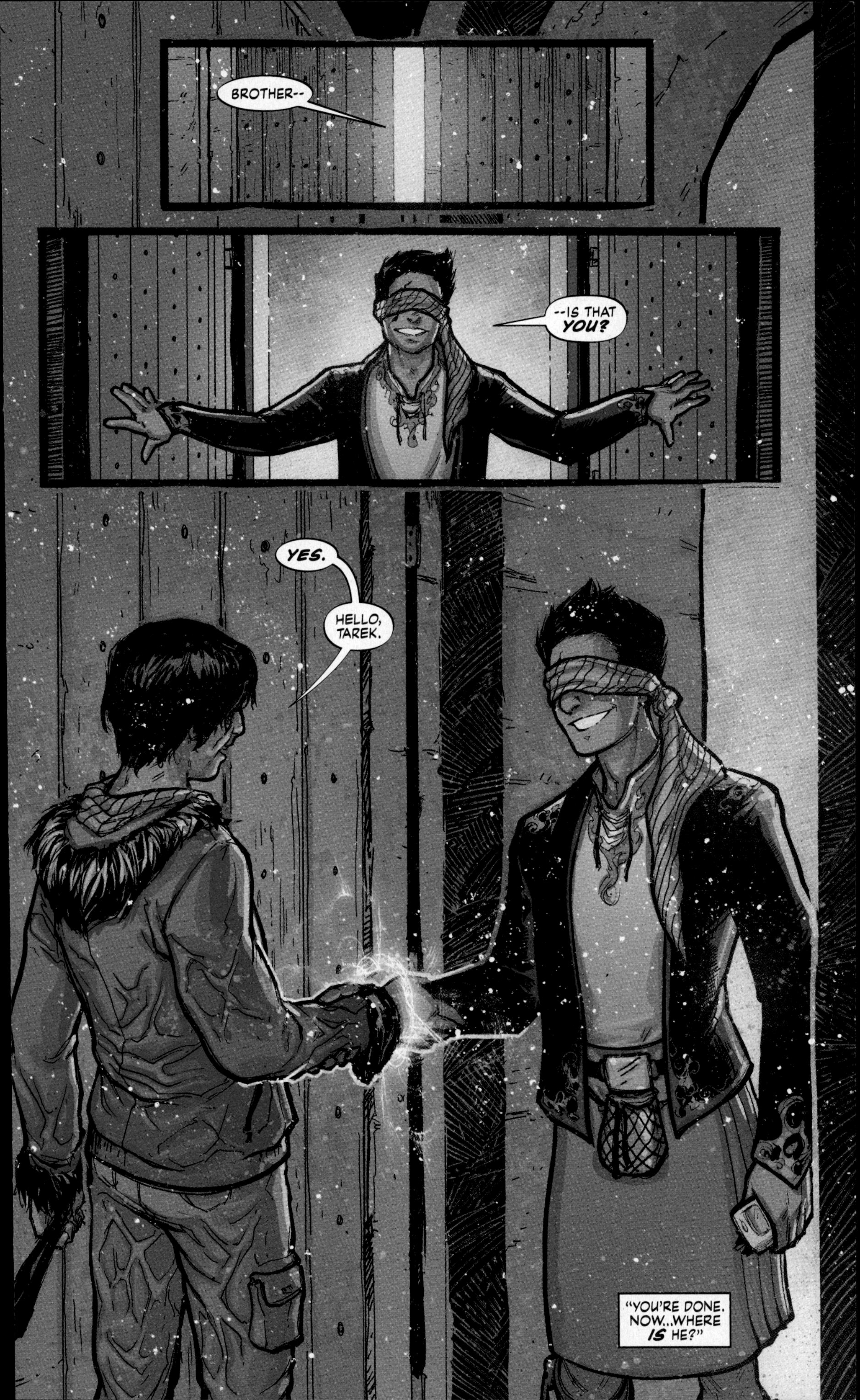
BROTHER--
--IS THAT YOU?
YES.
HELLO, TAREK.
"YOU'RE DONE. NOW...WHERE IS HE?"

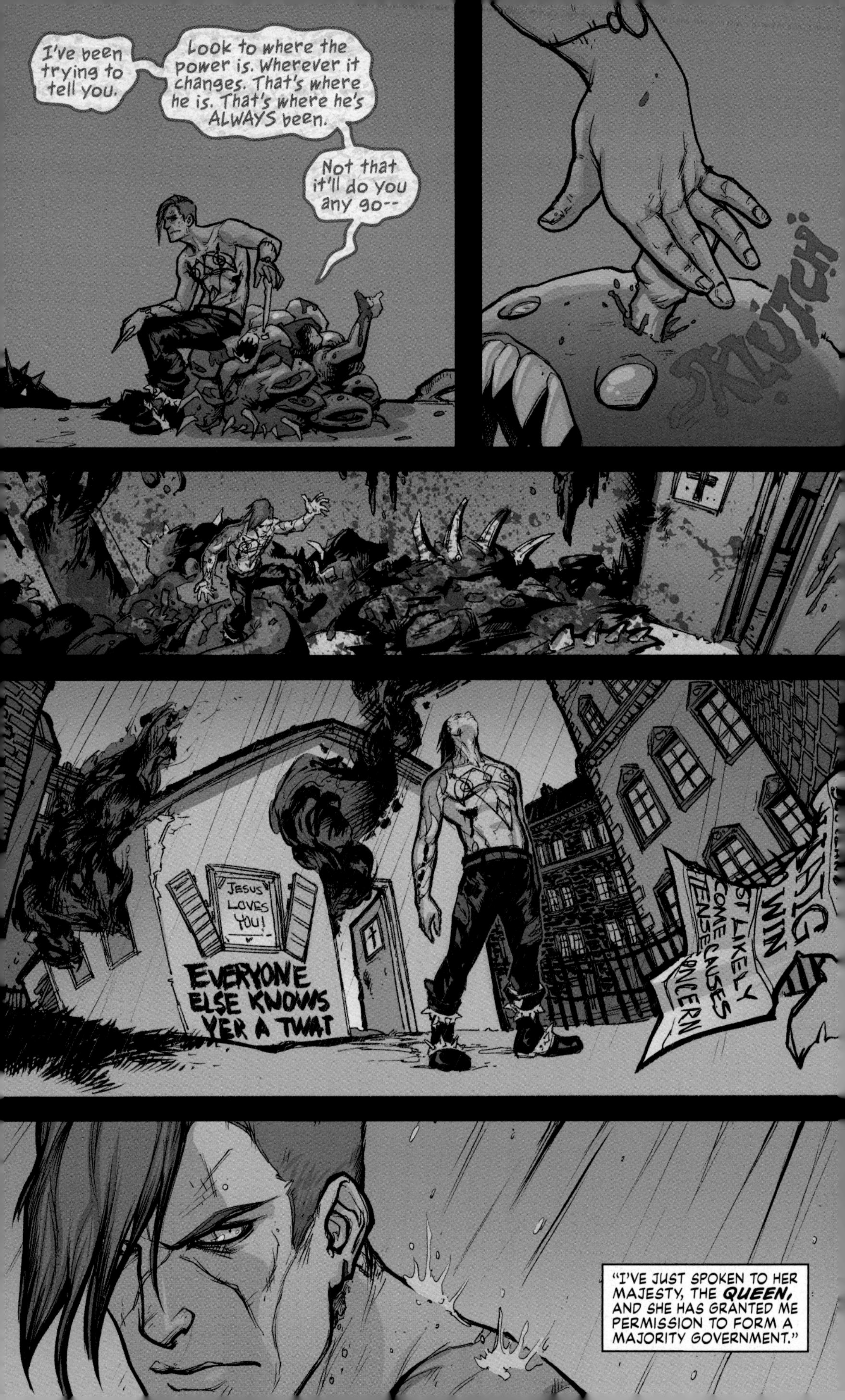
I've been trying to tell you.
Look to where the power is. Wherever it changes. That's where he is. That's where he's ALWAYS been.
Not that it'll do you any go--
SKLUTCH
JESUS LOVES YOU!
EVERYONE ELSE KNOWS YER A TWAT
"I'VE JUST SPOKEN TO HER MAJESTY, THE QUEEN, AND SHE HAS GRANTED ME PERMISSION TO FORM A MAJORITY GOVERNMENT."

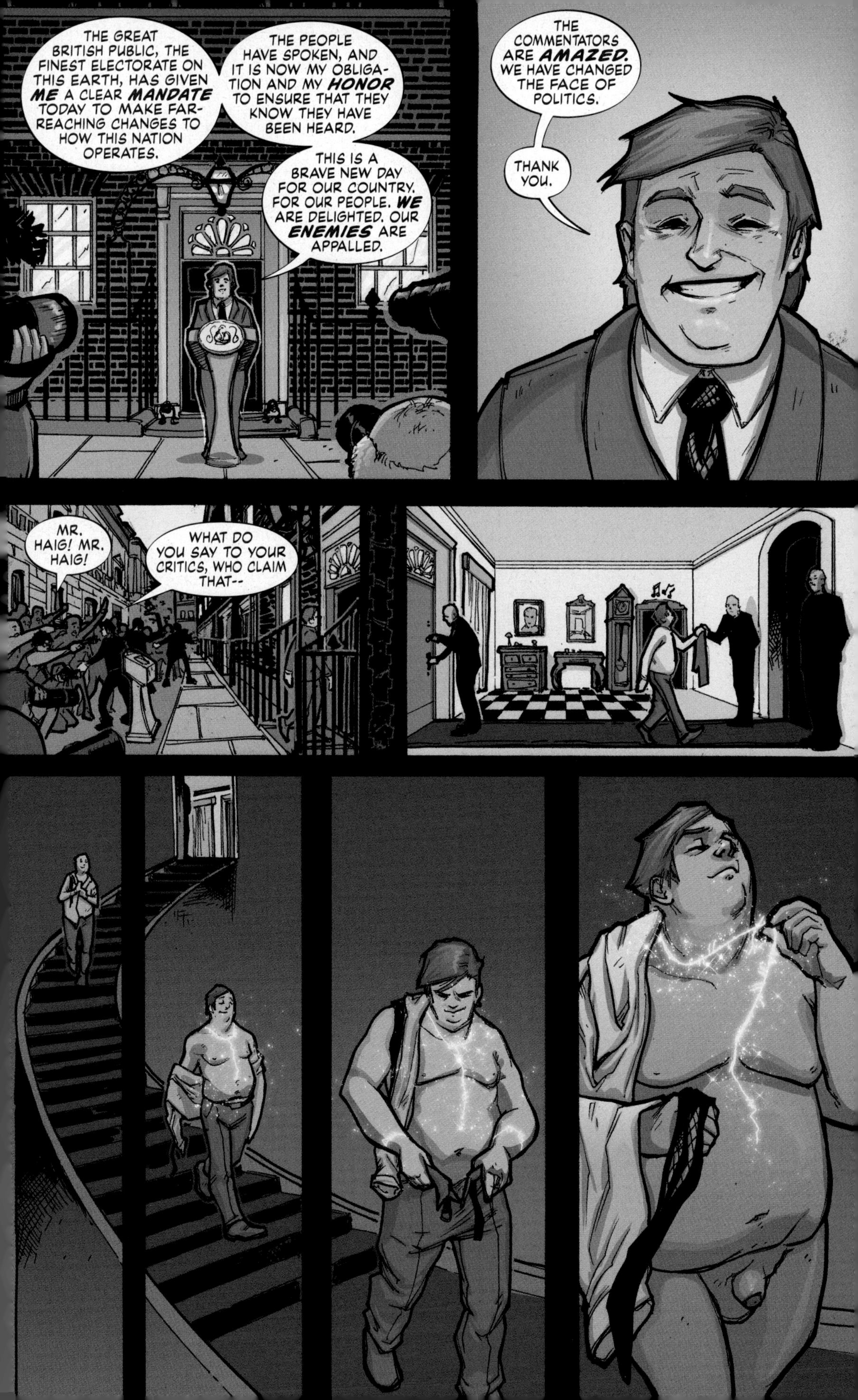
THE GREAT BRITISH PUBLIC, THE FINEST ELECTORATE ON THIS EARTH, HAS GIVEN **ME** A CLEAR **MANDATE** TODAY TO MAKE FAR-REACHING CHANGES TO HOW THIS NATION OPERATES.
THE PEOPLE HAVE SPOKEN, AND IT IS NOW MY OBLIGATION AND MY **HONOR** TO ENSURE THAT THEY KNOW THEY HAVE BEEN HEARD.
THIS IS A BRAVE NEW DAY FOR OUR COUNTRY. FOR OUR PEOPLE. **WE** ARE DELIGHTED. OUR **ENEMIES** ARE APPALLED.
THE COMMENTATORS ARE **AMAZED.** WE HAVE CHANGED THE FACE OF POLITICS.
THANK YOU.
MR. HAIG! MR. HAIG!
WHAT DO YOU SAY TO YOUR CRITICS, WHO CLAIM THAT--

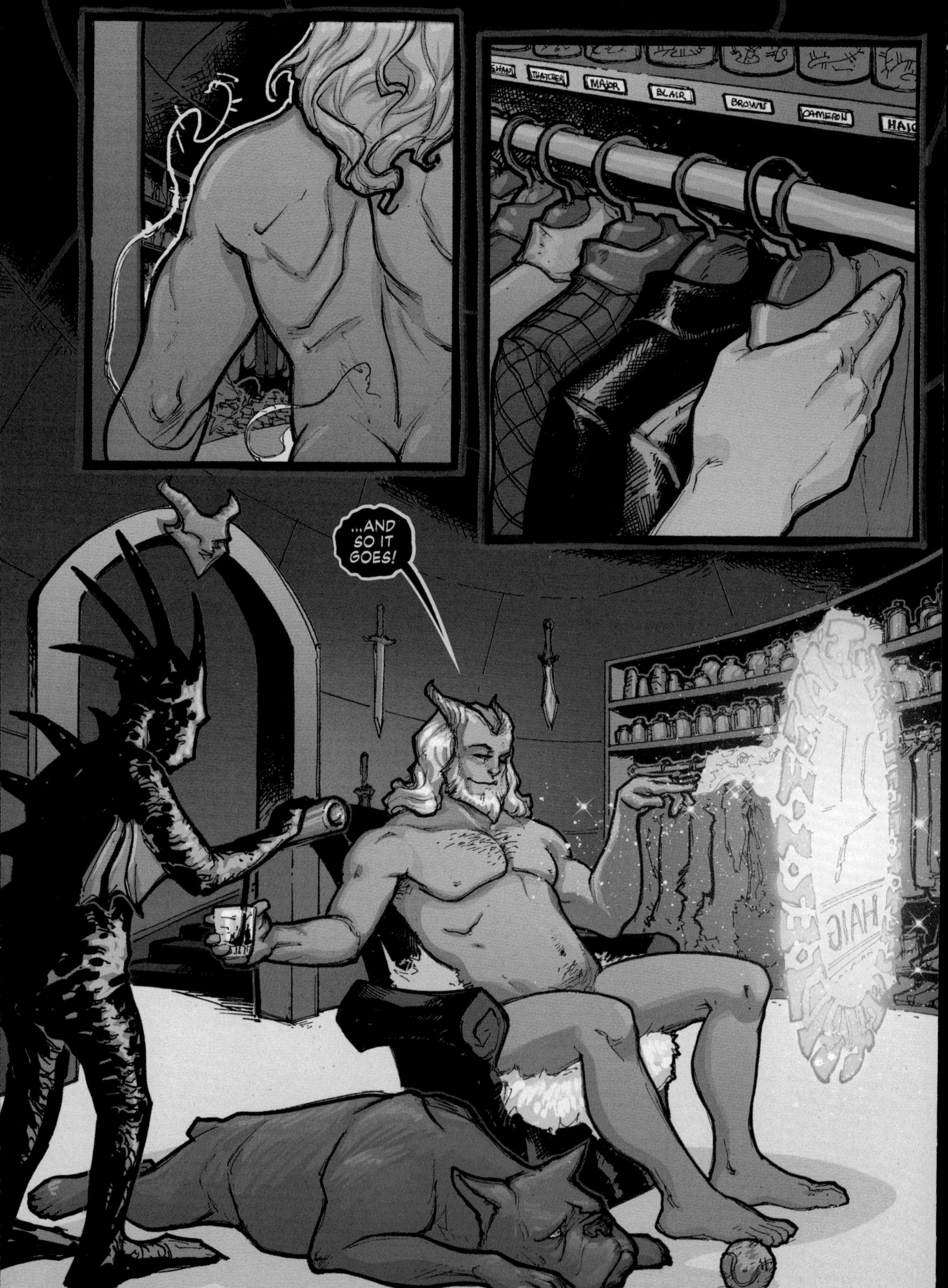
THATCHER
MAJOR
BLAIR
BROWN
CAMERON
...AND SO IT GOES!

ENDLESS, NAMELESS

Next: into the dirt

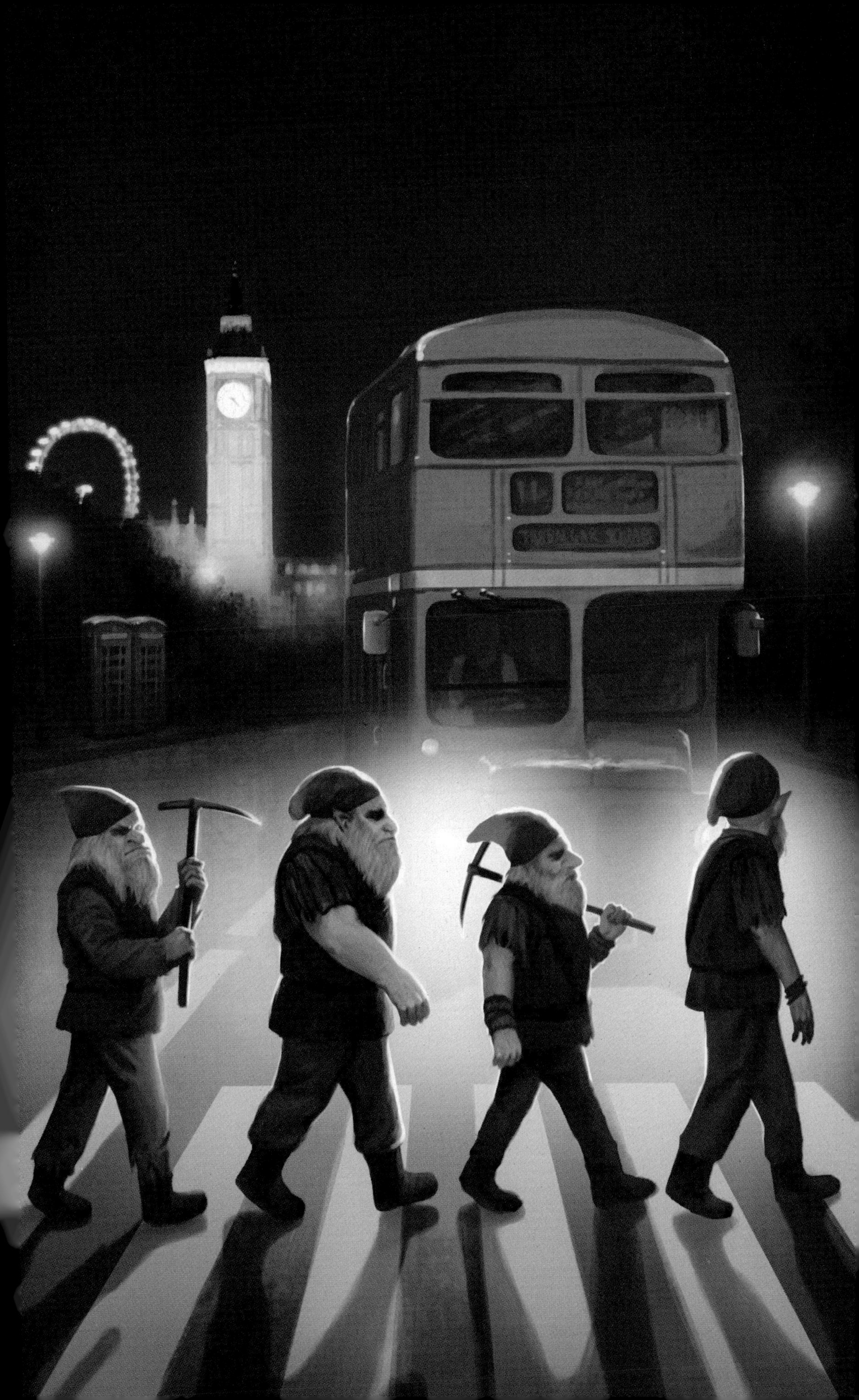

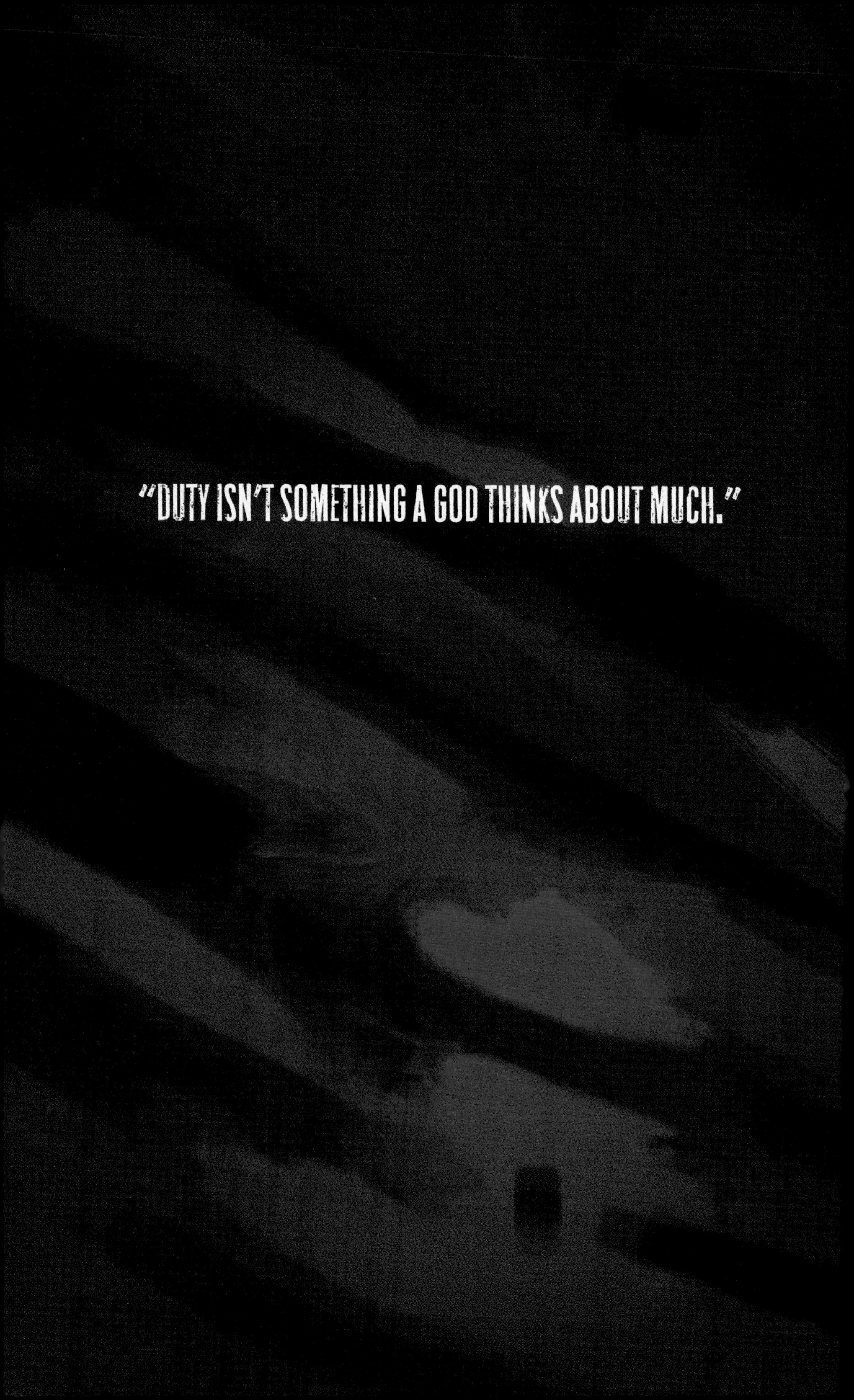
"DUTY ISN'T SOMETHING A GOD THINKS ABOUT MUCH."

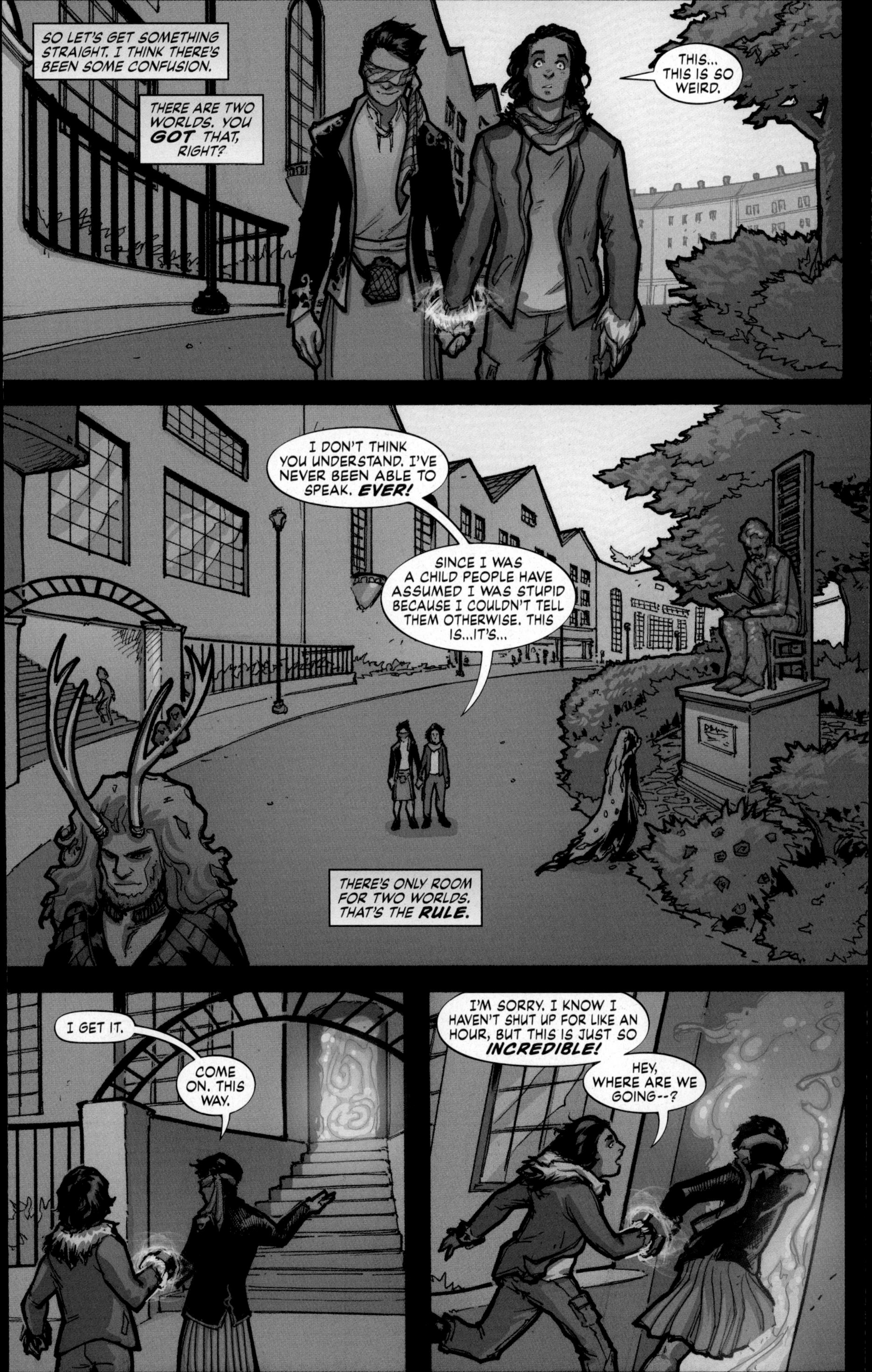
SO LET'S GET SOMETHING STRAIGHT. I THINK THERE'S BEEN SOME CONFUSION.
THERE ARE TWO WORLDS. YOU GOT THAT, RIGHT?
THIS... THIS IS SO WEIRD.
I DON'T THINK YOU UNDERSTAND. I'VE NEVER BEEN ABLE TO SPEAK. EVER!
SINCE I WAS A CHILD PEOPLE HAVE ASSUMED I WAS STUPID BECAUSE I COULDN'T TELL THEM OTHERWISE. THIS IS...IT'S...
THERE'S ONLY ROOM FOR TWO WORLDS. THAT'S THE RULE.
I GET IT.
COME ON. THIS WAY.
I'M SORRY. I KNOW I HAVEN'T SHUT UP FOR LIKE AN HOUR, BUT THIS IS JUST SO INCREDIBLE!
HEY, WHERE ARE WE GOING--?

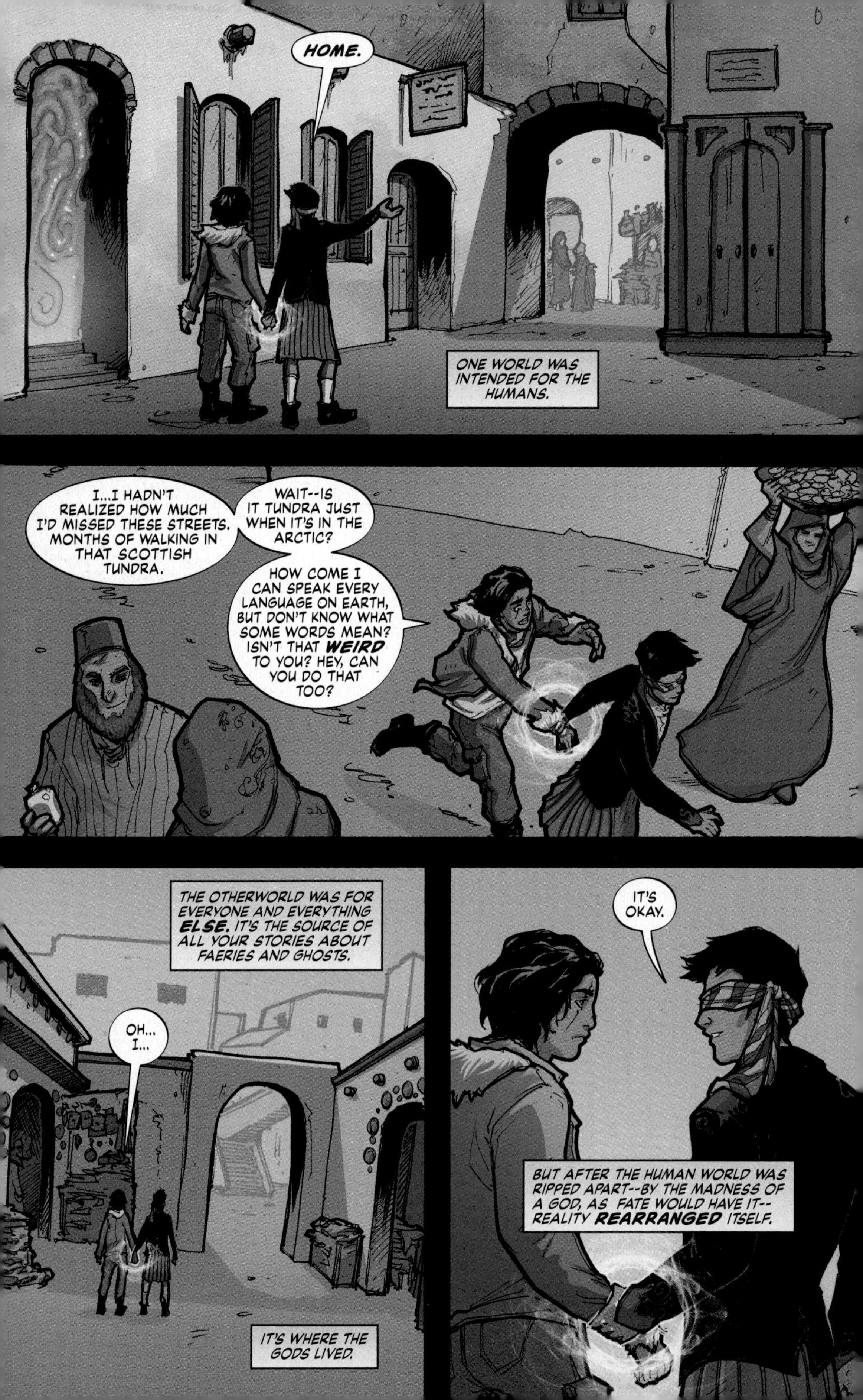
HOME.
ONE WORLD WAS INTENDED FOR THE HUMANS.
I...I HADN'T REALIZED HOW MUCH I'D MISSED THESE STREETS. MONTHS OF WALKING IN THAT SCOTTISH TUNDRA.
WAIT--IS IT TUNDRA JUST WHEN IT'S IN THE ARCTIC?
HOW COME I CAN SPEAK EVERY LANGUAGE ON EARTH, BUT DON'T KNOW WHAT SOME WORDS MEAN? ISN'T THAT WEIRD TO YOU? HEY, CAN YOU DO THAT TOO?
THE OTHERWORLD WAS FOR EVERYONE AND EVERYTHING ELSE. IT'S THE SOURCE OF ALL YOUR STORIES ABOUT FAERIES AND GHOSTS.
OH... I...
IT'S WHERE THE GODS LIVED.
IT'S OKAY.
BUT AFTER THE HUMAN WORLD WAS RIPPED APART--BY THE MADNESS OF A GOD, AS FATE WOULD HAVE IT--REALITY REARRANGED ITSELF.

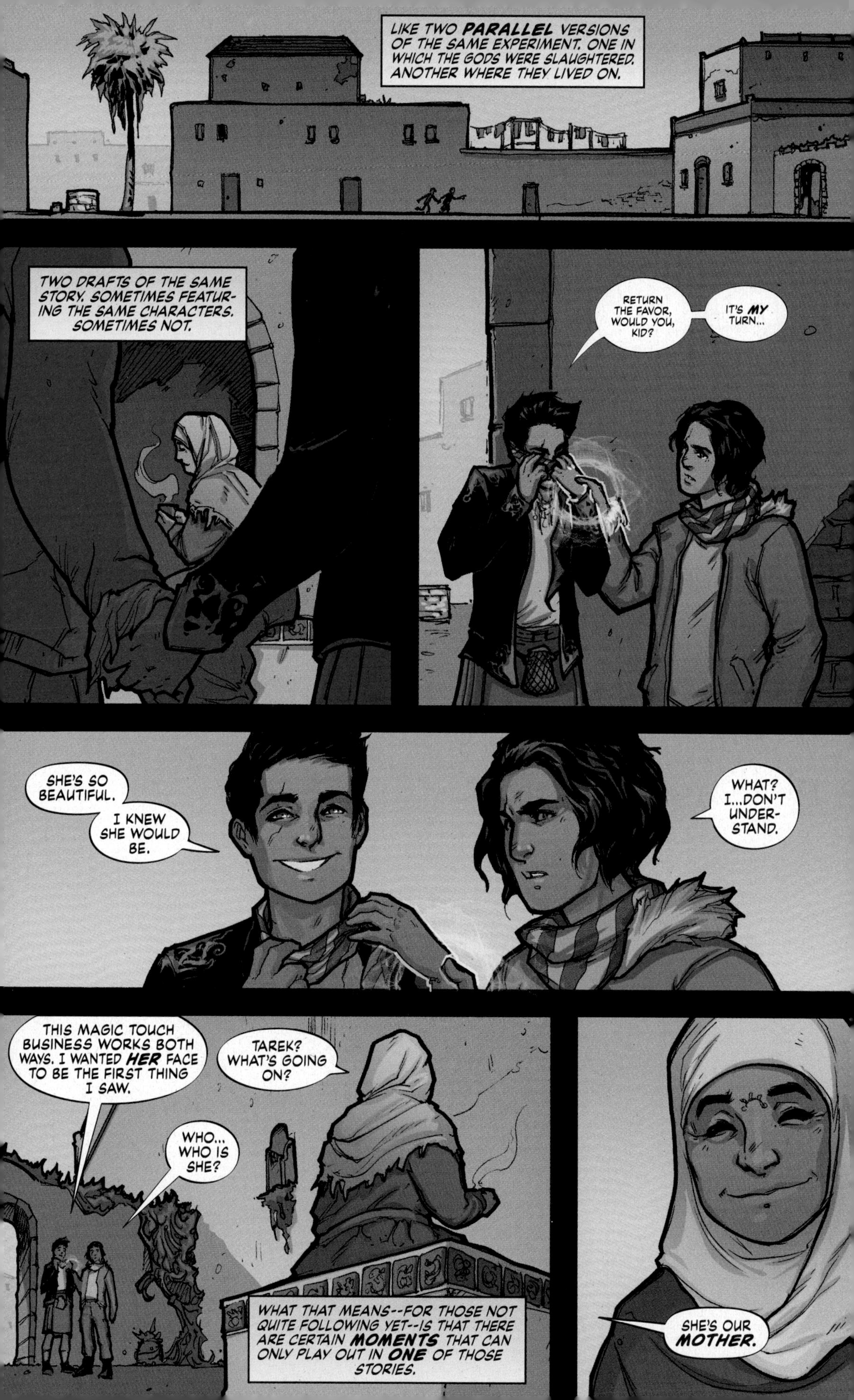
LIKE TWO PARALLEL VERSIONS OF THE SAME EXPERIMENT. ONE IN WHICH THE GODS WERE SLAUGHTERED. ANOTHER WHERE THEY LIVED ON.
TWO DRAFTS OF THE SAME STORY. SOMETIMES FEATURING THE SAME CHARACTERS. SOMETIMES NOT.
RETURN THE FAVOR, WOULD YOU, KID?
IT'S MY TURN...
SHE'S SO BEAUTIFUL.
I KNEW SHE WOULD BE.
WHAT? I...DON'T UNDERSTAND.
THIS MAGIC TOUCH BUSINESS WORKS BOTH WAYS. I WANTED HER FACE TO BE THE FIRST THING I SAW.
TAREK? WHAT'S GOING ON?
WHO... WHO IS SHE?
WHAT THAT MEANS--FOR THOSE NOT QUITE FOLLOWING YET--IS THAT THERE ARE CERTAIN MOMENTS THAT CAN ONLY PLAY OUT IN ONE OF THOSE STORIES.
SHE'S OUR MOTHER.

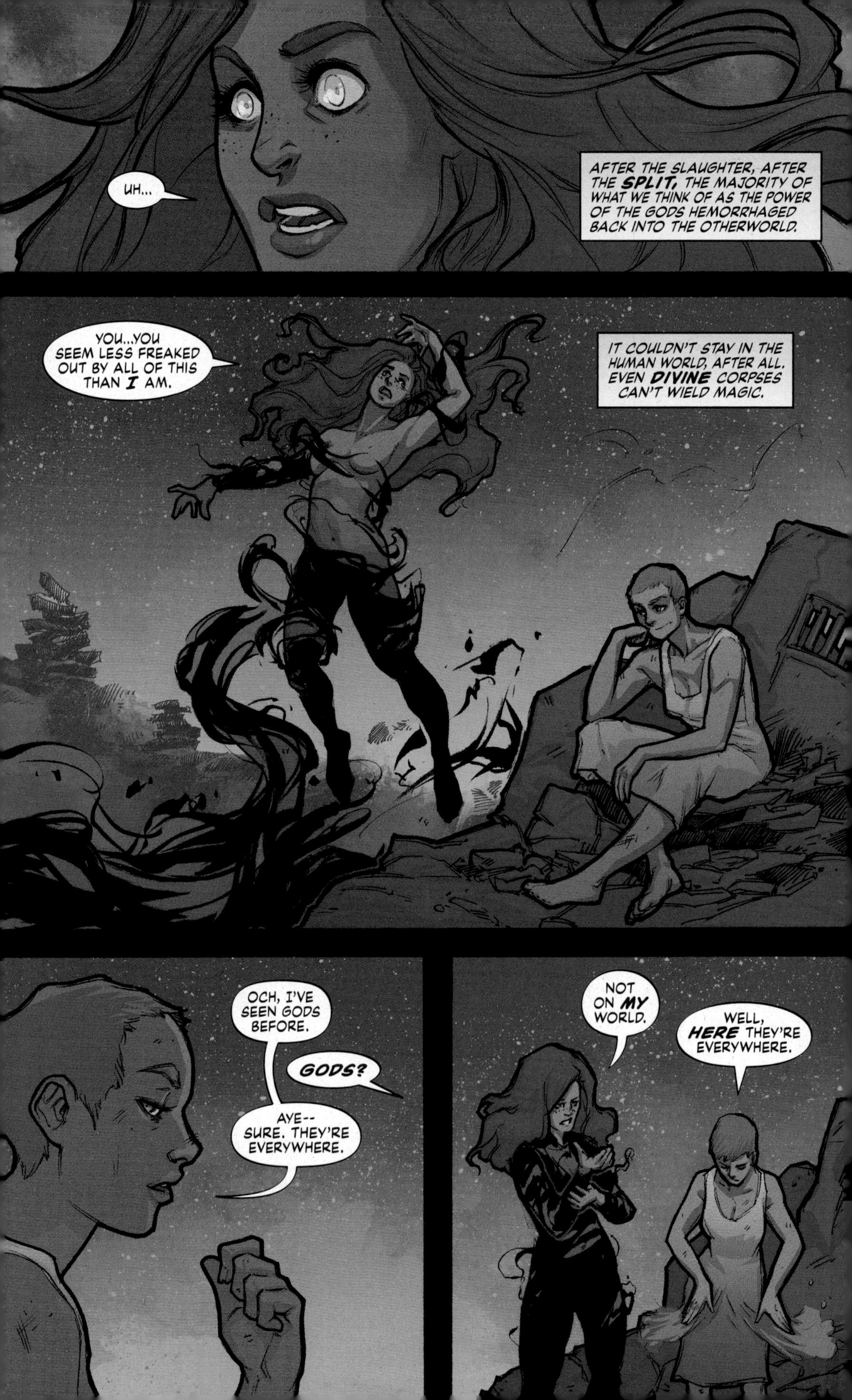
UH...
AFTER THE SLAUGHTER, AFTER THE SPLIT, THE MAJORITY OF WHAT WE THINK OF AS THE POWER OF THE GODS HEMORRHAGED BACK INTO THE OTHERWORLD.
YOU...YOU SEEM LESS FREAKED OUT BY ALL OF THIS THAN I AM.
IT COULDN'T STAY IN THE HUMAN WORLD, AFTER ALL. EVEN DIVINE CORPSES CAN'T WIELD MAGIC.
OCH, I'VE SEEN GODS BEFORE.
GODS?
AYE-- SURE. THEY'RE EVERYWHERE.
NOT ON MY WORLD.
WELL, HERE THEY'RE EVERYWHERE.

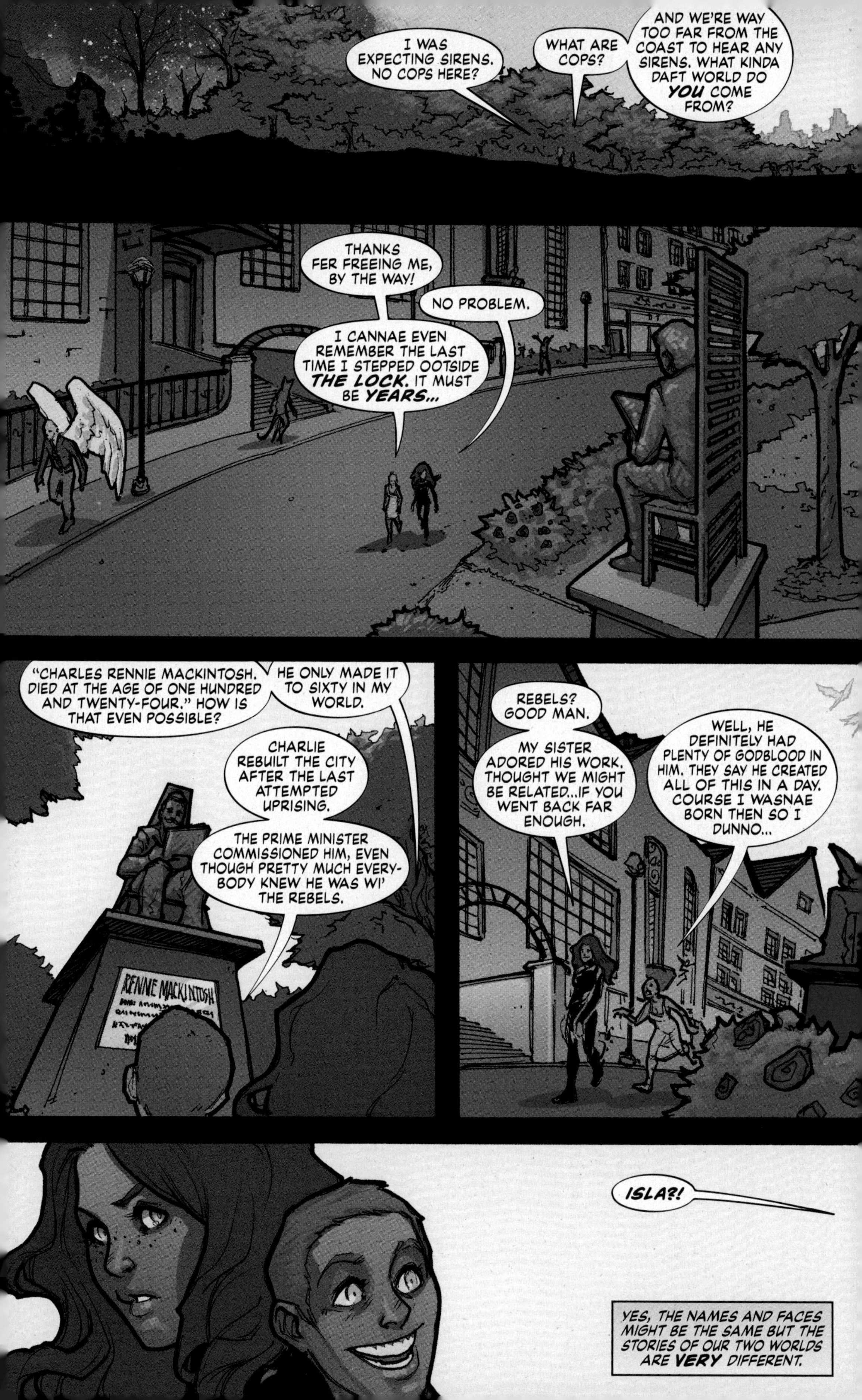
I WAS EXPECTING SIRENS. NO COPS HERE?
WHAT ARE COPS?
AND WE'RE WAY TOO FAR FROM THE COAST TO HEAR ANY SIRENS. WHAT KINDA DAFT WORLD DO *YOU* COME FROM?
THANKS FER FREEING ME, BY THE WAY!
NO PROBLEM.
I CANNAE EVEN REMEMBER THE LAST TIME I STEPPED OOTSIDE *THE LOCK.* IT MUST BE *YEARS...*
"CHARLES RENNIE MACKINTOSH. DIED AT THE AGE OF ONE HUNDRED AND TWENTY-FOUR." HOW IS THAT EVEN POSSIBLE?
HE ONLY MADE IT TO SIXTY IN MY WORLD.
CHARLIE REBUILT THE CITY AFTER THE LAST ATTEMPTED UPRISING.
THE PRIME MINISTER COMMISSIONED HIM, EVEN THOUGH PRETTY MUCH EVERY-BODY KNEW HE WAS WI' THE REBELS.
RENNIE MACKINTOSH
REBELS? GOOD MAN.
MY SISTER ADORED HIS WORK. THOUGHT WE MIGHT BE RELATED...IF YOU WENT BACK FAR ENOUGH.
WELL, HE DEFINITELY HAD PLENTY OF GODBLOOD IN HIM. THEY SAY HE CREATED ALL OF THIS IN A DAY. COURSE I WASNAE BORN THEN SO I DUNNO...
ISLA?!
YES, THE NAMES AND FACES MIGHT BE THE SAME BUT THE STORIES OF OUR TWO WORLDS ARE *VERY* DIFFERENT.

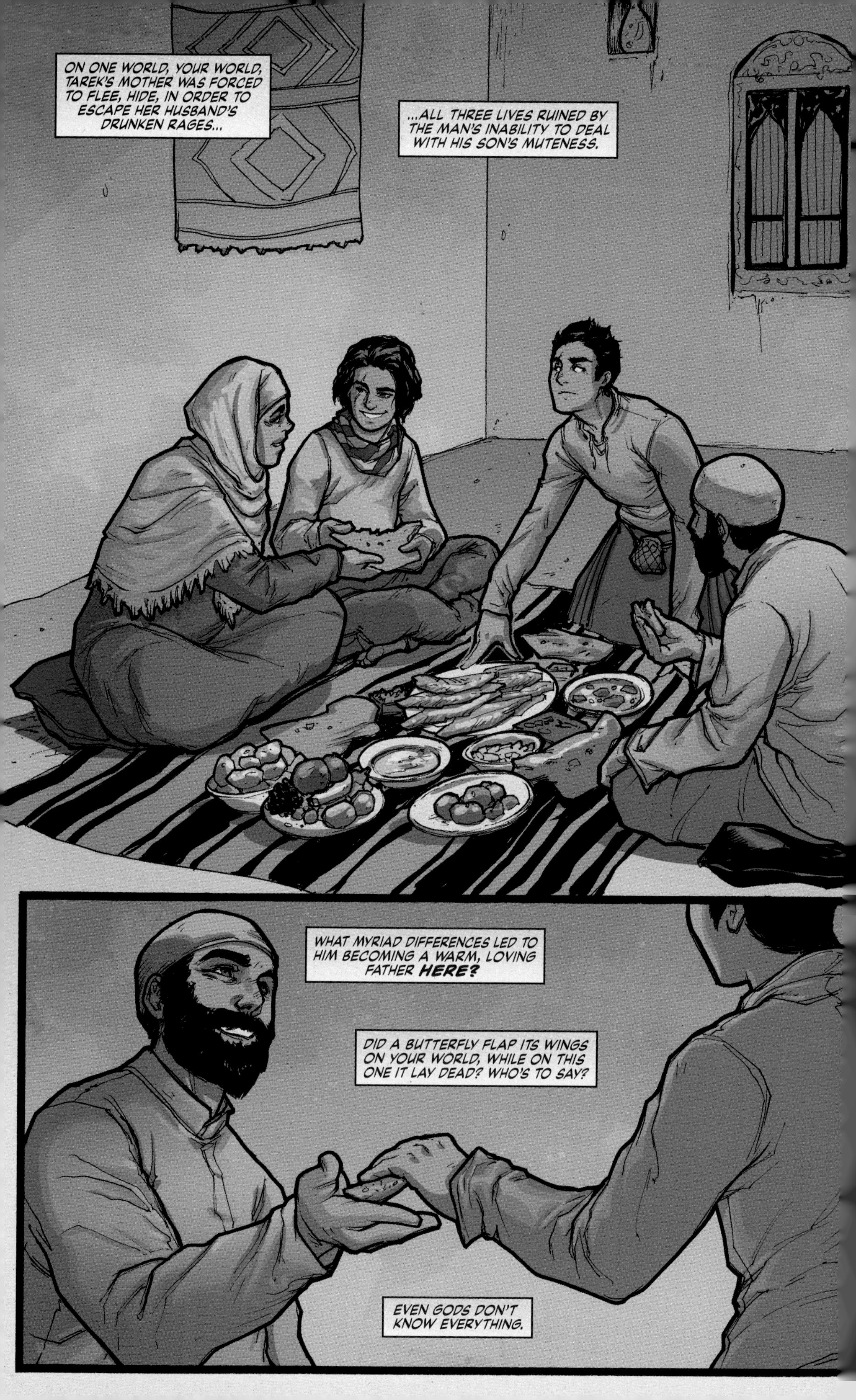
ON ONE WORLD, YOUR WORLD, TAREK'S MOTHER WAS FORCED TO FLEE, HIDE, IN ORDER TO ESCAPE HER HUSBAND'S DRUNKEN RAGES...
...ALL THREE LIVES RUINED BY THE MAN'S INABILITY TO DEAL WITH HIS SON'S MUTENESS.
WHAT MYRIAD DIFFERENCES LED TO HIM BECOMING A WARM, LOVING FATHER HERE?
DID A BUTTERFLY FLAP ITS WINGS ON YOUR WORLD, WHILE ON THIS ONE IT LAY DEAD? WHO'S TO SAY?
EVEN GODS DON'T KNOW EVERYTHING.

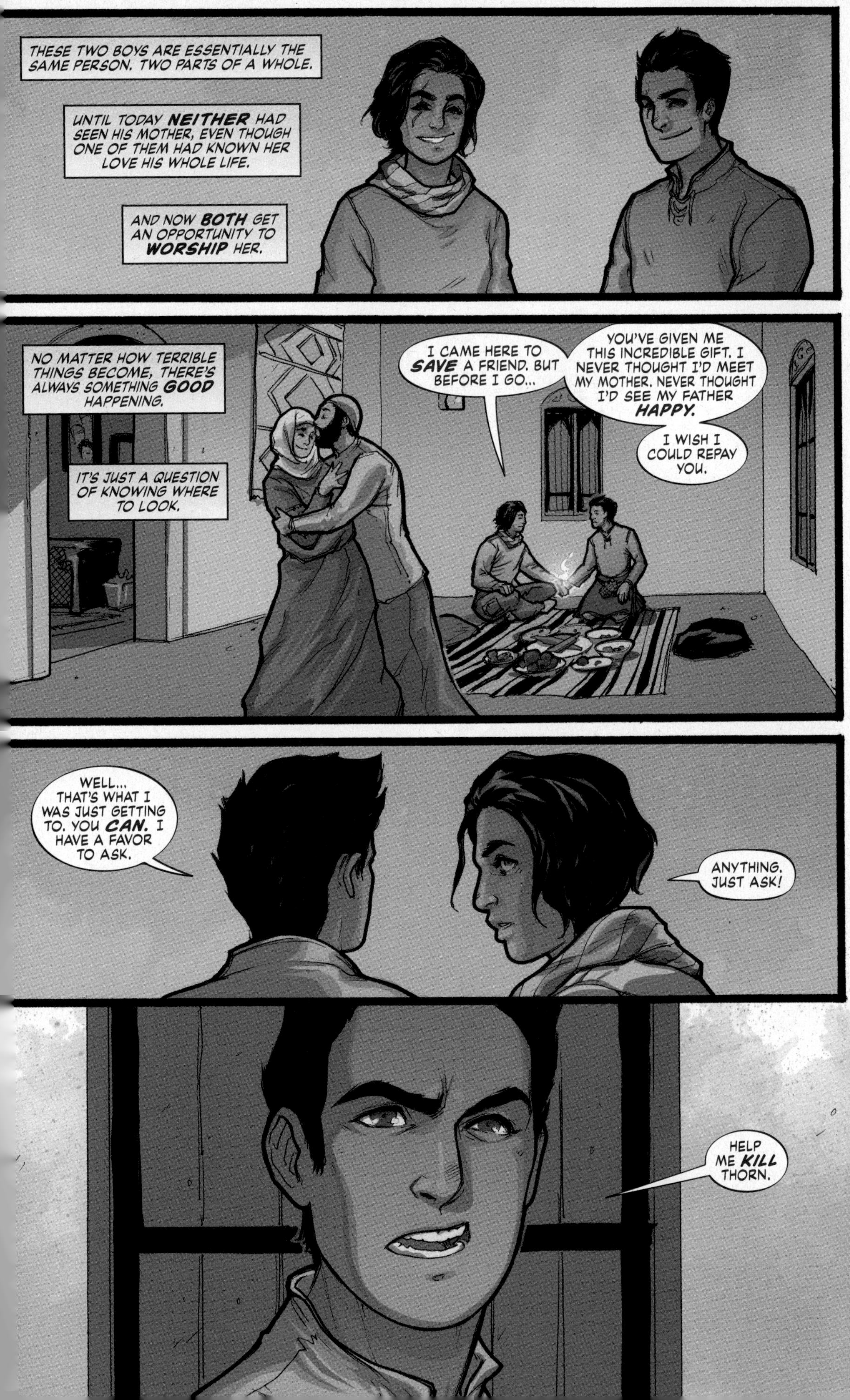
THESE TWO BOYS ARE ESSENTIALLY THE SAME PERSON. TWO PARTS OF A WHOLE.
UNTIL TODAY NEITHER HAD SEEN HIS MOTHER, EVEN THOUGH ONE OF THEM HAD KNOWN HER LOVE HIS WHOLE LIFE.
AND NOW BOTH GET AN OPPORTUNITY TO WORSHIP HER.
NO MATTER HOW TERRIBLE THINGS BECOME, THERE'S ALWAYS SOMETHING GOOD HAPPENING.
IT'S JUST A QUESTION OF KNOWING WHERE TO LOOK.
I CAME HERE TO SAVE A FRIEND. BUT BEFORE I GO...
YOU'VE GIVEN ME THIS INCREDIBLE GIFT. I NEVER THOUGHT I'D MEET MY MOTHER. NEVER THOUGHT I'D SEE MY FATHER HAPPY.
I WISH I COULD REPAY YOU.
WELL... THAT'S WHAT I WAS JUST GETTING TO. YOU CAN. I HAVE A FAVOR TO ASK.
ANYTHING. JUST ASK!
HELP ME KILL THORN.

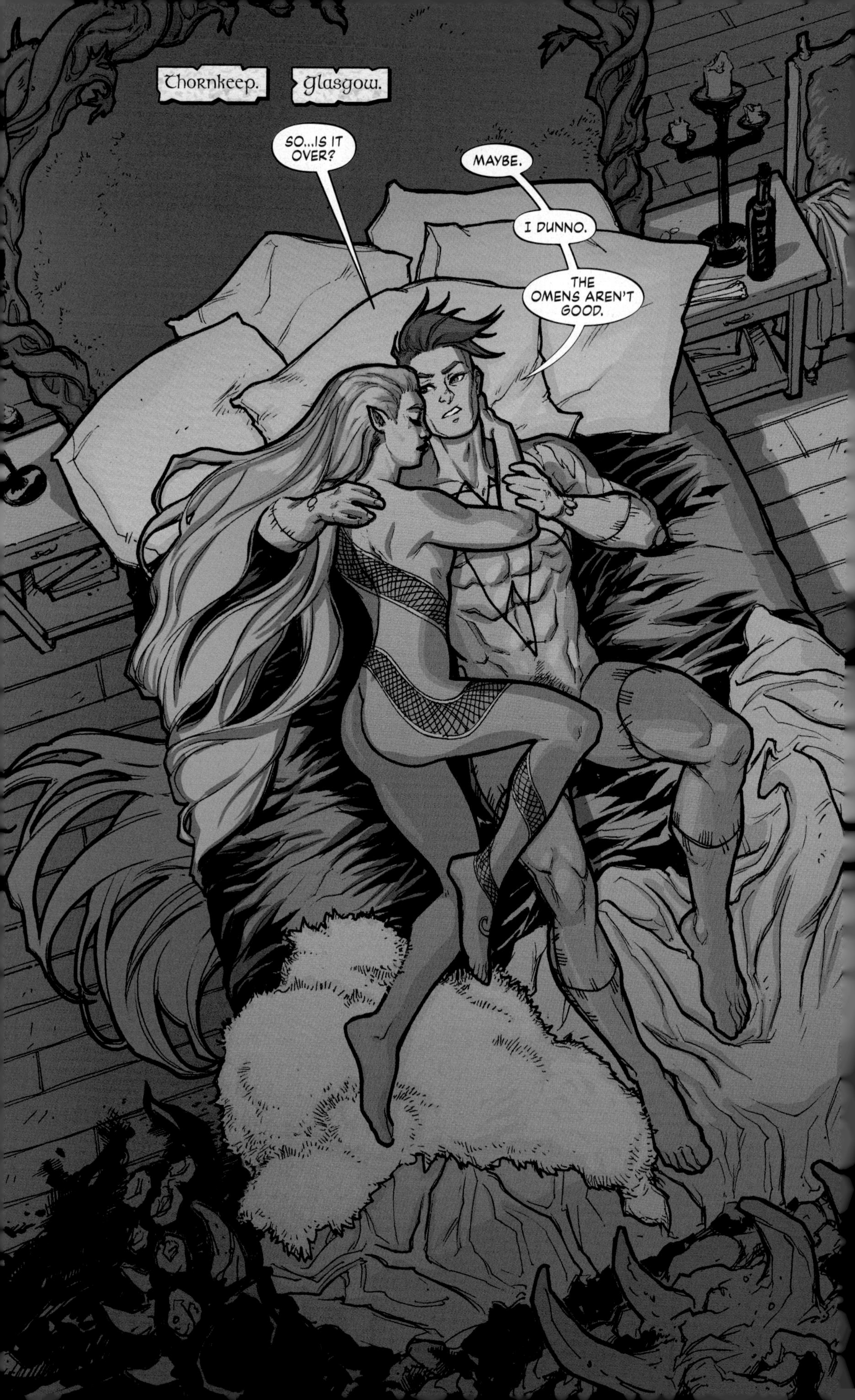
Thornkeep.
Glasgow.
SO...IS IT OVER?
MAYBE.
I DUNNO.
THE OMENS AREN'T GOOD.

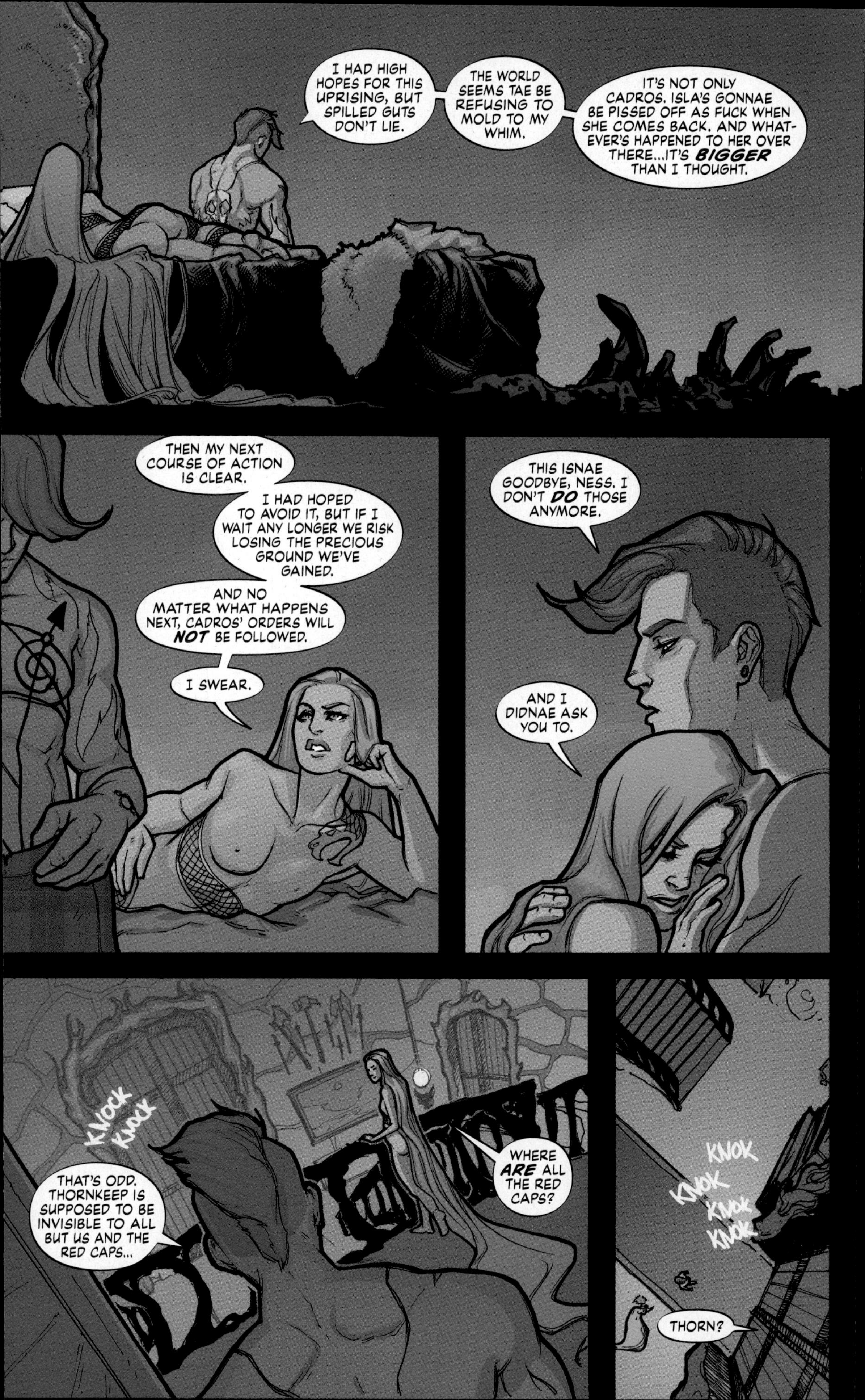
I HAD HIGH HOPES FOR THIS UPRISING, BUT SPILLED GUTS DON'T LIE.
THE WORLD SEEMS TAE BE REFUSING TO MOLD TO MY WHIM.
IT'S NOT ONLY CADROS. ISLA'S GONNAE BE PISSED OFF AS FUCK WHEN SHE COMES BACK. AND WHATEVER'S HAPPENED TO HER OVER THERE...IT'S **BIGGER** THAN I THOUGHT.
THEN MY NEXT COURSE OF ACTION IS CLEAR.
I HAD HOPED TO AVOID IT, BUT IF I WAIT ANY LONGER WE RISK LOSING THE PRECIOUS GROUND WE'VE GAINED.
AND NO MATTER WHAT HAPPENS NEXT, CADROS' ORDERS WILL **NOT** BE FOLLOWED.
I SWEAR.
THIS ISNAE GOODBYE, NESS. I DON'T **DO** THOSE ANYMORE.
AND I DIDNAE ASK YOU TO.
KNOCK KNOCK
THAT'S ODD. THORNKEEP IS SUPPOSED TO BE INVISIBLE TO ALL BUT US AND THE RED CAPS...
WHERE **ARE** ALL THE RED CAPS?
KNOK KNOK KNOK KNOK
THORN?

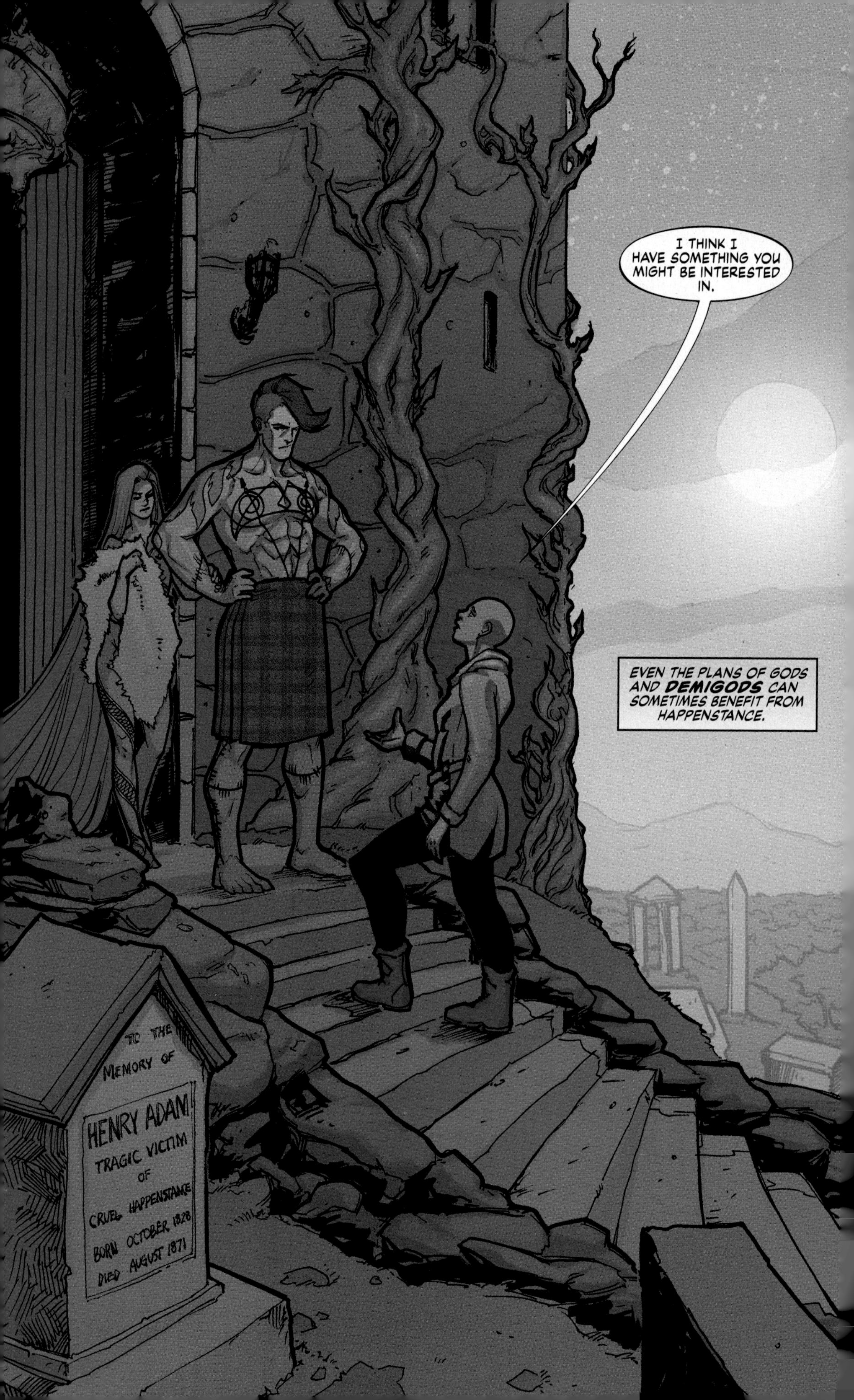
I THINK I HAVE SOMETHING YOU MIGHT BE INTERESTED IN.
EVEN THE PLANS OF GODS AND DEMIGODS CAN SOMETIMES BENEFIT FROM HAPPENSTANCE.
TO THE MEMORY OF HENRY ADAM TRAGIC VICTIM OF CRUEL HAPPENSTANCE BORN OCTOBER 1828 DIED AUGUST 1871

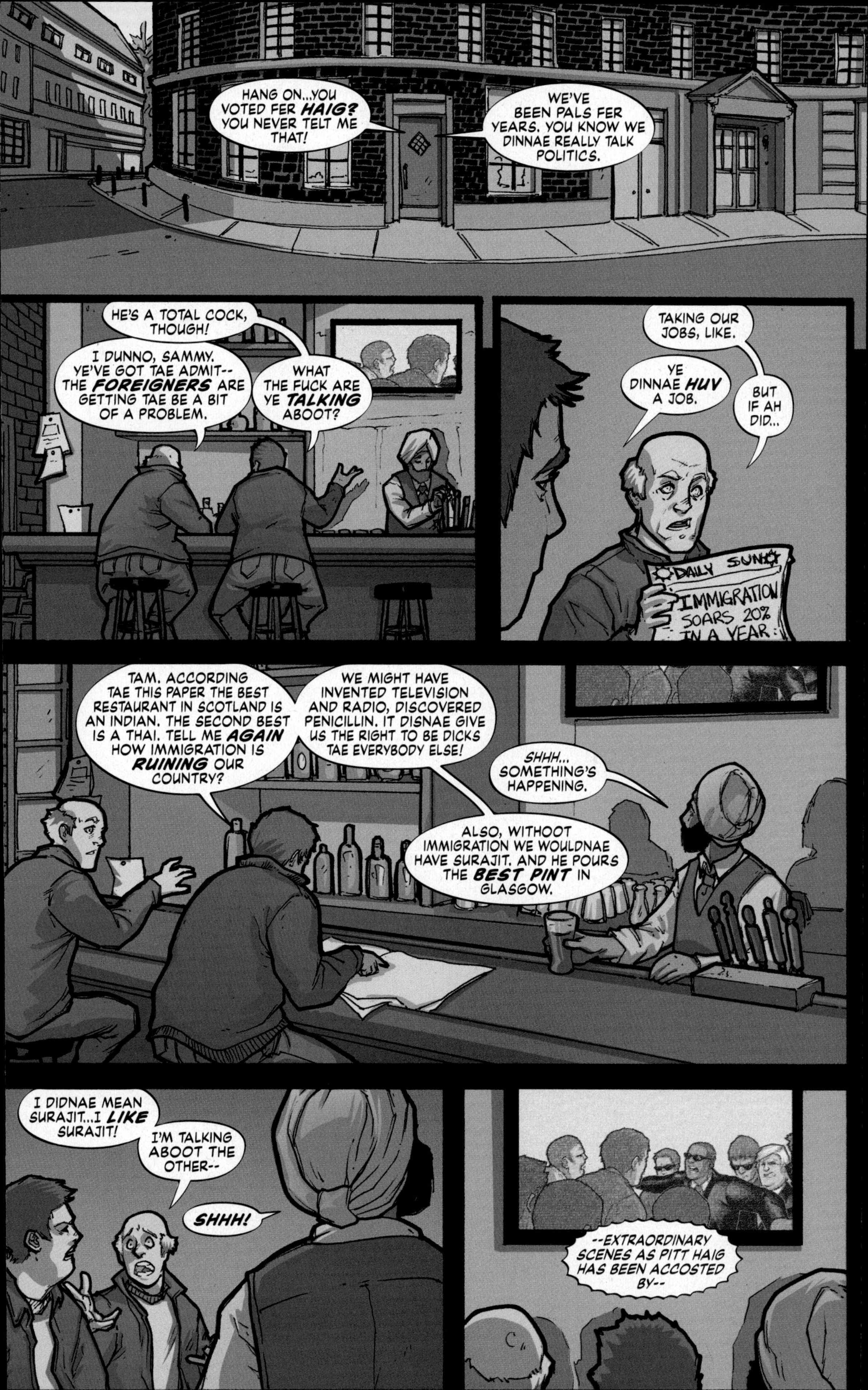
HANG ON...YOU VOTED FER HAIG? YOU NEVER TELT ME THAT!
WE'VE BEEN PALS FER YEARS. YOU KNOW WE DINNAE REALLY TALK POLITICS.
HE'S A TOTAL COCK, THOUGH!
I DUNNO, SAMMY. YE'VE GOT TAE ADMIT-- THE FOREIGNERS ARE GETTING TAE BE A BIT OF A PROBLEM.
WHAT THE FUCK ARE YE TALKING ABOOT?
TAKING OUR JOBS, LIKE.
YE DINNAE HUV A JOB.
BUT IF AH DID...
DAILY SUN
IMMIGRATION SOARS 20% IN A YEAR
TAM. ACCORDING TAE THIS PAPER THE BEST RESTAURANT IN SCOTLAND IS AN INDIAN. THE SECOND BEST IS A THAI. TELL ME AGAIN HOW IMMIGRATION IS RUINING OUR COUNTRY?
WE MIGHT HAVE INVENTED TELEVISION AND RADIO, DISCOVERED PENICILLIN. IT DISNAE GIVE US THE RIGHT TO BE DICKS TAE EVERYBODY ELSE!
ALSO, WITHOOT IMMIGRATION WE WOULDNAE HAVE SURAJIT. AND HE POURS THE BEST PINT IN GLASGOW.
SHHH... SOMETHING'S HAPPENING.
I DIDNAE MEAN SURAJIT...I LIKE SURAJIT!
I'M TALKING ABOOT THE OTHER--
SHHH!
--EXTRAORDINARY SCENES AS PITT HAIG HAS BEEN ACCOSTED BY--

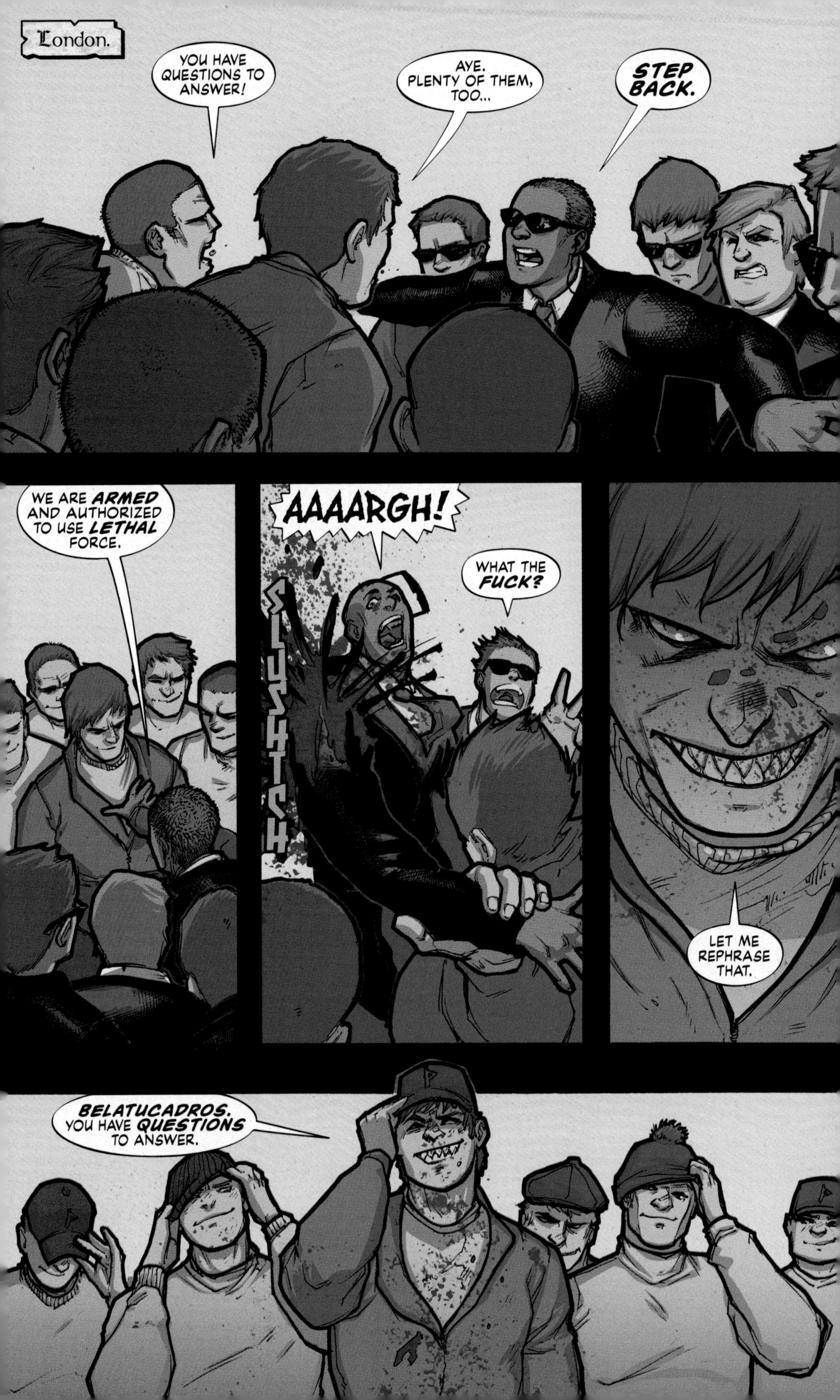
London.
YOU HAVE QUESTIONS TO ANSWER!
AYE. PLENTY OF THEM, TOO...
STEP BACK.
WE ARE ARMED AND AUTHORIZED TO USE LETHAL FORCE.
AAAARGH!
SLUSHTCH
WHAT THE FUCK?
LET ME REPHRASE THAT.
BELATUCADROS. YOU HAVE QUESTIONS TO ANSWER.

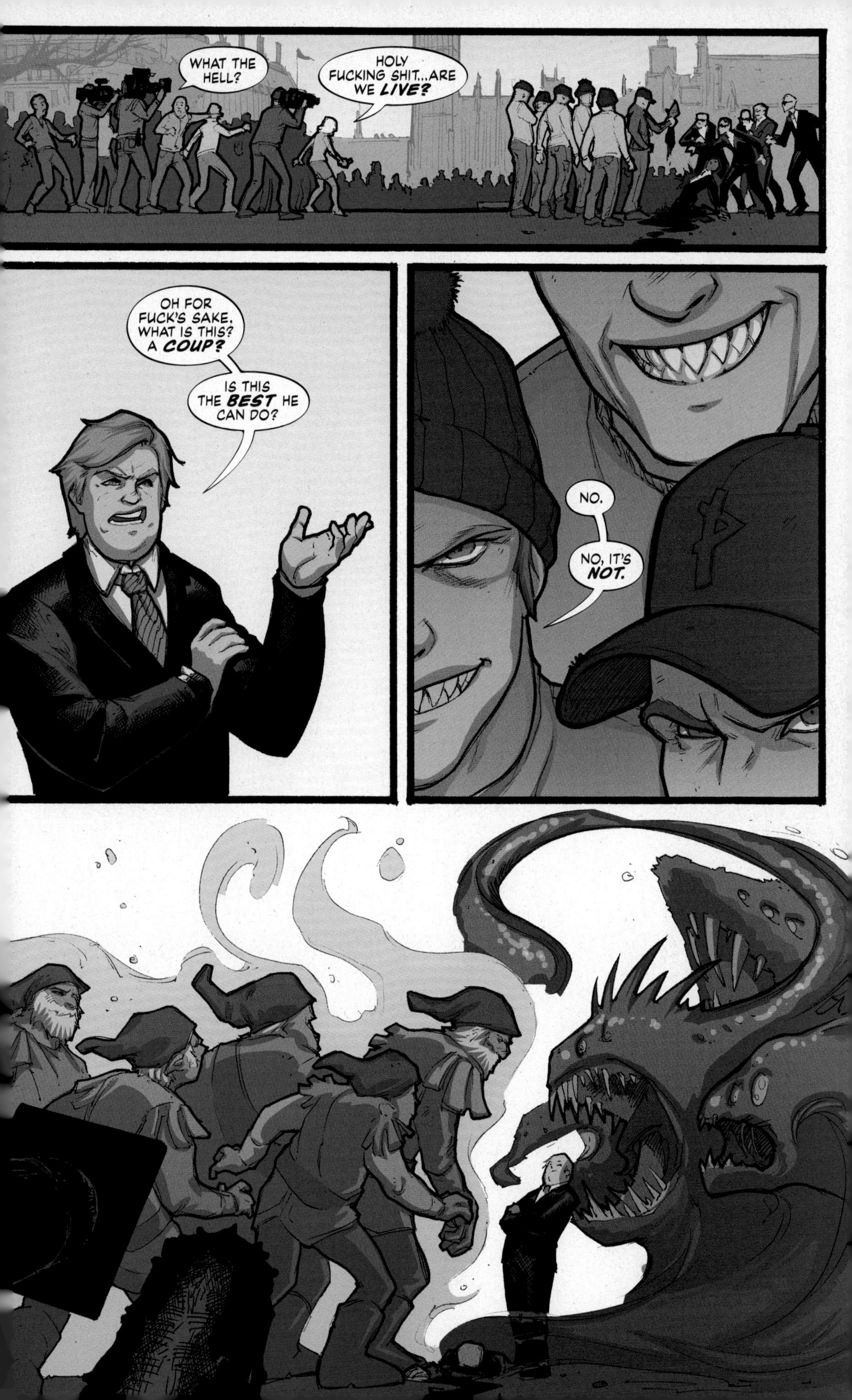
WHAT THE HELL?
HOLY FUCKING SHIT...ARE WE LIVE?
OH FOR FUCK'S SAKE. WHAT IS THIS? A COUP?
IS THIS THE BEST HE CAN DO?
NO.
NO, IT'S NOT.

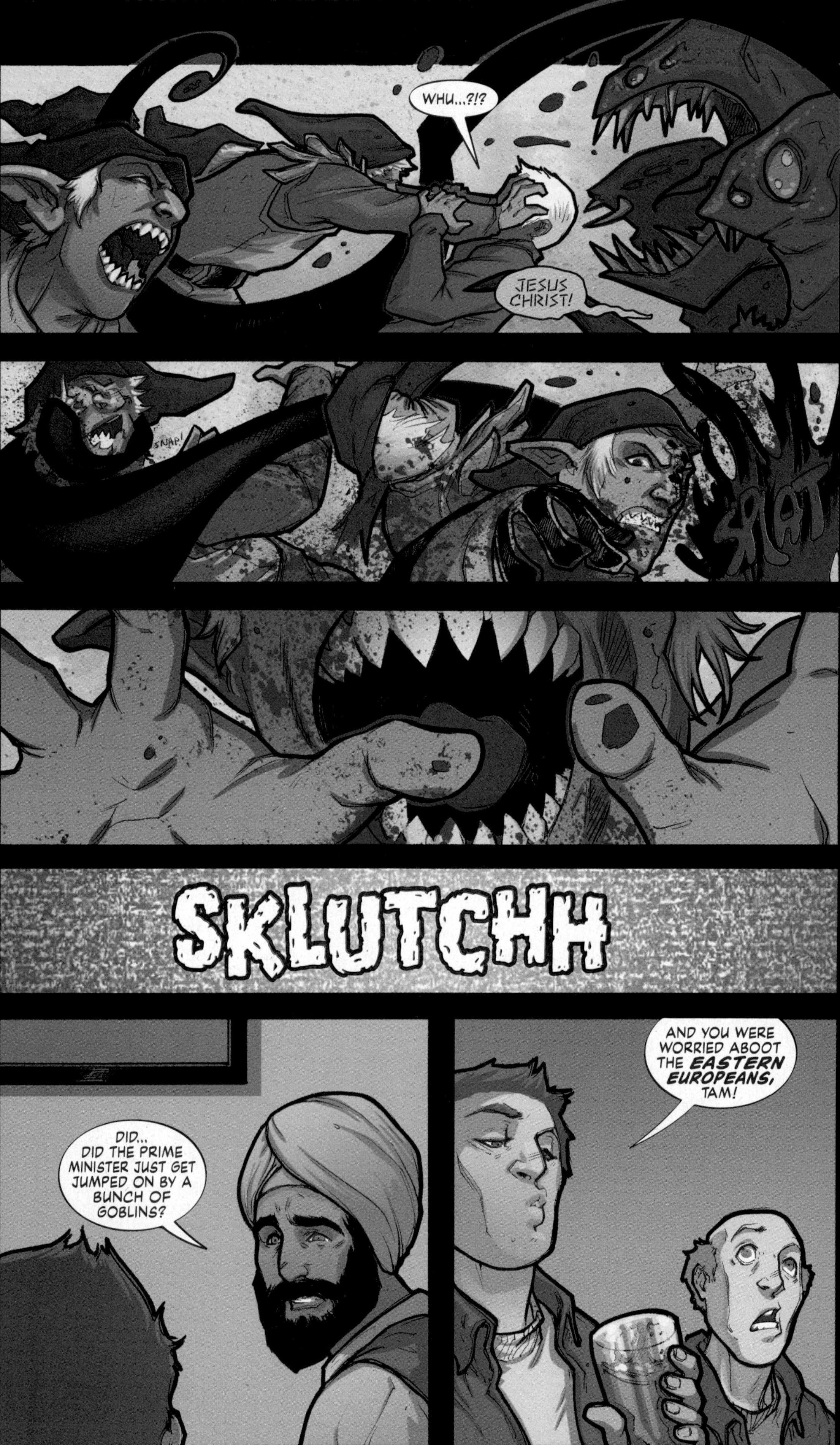
WHU...?!?
JESUS CHRIST!
SNAP!
SPLAT
SKLUTCHH
DID... DID THE PRIME MINISTER JUST GET JUMPED ON BY A BUNCH OF GOBLINS?
AND YOU WERE WORRIED ABOOT THE EASTERN EUROPEANS, TAM!

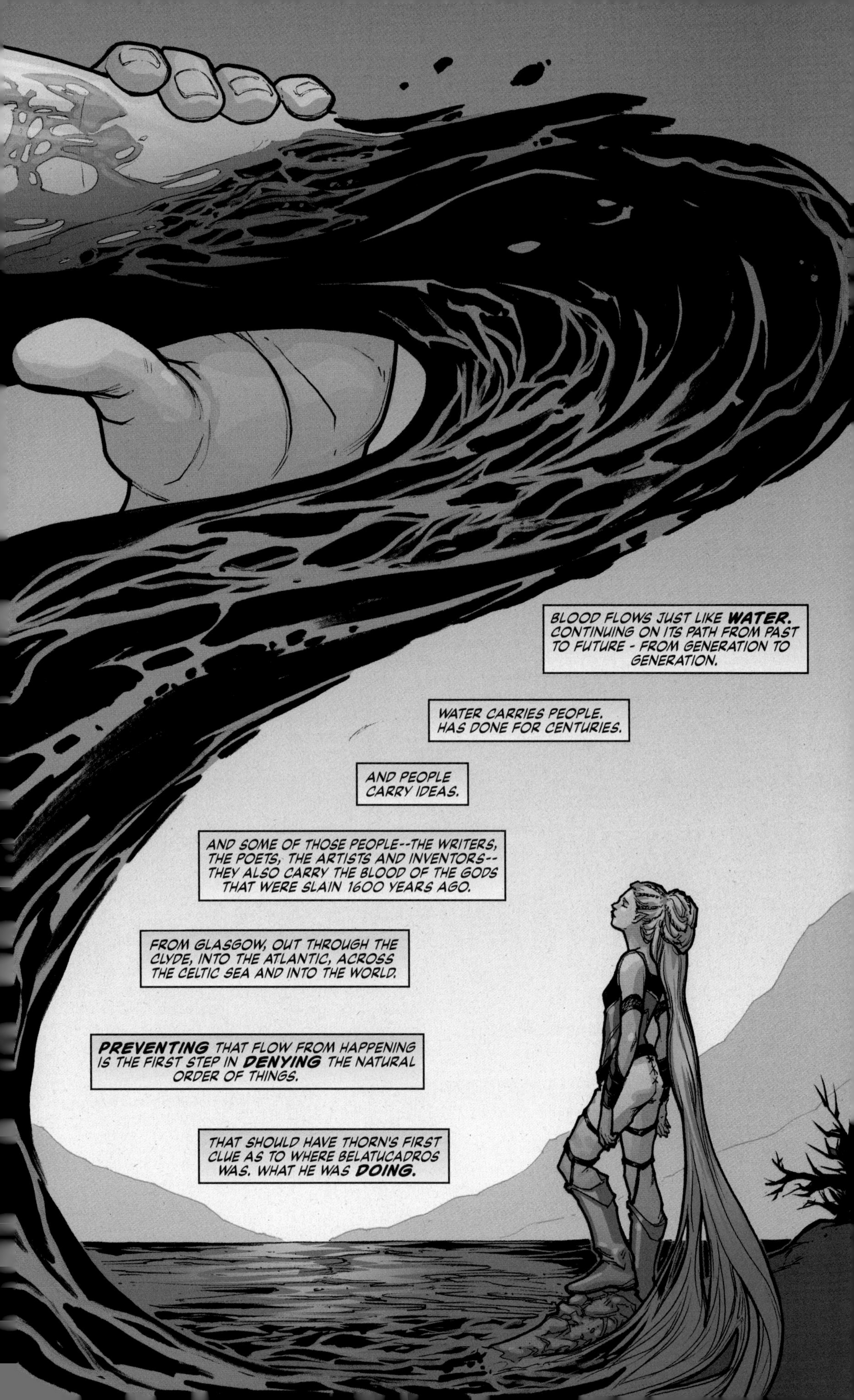
BLOOD FLOWS JUST LIKE WATER. CONTINUING ON ITS PATH FROM PAST TO FUTURE - FROM GENERATION TO GENERATION.
WATER CARRIES PEOPLE. HAS DONE FOR CENTURIES.
AND PEOPLE CARRY IDEAS.
AND SOME OF THOSE PEOPLE--THE WRITERS, THE POETS, THE ARTISTS AND INVENTORS--THEY ALSO CARRY THE BLOOD OF THE GODS THAT WERE SLAIN 1600 YEARS AGO.
FROM GLASGOW, OUT THROUGH THE CLYDE, INTO THE ATLANTIC, ACROSS THE CELTIC SEA AND INTO THE WORLD.
PREVENTING THAT FLOW FROM HAPPENING IS THE FIRST STEP IN DENYING THE NATURAL ORDER OF THINGS.
THAT SHOULD HAVE THORN'S FIRST CLUE AS TO WHERE BELATUCADROS WAS. WHAT HE WAS DOING.

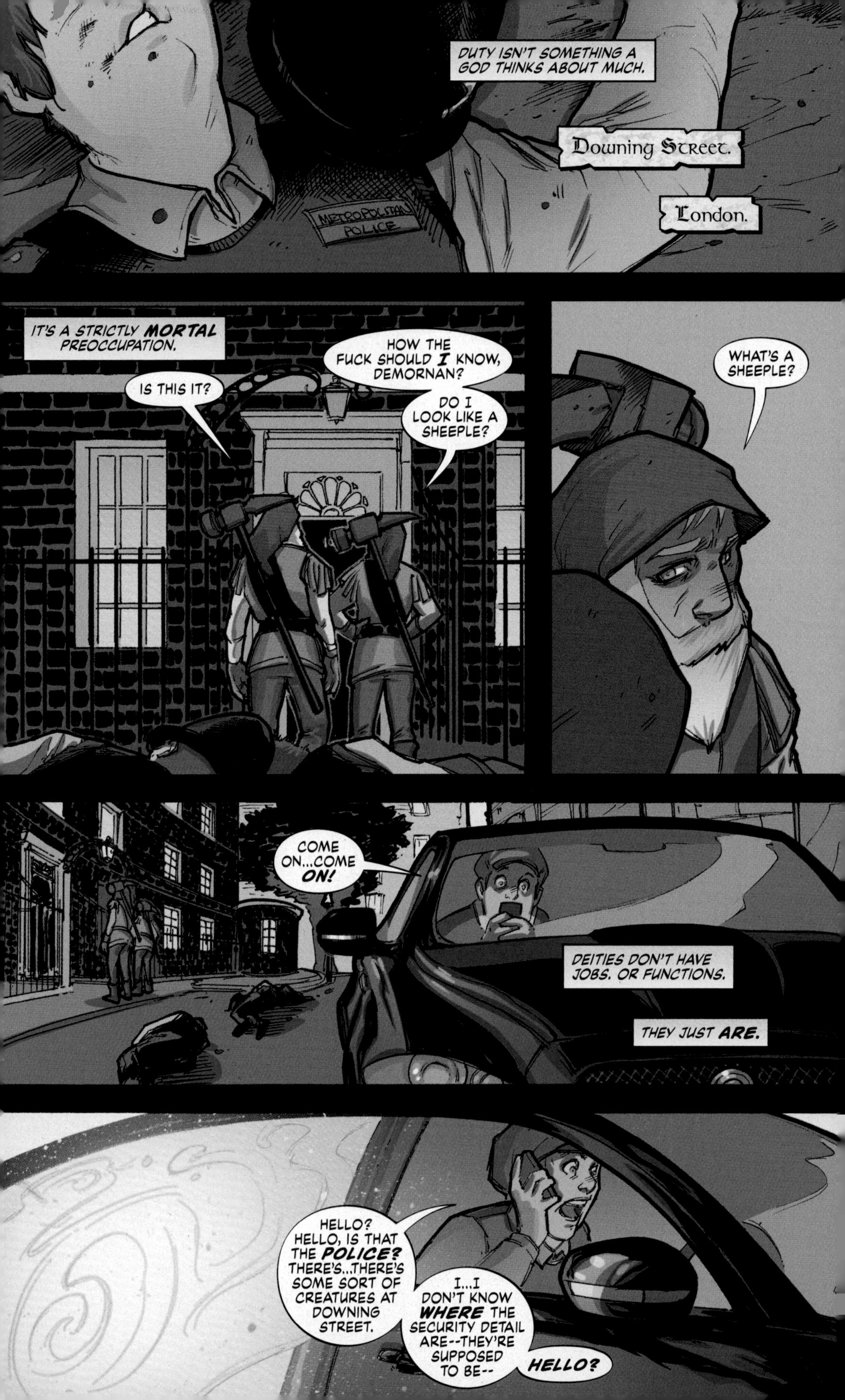
DUTY ISN'T SOMETHING A GOD THINKS ABOUT MUCH.
Downing Street.
London.
METROPOLITAN POLICE
IT'S A STRICTLY MORTAL PREOCCUPATION.
IS THIS IT?
HOW THE FUCK SHOULD I KNOW, DEMORNAN?
DO I LOOK LIKE A SHEEPLE?
WHAT'S A SHEEPLE?
COME ON...COME ON!
DEITIES DON'T HAVE JOBS. OR FUNCTIONS.
THEY JUST ARE.
HELLO? HELLO, IS THAT THE POLICE? THERE'S...THERE'S SOME SORT OF CREATURES AT DOWNING STREET.
I...I DON'T KNOW WHERE THE SECURITY DETAIL ARE--THEY'RE SUPPOSED TO BE--
HELLO?

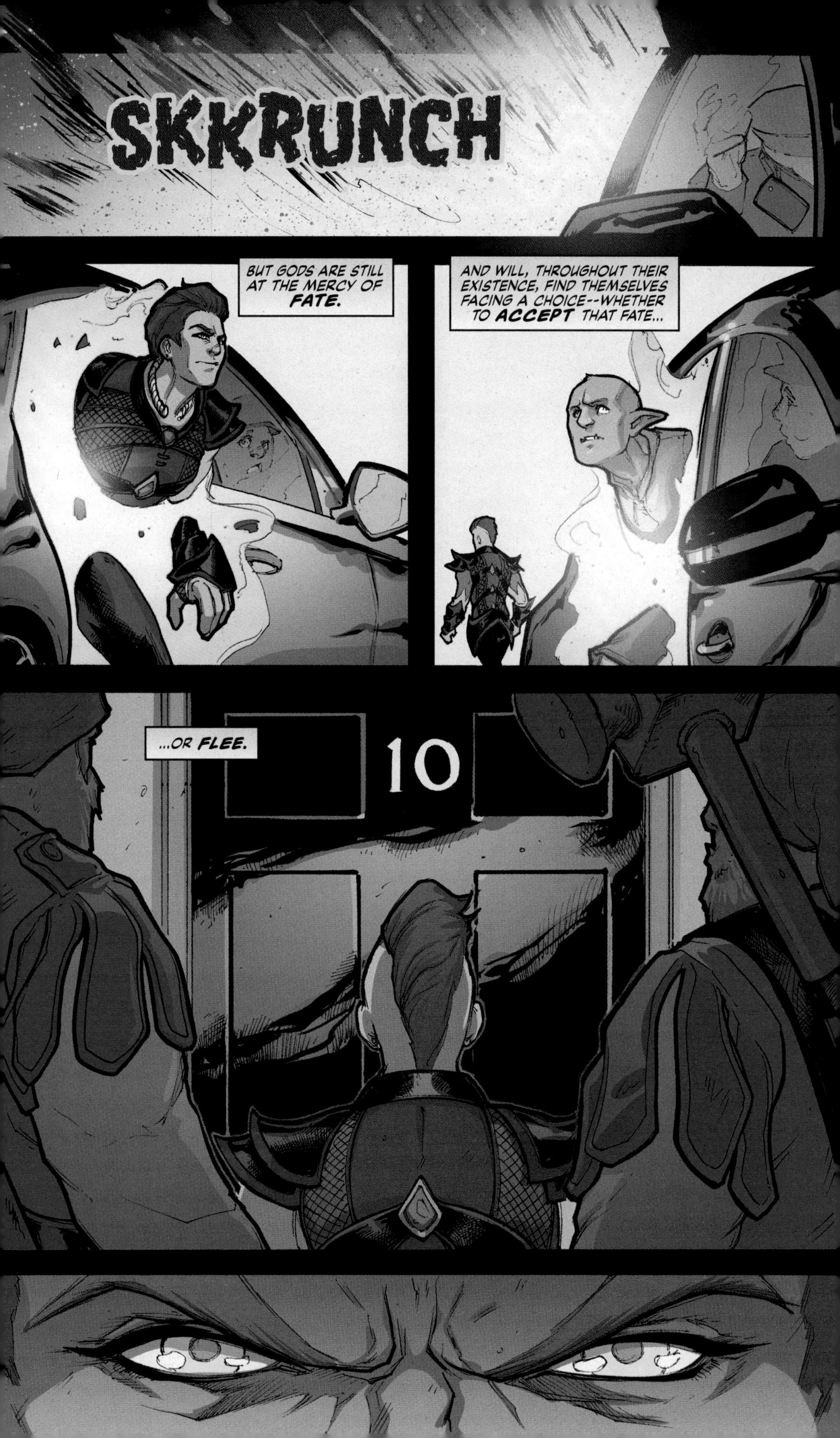
SKKRUNCH
BUT GODS ARE STILL AT THE MERCY OF FATE.
AND WILL, THROUGHOUT THEIR EXISTENCE, FIND THEMSELVES FACING A CHOICE--WHETHER TO ACCEPT THAT FATE...
...OR FLEE.
10

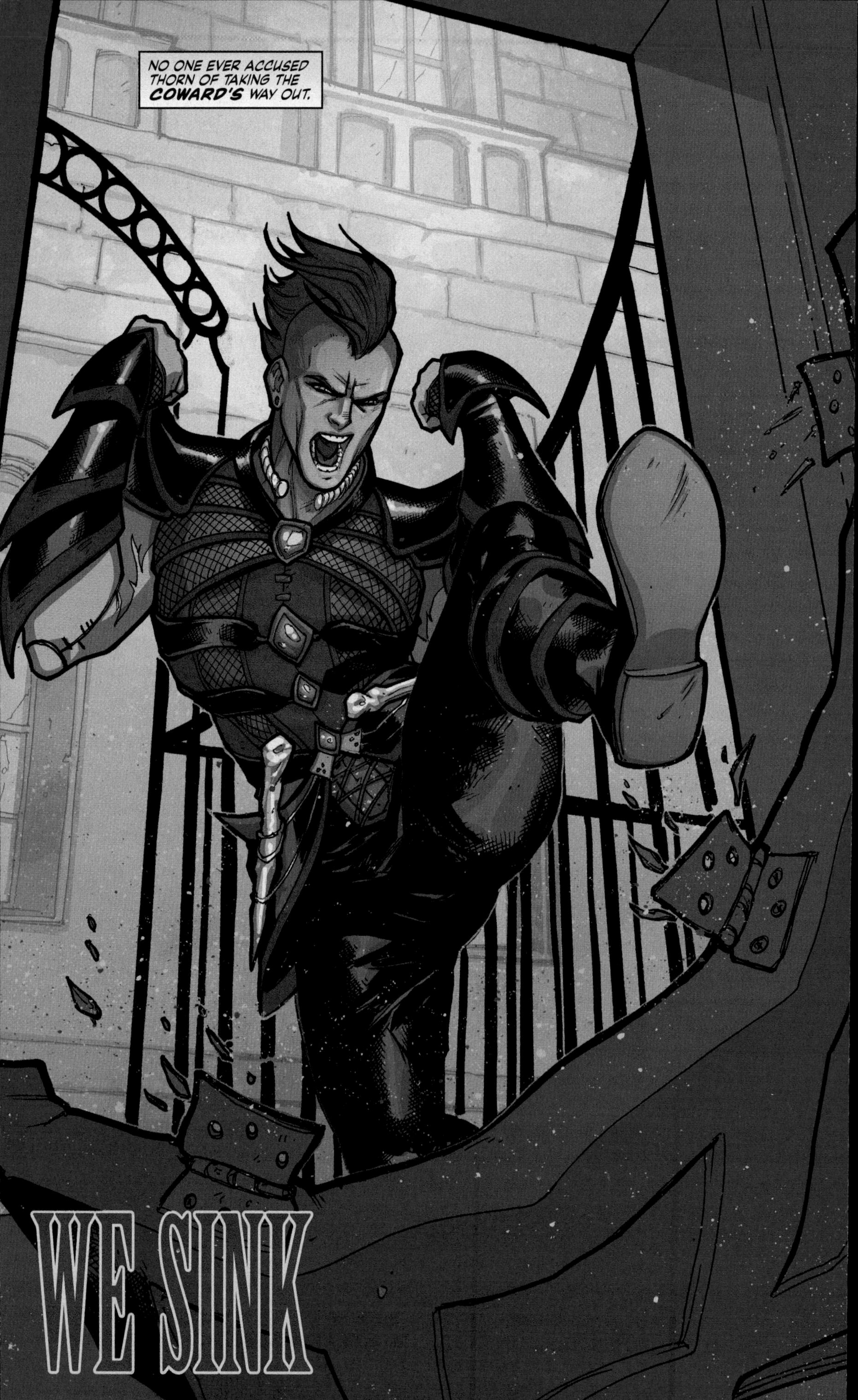
NO ONE EVER ACCUSED THORN OF TAKING THE COWARD'S WAY OUT.
WE SINK

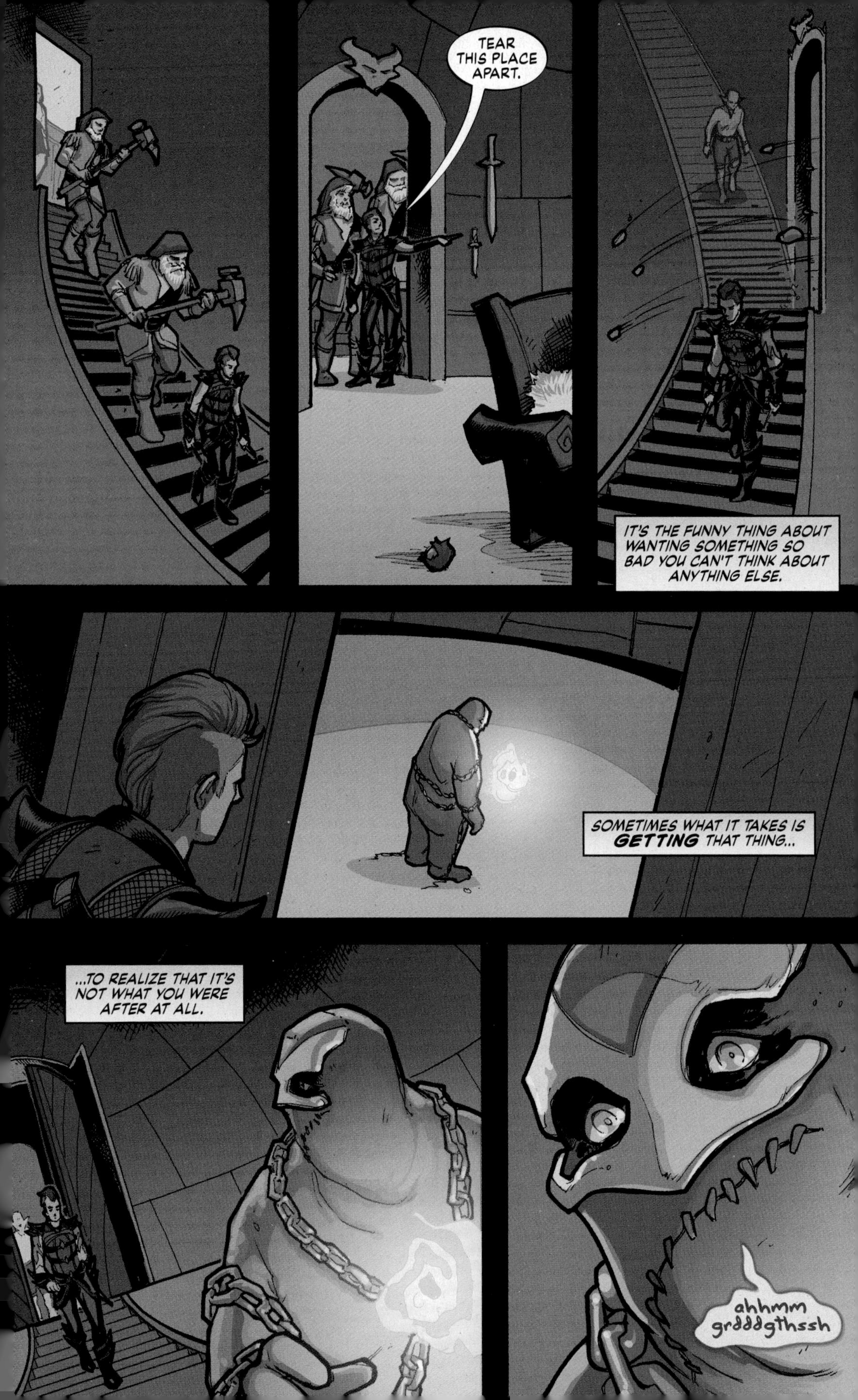
TEAR THIS PLACE APART.
IT'S THE FUNNY THING ABOUT WANTING SOMETHING SO BAD YOU CAN'T THINK ABOUT ANYTHING ELSE.
SOMETIMES WHAT IT TAKES IS GETTING THAT THING...
...TO REALIZE THAT IT'S NOT WHAT YOU WERE AFTER AT ALL.
ahhmm grdddgthssh

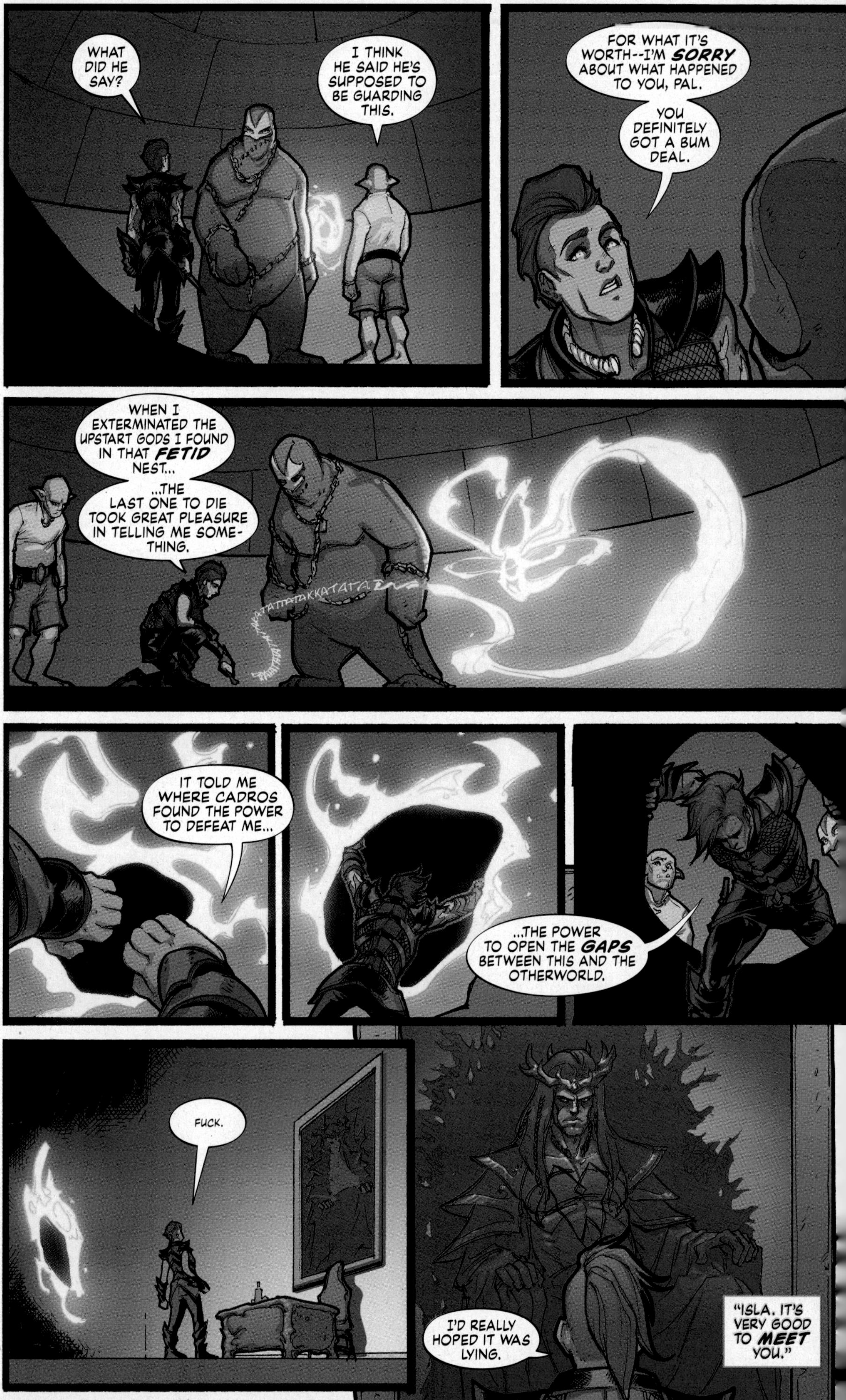
WHAT DID HE SAY?
I THINK HE SAID HE'S SUPPOSED TO BE GUARDING THIS.
FOR WHAT IT'S WORTH--I'M SORRY ABOUT WHAT HAPPENED TO YOU, PAL.
YOU DEFINITELY GOT A BUM DEAL.
WHEN I EXTERMINATED THE UPSTART GODS I FOUND IN THAT FETID NEST...
...THE LAST ONE TO DIE TOOK GREAT PLEASURE IN TELLING ME SOME-THING.
IT TOLD ME WHERE CADROS FOUND THE POWER TO DEFEAT ME...
...THE POWER TO OPEN THE GAPS BETWEEN THIS AND THE OTHERWORLD.
FUCK.
I'D REALLY HOPED IT WAS LYING.
"ISLA. IT'S VERY GOOD TO MEET YOU."

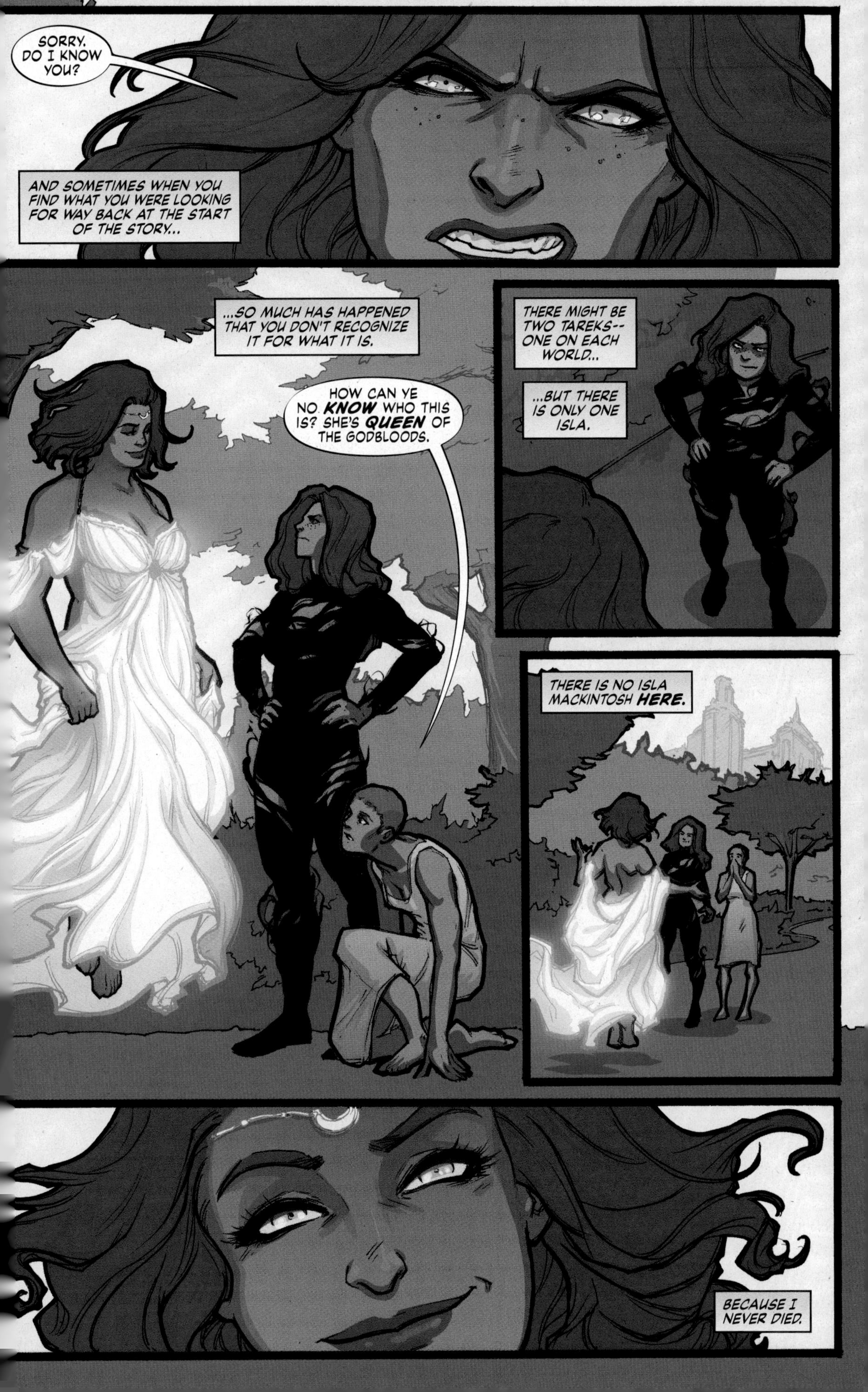
SORRY. DO I KNOW YOU?
AND SOMETIMES WHEN YOU FIND WHAT YOU WERE LOOKING FOR WAY BACK AT THE START OF THE STORY...
...SO MUCH HAS HAPPENED THAT YOU DON'T RECOGNIZE IT FOR WHAT IT IS.
HOW CAN YE NO **KNOW** WHO THIS IS? SHE'S **QUEEN** OF THE GODBLOODS.
THERE MIGHT BE TWO TAREKS-- ONE ON EACH WORLD...
...BUT THERE IS ONLY ONE ISLA.
THERE IS NO ISLA MACKINTOSH **HERE.**
BECAUSE I NEVER DIED.

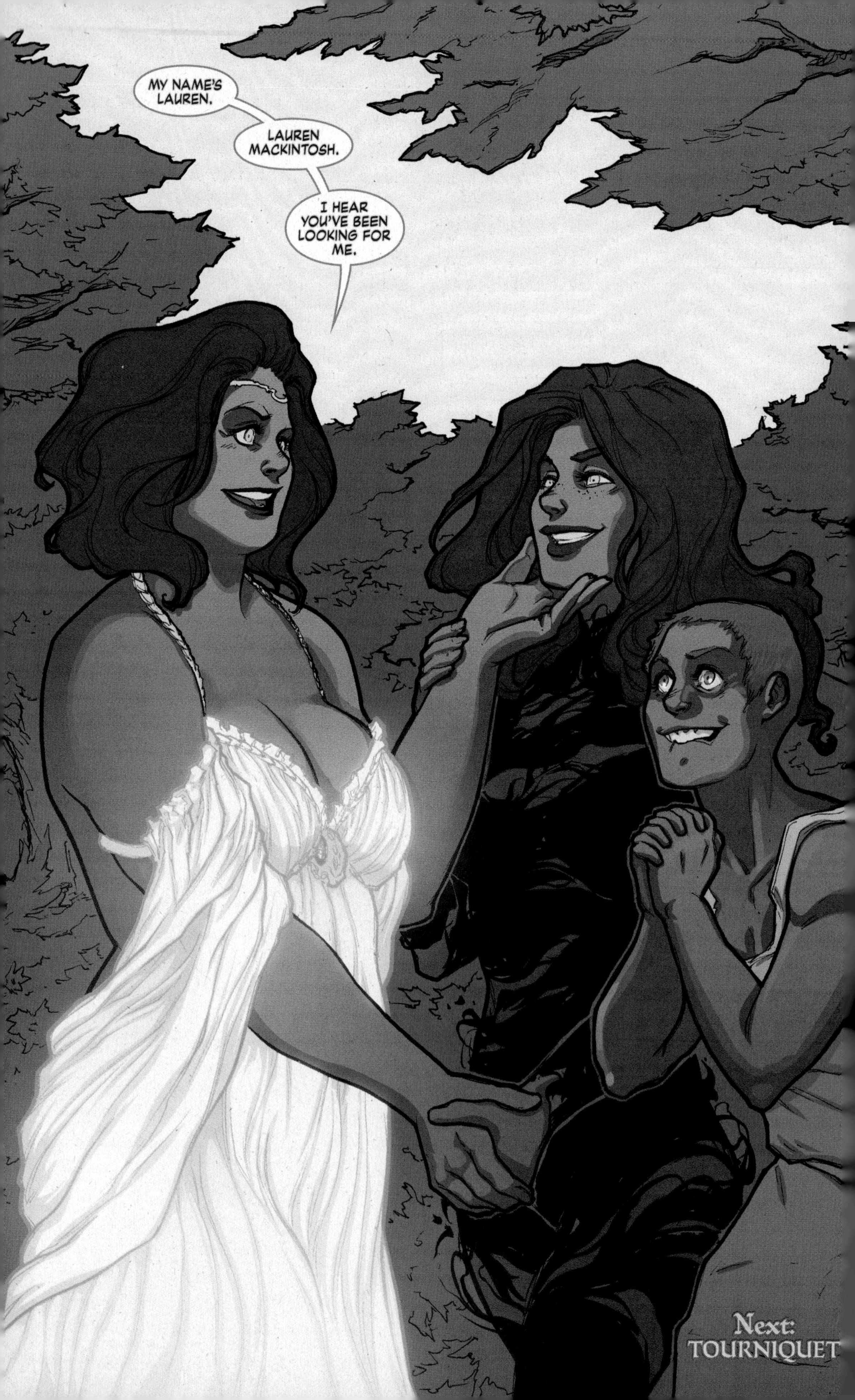
MY NAME'S LAUREN.
LAUREN MACKINTOSH.
I HEAR YOU'VE BEEN LOOKING FOR ME.
Next: TOURNIQUET

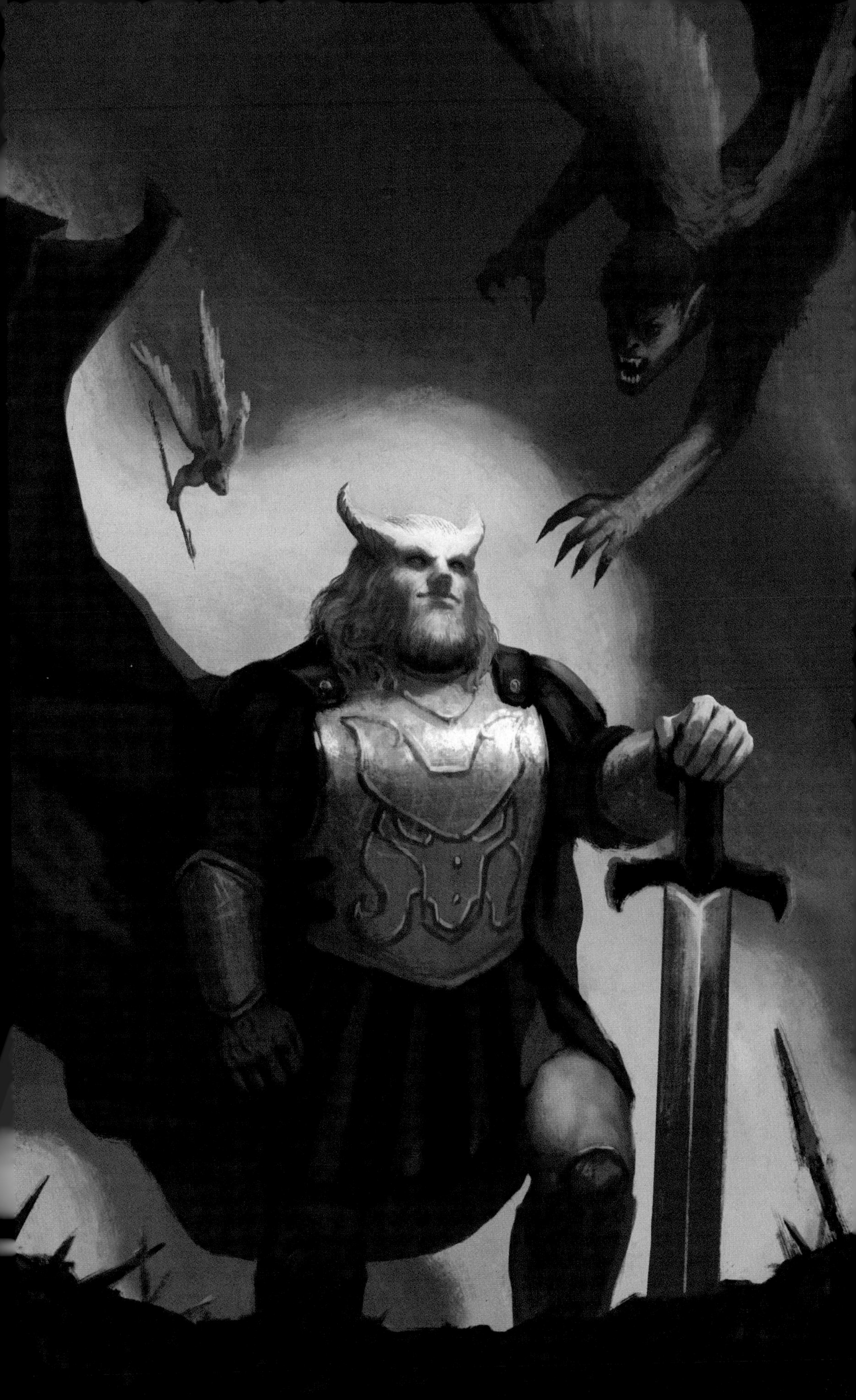

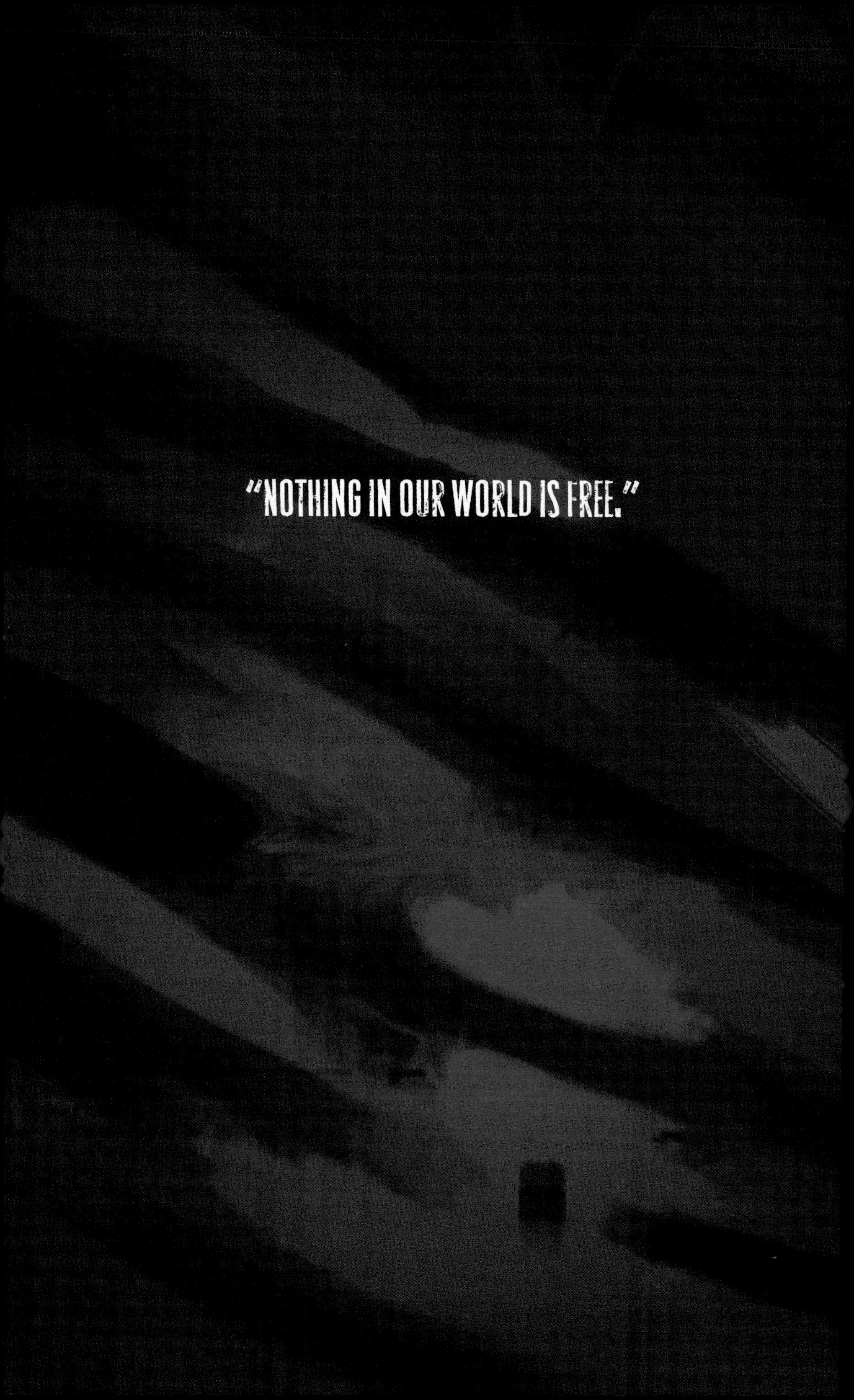
"NOTHING IN OUR WORLD IS FREE."

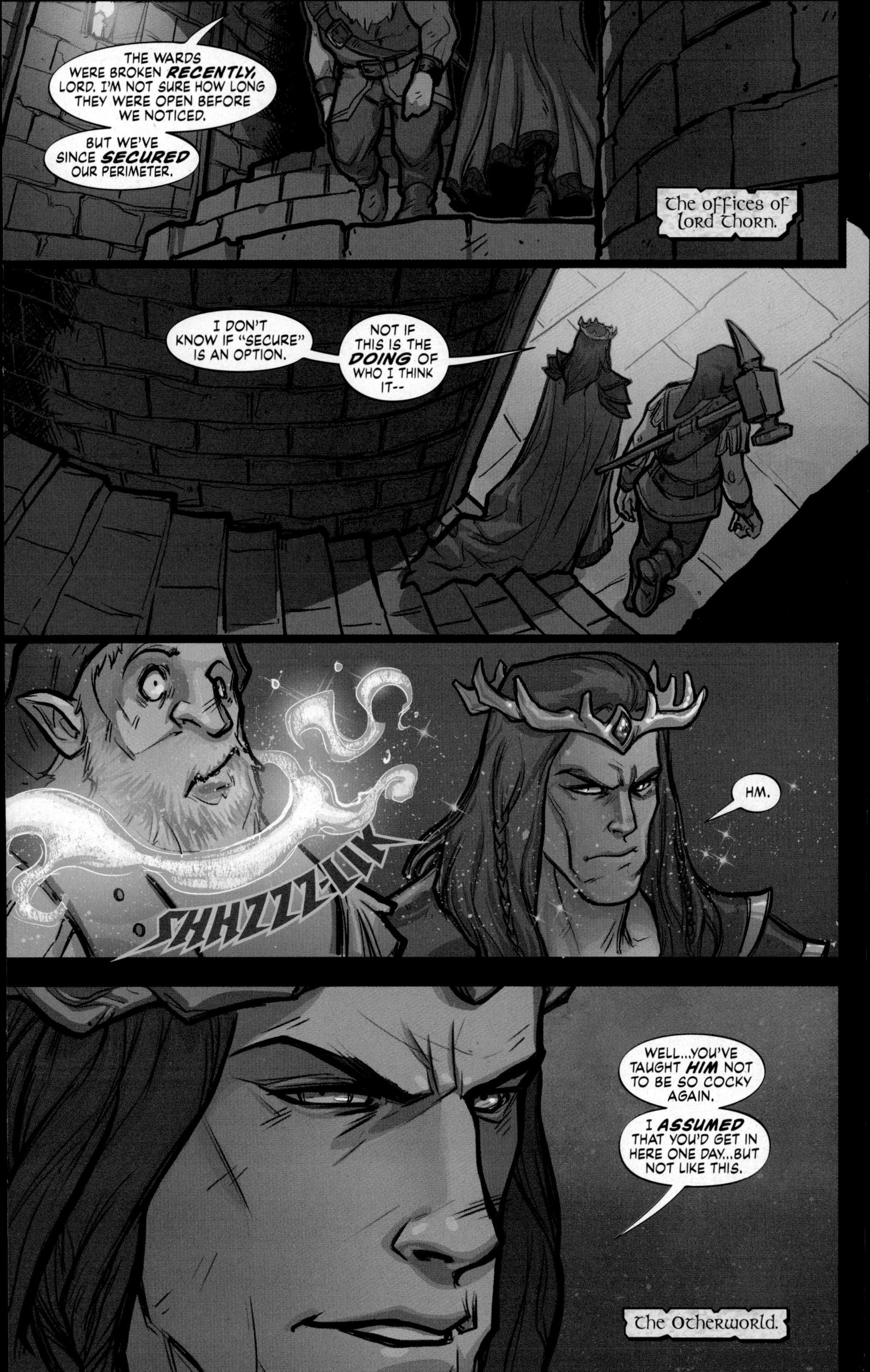
THE WARDS WERE BROKEN RECENTLY, LORD. I'M NOT SURE HOW LONG THEY WERE OPEN BEFORE WE NOTICED.
BUT WE'VE SINCE SECURED OUR PERIMETER.
The offices of Lord Thorn.
I DON'T KNOW IF "SECURE" IS AN OPTION.
NOT IF THIS IS THE DOING OF WHO I THINK IT--
SHHZZZZ-LIK
HM.
WELL...YOU'VE TAUGHT HIM NOT TO BE SO COCKY AGAIN.
I ASSUMED THAT YOU'D GET IN HERE ONE DAY...BUT NOT LIKE THIS.
The Otherworld.

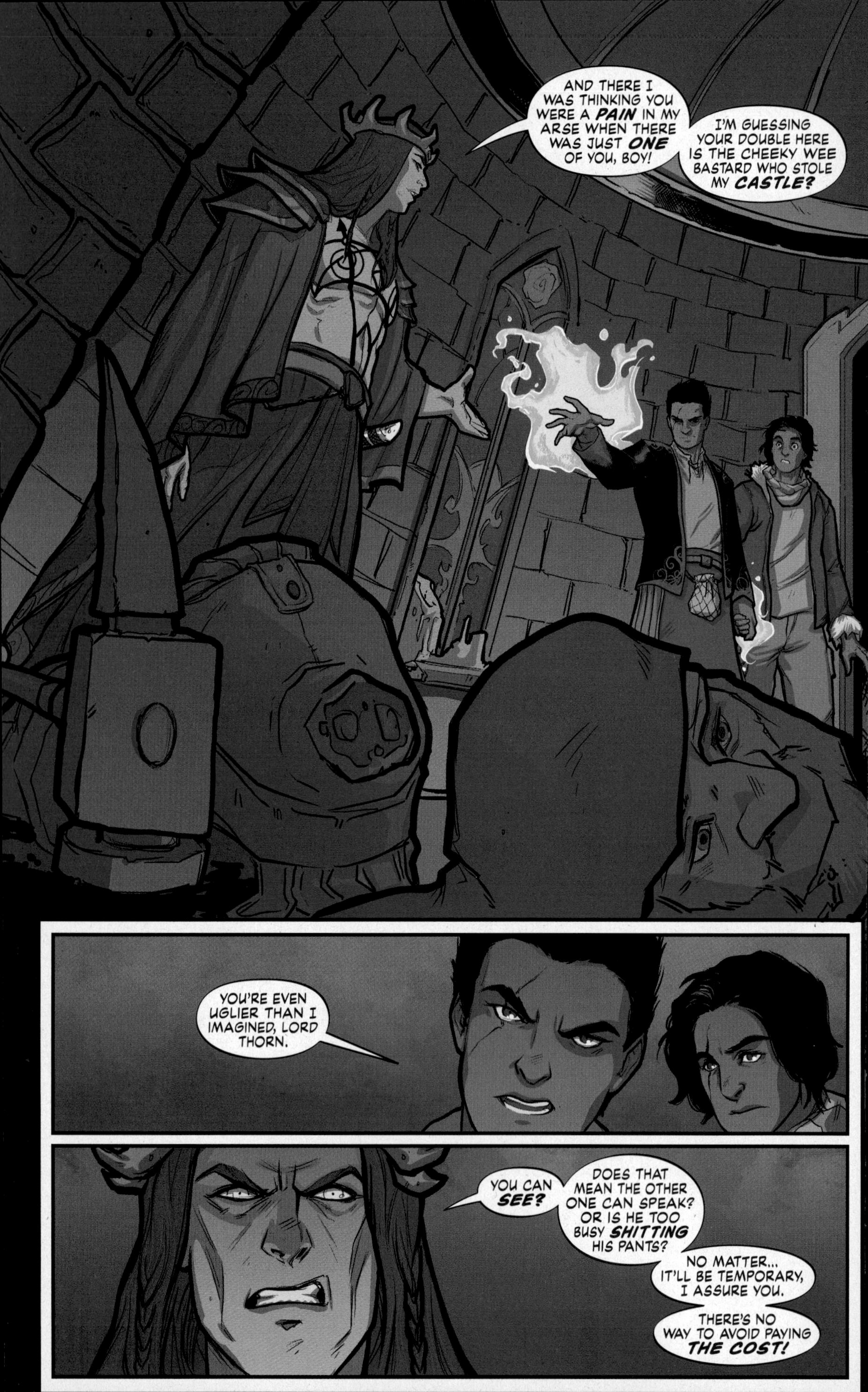
AND THERE I WAS THINKING YOU WERE A PAIN IN MY ARSE WHEN THERE WAS JUST ONE OF YOU, BOY!
I'M GUESSING YOUR DOUBLE HERE IS THE CHEEKY WEE BASTARD WHO STOLE MY CASTLE?
YOU'RE EVEN UGLIER THAN I IMAGINED, LORD THORN.
YOU CAN SEE?
DOES THAT MEAN THE OTHER ONE CAN SPEAK? OR IS HE TOO BUSY SHITTING HIS PANTS?
NO MATTER... IT'LL BE TEMPORARY, I ASSURE YOU.
THERE'S NO WAY TO AVOID PAYING THE COST!

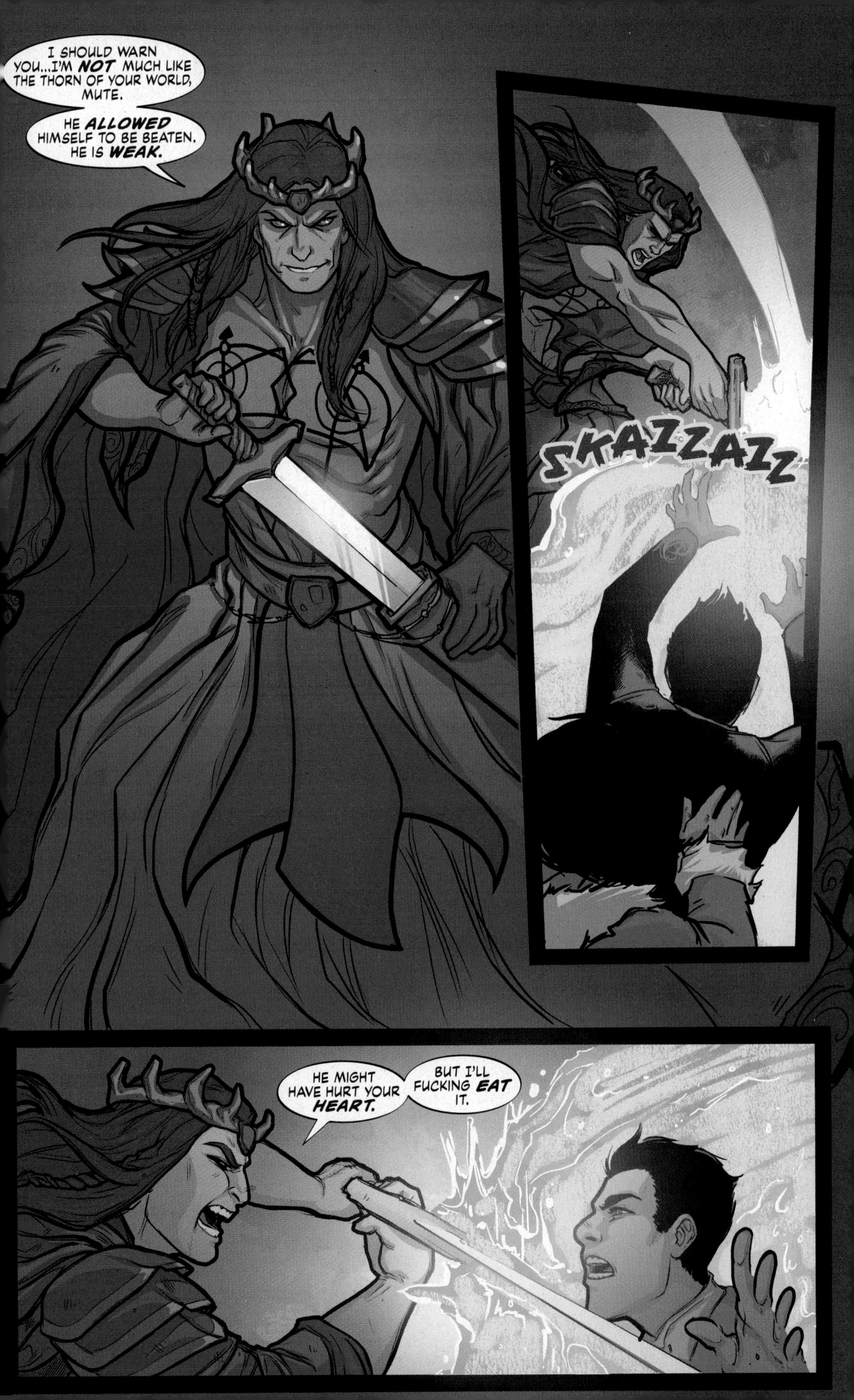
I SHOULD WARN YOU...I'M NOT MUCH LIKE THE THORN OF YOUR WORLD, MUTE.
HE ALLOWED HIMSELF TO BE BEATEN. HE IS WEAK.
SKAZZAZZ
HE MIGHT HAVE HURT YOUR HEART.
BUT I'LL FUCKING EAT IT.

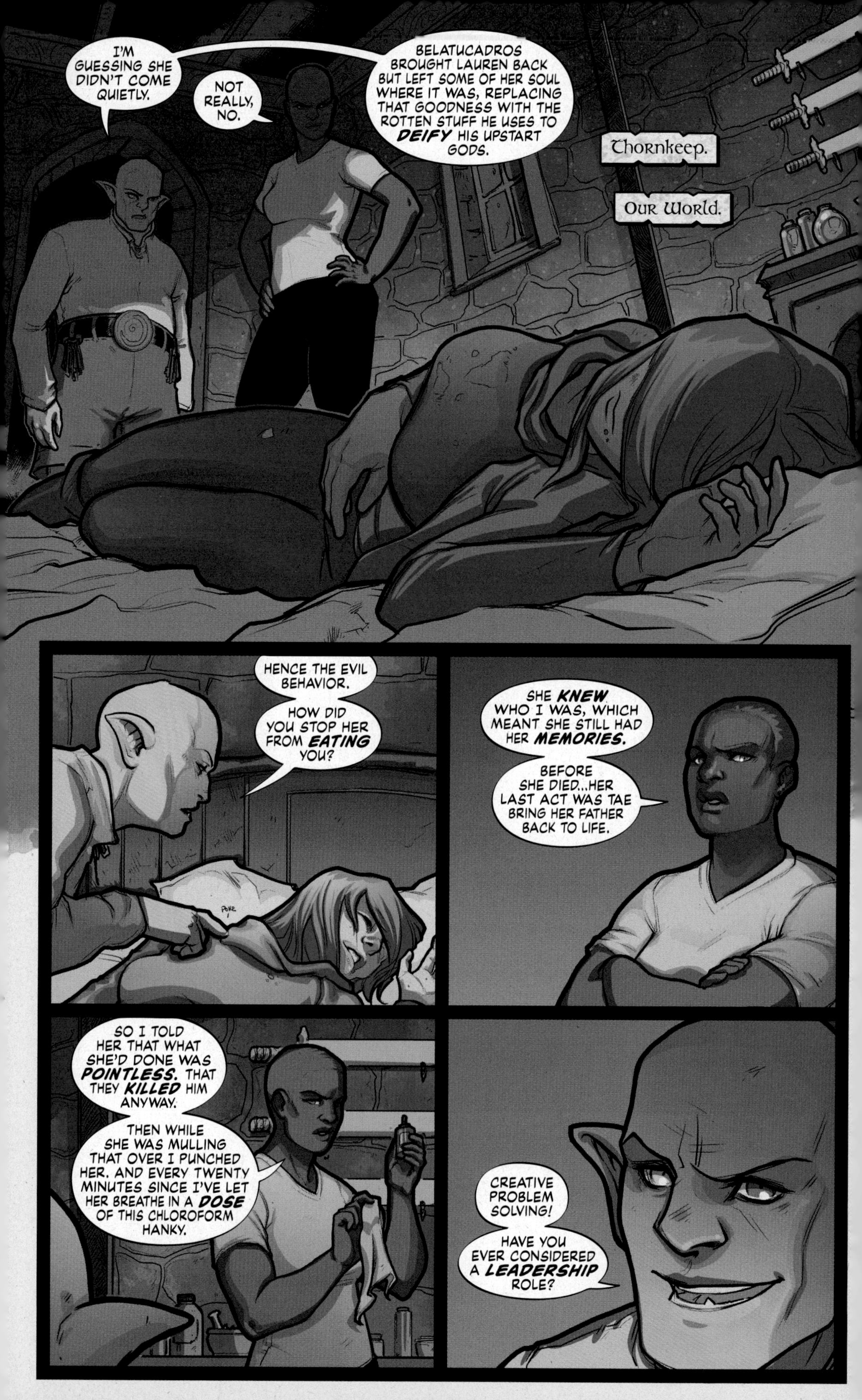
I'M GUESSING SHE DIDN'T COME QUIETLY.
NOT REALLY, NO.
BELATUCADROS BROUGHT LAUREN BACK BUT LEFT SOME OF HER SOUL WHERE IT WAS, REPLACING THAT GOODNESS WITH THE ROTTEN STUFF HE USES TO DEIFY HIS UPSTART GODS.
Thornkeep.
Our World.
HENCE THE EVIL BEHAVIOR.
HOW DID YOU STOP HER FROM EATING YOU?
SHE KNEW WHO I WAS, WHICH MEANT SHE STILL HAD HER MEMORIES.
BEFORE SHE DIED...HER LAST ACT WAS TAE BRING HER FATHER BACK TO LIFE.
SO I TOLD HER THAT WHAT SHE'D DONE WAS POINTLESS. THAT THEY KILLED HIM ANYWAY.
THEN WHILE SHE WAS MULLING THAT OVER I PUNCHED HER. AND EVERY TWENTY MINUTES SINCE I'VE LET HER BREATHE IN A DOSE OF THIS CHLOROFORM HANKY.
CREATIVE PROBLEM SOLVING!
HAVE YOU EVER CONSIDERED A LEADERSHIP ROLE?

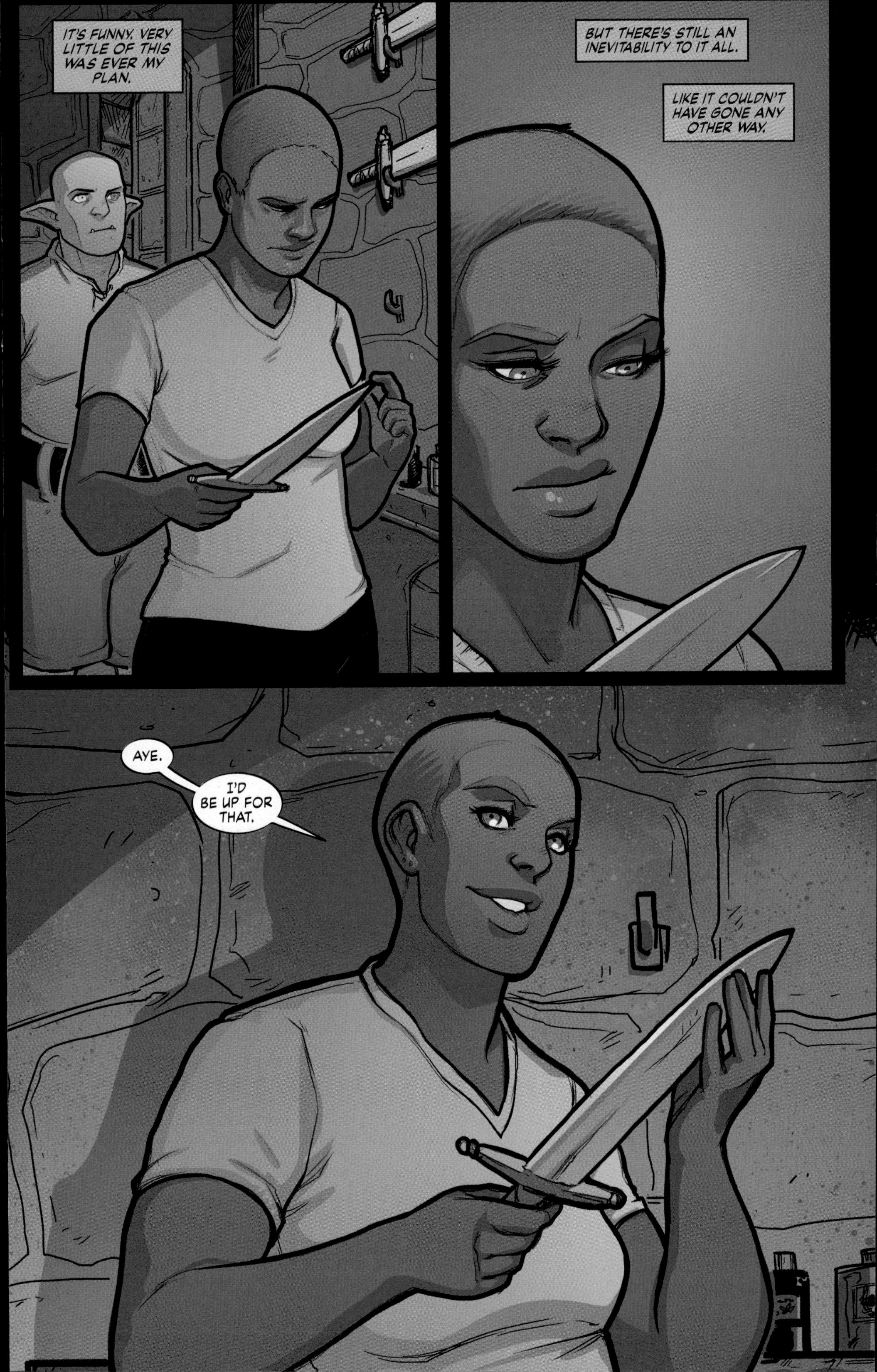
IT'S FUNNY. VERY LITTLE OF THIS WAS EVER MY PLAN.
BUT THERE'S STILL AN INEVITABILITY TO IT ALL.
LIKE IT COULDN'T HAVE GONE ANY OTHER WAY.
AYE.
I'D BE UP FOR THAT.

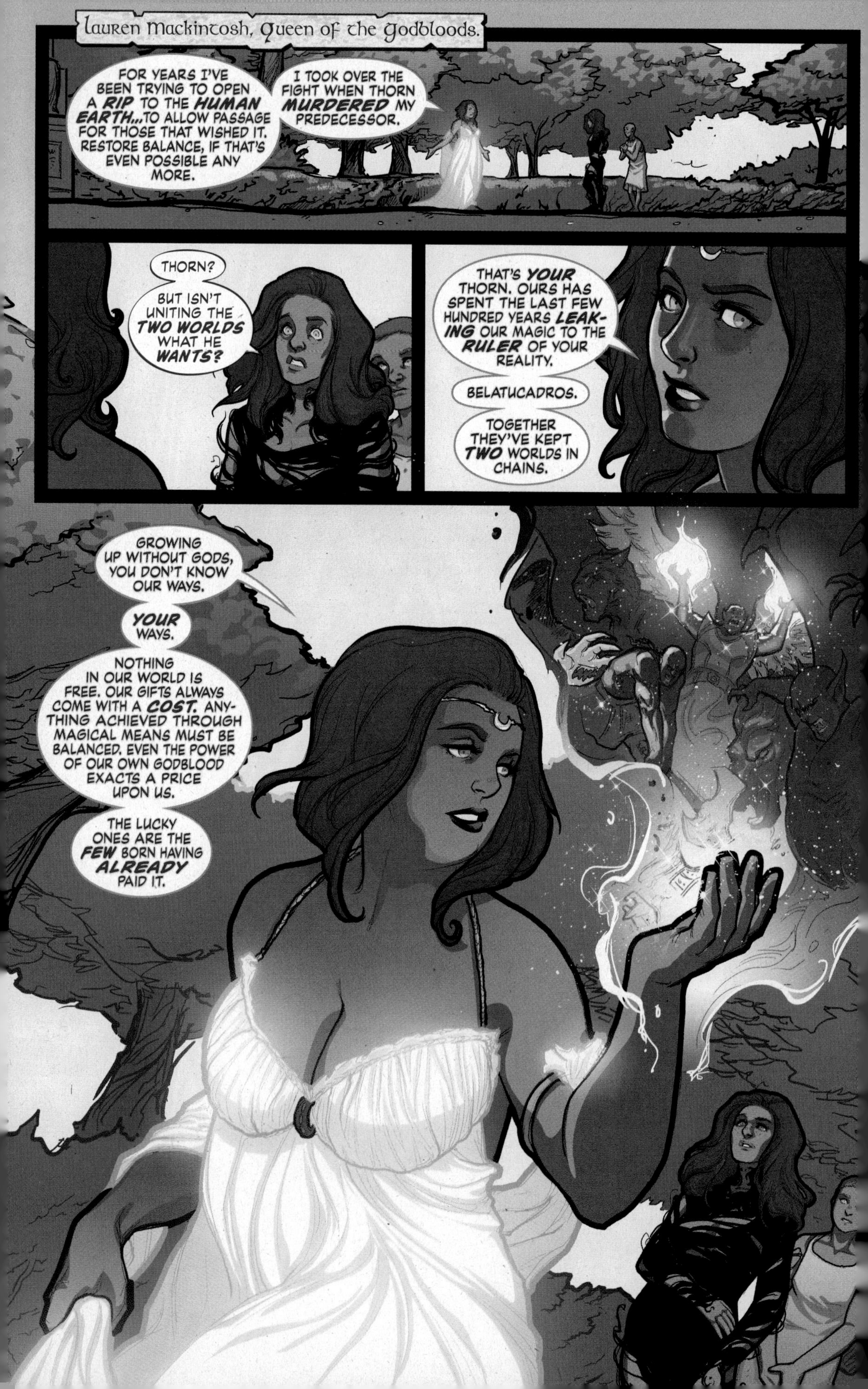
Lauren Mackintosh, Queen of the Godbloods.
FOR YEARS I'VE BEEN TRYING TO OPEN A RIP TO THE HUMAN EARTH...TO ALLOW PASSAGE FOR THOSE THAT WISHED IT. RESTORE BALANCE, IF THAT'S EVEN POSSIBLE ANY MORE.
I TOOK OVER THE FIGHT WHEN THORN MURDERED MY PREDECESSOR.
THORN?
BUT ISN'T UNITING THE TWO WORLDS WHAT HE WANTS?
THAT'S YOUR THORN. OURS HAS SPENT THE LAST FEW HUNDRED YEARS LEAKING OUR MAGIC TO THE RULER OF YOUR REALITY.
BELATUCADROS.
TOGETHER THEY'VE KEPT TWO WORLDS IN CHAINS.
GROWING UP WITHOUT GODS, YOU DON'T KNOW OUR WAYS.
YOUR WAYS.
NOTHING IN OUR WORLD IS FREE. OUR GIFTS ALWAYS COME WITH A COST. ANYTHING ACHIEVED THROUGH MAGICAL MEANS MUST BE BALANCED. EVEN THE POWER OF OUR OWN GODBLOOD EXACTS A PRICE UPON US.
THE LUCKY ONES ARE THE FEW BORN HAVING ALREADY PAID IT.

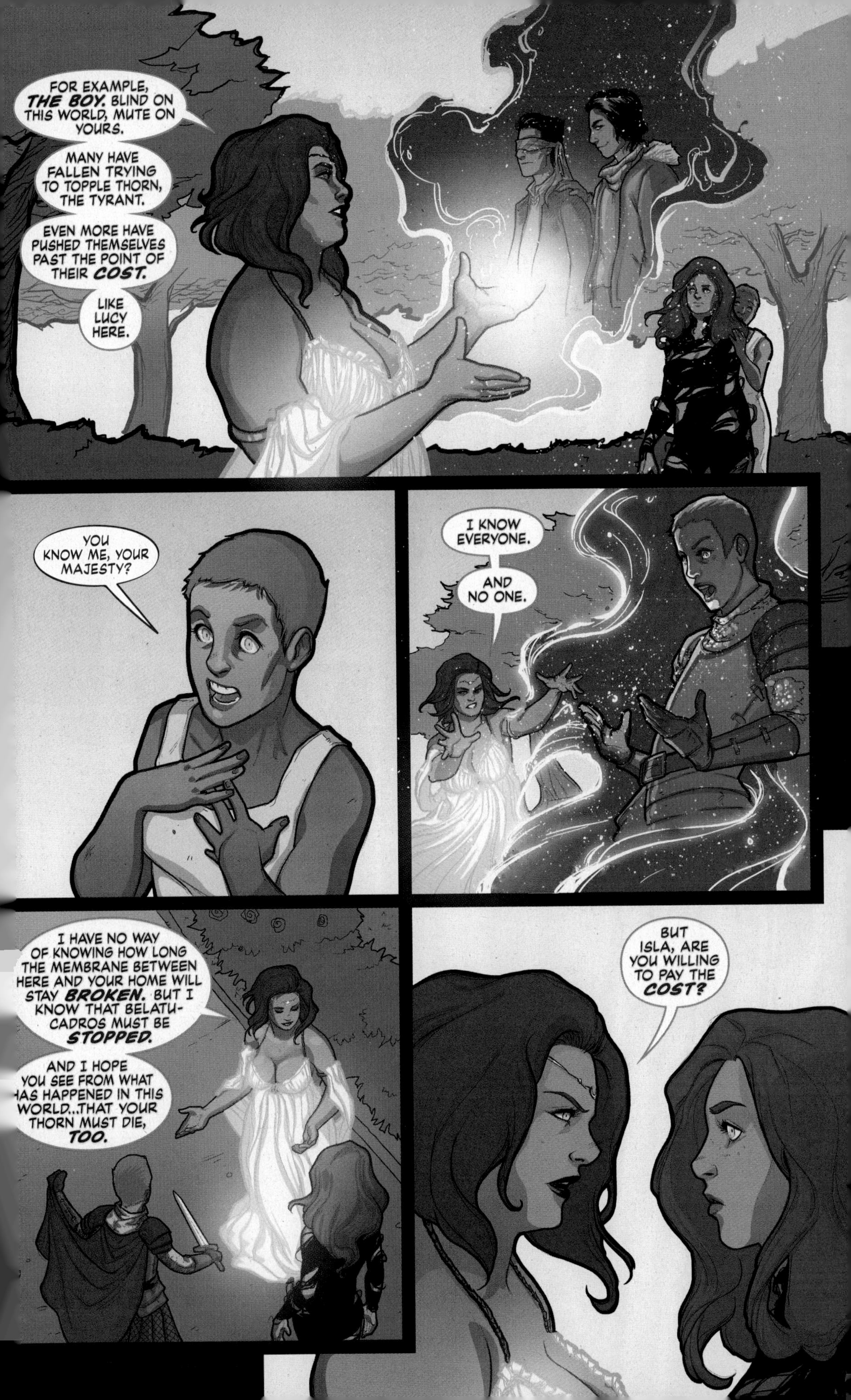
FOR EXAMPLE, THE BOY. BLIND ON THIS WORLD, MUTE ON YOURS.
MANY HAVE FALLEN TRYING TO TOPPLE THORN, THE TYRANT.
EVEN MORE HAVE PUSHED THEMSELVES PAST THE POINT OF THEIR COST.
LIKE LUCY HERE.
YOU KNOW ME, YOUR MAJESTY?
I KNOW EVERYONE.
AND NO ONE.
I HAVE NO WAY OF KNOWING HOW LONG THE MEMBRANE BETWEEN HERE AND YOUR HOME WILL STAY BROKEN. BUT I KNOW THAT BELATU-CADROS MUST BE STOPPED.
AND I HOPE YOU SEE FROM WHAT HAS HAPPENED IN THIS WORLD...THAT YOUR THORN MUST DIE, TOO.
BUT ISLA, ARE YOU WILLING TO PAY THE COST?

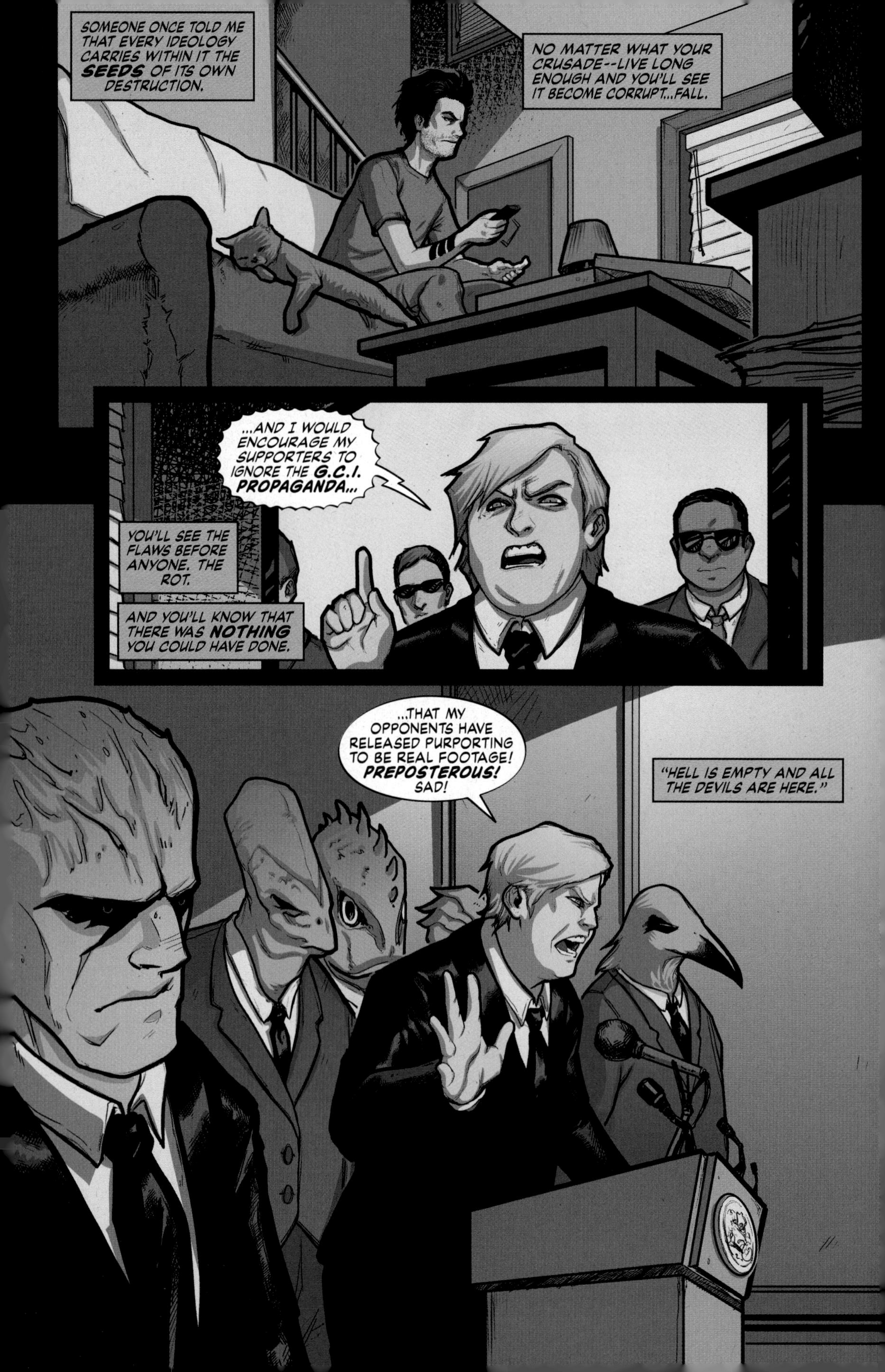
SOMEONE ONCE TOLD ME THAT EVERY IDEOLOGY CARRIES WITHIN IT THE SEEDS OF ITS OWN DESTRUCTION.
NO MATTER WHAT YOUR CRUSADE--LIVE LONG ENOUGH AND YOU'LL SEE IT BECOME CORRUPT...FALL.
...AND I WOULD ENCOURAGE MY SUPPORTERS TO IGNORE THE G.C.I. PROPAGANDA...
YOU'LL SEE THE FLAWS BEFORE ANYONE. THE ROT.
AND YOU'LL KNOW THAT THERE WAS NOTHING YOU COULD HAVE DONE.
...THAT MY OPPONENTS HAVE RELEASED PURPORTING TO BE REAL FOOTAGE! PREPOSTEROUS! SAD!
"HELL IS EMPTY AND ALL THE DEVILS ARE HERE."

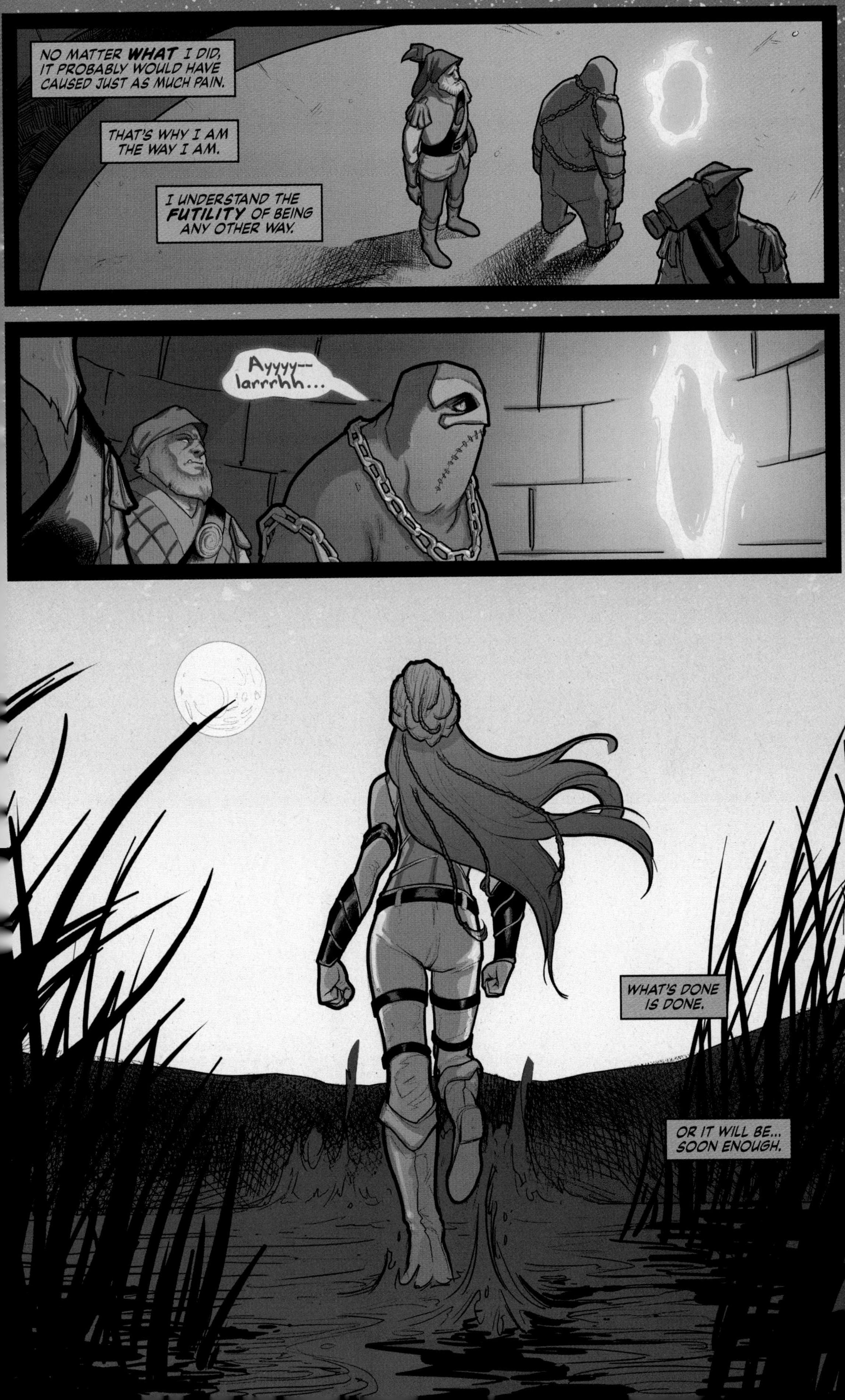
NO MATTER WHAT I DID, IT PROBABLY WOULD HAVE CAUSED JUST AS MUCH PAIN.
THAT'S WHY I AM THE WAY I AM.
I UNDERSTAND THE FUTILITY OF BEING ANY OTHER WAY.
Ayyyy-- larrrhh...
WHAT'S DONE IS DONE.
OR IT WILL BE... SOON ENOUGH.

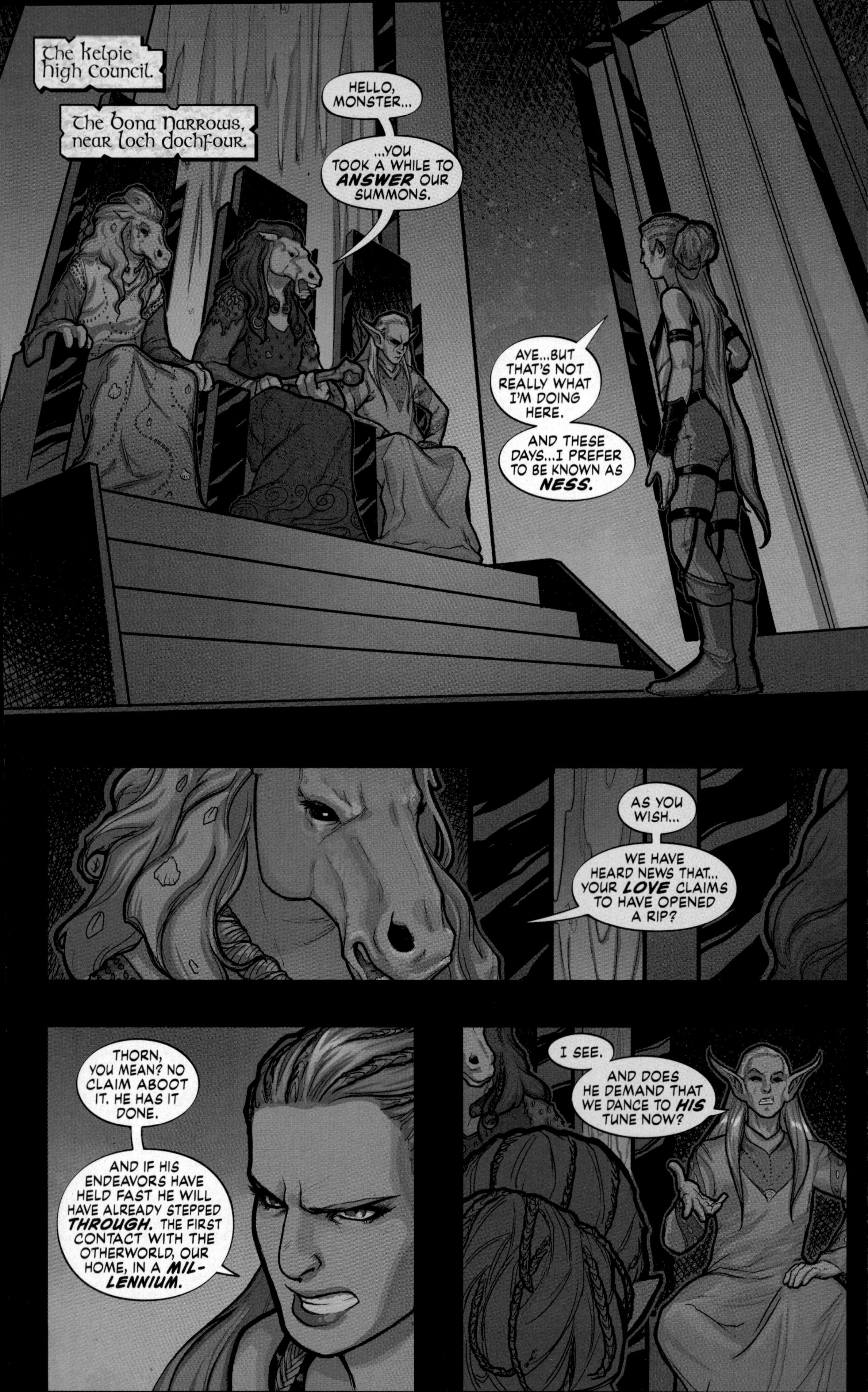
The kelpie high council.
The bona narrows, near loch dochfour.
HELLO, MONSTER...
...YOU TOOK A WHILE TO ANSWER OUR SUMMONS.
AYE...BUT THAT'S NOT REALLY WHAT I'M DOING HERE.
AND THESE DAYS...I PREFER TO BE KNOWN AS NESS.
AS YOU WISH...
WE HAVE HEARD NEWS THAT... YOUR LOVE CLAIMS TO HAVE OPENED A RIP?
THORN, YOU MEAN? NO CLAIM ABOUT IT. HE HAS IT DONE.
AND IF HIS ENDEAVORS HAVE HELD FAST HE WILL HAVE ALREADY STEPPED THROUGH. THE FIRST CONTACT WITH THE OTHERWORLD, OUR HOME, IN A MIL-LENNIUM.
I SEE.
AND DOES HE DEMAND THAT WE DANCE TO HIS TUNE NOW?

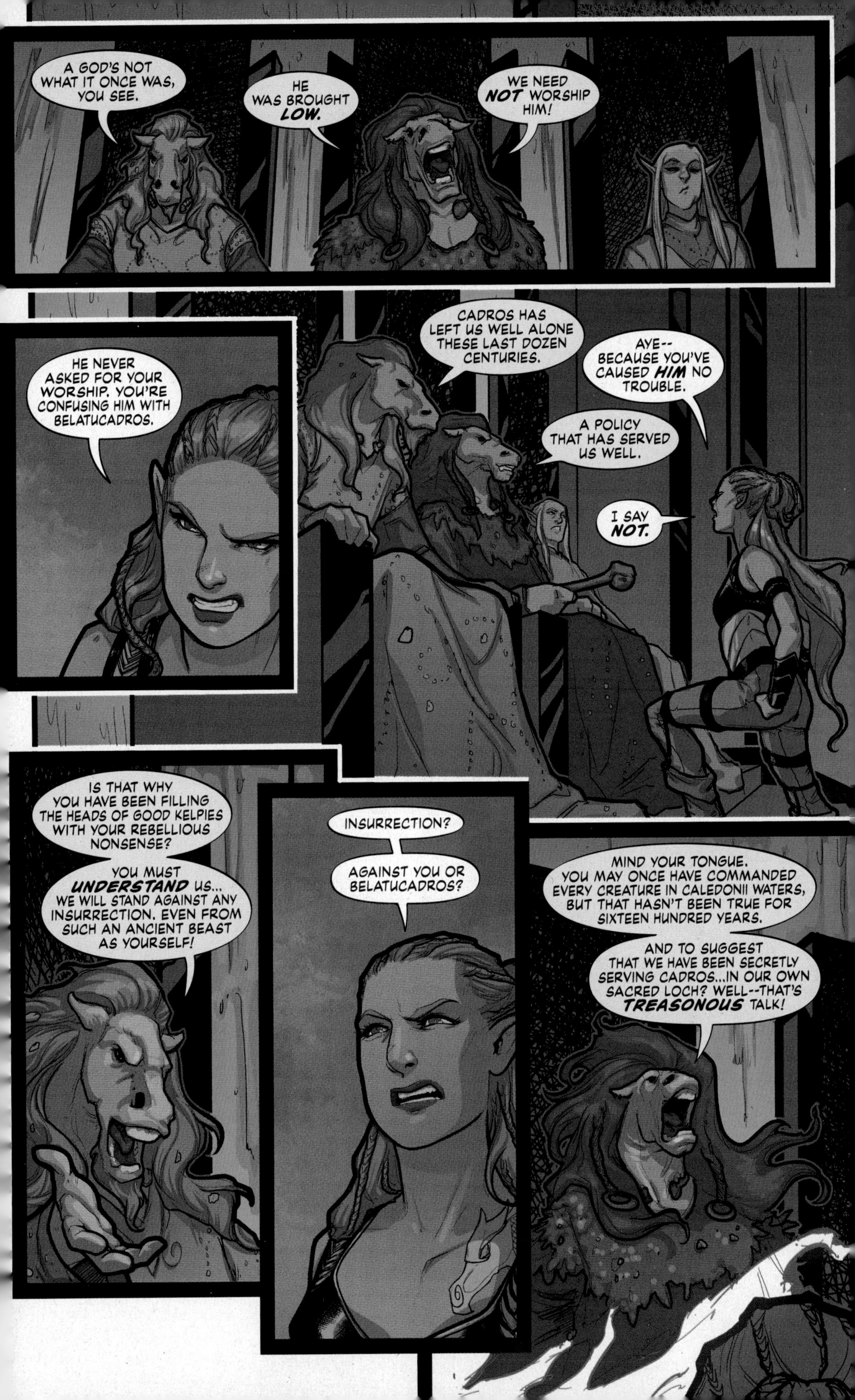
A GOD'S NOT WHAT IT ONCE WAS, YOU SEE.
HE WAS BROUGHT LOW.
WE NEED NOT WORSHIP HIM!
HE NEVER ASKED FOR YOUR WORSHIP. YOU'RE CONFUSING HIM WITH BELATUCADROS.
CADROS HAS LEFT US WELL ALONE THESE LAST DOZEN CENTURIES.
AYE-- BECAUSE YOU'VE CAUSED HIM NO TROUBLE.
A POLICY THAT HAS SERVED US WELL.
I SAY NOT.
IS THAT WHY YOU HAVE BEEN FILLING THE HEADS OF GOOD KELPIES WITH YOUR REBELLIOUS NONSENSE?
YOU MUST UNDERSTAND US... WE WILL STAND AGAINST ANY INSURRECTION. EVEN FROM SUCH AN ANCIENT BEAST AS YOURSELF!
INSURRECTION?
AGAINST YOU OR BELATUCADROS?
MIND YOUR TONGUE. YOU MAY ONCE HAVE COMMANDED EVERY CREATURE IN CALEDONII WATERS, BUT THAT HASN'T BEEN TRUE FOR SIXTEEN HUNDRED YEARS.
AND TO SUGGEST THAT WE HAVE BEEN SECRETLY SERVING CADROS...IN OUR OWN SACRED LOCH? WELL--THAT'S TREASONOUS TALK!

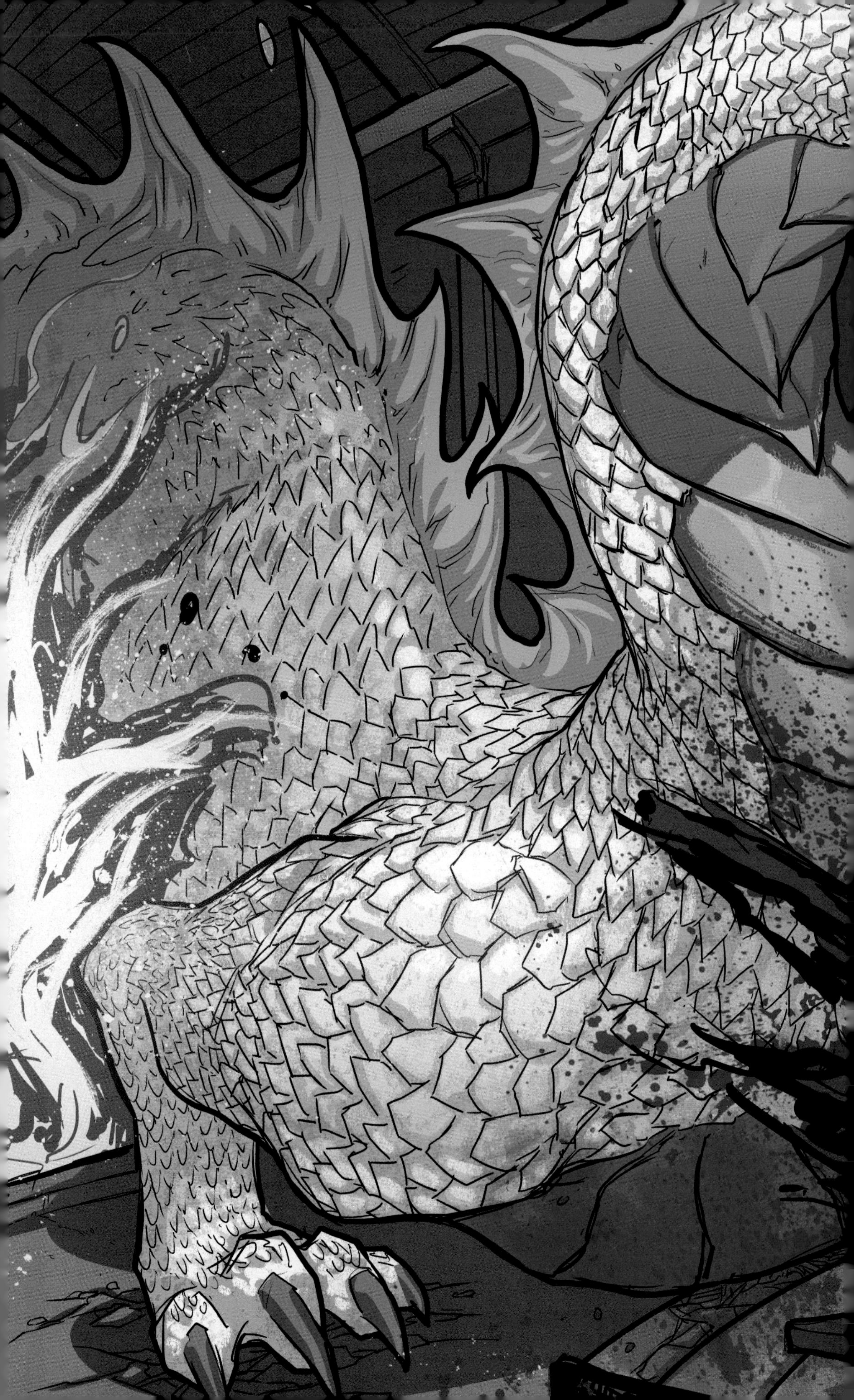

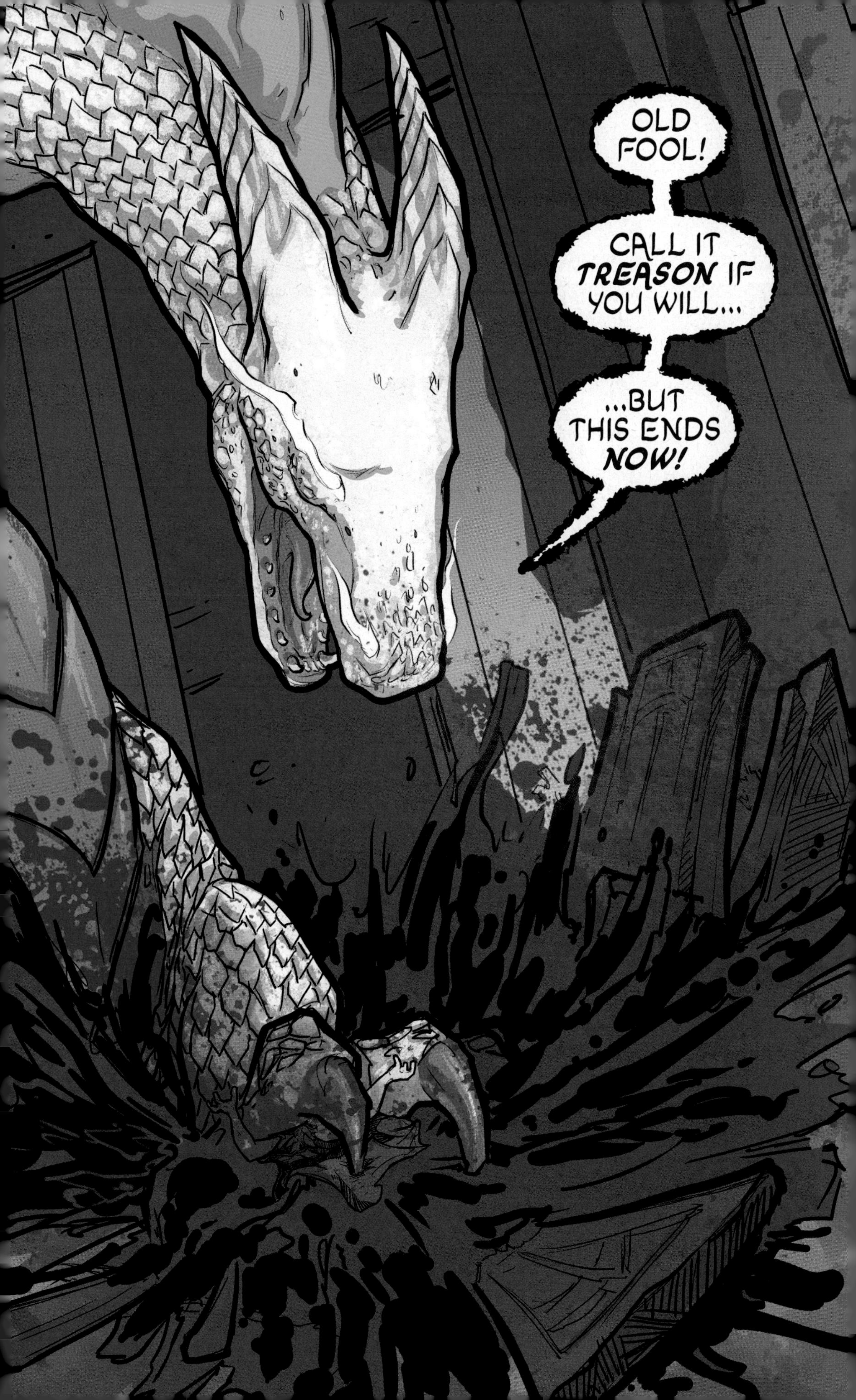
OLD FOOL!
CALL IT *TREASON* IF YOU WILL...
...BUT THIS ENDS *NOW!*

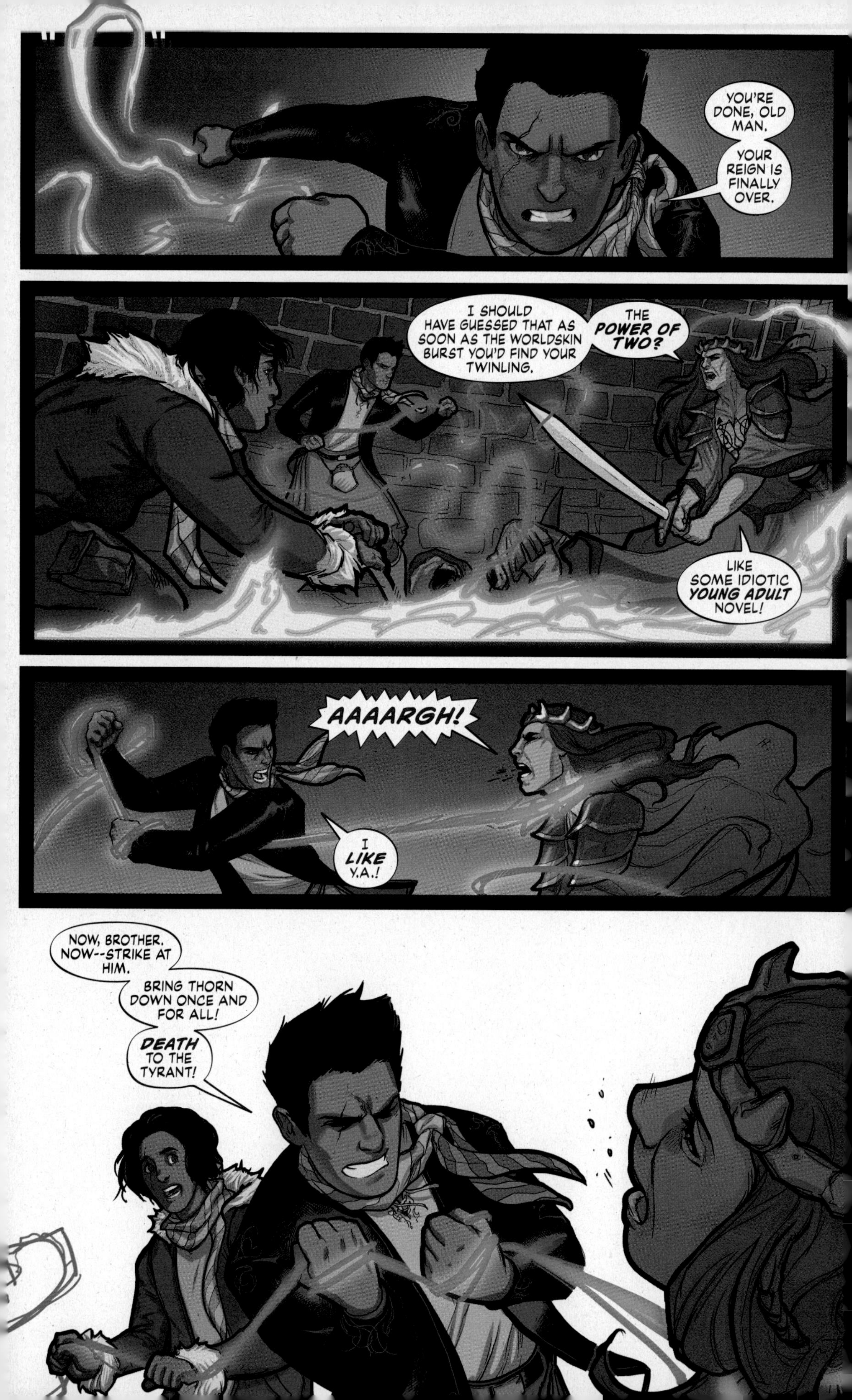
YOU'RE DONE, OLD MAN.
YOUR REIGN IS FINALLY OVER.
I SHOULD HAVE GUESSED THAT AS SOON AS THE WORLDSKIN BURST YOU'D FIND YOUR TWINLING.
THE POWER OF TWO?
LIKE SOME IDIOTIC YOUNG ADULT NOVEL!
AAAARGH!
I LIKE Y.A.!
NOW, BROTHER. NOW--STRIKE AT HIM.
BRING THORN DOWN ONCE AND FOR ALL!
DEATH TO THE TYRANT!

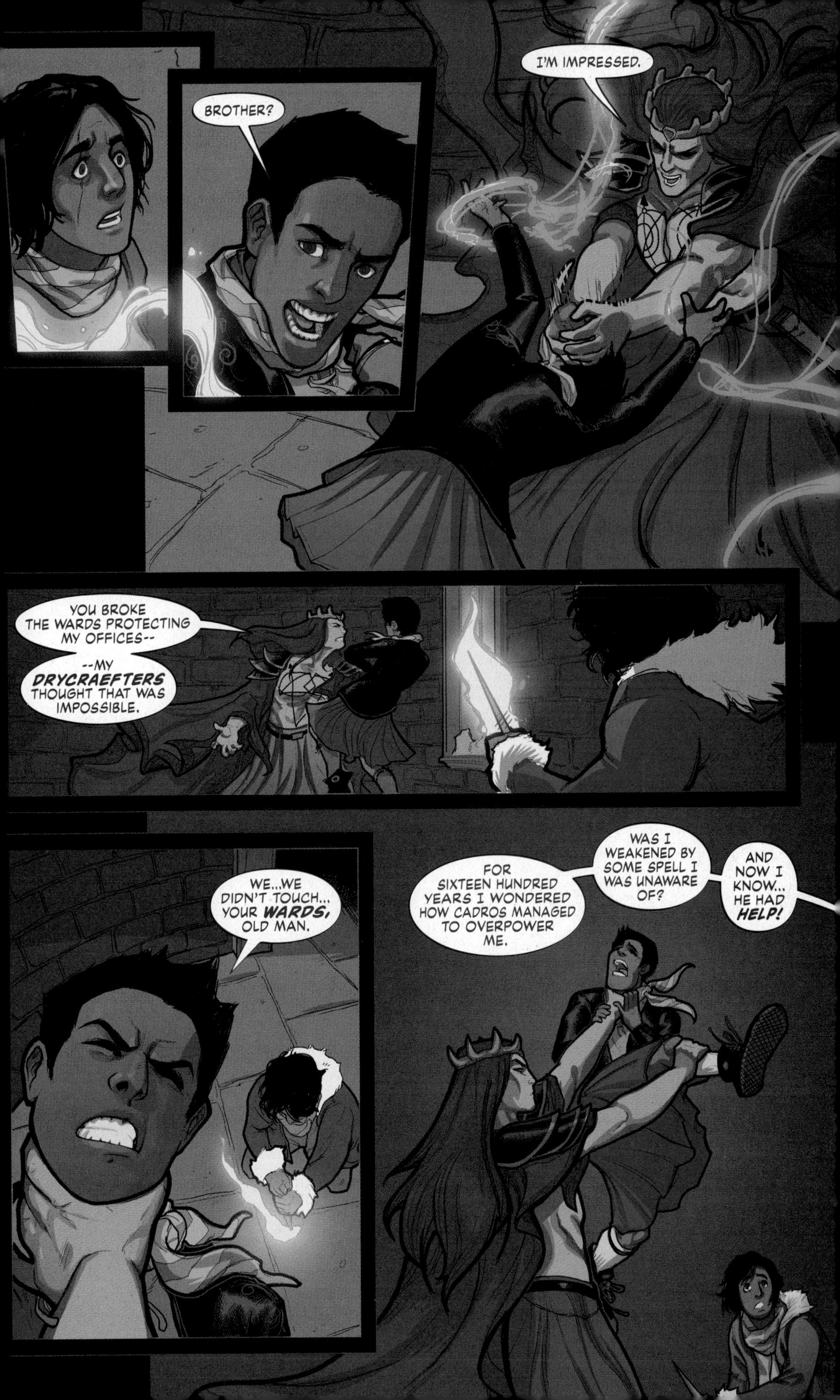
BROTHER?
I'M IMPRESSED.
YOU BROKE THE WARDS PROTECTING MY OFFICES--
--MY DRYCRAEFTERS THOUGHT THAT WAS IMPOSSIBLE.
WE...WE DIDN'T TOUCH... YOUR WARDS, OLD MAN.
FOR SIXTEEN HUNDRED YEARS I WONDERED HOW CADROS MANAGED TO OVERPOWER ME.
WAS I WEAKENED BY SOME SPELL I WAS UNAWARE OF?
AND NOW I KNOW... HE HAD HELP!

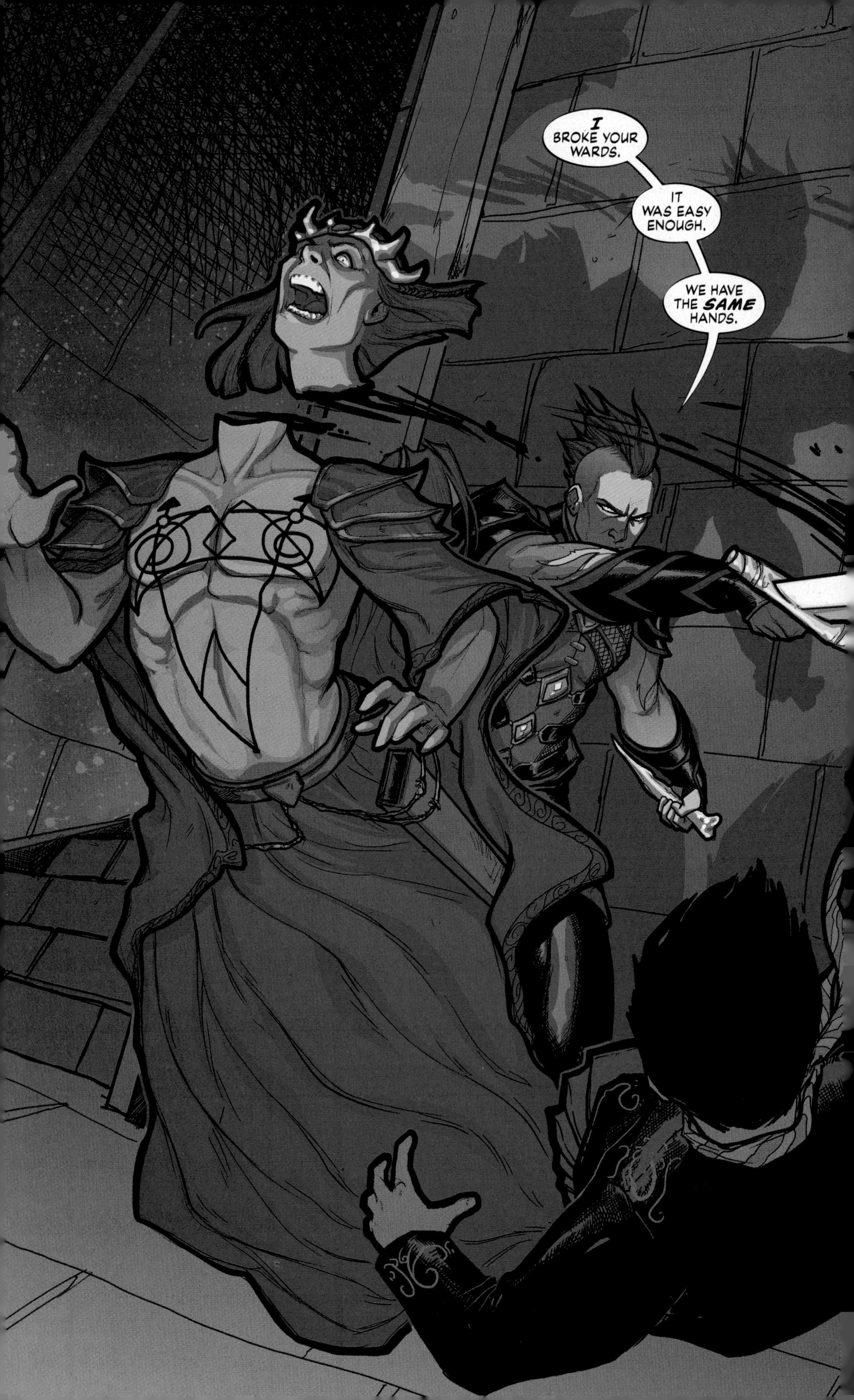
I BROKE YOUR WARDS.
IT WAS EASY ENOUGH.
WE HAVE THE SAME HANDS.

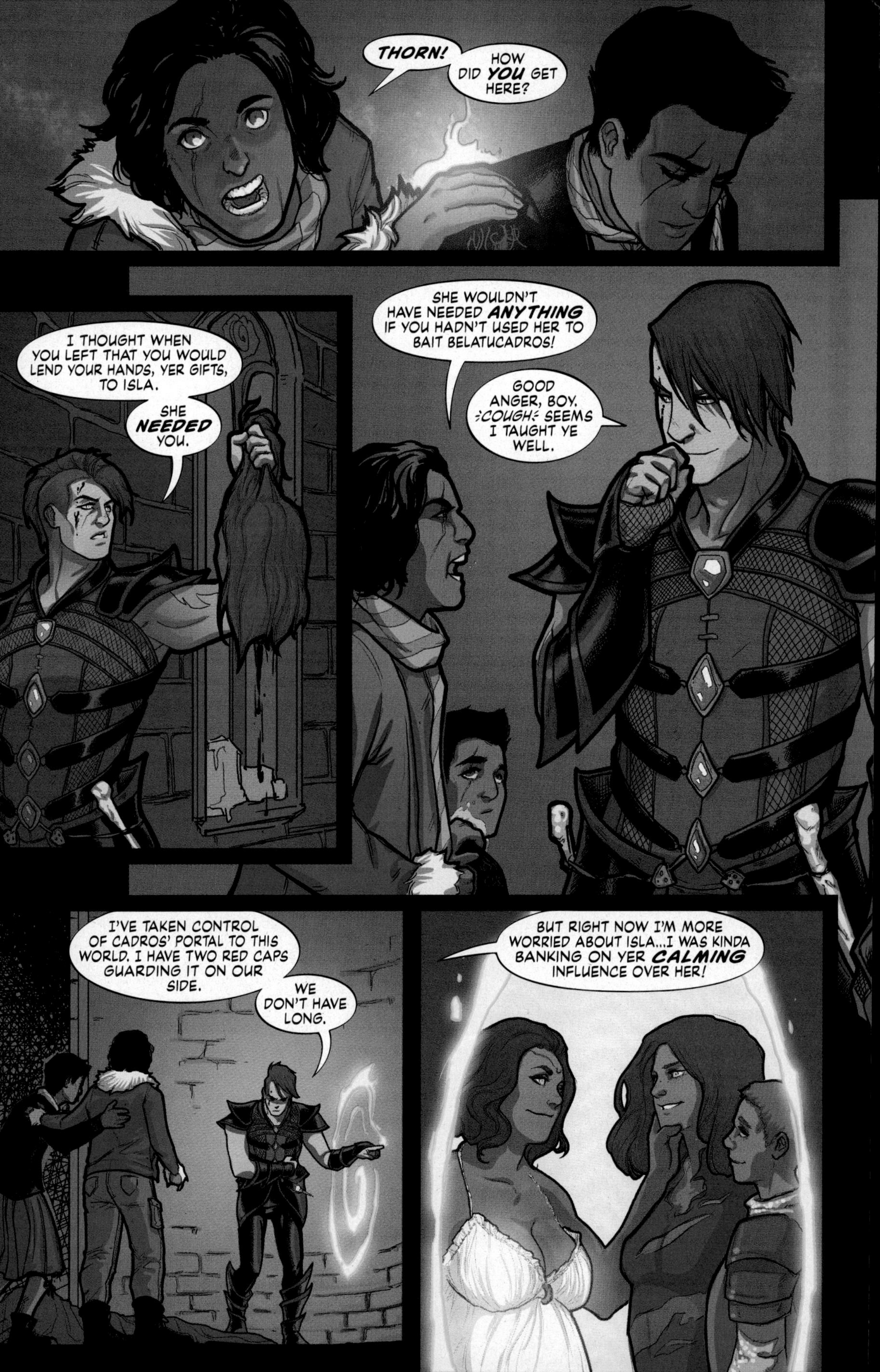
THORN!
HOW DID YOU GET HERE?
I THOUGHT WHEN YOU LEFT THAT YOU WOULD LEND YOUR HANDS, YER GIFTS, TO ISLA.
SHE NEEDED YOU.
SHE WOULDN'T HAVE NEEDED ANYTHING IF YOU HADN'T USED HER TO BAIT BELATUCADROS!
GOOD ANGER, BOY. COUGH SEEMS I TAUGHT YE WELL.
I'VE TAKEN CONTROL OF CADROS' PORTAL TO THIS WORLD. I HAVE TWO RED CAPS GUARDING IT ON OUR SIDE.
WE DON'T HAVE LONG.
BUT RIGHT NOW I'M MORE WORRIED ABOUT ISLA...I WAS KINDA BANKING ON YER CALMING INFLUENCE OVER HER!

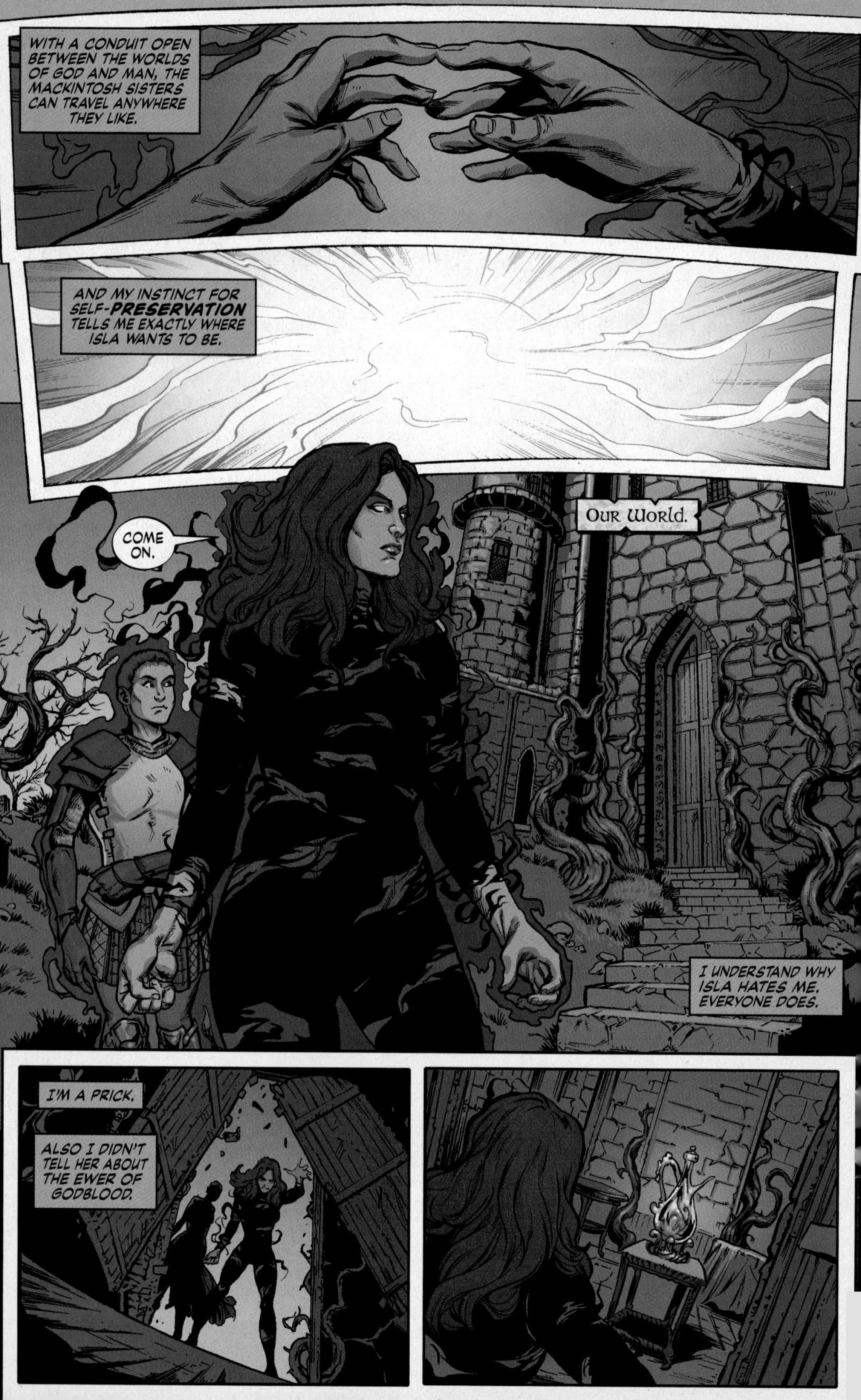
WITH A CONDUIT OPEN BETWEEN THE WORLDS OF GOD AND MAN, THE MACKINTOSH SISTERS CAN TRAVEL ANYWHERE THEY LIKE.
AND MY INSTINCT FOR SELF-PRESERVATION TELLS ME EXACTLY WHERE ISLA WANTS TO BE.
COME ON.
OUR WORLD.
I UNDERSTAND WHY ISLA HATES ME. EVERYONE DOES.
I'M A PRICK.
ALSO I DIDN'T TELL HER ABOUT THE EWER OF GODBLOOD.

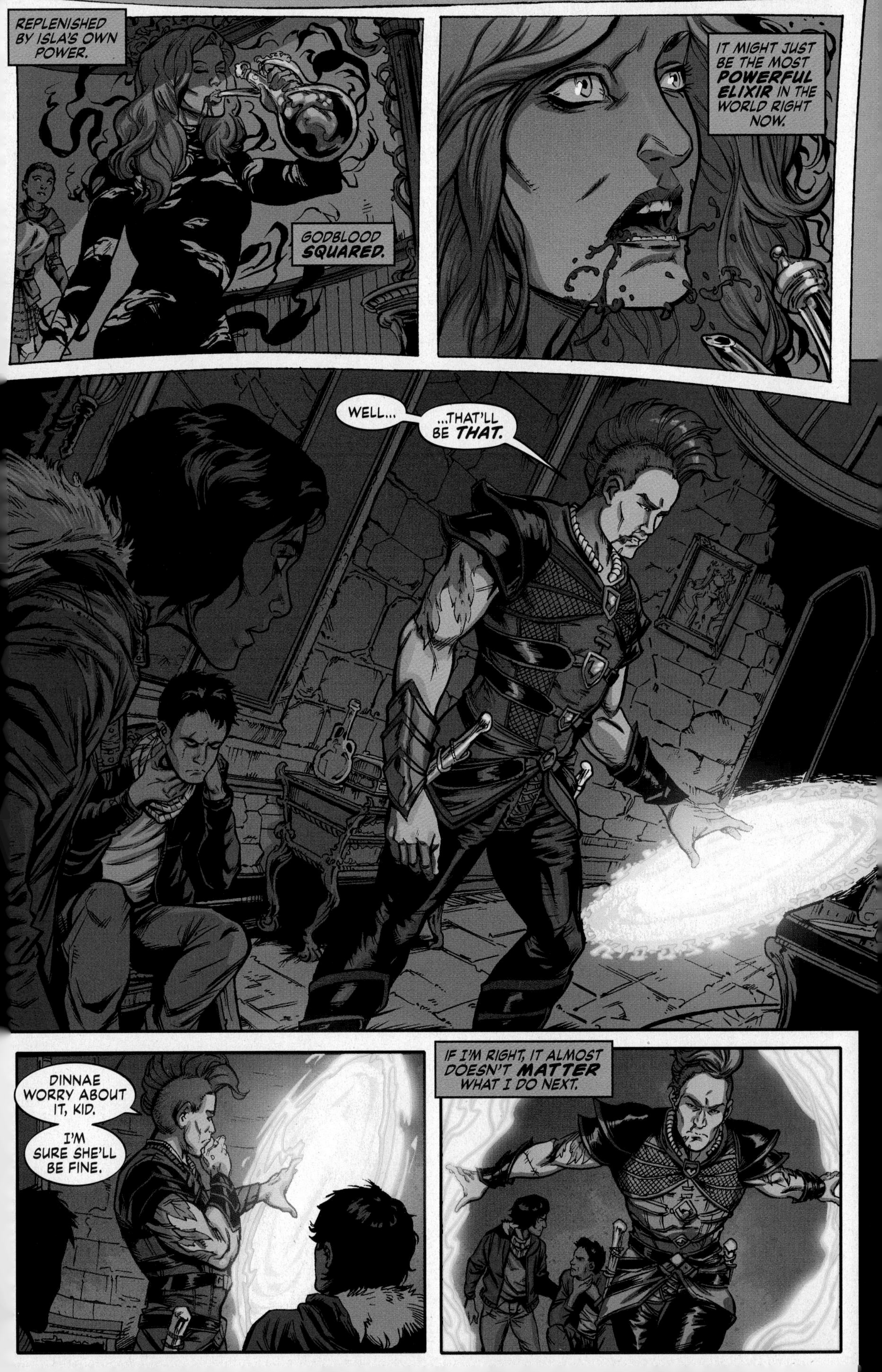
REPLENISHED BY ISLA'S OWN POWER.
GODBLOOD SQUARED.
IT MIGHT JUST BE THE MOST POWERFUL ELIXIR IN THE WORLD RIGHT NOW.
WELL...
...THAT'LL BE THAT.
DINNAE WORRY ABOUT IT, KID.
I'M SURE SHE'LL BE FINE.
IF I'M RIGHT, IT ALMOST DOESN'T MATTER WHAT I DO NEXT.

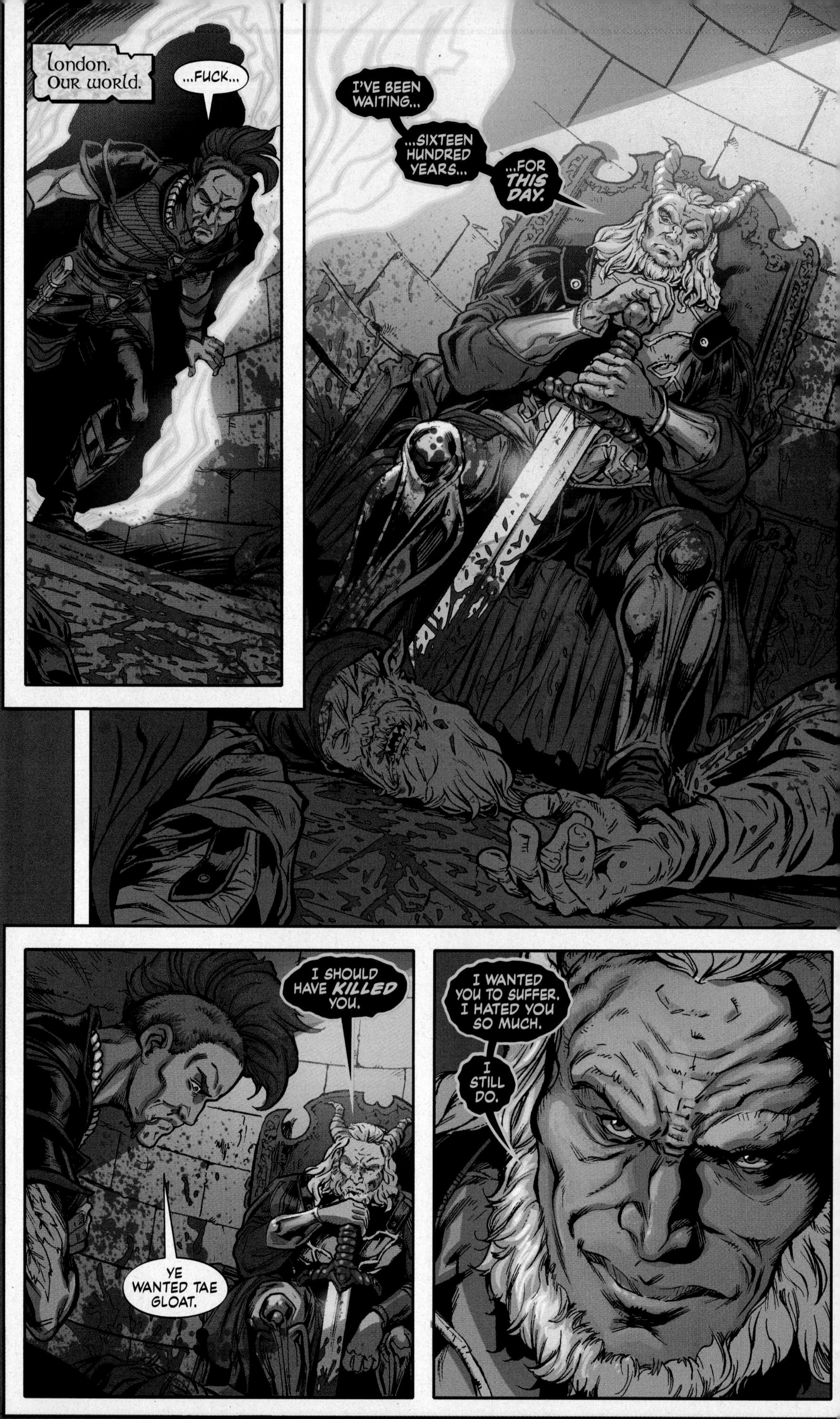
london.
Our world.
...FUCK...
I'VE BEEN WAITING...
...SIXTEEN HUNDRED YEARS...
...FOR THIS DAY.
I SHOULD HAVE KILLED YOU.
YE WANTED TAE GLOAT.
I WANTED YOU TO SUFFER. I HATED YOU SO MUCH.
I STILL DO.

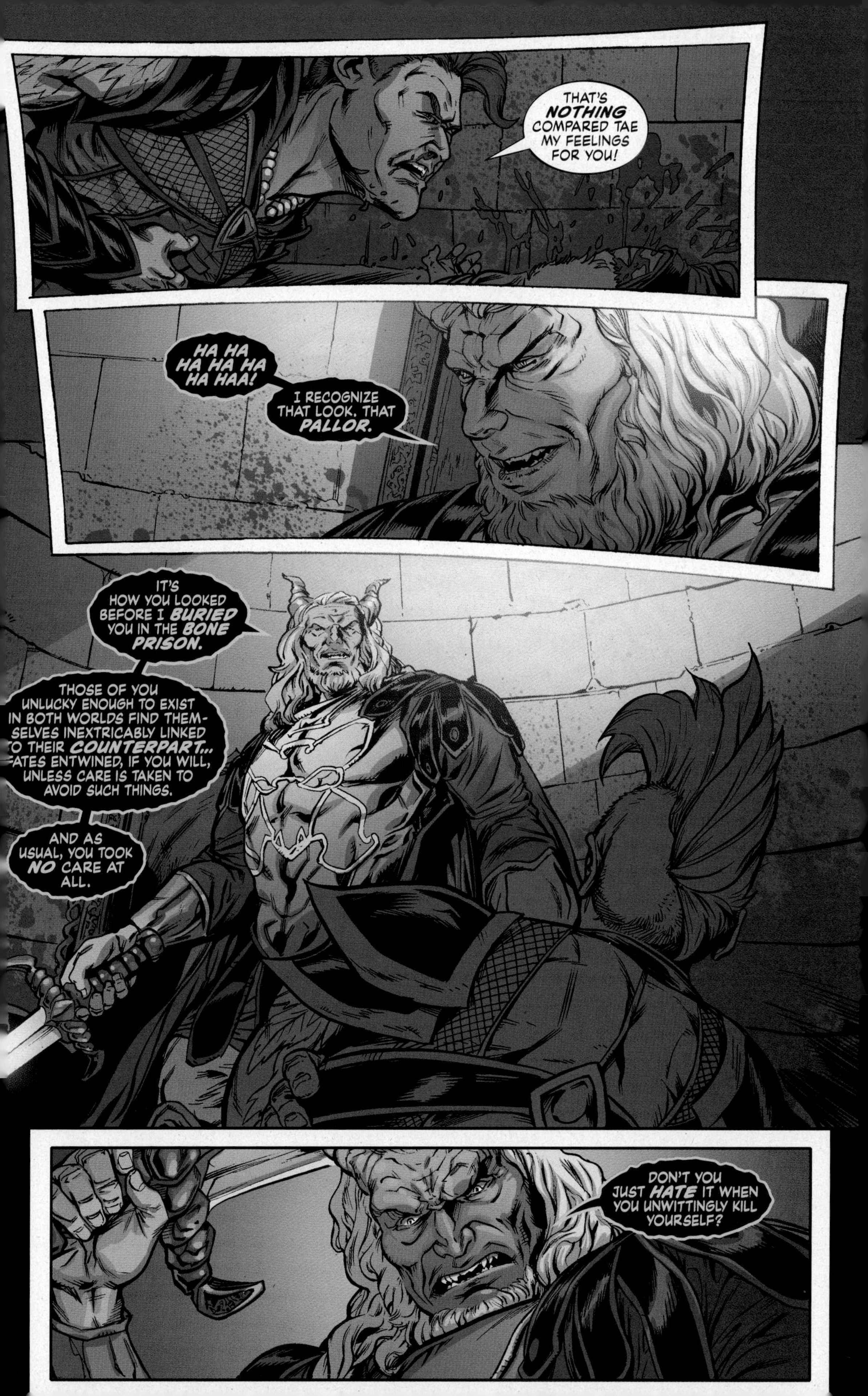
THAT'S NOTHING COMPARED TAE MY FEELINGS FOR YOU!
HA HA HA HA HA HA HAA!
I RECOGNIZE THAT LOOK. THAT PALLOR.
IT'S HOW YOU LOOKED BEFORE I BURIED YOU IN THE BONE PRISON.
THOSE OF YOU UNLUCKY ENOUGH TO EXIST IN BOTH WORLDS FIND THEMSELVES INEXTRICABLY LINKED TO THEIR COUNTERPART... FATES ENTWINED, IF YOU WILL, UNLESS CARE IS TAKEN TO AVOID SUCH THINGS.
AND AS USUAL, YOU TOOK NO CARE AT ALL.
DON'T YOU JUST HATE IT WHEN YOU UNWITTINGLY KILL YOURSELF?

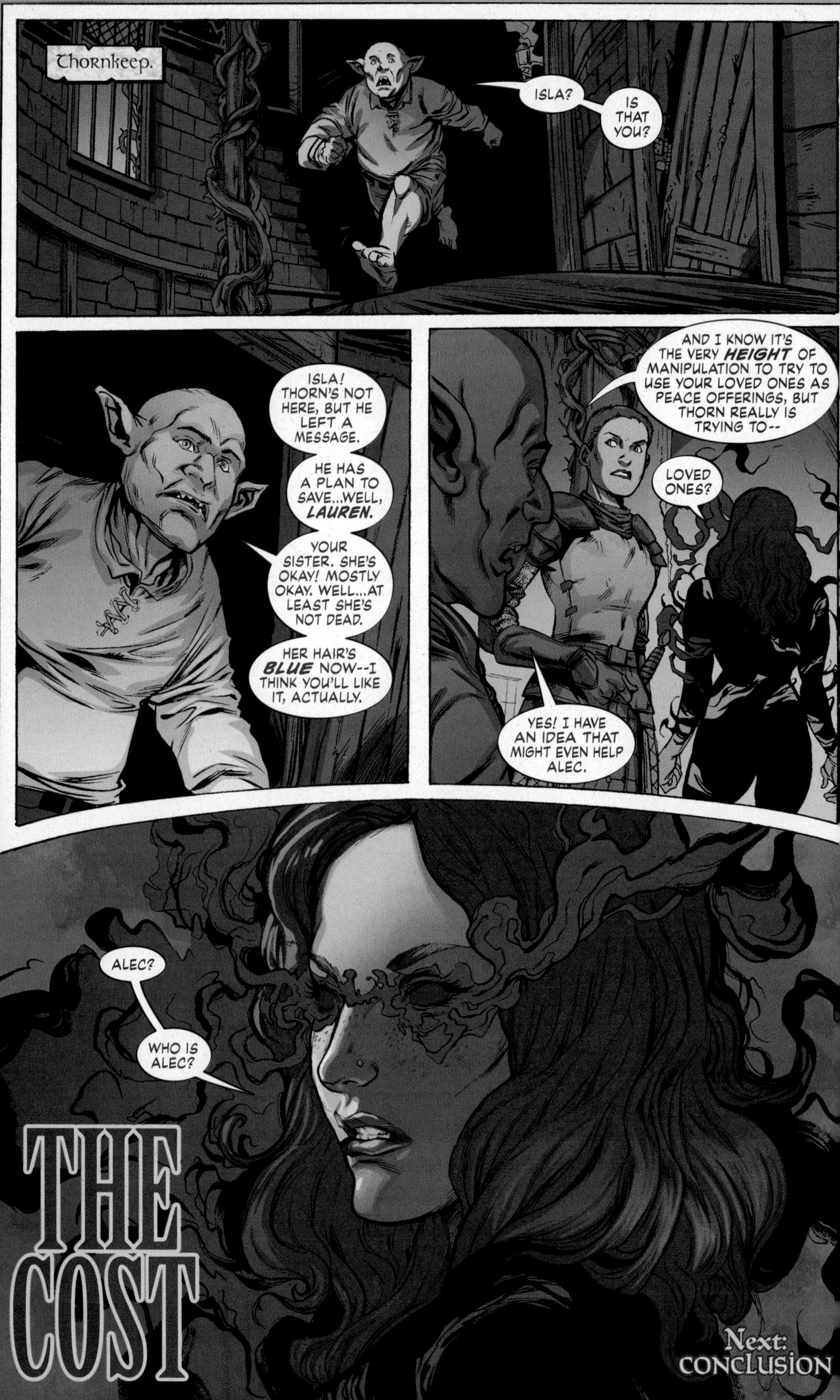
Thornkeep.
ISLA?
IS THAT YOU?
ISLA! THORN'S NOT HERE, BUT HE LEFT A MESSAGE.
HE HAS A PLAN TO SAVE...WELL, LAUREN.
YOUR SISTER. SHE'S OKAY! MOSTLY OKAY. WELL...AT LEAST SHE'S NOT DEAD.
HER HAIR'S BLUE NOW--I THINK YOU'LL LIKE IT, ACTUALLY.
AND I KNOW IT'S THE VERY HEIGHT OF MANIPULATION TO TRY TO USE YOUR LOVED ONES AS PEACE OFFERINGS, BUT THORN REALLY IS TRYING TO--
LOVED ONES?
YES! I HAVE AN IDEA THAT MIGHT EVEN HELP ALEC.
ALEC?
WHO IS ALEC?
THE COST
Next: CONCLUSION

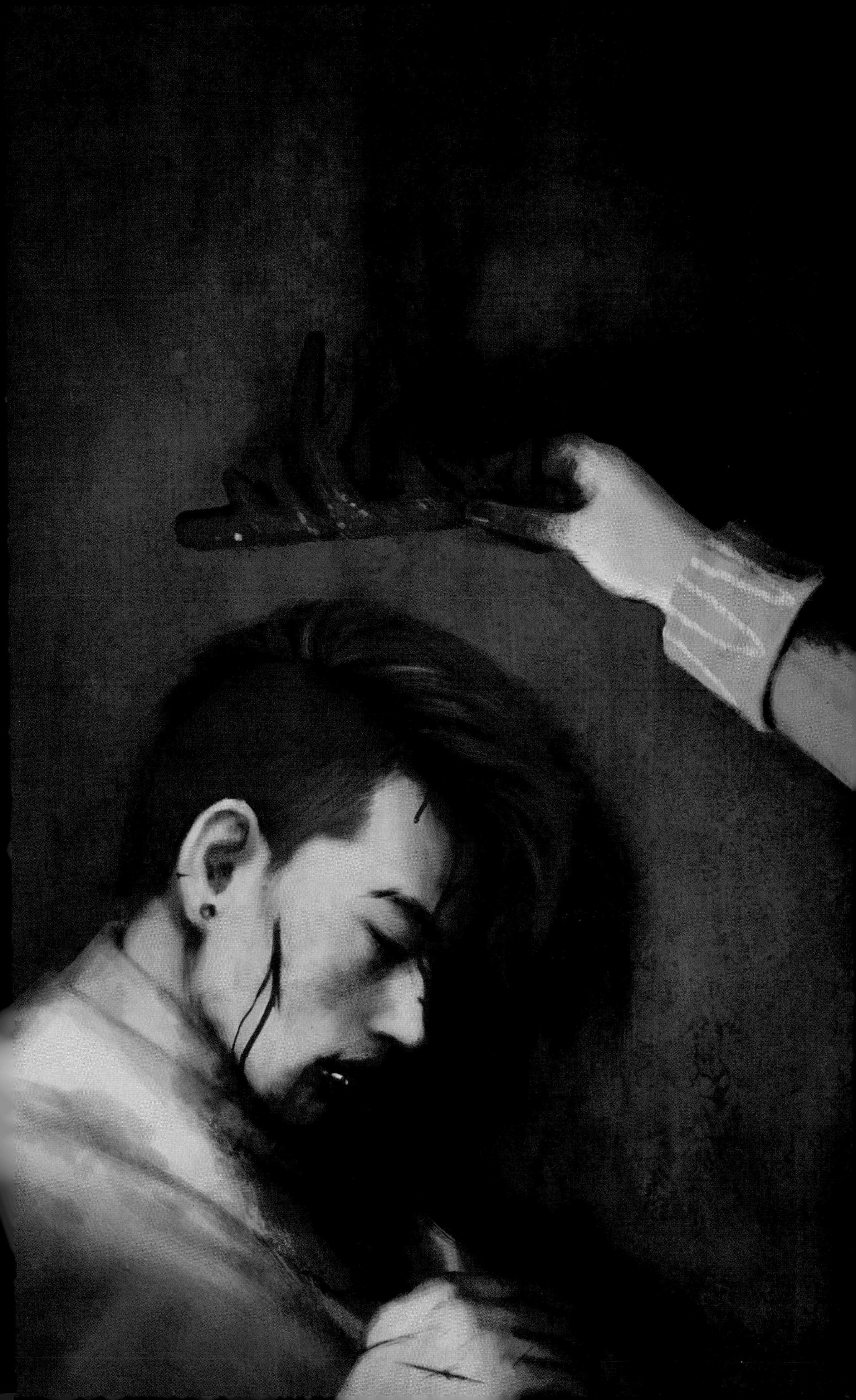

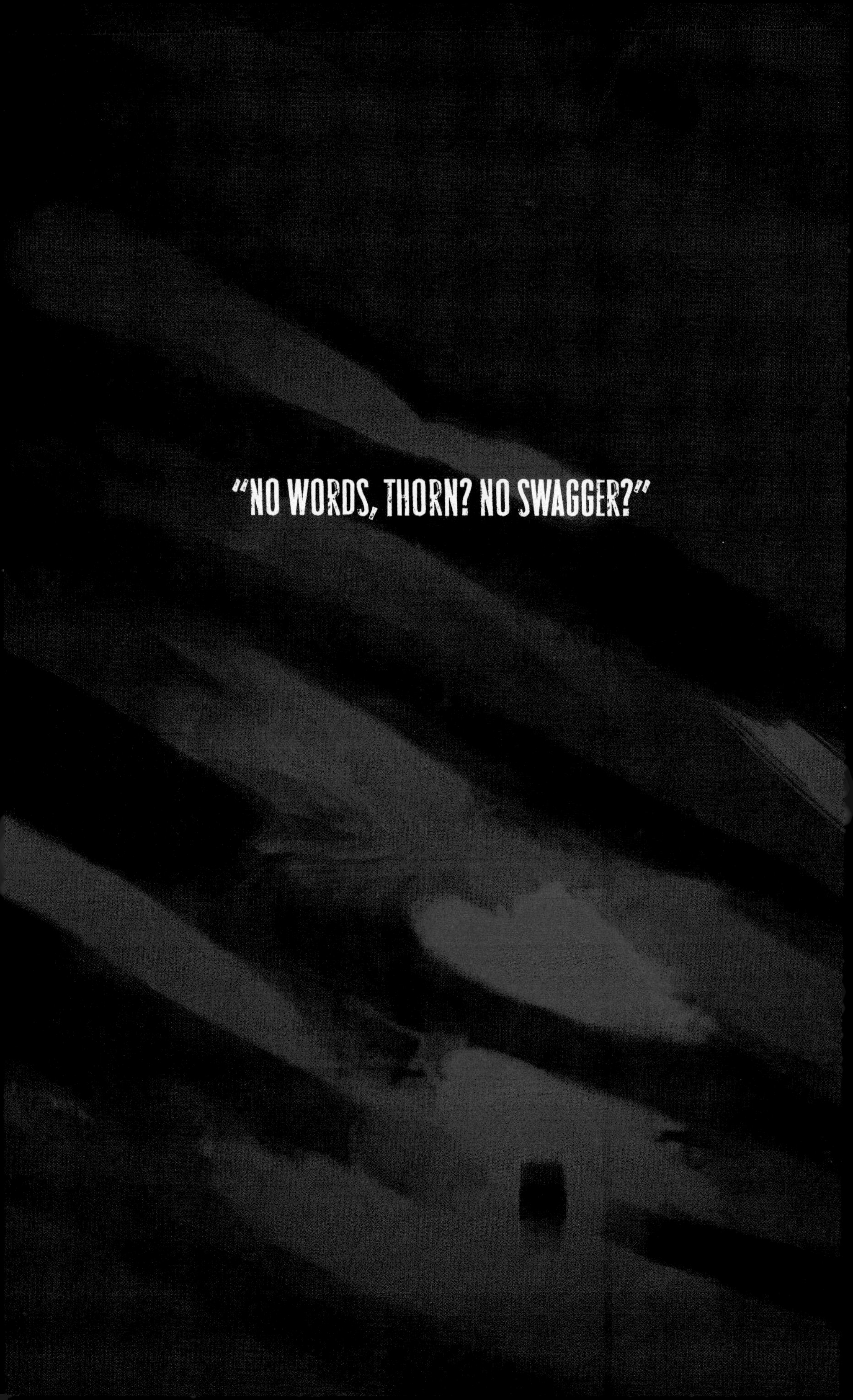
"NO WORDS, THORN? NO SWAGGER?"

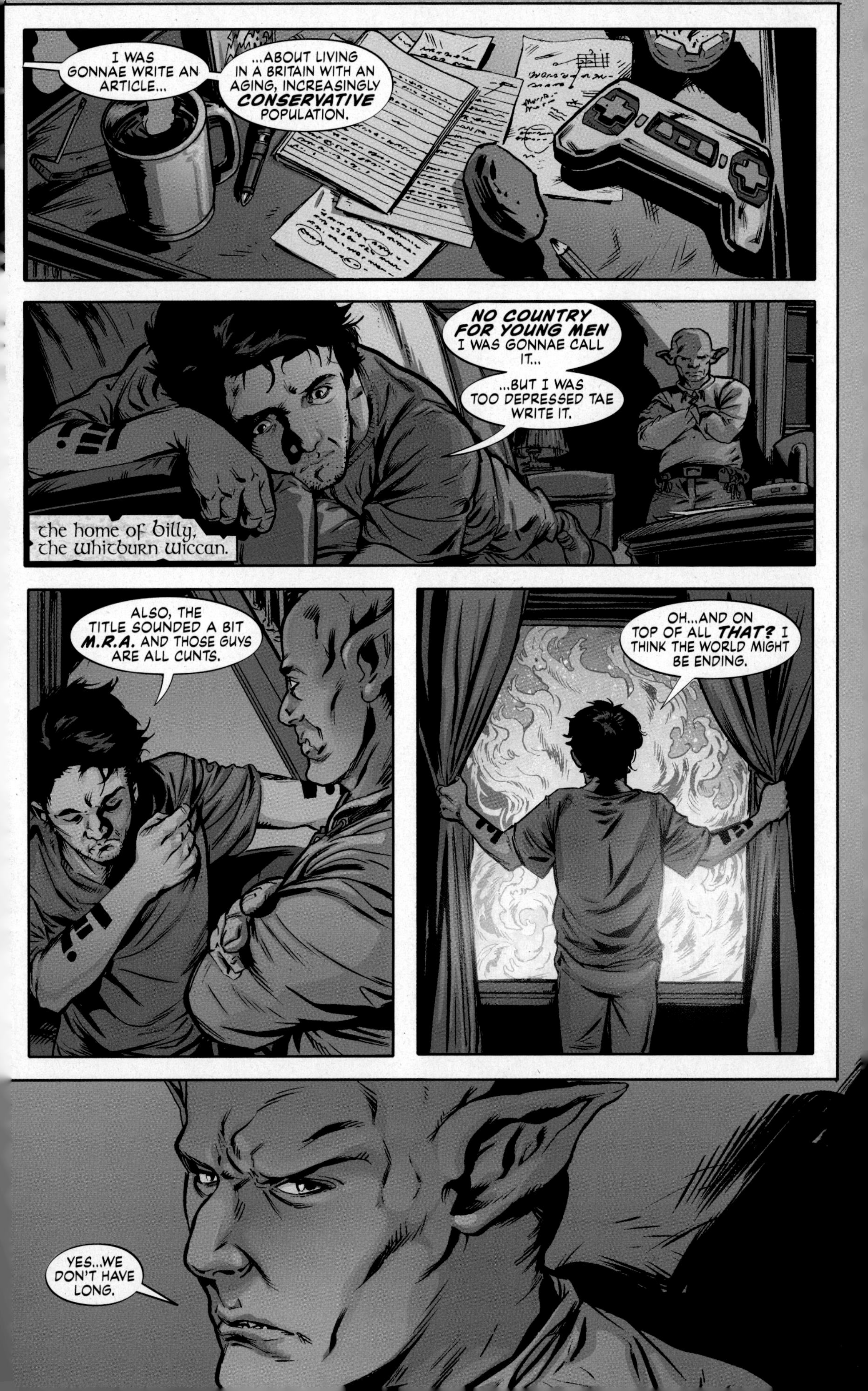
I WAS GONNAE WRITE AN ARTICLE...
...ABOUT LIVING IN A BRITAIN WITH AN AGING, INCREASINGLY CONSERVATIVE POPULATION.
NO COUNTRY FOR YOUNG MEN I WAS GONNAE CALL IT...
...BUT I WAS TOO DEPRESSED TAE WRITE IT.
the home of billy, the Whitburn Wiccan.
ALSO, THE TITLE SOUNDED A BIT M.R.A. AND THOSE GUYS ARE ALL CUNTS.
OH...AND ON TOP OF ALL THAT? I THINK THE WORLD MIGHT BE ENDING.
YES...WE DON'T HAVE LONG.

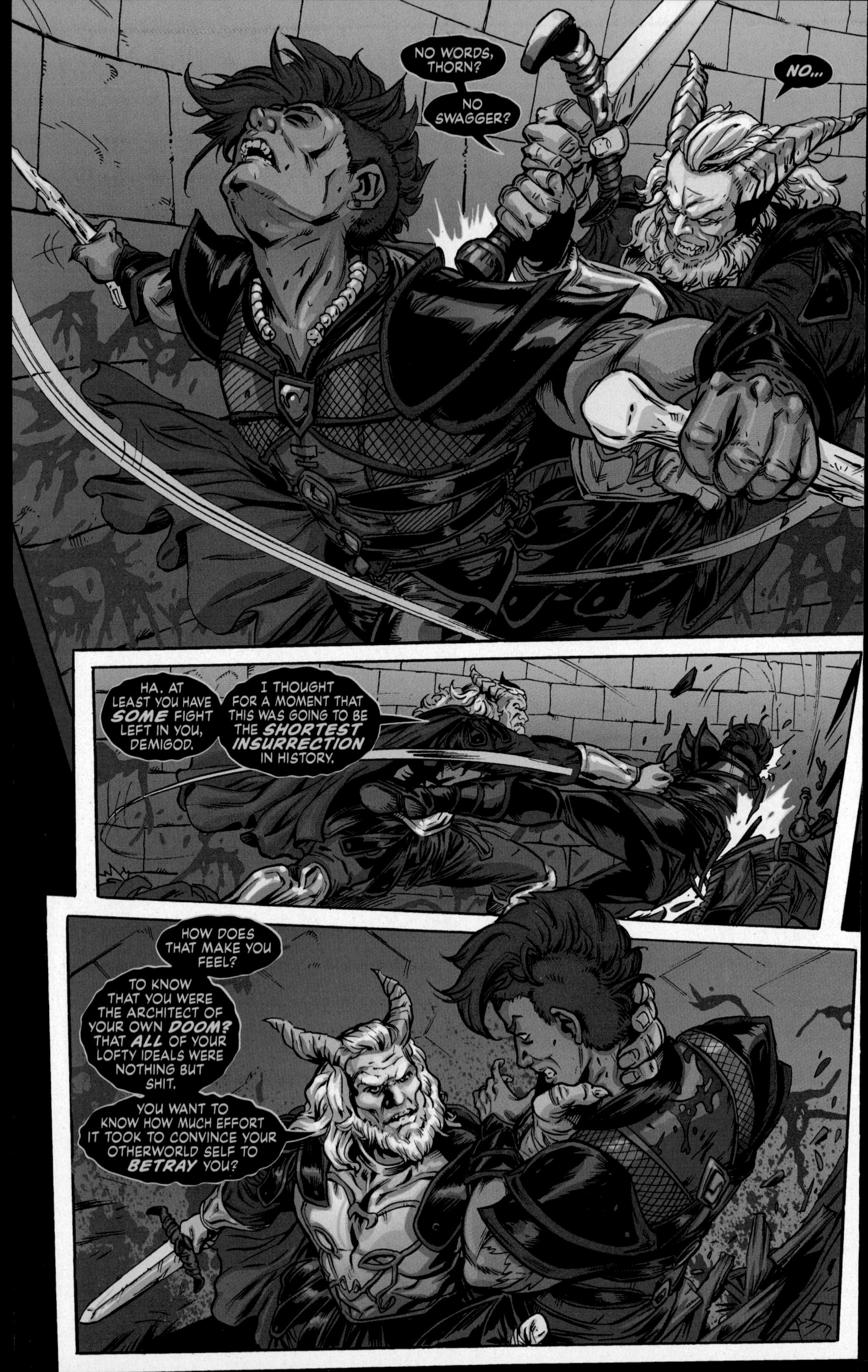
NO WORDS, THORN?
NO SWAGGER?
NO...
HA. AT LEAST YOU HAVE SOME FIGHT LEFT IN YOU, DEMIGOD.
I THOUGHT FOR A MOMENT THAT THIS WAS GOING TO BE THE SHORTEST INSURRECTION IN HISTORY.
HOW DOES THAT MAKE YOU FEEL?
TO KNOW THAT YOU WERE THE ARCHITECT OF YOUR OWN DOOM? THAT ALL OF YOUR LOFTY IDEALS WERE NOTHING BUT SHIT.
YOU WANT TO KNOW HOW MUCH EFFORT IT TOOK TO CONVINCE YOUR OTHERWORLD SELF TO BETRAY YOU?

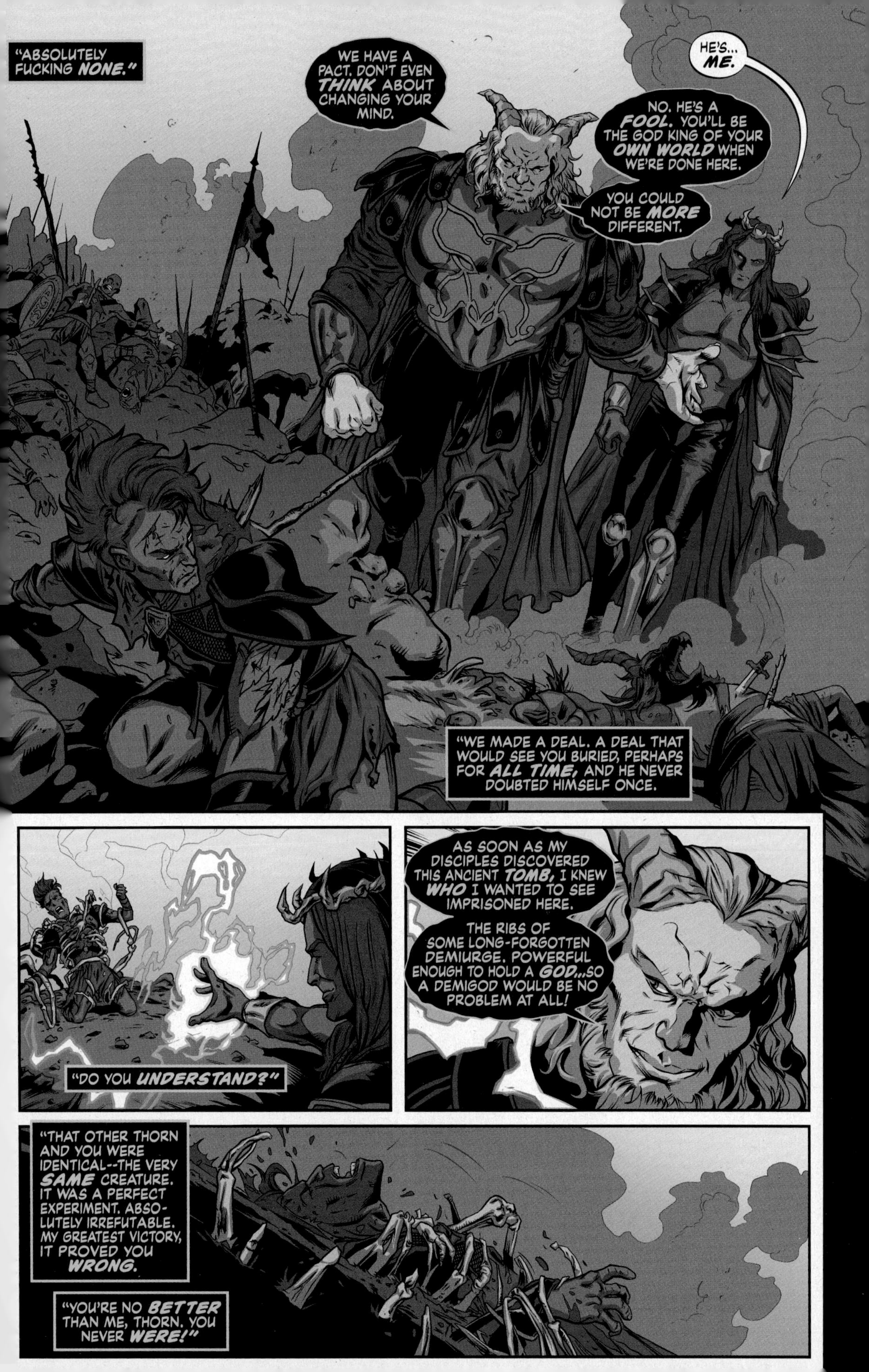
"ABSOLUTELY FUCKING NONE."
WE HAVE A PACT. DON'T EVEN THINK ABOUT CHANGING YOUR MIND.
HE'S... ME.
NO. HE'S A FOOL. YOU'LL BE THE GOD KING OF YOUR OWN WORLD WHEN WE'RE DONE HERE.
YOU COULD NOT BE MORE DIFFERENT.
"WE MADE A DEAL. A DEAL THAT WOULD SEE YOU BURIED, PERHAPS FOR ALL TIME, AND HE NEVER DOUBTED HIMSELF ONCE.
"DO YOU UNDERSTAND?"
AS SOON AS MY DISCIPLES DISCOVERED THIS ANCIENT TOMB, I KNEW WHO I WANTED TO SEE IMPRISONED HERE.
THE RIBS OF SOME LONG-FORGOTTEN DEMIURGE. POWERFUL ENOUGH TO HOLD A GOD...SO A DEMIGOD WOULD BE NO PROBLEM AT ALL!
"THAT OTHER THORN AND YOU WERE IDENTICAL--THE VERY SAME CREATURE. IT WAS A PERFECT EXPERIMENT. ABSO-LUTELY IRREFUTABLE. MY GREATEST VICTORY, IT PROVED YOU WRONG.
"YOU'RE NO BETTER THAN ME, THORN. YOU NEVER WERE!"

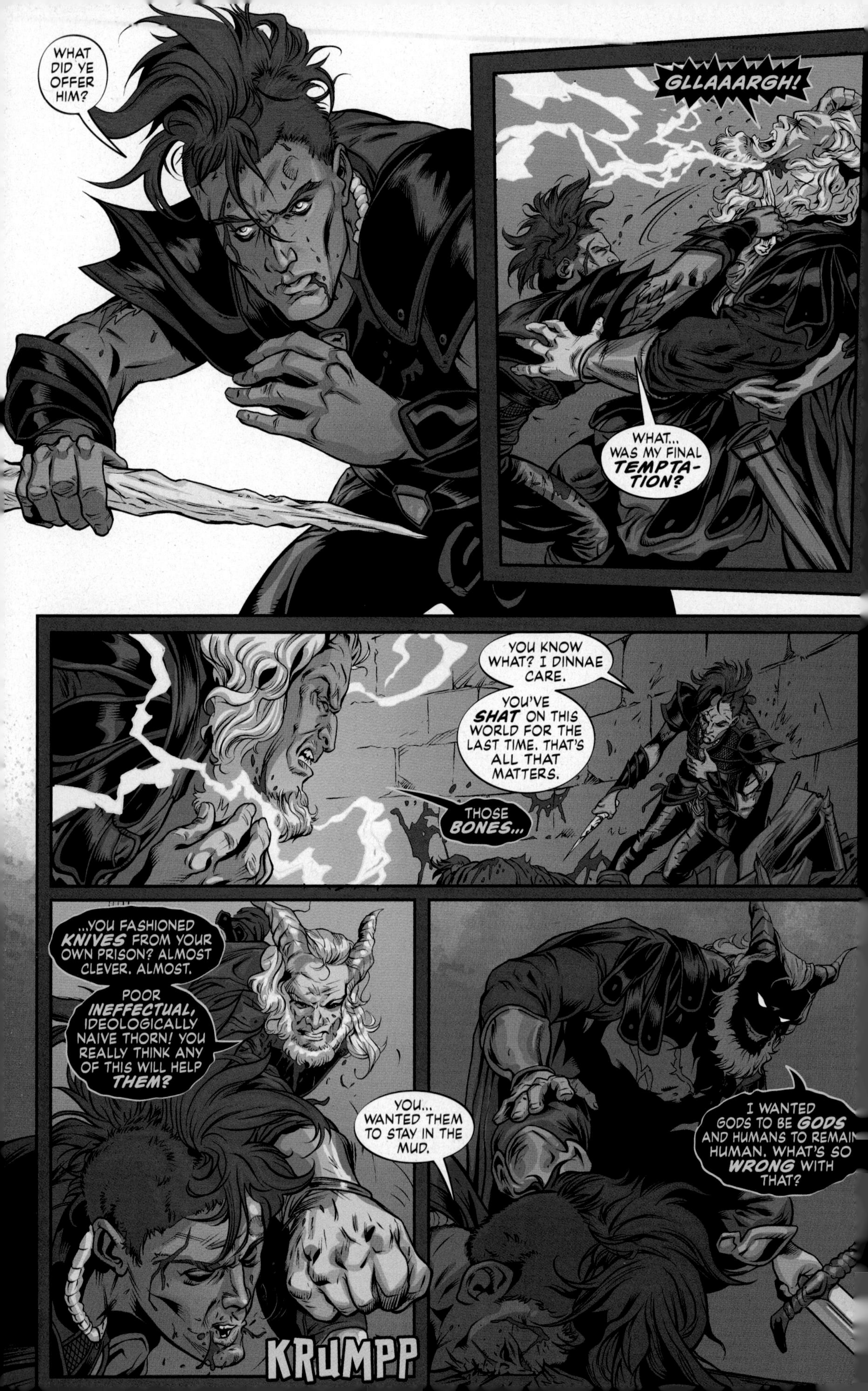

WHAT DID YE OFFER HIM?
GLLAAARGH!
WHAT... WAS MY FINAL TEMPTA-TION?
YOU KNOW WHAT? I DINNAE CARE.
YOU'VE SHAT ON THIS WORLD FOR THE LAST TIME. THAT'S ALL THAT MATTERS.
THOSE BONES...
...YOU FASHIONED KNIVES FROM YOUR OWN PRISON? ALMOST CLEVER. ALMOST.
POOR INEFFECTUAL, IDEOLOGICALLY NAIVE THORN! YOU REALLY THINK ANY OF THIS WILL HELP THEM?
YOU... WANTED THEM TO STAY IN THE MUD.
KRUMPP
I WANTED GODS TO BE GODS AND HUMANS TO REMAIN HUMAN. WHAT'S SO WRONG WITH THAT?

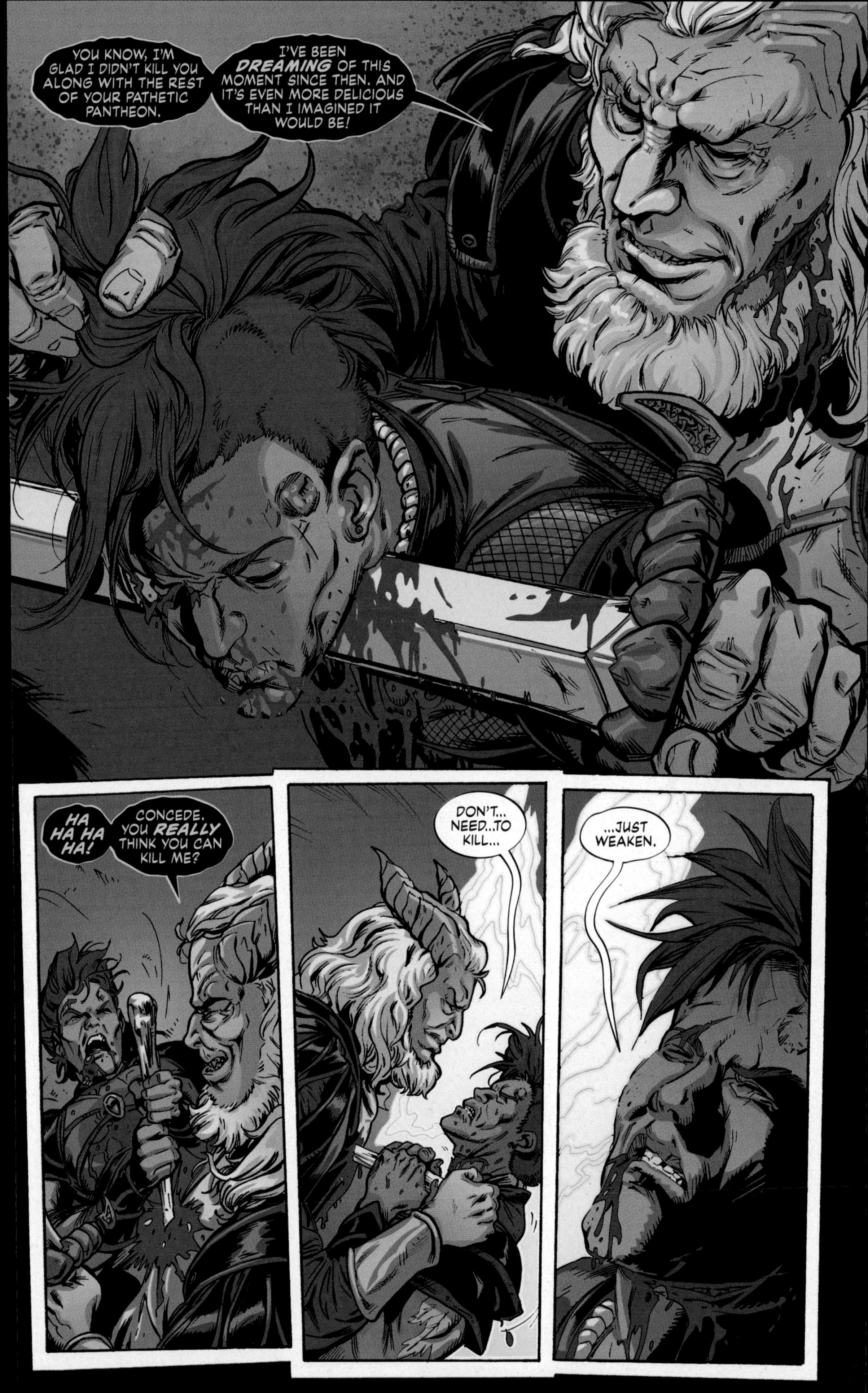
YOU KNOW, I'M GLAD I DIDN'T KILL YOU ALONG WITH THE REST OF YOUR PATHETIC PANTHEON.
I'VE BEEN *DREAMING* OF THIS MOMENT SINCE THEN. AND IT'S EVEN MORE DELICIOUS THAN I IMAGINED IT WOULD BE!
HA HA HA HA!
CONCEDE. YOU *REALLY* THINK YOU CAN KILL ME?
DON'T... NEED...TO KILL...
...JUST WEAKEN.

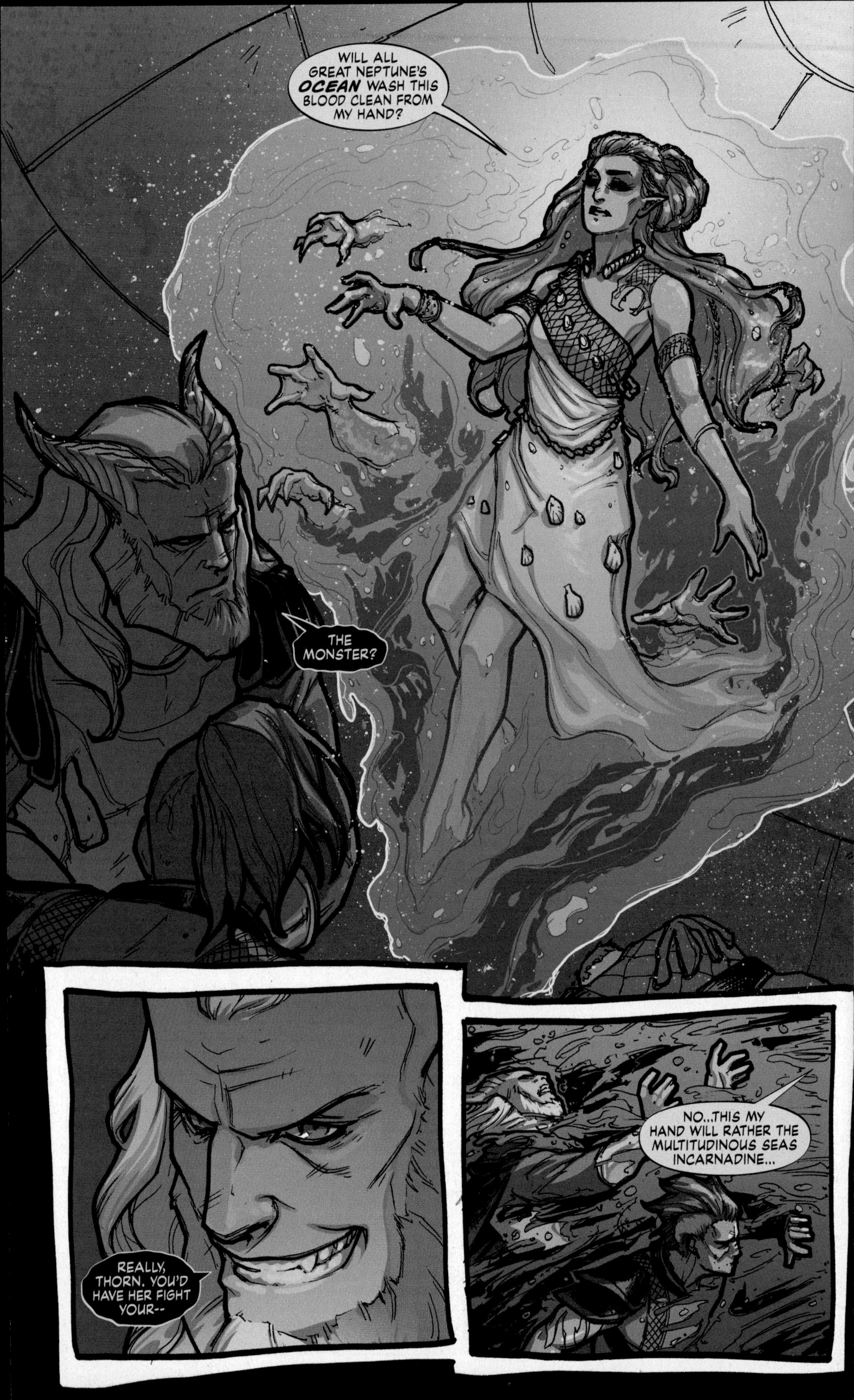
WILL ALL GREAT NEPTUNE'S OCEAN WASH THIS BLOOD CLEAN FROM MY HAND?
THE MONSTER?
REALLY, THORN. YOU'D HAVE HER FIGHT YOUR--
NO...THIS MY HAND WILL RATHER THE MULTITUDINOUS SEAS INCARNADINE...

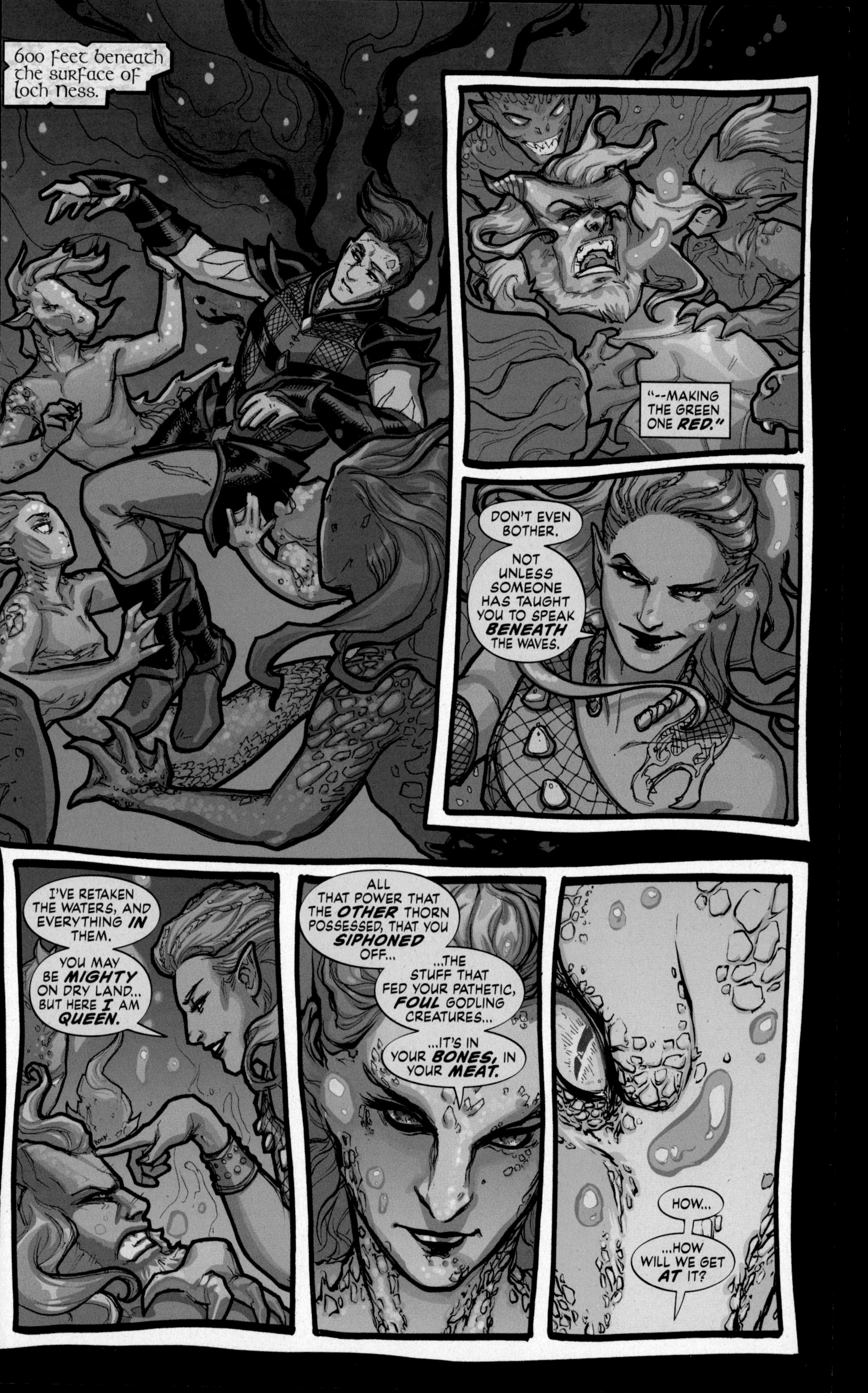
600 feet beneath the surface of loch Ness.
"--MAKING THE GREEN ONE RED."
DON'T EVEN BOTHER.
NOT UNLESS SOMEONE HAS TAUGHT YOU TO SPEAK BENEATH THE WAVES.
I'VE RETAKEN THE WATERS, AND EVERYTHING IN THEM.
YOU MAY BE MIGHTY ON DRY LAND... BUT HERE I AM QUEEN.
ALL THAT POWER THAT THE OTHER THORN POSSESSED, THAT YOU SIPHONED OFF...
...THE STUFF THAT FED YOUR PATHETIC, FOUL GODLING CREATURES...
...IT'S IN YOUR BONES, IN YOUR MEAT.
HOW...
...HOW WILL WE GET AT IT?

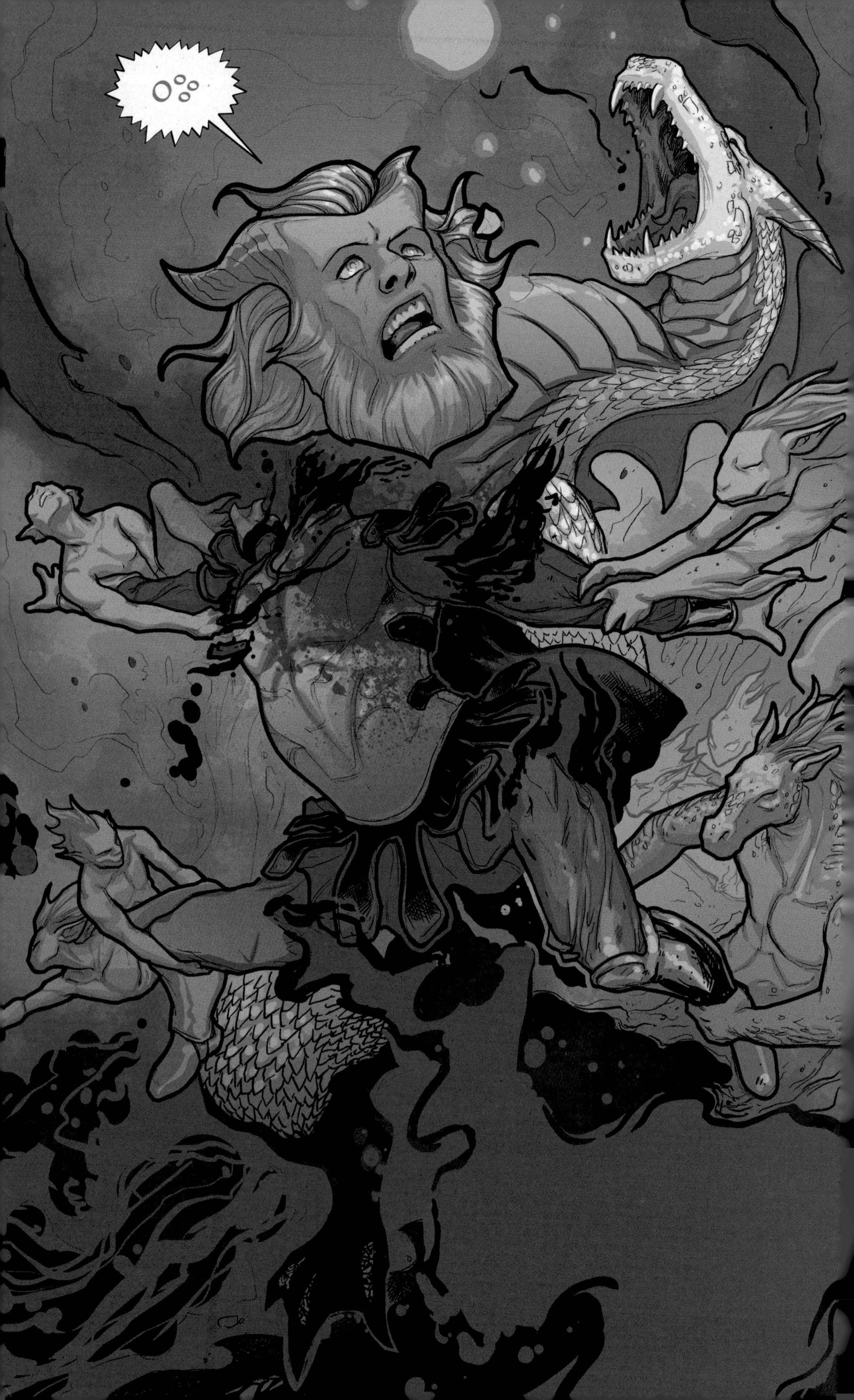

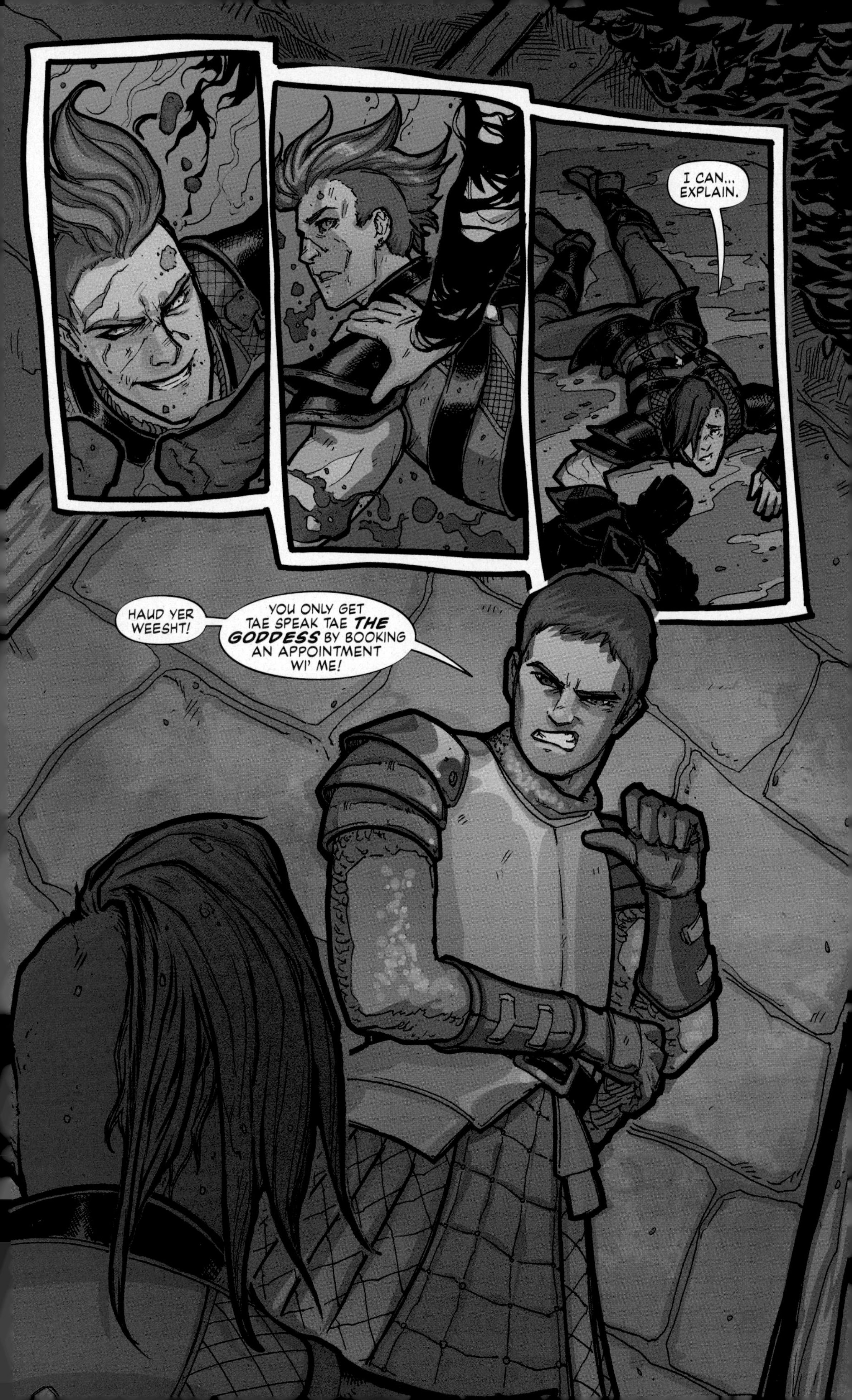
I CAN... EXPLAIN.
HAUD YER WEESHT!
YOU ONLY GET TAE SPEAK TAE THE GODDESS BY BOOKING AN APPOINTMENT WI' ME!

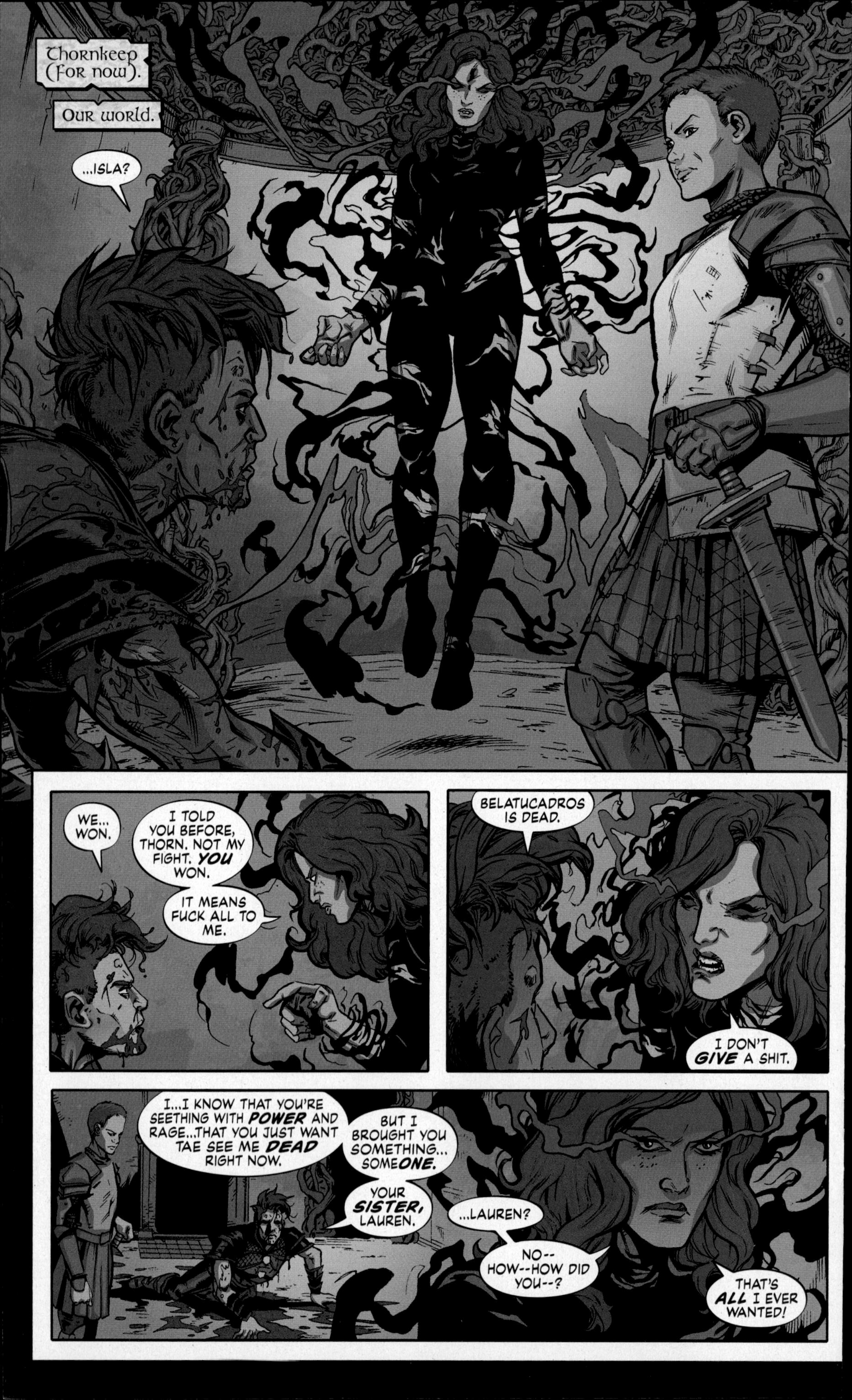
Thornkeep (For now).
Our world.
...ISLA?
WE... WON.
I TOLD YOU BEFORE, THORN. NOT MY FIGHT. YOU WON.
IT MEANS FUCK ALL TO ME.
BELATUCADROS IS DEAD.
I DON'T GIVE A SHIT.
I...I KNOW THAT YOU'RE SEETHING WITH POWER AND RAGE...THAT YOU JUST WANT TAE SEE ME DEAD RIGHT NOW.
BUT I BROUGHT YOU SOMETHING... SOMEONE.
YOUR SISTER, LAUREN.
...LAUREN?
NO-- HOW--HOW DID YOU--?
THAT'S ALL I EVER WANTED!

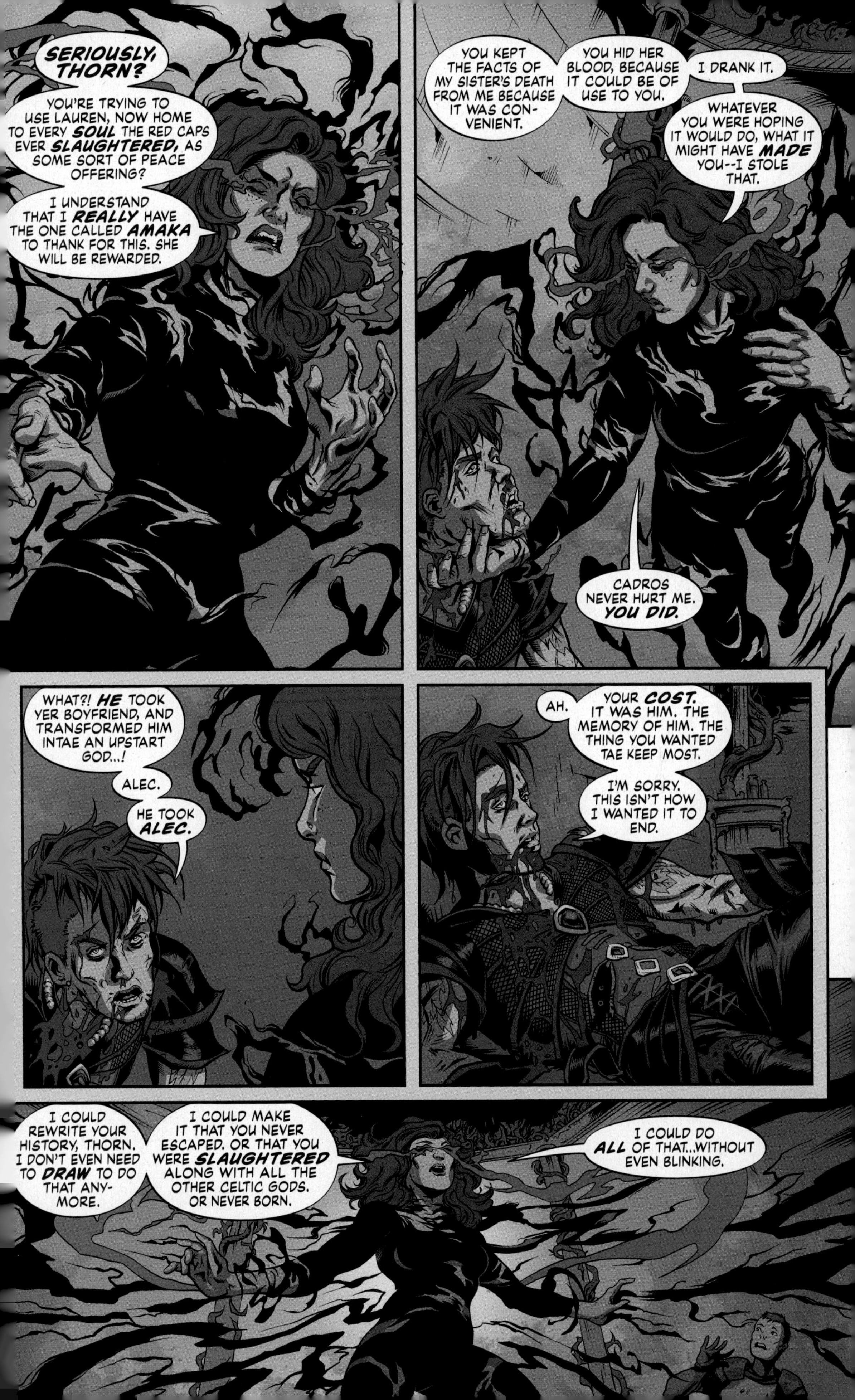
SERIOUSLY, THORN?
YOU'RE TRYING TO USE LAUREN, NOW HOME TO EVERY SOUL THE RED CAPS EVER SLAUGHTERED, AS SOME SORT OF PEACE OFFERING?
I UNDERSTAND THAT I REALLY HAVE THE ONE CALLED AMAKA TO THANK FOR THIS. SHE WILL BE REWARDED.
YOU KEPT THE FACTS OF MY SISTER'S DEATH FROM ME BECAUSE IT WAS CON-VENIENT.
YOU HID HER BLOOD, BECAUSE IT COULD BE OF USE TO YOU.
I DRANK IT.
WHATEVER YOU WERE HOPING IT WOULD DO, WHAT IT MIGHT HAVE MADE YOU--I STOLE THAT.
CADROS NEVER HURT ME. YOU DID.
WHAT?! HE TOOK YER BOYFRIEND, AND TRANSFORMED HIM INTAE AN UPSTART GOD...!
ALEC.
HE TOOK ALEC.
AH.
YOUR COST. IT WAS HIM. THE MEMORY OF HIM. THE THING YOU WANTED TAE KEEP MOST.
I'M SORRY. THIS ISN'T HOW I WANTED IT TO END.
I COULD REWRITE YOUR HISTORY, THORN. I DON'T EVEN NEED TO DRAW TO DO THAT ANY-MORE.
I COULD MAKE IT THAT YOU NEVER ESCAPED. OR THAT YOU WERE SLAUGHTERED ALONG WITH ALL THE OTHER CELTIC GODS. OR NEVER BORN.
I COULD DO ALL OF THAT...WITHOUT EVEN BLINKING.

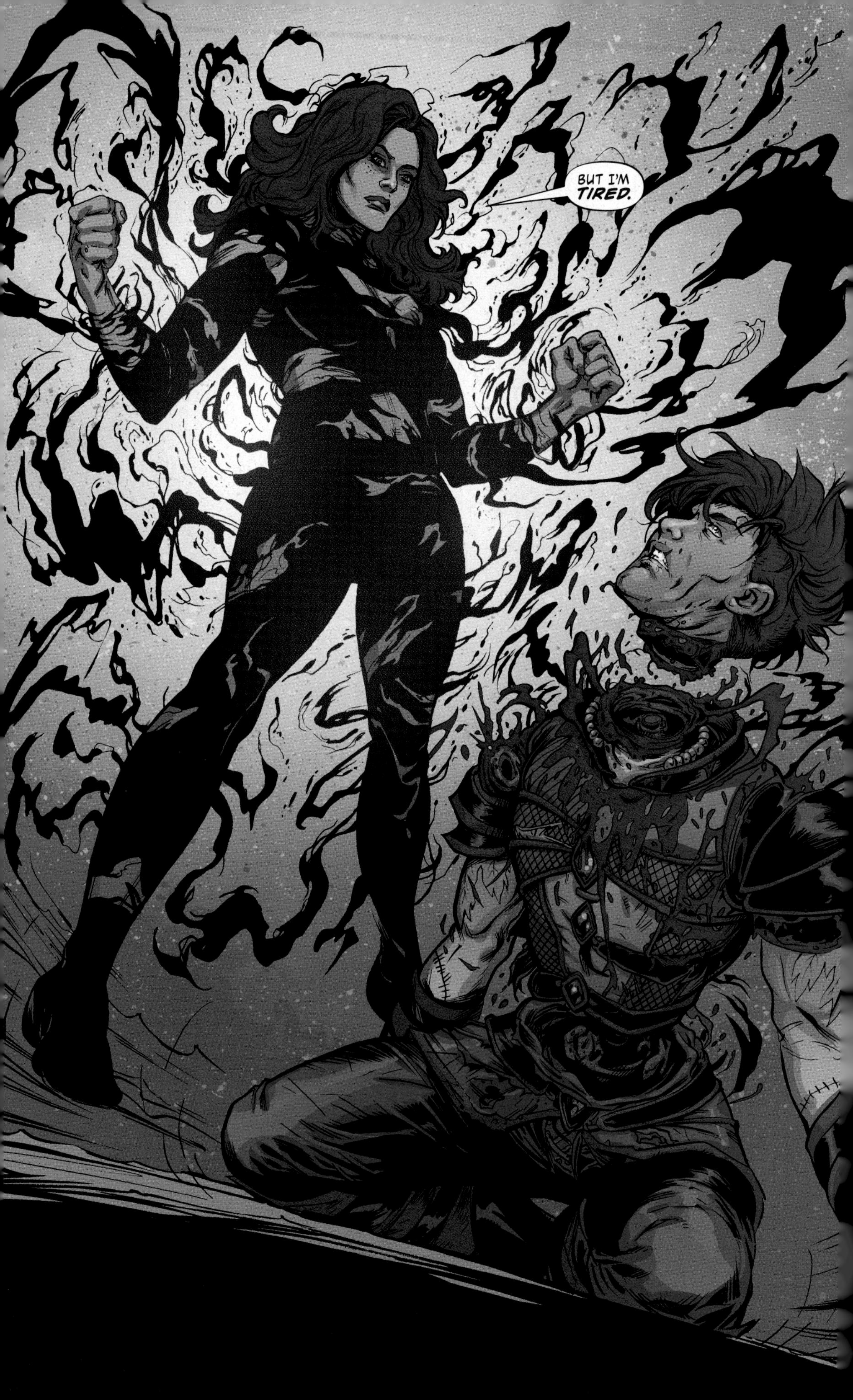
BUT I'M
TIRED.

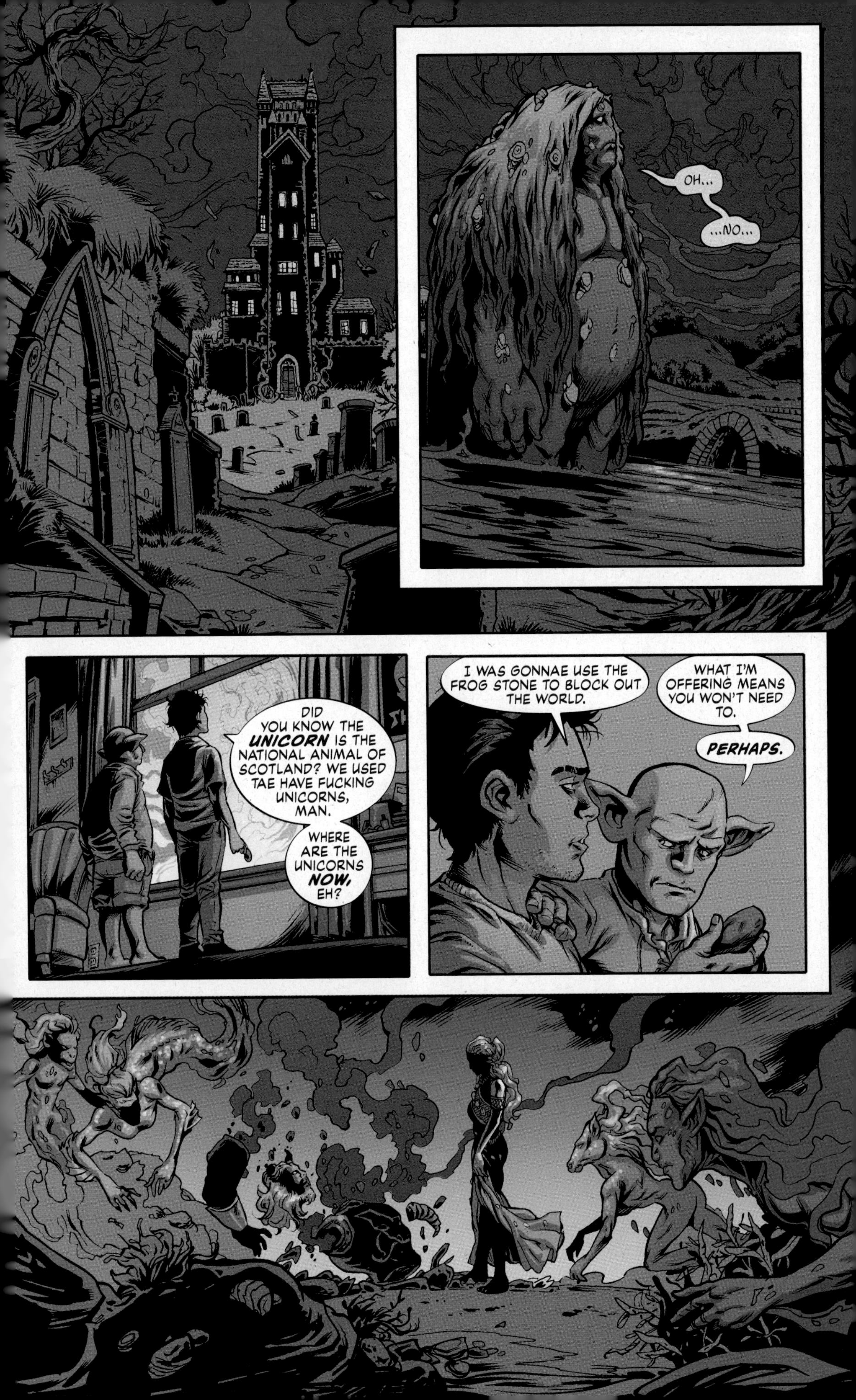
OH...
...NO...
DID YOU KNOW THE UNICORN IS THE NATIONAL ANIMAL OF SCOTLAND? WE USED TAE HAVE FUCKING UNICORNS, MAN.
WHERE ARE THE UNICORNS NOW, EH?
I WAS GONNAE USE THE FROG STONE TO BLOCK OUT THE WORLD.
WHAT I'M OFFERING MEANS YOU WON'T NEED TO.
PERHAPS.

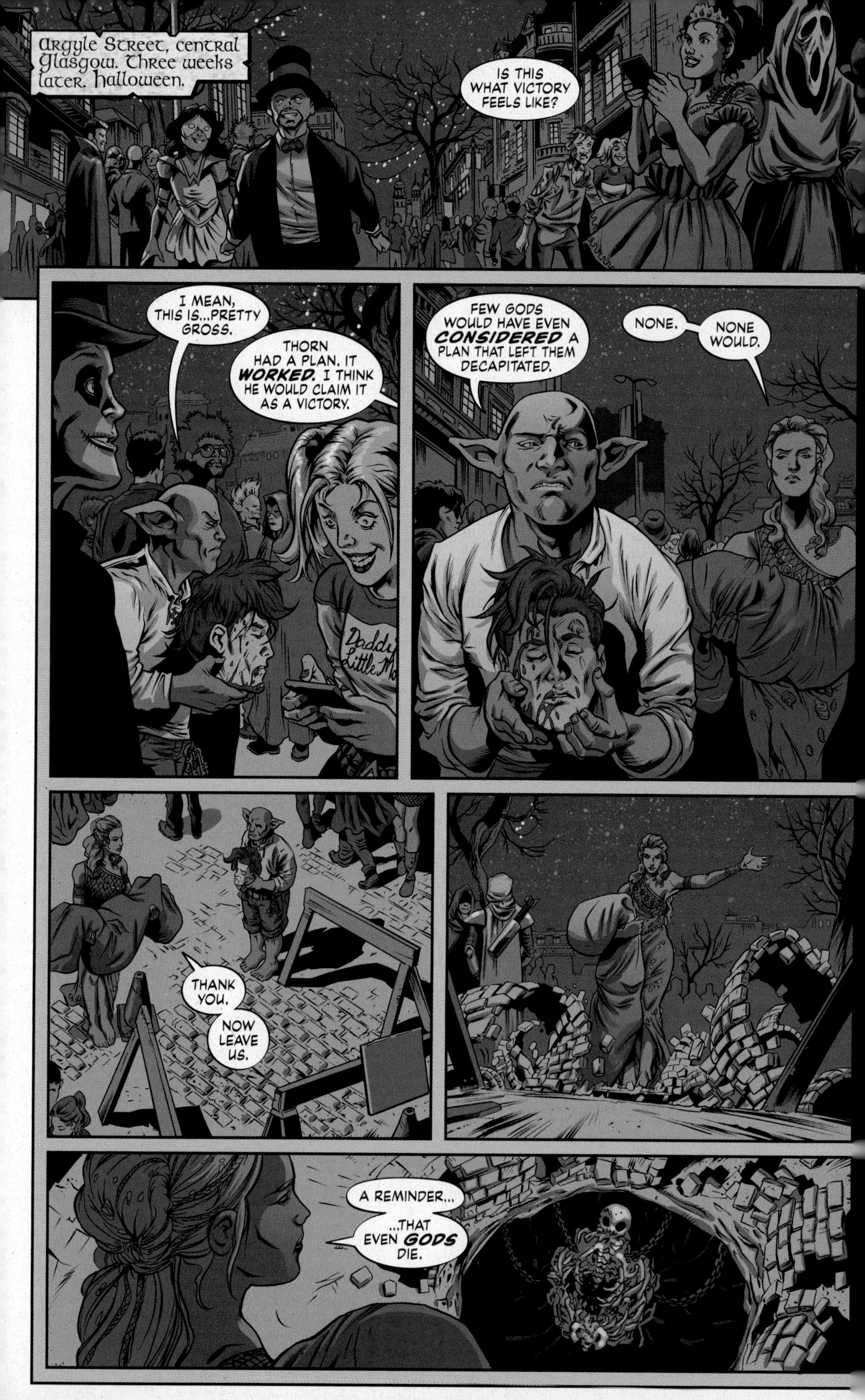
Argyle Street, central Glasgow. Three weeks later. Halloween.
IS THIS WHAT VICTORY FEELS LIKE?
I MEAN, THIS IS...PRETTY GROSS.
THORN HAD A PLAN. IT WORKED. I THINK HE WOULD CLAIM IT AS A VICTORY.
FEW GODS WOULD HAVE EVEN CONSIDERED A PLAN THAT LEFT THEM DECAPITATED.
NONE.
NONE WOULD.
THANK YOU.
NOW LEAVE US.
A REMINDER...
...THAT EVEN GODS DIE.

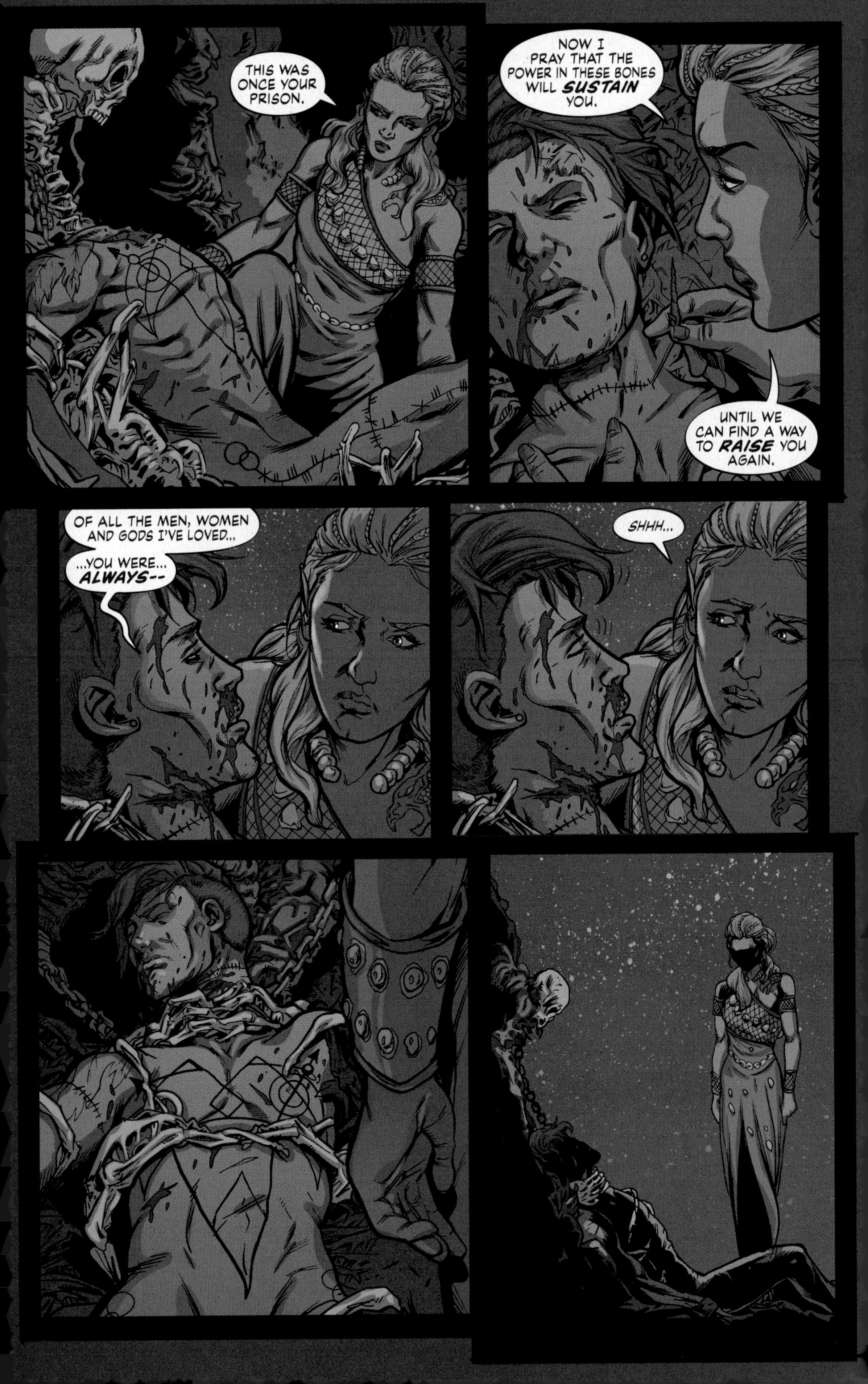
THIS WAS ONCE YOUR PRISON.
NOW I PRAY THAT THE POWER IN THESE BONES WILL SUSTAIN YOU.
UNTIL WE CAN FIND A WAY TO RAISE YOU AGAIN.
OF ALL THE MEN, WOMEN AND GODS I'VE LOVED...
...YOU WERE... ALWAYS--
SHHH...

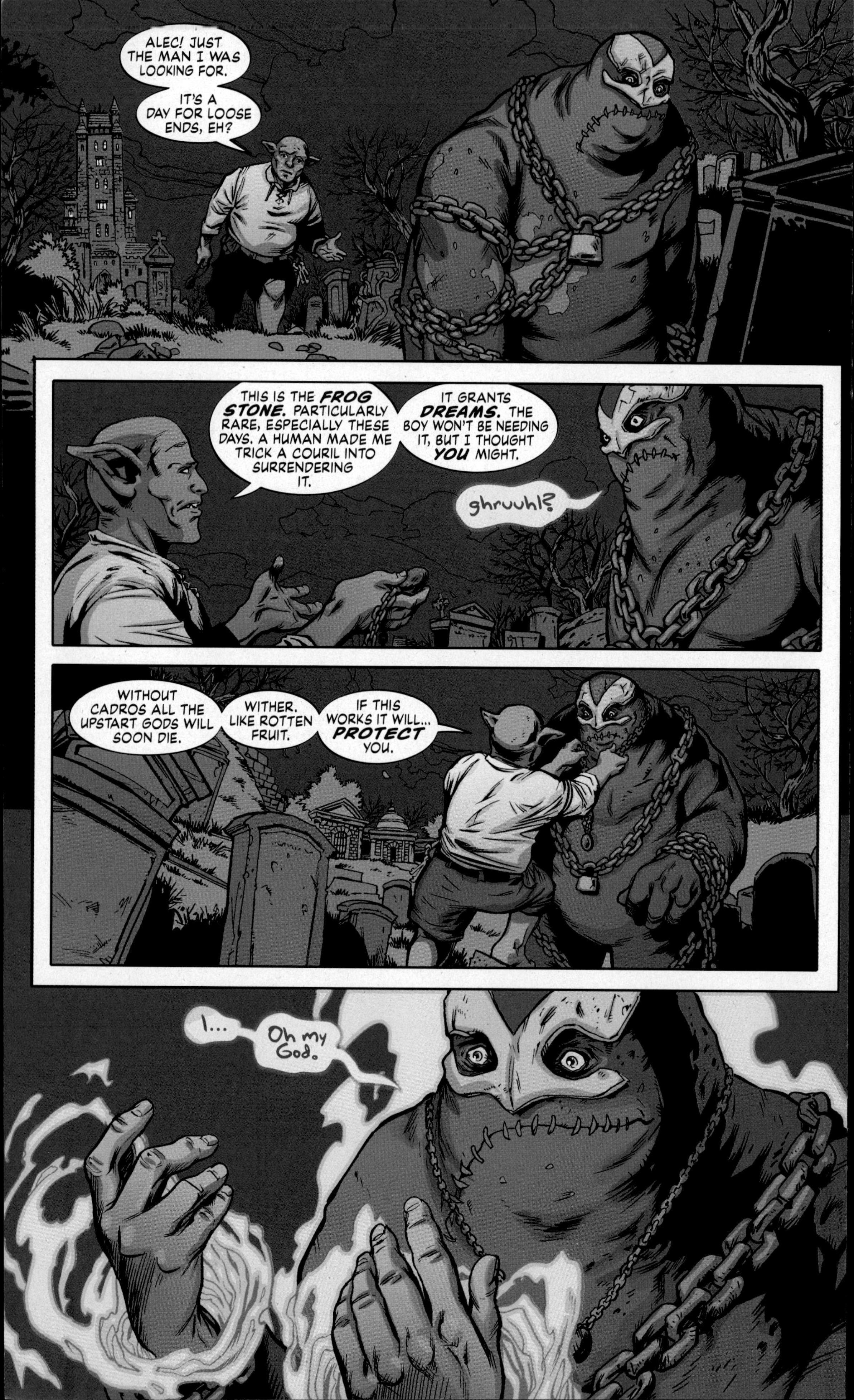
ALEC! JUST THE MAN I WAS LOOKING FOR.
IT'S A DAY FOR LOOSE ENDS, EH?
THIS IS THE **FROG STONE.** PARTICULARLY RARE, ESPECIALLY THESE DAYS. A HUMAN MADE ME TRICK A COURIL INTO SURRENDERING IT.
IT GRANTS **DREAMS.** THE BOY WON'T BE NEEDING IT, BUT I THOUGHT **YOU** MIGHT.
ghruuhl?
WITHOUT CADROS ALL THE UPSTART GODS WILL SOON DIE.
WITHER. LIKE ROTTEN FRUIT.
IF THIS WORKS IT WILL... **PROTECT** YOU.
I...
Oh my God.

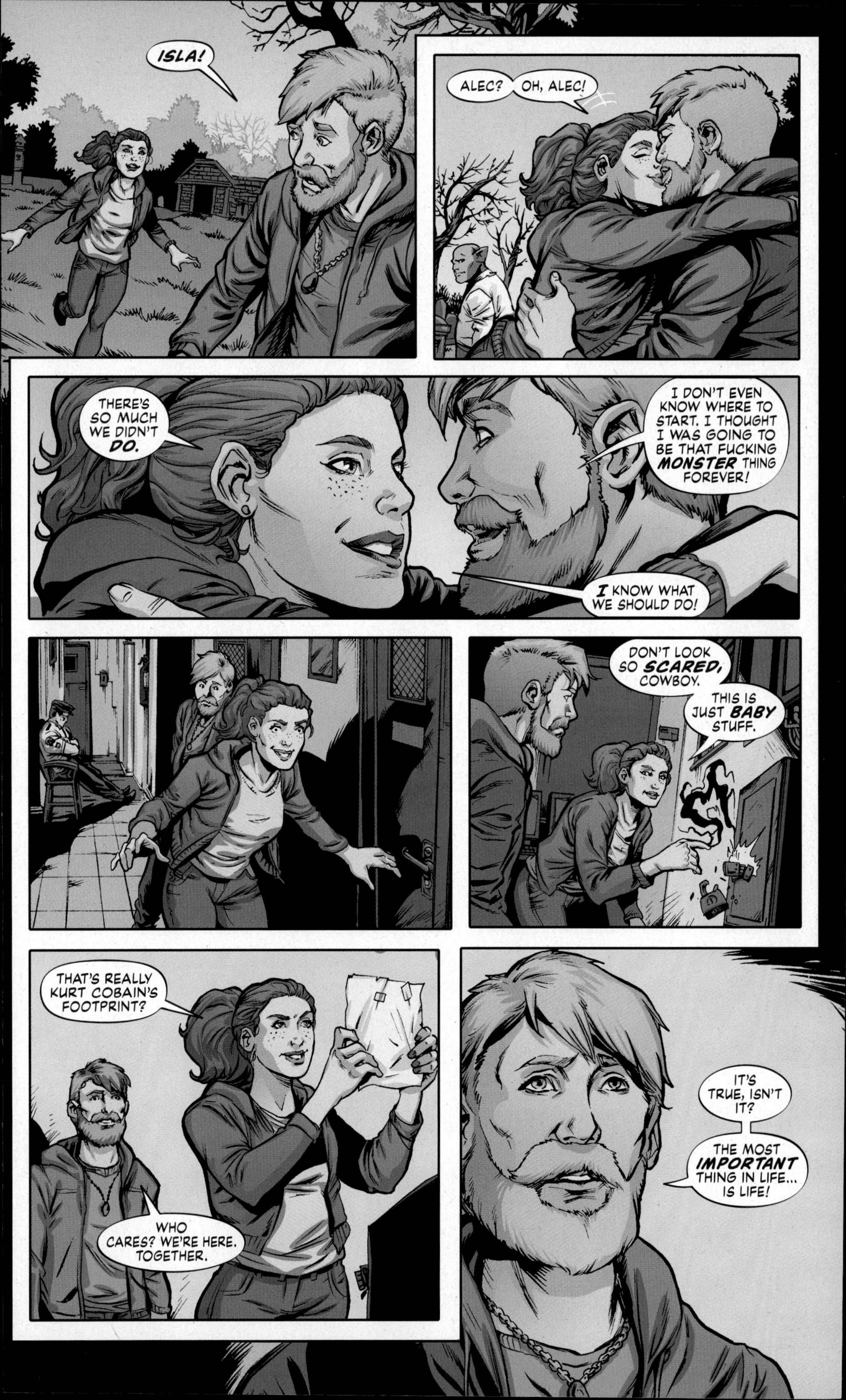
ISLA!
ALEC?
OH, ALEC!
THERE'S SO MUCH WE DIDN'T DO.
I DON'T EVEN KNOW WHERE TO START. I THOUGHT I WAS GOING TO BE THAT FUCKING MONSTER THING FOREVER!
I KNOW WHAT WE SHOULD DO!
DON'T LOOK SO SCARED, COWBOY.
THIS IS JUST BABY STUFF.
THAT'S REALLY KURT COBAIN'S FOOTPRINT?
WHO CARES? WE'RE HERE. TOGETHER.
IT'S TRUE, ISN'T IT?
THE MOST IMPORTANT THING IN LIFE... IS LIFE!

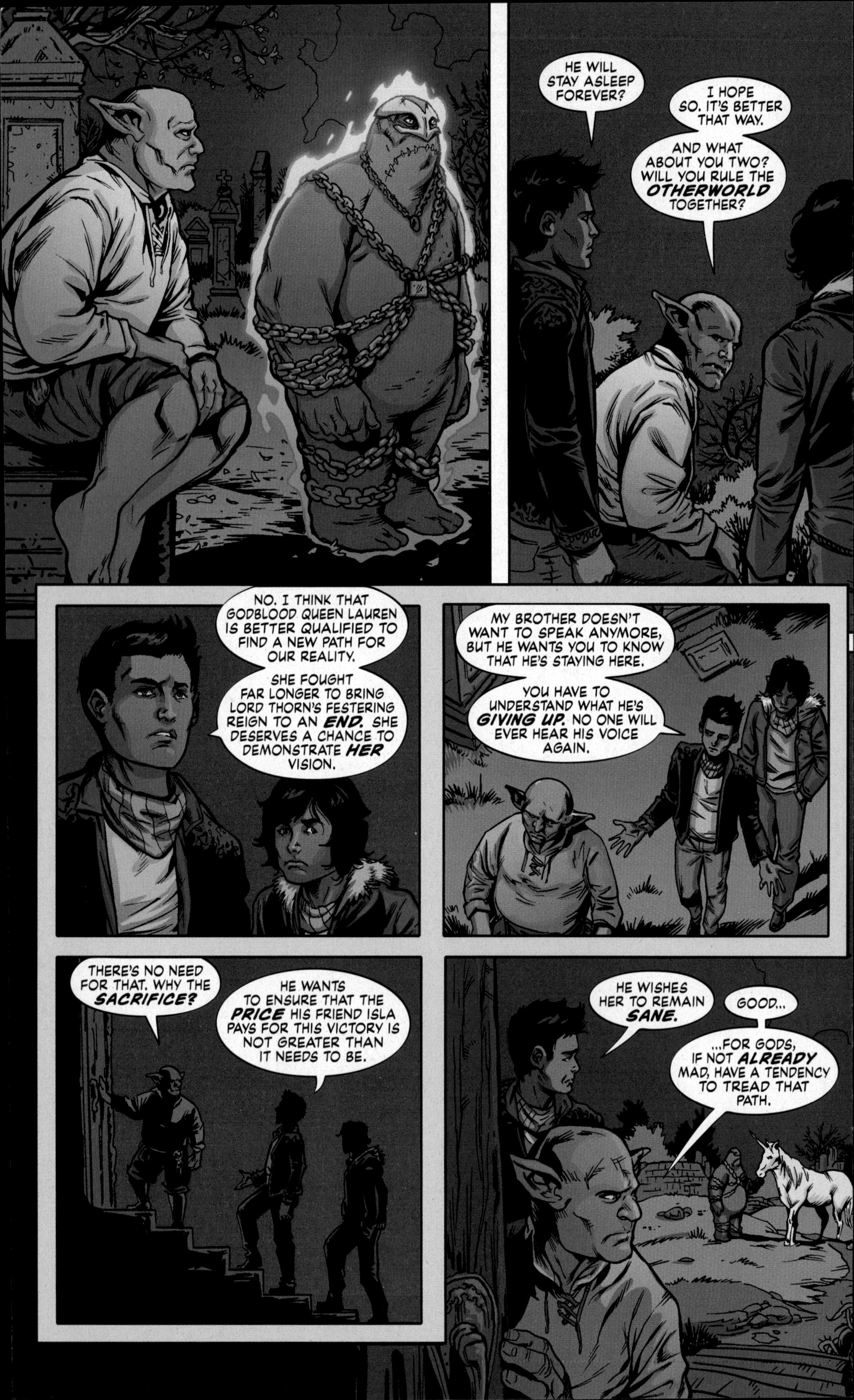
HE WILL STAY ASLEEP FOREVER?
I HOPE SO. IT'S BETTER THAT WAY.
AND WHAT ABOUT YOU TWO? WILL YOU RULE THE OTHERWORLD TOGETHER?
NO. I THINK THAT GODBLOOD QUEEN LAUREN IS BETTER QUALIFIED TO FIND A NEW PATH FOR OUR REALITY.
SHE FOUGHT FAR LONGER TO BRING LORD THORN'S FESTERING REIGN TO AN END. SHE DESERVES A CHANCE TO DEMONSTRATE HER VISION.
MY BROTHER DOESN'T WANT TO SPEAK ANYMORE, BUT HE WANTS YOU TO KNOW THAT HE'S STAYING HERE.
YOU HAVE TO UNDERSTAND WHAT HE'S GIVING UP. NO ONE WILL EVER HEAR HIS VOICE AGAIN.
THERE'S NO NEED FOR THAT. WHY THE SACRIFICE?
HE WANTS TO ENSURE THAT THE PRICE HIS FRIEND ISLA PAYS FOR THIS VICTORY IS NOT GREATER THAN IT NEEDS TO BE.
HE WISHES HER TO REMAIN SANE.
GOOD...
...FOR GODS, IF NOT ALREADY MAD, HAVE A TENDENCY TO TREAD THAT PATH.

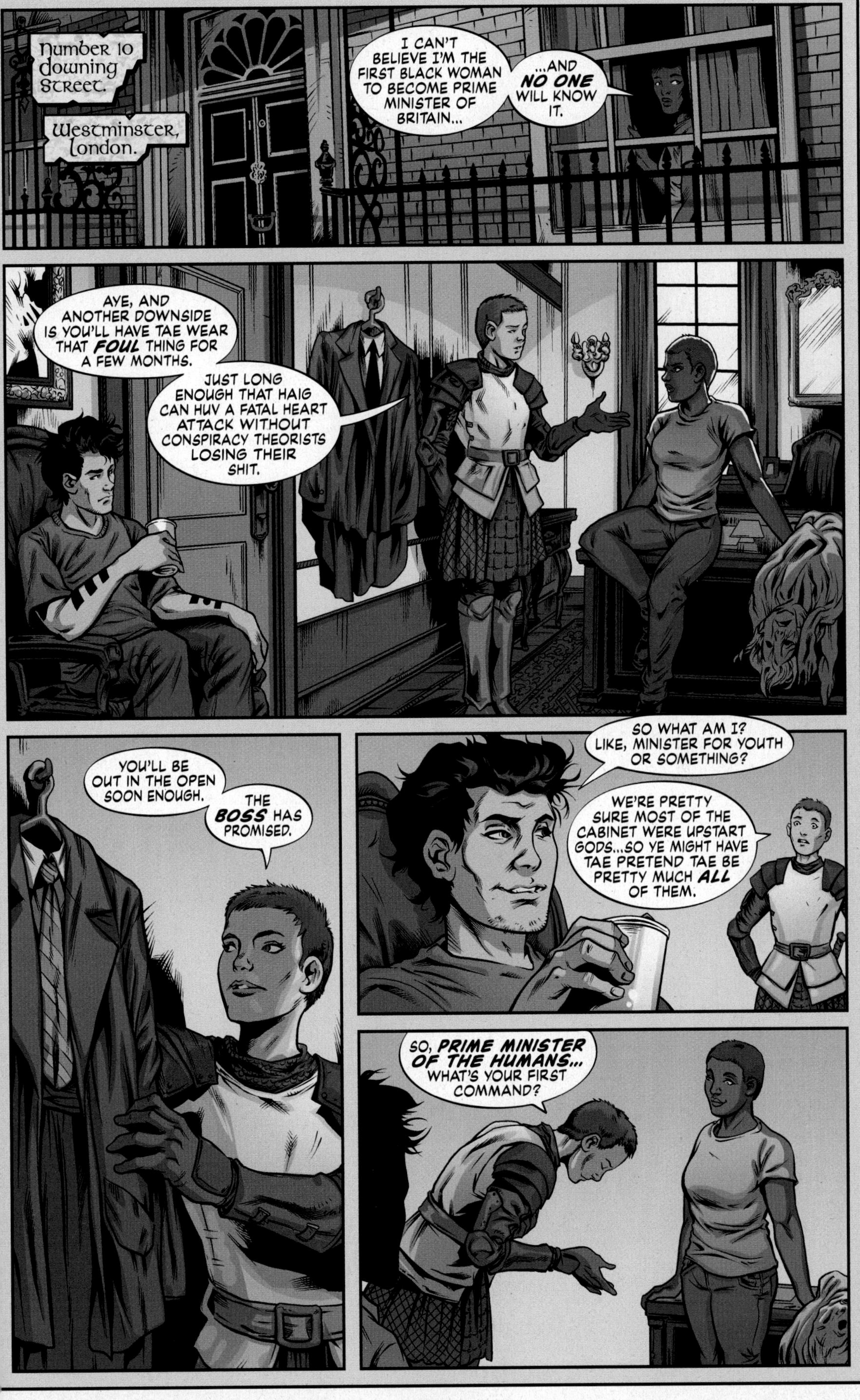

Number 10 downing Street.
Westminster, London.
I CAN'T BELIEVE I'M THE FIRST BLACK WOMAN TO BECOME PRIME MINISTER OF BRITAIN...
...AND NO ONE WILL KNOW IT.
AYE, AND ANOTHER DOWNSIDE IS YOU'LL HAVE TAE WEAR THAT FOUL THING FOR A FEW MONTHS.
JUST LONG ENOUGH THAT HAIG CAN HUV A FATAL HEART ATTACK WITHOUT CONSPIRACY THEORISTS LOSING THEIR SHIT.
YOU'LL BE OUT IN THE OPEN SOON ENOUGH.
THE BOSS HAS PROMISED.
SO WHAT AM I? LIKE, MINISTER FOR YOUTH OR SOMETHING?
WE'RE PRETTY SURE MOST OF THE CABINET WERE UPSTART GODS...SO YE MIGHT HAVE TAE PRETEND TAE BE PRETTY MUCH ALL OF THEM.
SO, PRIME MINISTER OF THE HUMANS... WHAT'S YOUR FIRST COMMAND?

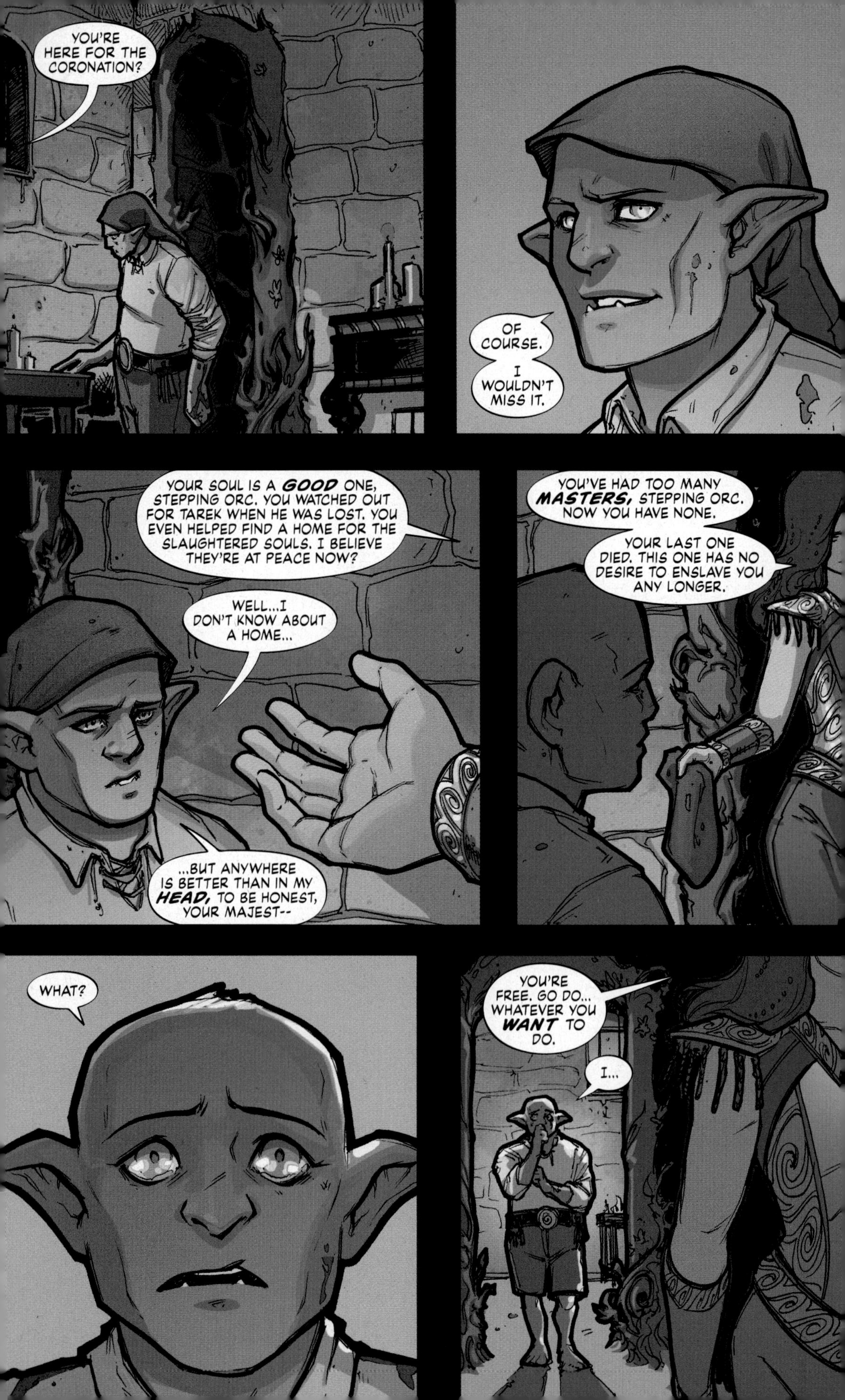
YOU'RE HERE FOR THE CORONATION?
OF COURSE.
I WOULDN'T MISS IT.
YOUR SOUL IS A **GOOD** ONE, STEPPING ORC. YOU WATCHED OUT FOR TAREK WHEN HE WAS LOST. YOU EVEN HELPED FIND A HOME FOR THE SLAUGHTERED SOULS. I BELIEVE THEY'RE AT PEACE NOW?
WELL...I DON'T KNOW ABOUT A HOME...
...BUT ANYWHERE IS BETTER THAN IN MY **HEAD,** TO BE HONEST, YOUR MAJEST--
YOU'VE HAD TOO MANY **MASTERS,** STEPPING ORC. NOW YOU HAVE NONE.
YOUR LAST ONE DIED. THIS ONE HAS NO DESIRE TO ENSLAVE YOU ANY LONGER.
WHAT?
YOU'RE FREE. GO DO... WHATEVER YOU **WANT** TO DO.
I...

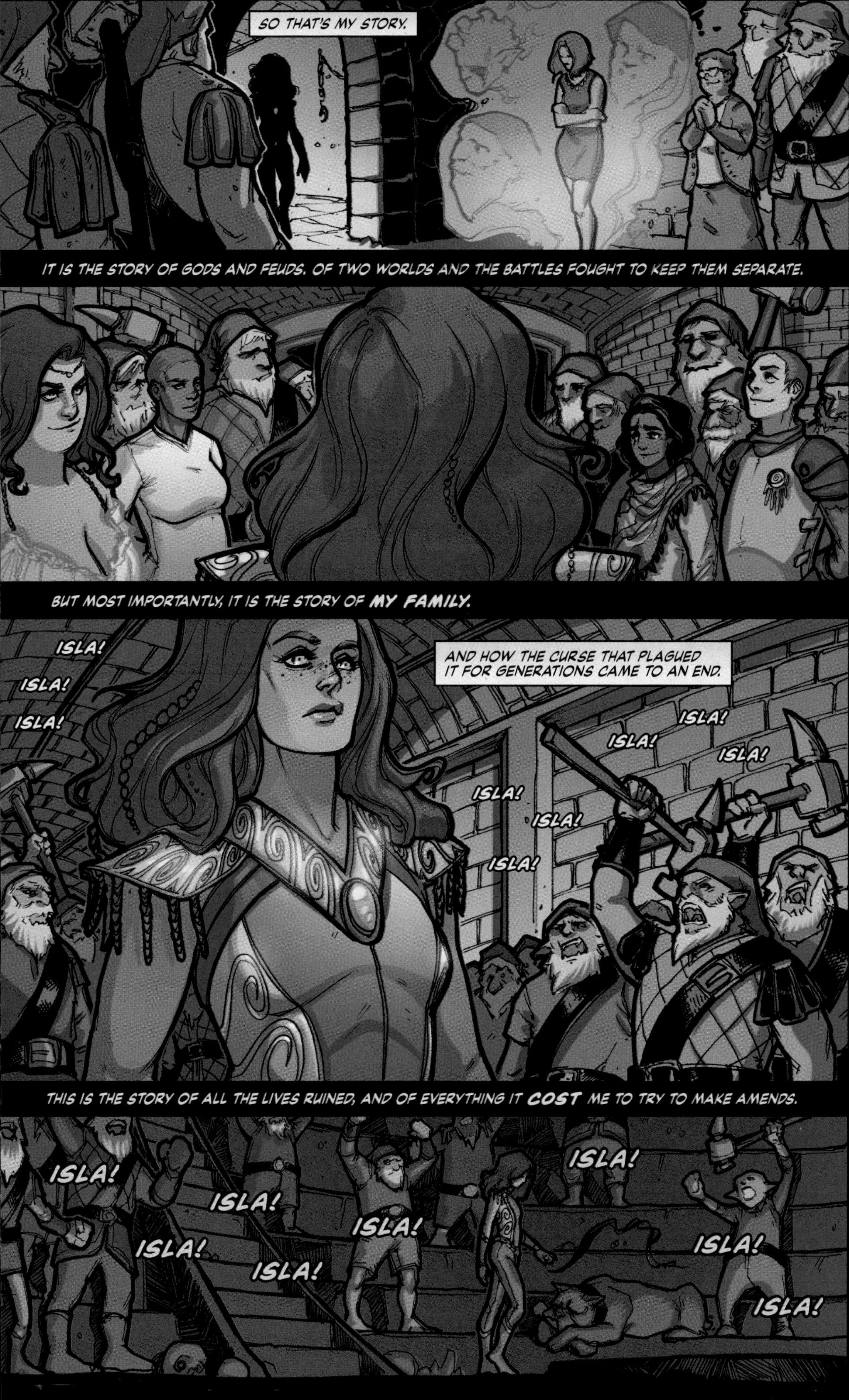
SO THAT'S MY STORY.
IT IS THE STORY OF GODS AND FEUDS. OF TWO WORLDS AND THE BATTLES FOUGHT TO KEEP THEM SEPARATE.
BUT MOST IMPORTANTLY, IT IS THE STORY OF MY FAMILY.
AND HOW THE CURSE THAT PLAGUED IT FOR GENERATIONS CAME TO AN END.
ISLA!
ISLA!
ISLA!
ISLA!
ISLA!
ISLA!
ISLA!
ISLA!
ISLA!
THIS IS THE STORY OF ALL THE LIVES RUINED, AND OF EVERYTHING IT COST ME TO TRY TO MAKE AMENDS.
ISLA!
ISLA!
ISLA!
ISLA!
ISLA!
ISLA!
ISLA!
ISLA!

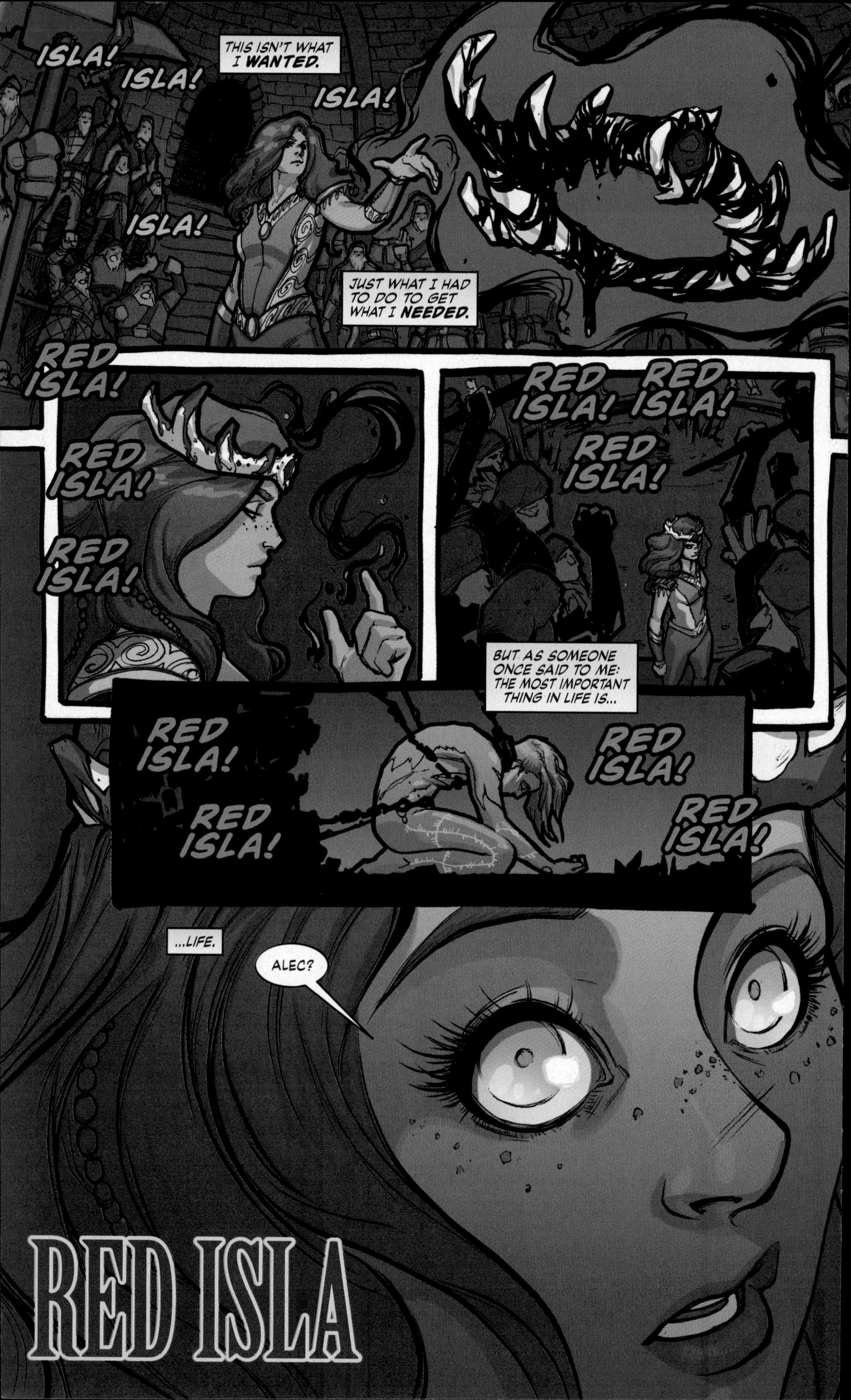
ISLA!
ISLA!
THIS ISN'T WHAT I WANTED.
ISLA!
ISLA!
JUST WHAT I HAD TO DO TO GET WHAT I NEEDED.
RED ISLA!
RED ISLA!
RED ISLA!
RED ISLA!
RED ISLA!
RED ISLA!
BUT AS SOMEONE ONCE SAID TO ME: THE MOST IMPORTANT THING IN LIFE IS...
RED ISLA!
RED ISLA!
RED ISLA!
RED ISLA!
...LIFE.
ALEC?
RED ISLA

KILT OR BE KILLED!

Character designs and sketches from Meghan Hetrick

THORN

RAVEN SKULL
BACK WRAP

CLOSELY CROPPED SIDES
NOT SKINNED

MUSCULAR, LEAN BUILD

MOVES LIKE A PREDATOR
LOTS OF HIP ACTION

MODIFIED V-ROD
ONGE PIPES

OGHAM ON FORBARMS
& LEGS

 THURSAZ-
THORN RUNE

MIRROR & TRIPLE
DISC MOTIFF

DOUBLE GOD BONE
BLADES

THORN MOTIFF
THROUGHOUT

BOUND
CHEANGAL

VENGEANCE
DIOFELTE

JUSTICE
CEARTAIS

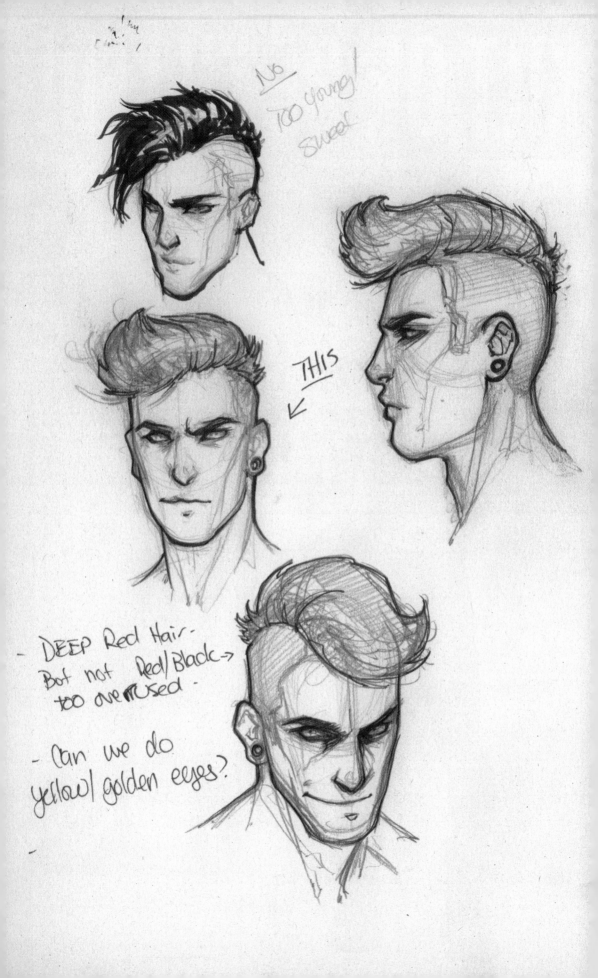

No
Too young!
sweet

THIS
←

- DEEP Red Hair-
But not Red/Black→
too overused-

- Can we do
yellow/golden eyes?

remove sleeves ?

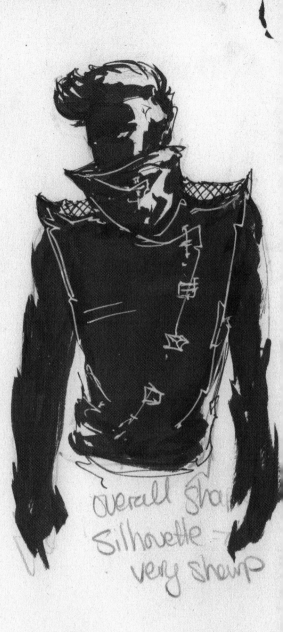

overall sha-
silhouette —
very sharp

outfits change —
But overall shape
is maintained.

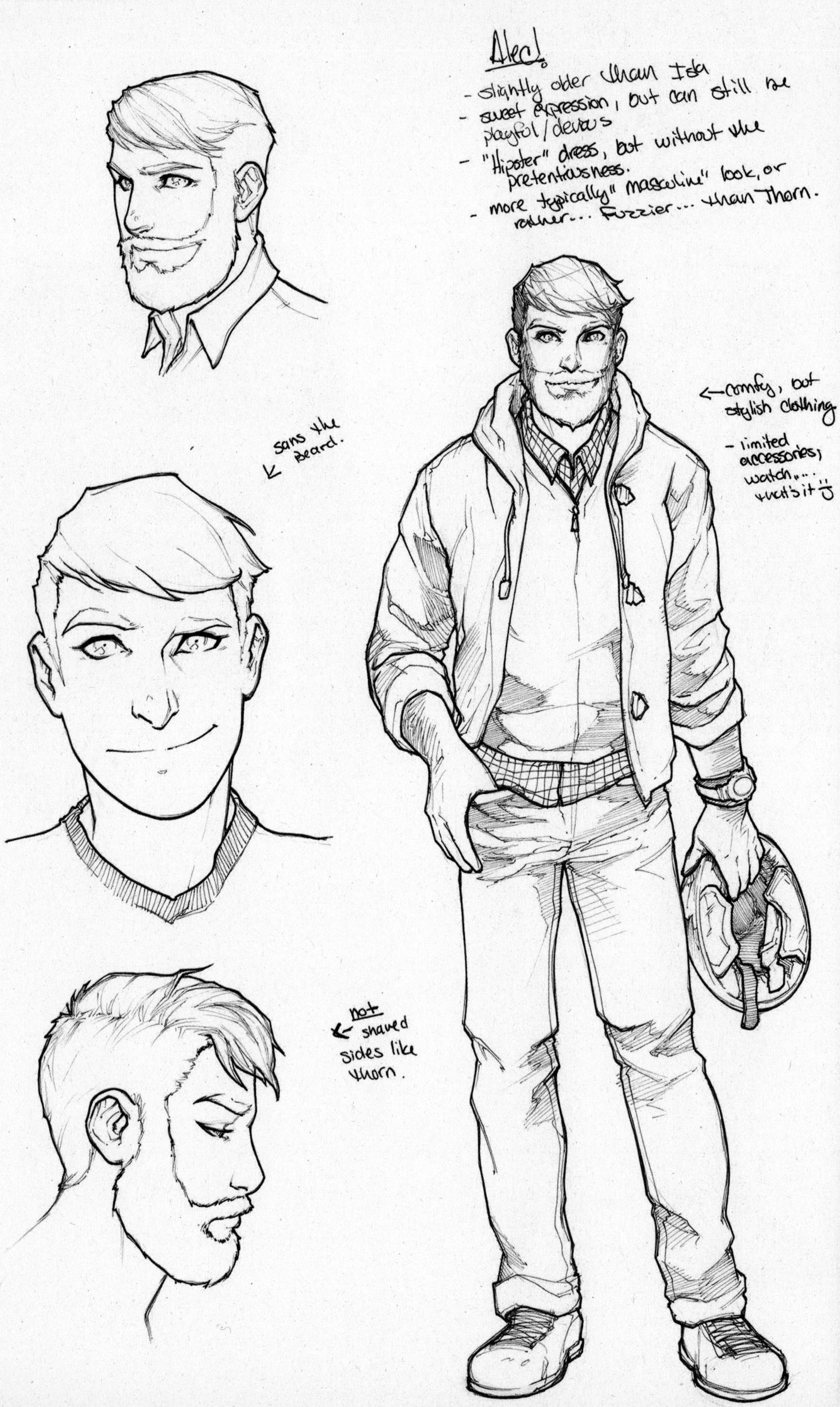
Alec!
- slightly older than Ida
- sweet expression, but can still be playful/devious
- "Hipster" dress, but without the pretentiousness.
- more typically "masculine" look, or rather... Fuzzier... than Thorn.
sans the beard.
← comfy, but stylish clothing
- limited accessories; watch... that's it
not shaved sides like thorn.

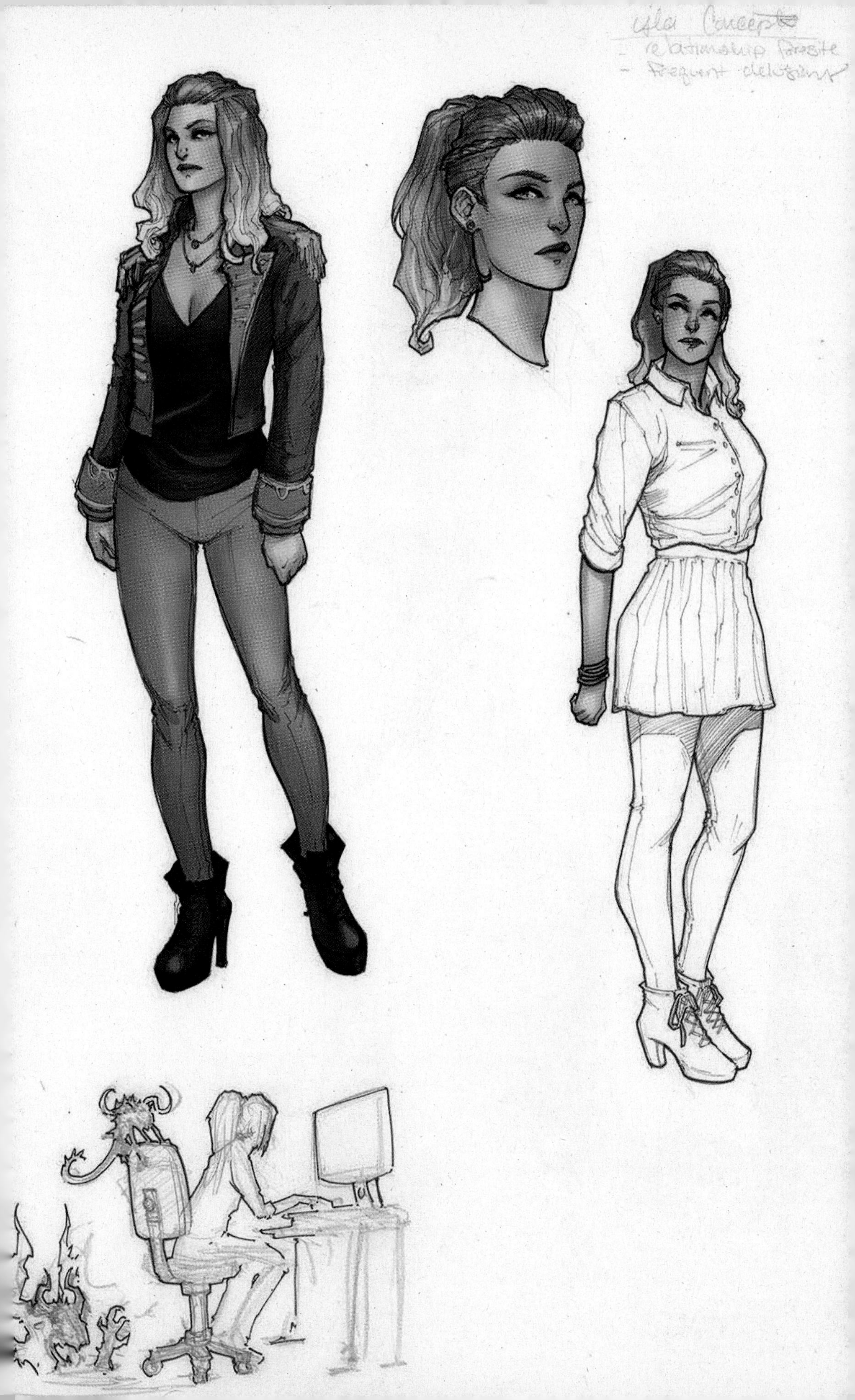
Lyla Concepts
- relationship parasite
- frequent delusions

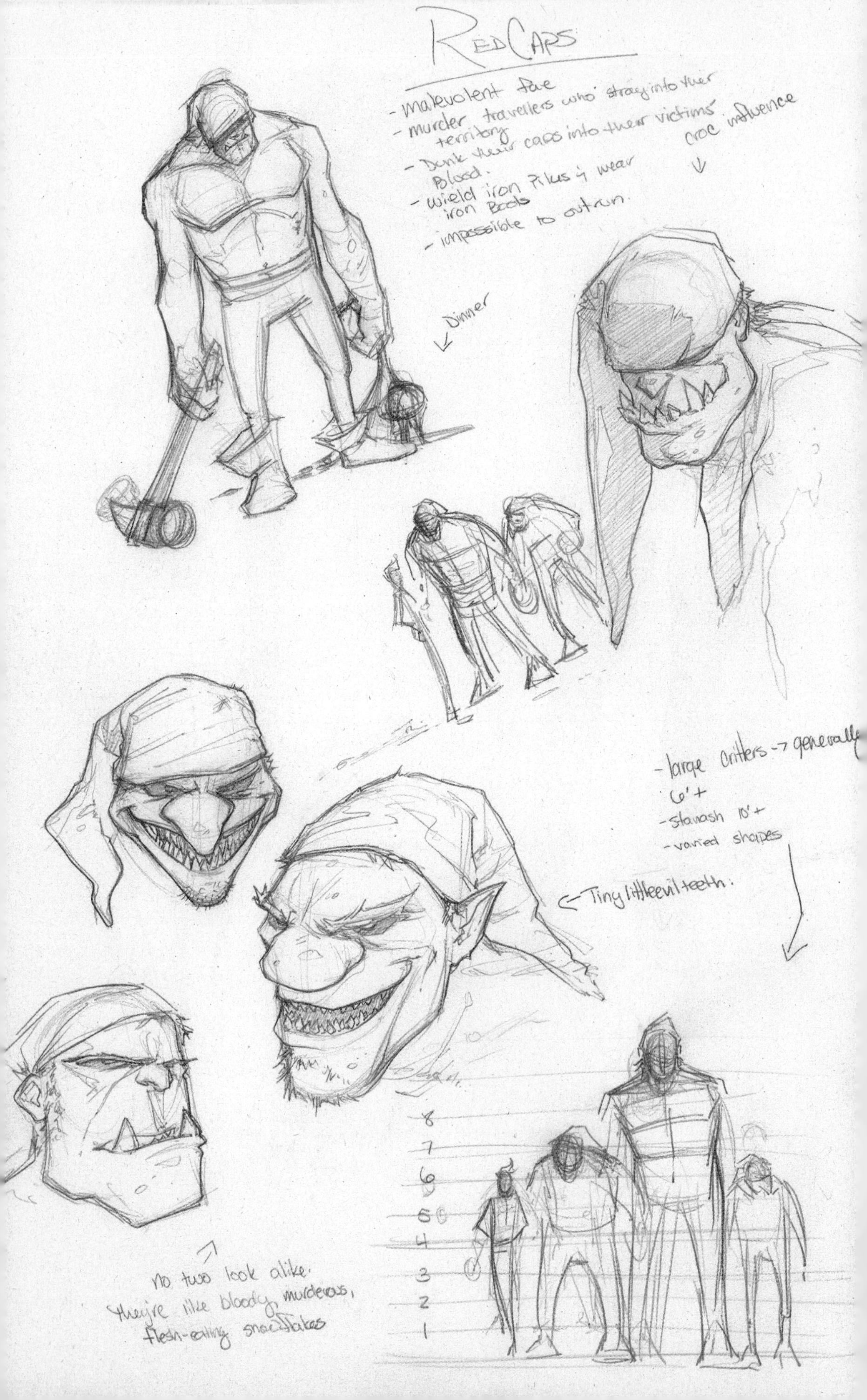
RedCaps
- malevolent fae
- murder travellers who stray into their territory
- Dunk their caps into their victims' Blood.
- wield iron Pikes & wear iron Boots
- impossible to outrun.
croc influence
Dinner
- large critters -> generally 6'+
- Slanash 10'+
- varied shapes
Tiny little evil teeth.
no two look alike.
they're like bloody, murderous, flesh-eating snowflakes
8
7
6
5
4
3
2
1

Tarek

teenage B?
Moroccan
cartographer
fictional
Maybe 14?

← messy, unkempt
crudely cut hair

gangly
antelope →
stage
all arms →
legs →

left handed?

← Blue Berber
scarf

→ maps on Napkin, newspaper
bags → whatever scraps
which could be written on

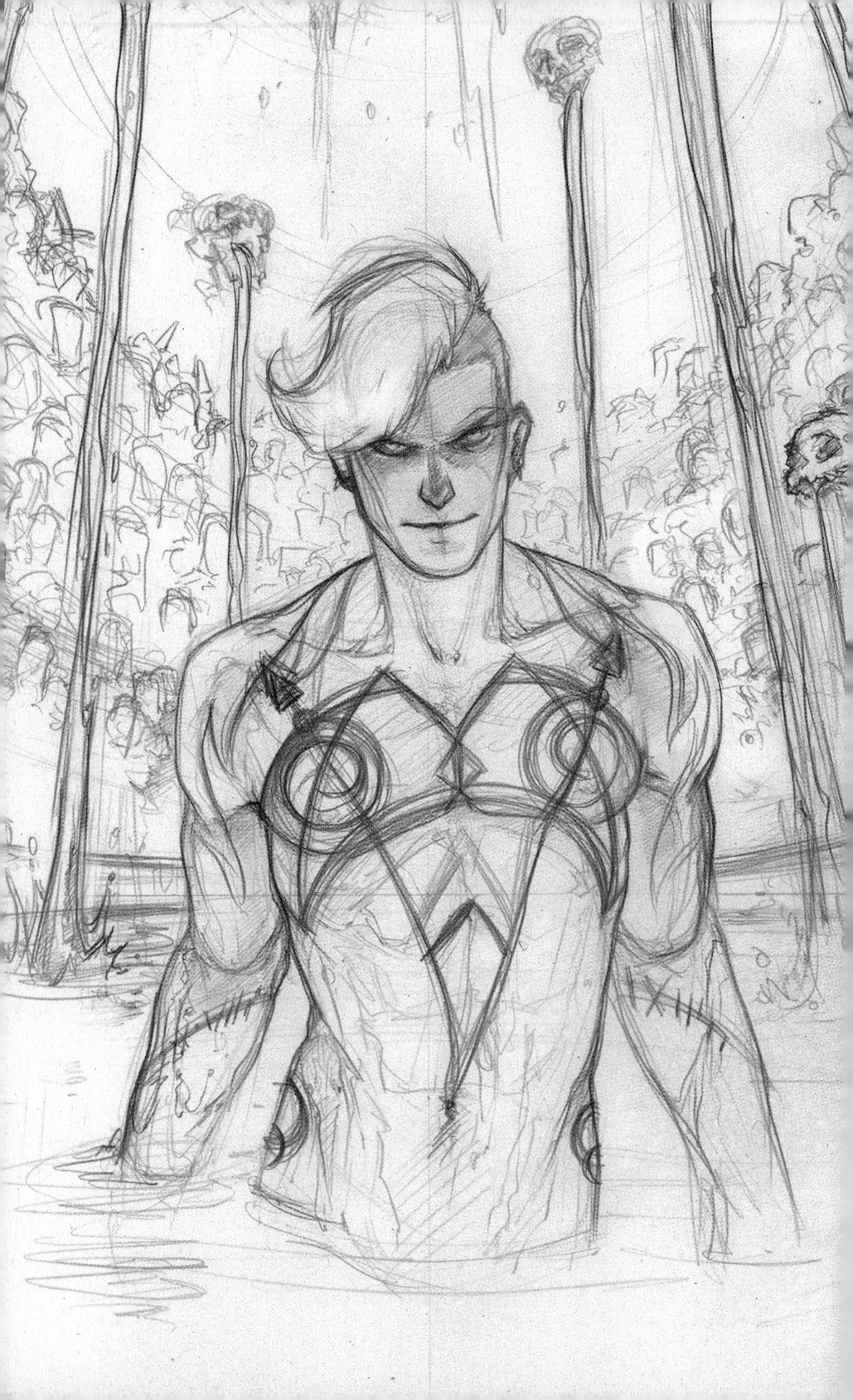

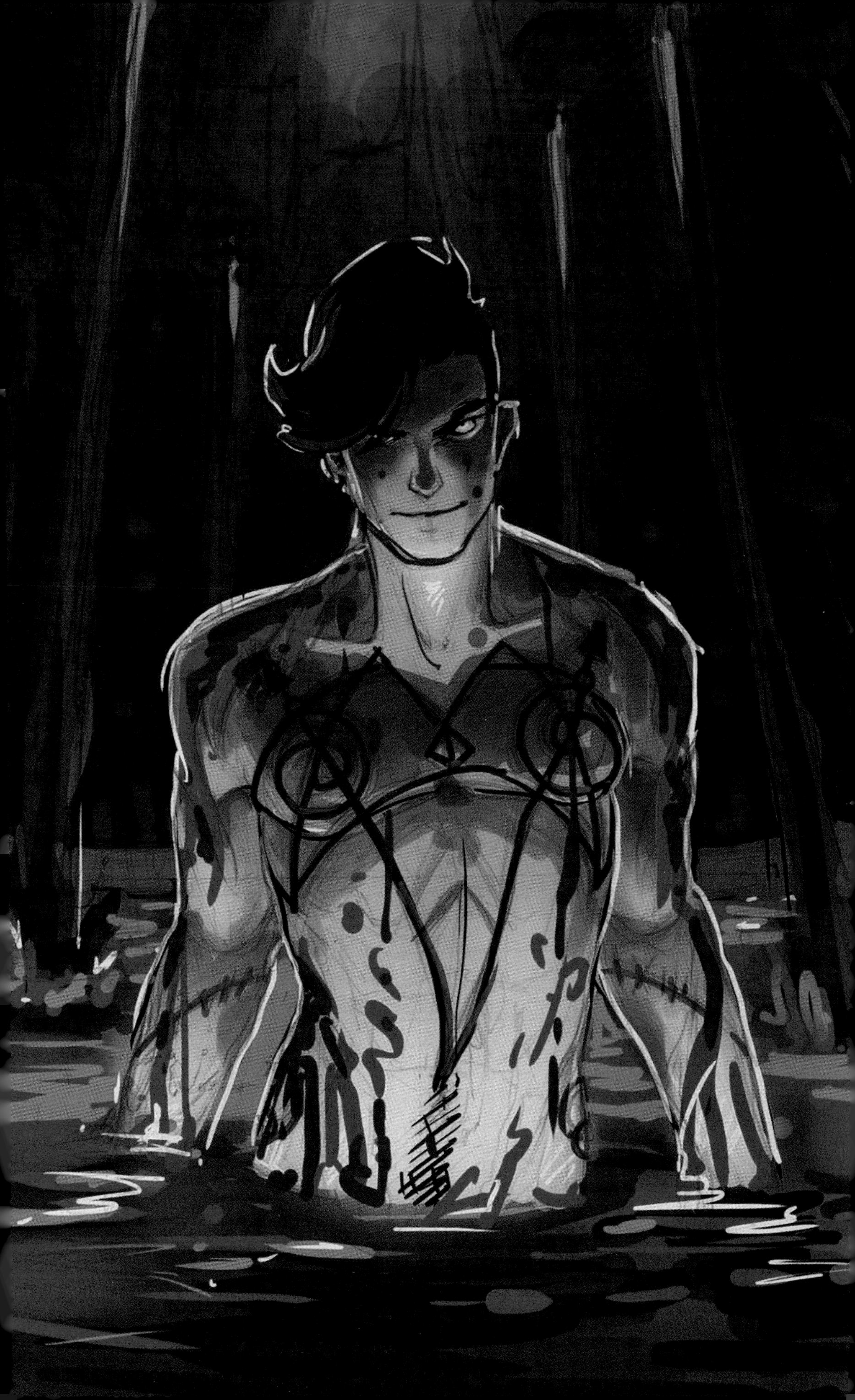

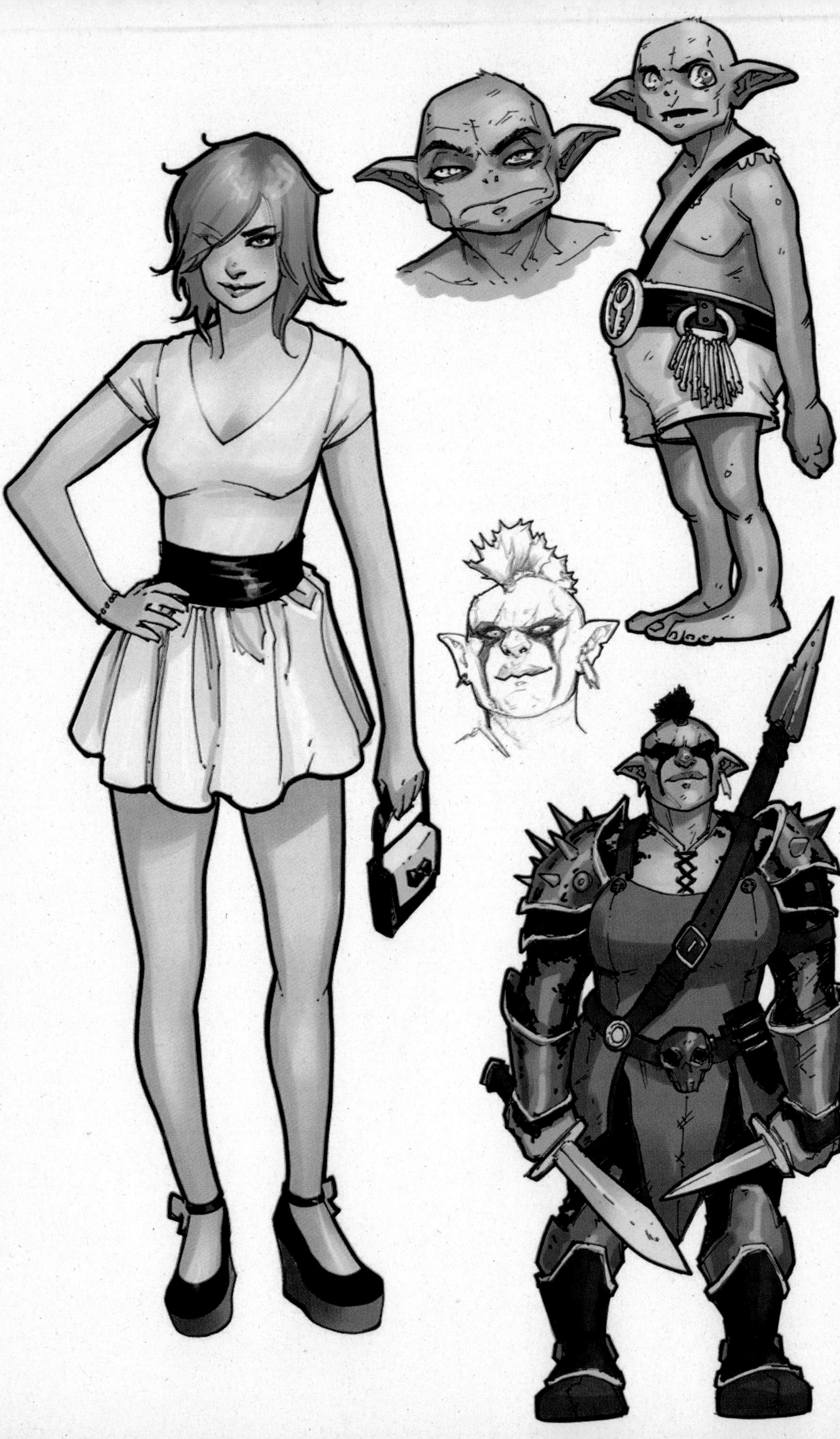

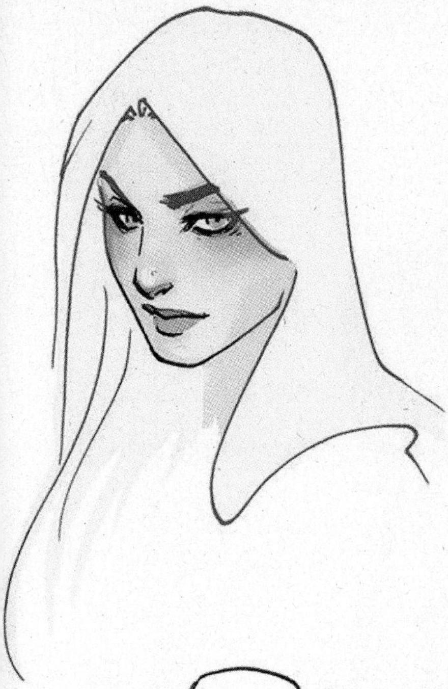
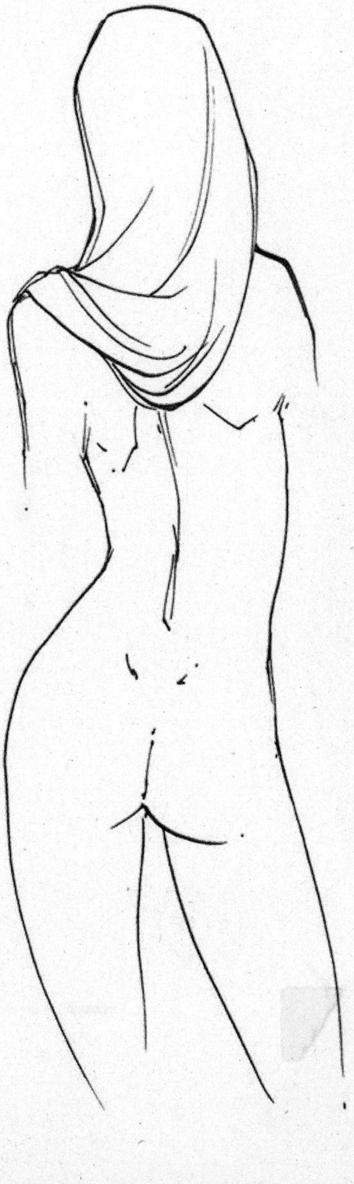
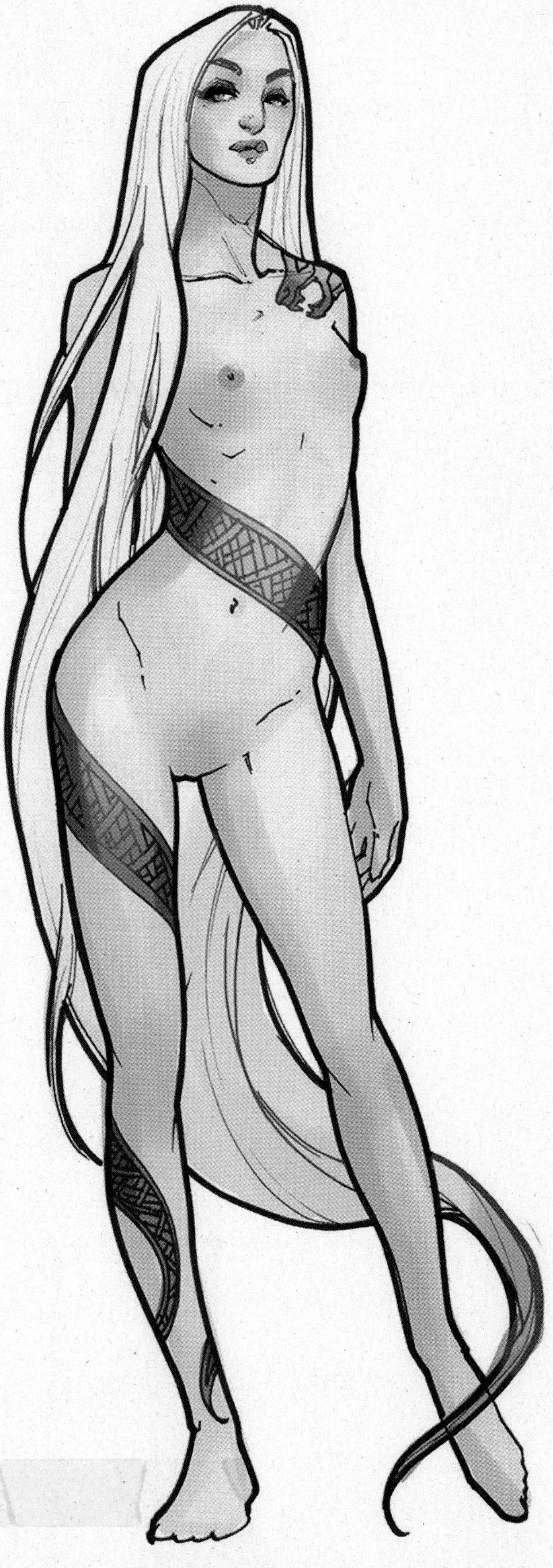

31901060204627